Public Administration

Also by R. A. W. Rhodes

Everyday Life in British Government

The State as Cultural Practice (with Mark Bevir)

Comparing Westminster (with J. Wanna and P. Weller)

Governance Stories (with Mark Bevir)

Interpreting British Governance (with Mark Bevir)

Understanding Governance

Beyond Westminster and Whitehall

The National World of Local Government

Control and Power in Central-Local Government Relationships

The Australian Study of Politics (editor)

Observing Government Elites (editor with Paul 't Hart and Mirko Noordegraaf)

The Oxford Handbook of Political Institutions (editor with S. Binder and B. Rockman)

The Changing World of Top Officials. Mandarins or Valets? (editor with P. Weller)

Transforming British Government. Volume 1. Changing Institutions. Volume 2. Changing Roles and Relationships

The Hollow Crown (editor with P. Weller and H. Bakvis)

Prime Minister, Cabinet and Core Executive (editor with P. Dunleavy)

Policy Networks in British Government (editor with D. Marsh)

Public Administration:

25 Years of Analysis and Debate

Edited by

R. A. W. Rhodes

Professor of Government
University of Tasmania

WILEY-
BLACKWELL

Blackwell Publishing was acquired by John Wiley & Sons in February 2007. Blackwell's publishing program has been merged with Wiley's global Scientific, Technical and Medical business to form Wiley-Blackwell.

Registered Office
John Wiley & Sons Ltd, The Atrium, Southern Gate, Chichester, West Sussex, PO19 8SQ, United Kingdom

Editorial Offices
350 Main Street, Malden, MA 02148-5.50, USA
9600 Garsington Road, Oxford, OX4 2DQ, UK
The Atrium, Southern Gate, Chichester, West Sussex, PO19 8SQ, UK

For details of our global editorial offices, for customer services, and for information about how to apply for permission to reuse the copyright material in this book please see our website at www.wiley.com/wiley-blackwell.

Library of Congress Cataloging-in-Publication Data
Public administration : 25 years of analysis and debate / edited by R. A. W. Rhodes.
    p. cm.
  Includes index.
  ISBN 978-1-4443-3216-2
1. Public administration. I. Rhodes, R. A. W. II. Public administration.
  JF1351.P8187 2011
  351--dc22

                                     2011006748

A catalogue record for this book is available from the British Library.

Set in 10 on 12pt, Palatino
by Laserwords Private Limited, Chennai, India

Contents

List of Figures, Tables, Boxes and Appendixes

Figures

Tables

Boxes

Appendixes

List of Sources

Baron Wilson of Dinton. 2003. 'Portrait of a Profession Revisited', *Public Administration*, 81, 2, 365–78.

Hay, C. 2004. 'Theory, Stylized Heuristic or Self-Fulfilling Prophecy? The Status of Rational Choice Theory in Public Administration', *Public Administration*, 82, 1, 39–62.

Hood, C. 1991. 'A Public Management For All Seasons', *Public Administration* 69, 1, 3–19.

Klijn, E.-H., J. Koppenjan and K. Termeer 1995. 'Managing Networks in the Public Sector: A Theoretical Study of Management Strategies in Policy Networks', *Public Administration*, 73, 3, 437–54.

Lowndes, V. and C. Skelcher. 1998. 'The Dynamics of Multi-organizational Partnerships: An Analysis of Changing Modes of Governance', *Public Administration* 76, 3, 313–33.

Mulgan, R. 2000. '"Accountability": An Ever-expanding Concept?', *Public Administration*, 78, 3, 555–73.

Rhodes, R. A.W. 2000. 'The Governance Narrative', *Public Administration*, 78, 2, 345–63.

Scharpf, F.W. 1988. 'The Joint-decision Trap: Lessons from German Federalism and European Integration', *Public Administration*, 66, 3, 239–78.

Stewart, J. and M. Clarke. 1987. 'The Public-service Orientation: Issues and Dilemmas', *Public Administration*, 65, 2, 161–77.

Thoenig, J.-C. 2005. 'Territorial Administration and Political Control: Decentralization in France', *Public Administration*, 83, 3, 685–708.

Weller, P. 2003. 'Cabinet Government: An Elusive Ideal?' *Public Administration*, 81, 4, 701–22.

Williams, P. 2002. 'The Competent Boundary Spanner', *Public Administration*, 80, 1, 103–24.

Acknowledgements

The acknowledgements of each author are in their chapter. Here I thank all those who made this volume possible. At Wiley-Blackwell, Gemma Johnson enthusiastically sponsored the book and Lucie Trarieux provided the data on citations. Sally Crawford was my editorial manager for *Public Administration: An International Quarterly*, and she applied the same skills to this volume. Now as ever she has been an invaluable helper. Eilidh St John provided research assistance for the contents analysis of the journal and helped with copy editing and proof reading. Laura Bevir did her usual excellent, and prompt, job in compiling the indexes.

List of Contributors

Michael Clarke retired as Deputy Vice-Chancellor of the University of Birmingham in the autumn of 2008. His career has spanned the world of local government practice, academic life (lecturing in politics at the University of Edinburgh in the early 1970s and going to Birmingham to their Chair of Public Policy in the early 1990s) and the leadership of two national support organizations for local government in the UK, one involved with training and the other with the development of management practice. Running through the whole has been his interest in understanding and improving public service organizations.

Colin Hay is Professor of Political Analysis, University of Sheffield. He is the author, coauthor or editor of a number of books, including most recently: *New Directions in Political Science* (editor, Palgrave 2010), *The Role of Ideas in Political Analysis* (joint editor, Routledge 2010); *The Oxford Handbook of British Politics* (joint editor, Oxford University Press 2009), *Why We Hate Politics* (Polity 2007, winner of the Political Studies Association's W. J. M. Mackenzie Prize in 2008), *European Politics* (joint editor, Oxford University Press 2007); *The State: Theories and Issues* (joint editor Palgrave 2006), and *Political Analysis* (Palgrave 2002). He is co-founder and co-editor of the journals *Comparative European Politics* and *British Politics* and an editor of *New Political Economy*. He was elected an Academician of the Academy of Social Science in 2009.

Christopher Hood is Gladstone Professor of Government and Fellow of All Souls College Oxford. When this article was published he was Professor of Public Administration and Public Policy at the LSE (1989–2000), and previously worked at the Universities of Sydney and Glasgow. More recently he was Director of ESRC's Public Services research programme (2005–10). His publications include *The Limits of Administration* (Wiley 1976), *Bureaumetrics* (joint author, Gower 1981), *The Art of the State* (Macmillan 1998), *Telecommunications Regulation* (joint author, Routledge 2000), *The Government of Risk* (joint author, Oxford University Press 2001), *The Politics of Public Service Bargains* (joint author, Oxford University Press 2006), and *The Blame Game* (Princeton University Press 2010).

Erik-Hans Klijn is Professor of Public Administration at Erasmus University Rotterdam, The Netherlands, and visiting professor at the School of Public Policy at the University of Birmingham. His research and teaching activities focus on complex decision-making and management in networks, institutional design and public private partnerships, mainly in the area of environmental and housing policy. He has published extensively in international journals and is co-author with Joop Koppenjan of *Managing Complex Networks: Strategies for the Public Sector* (Sage 1997), and *Managing Uncertainties in Networks: A Network Approach to Problem Solving and Decision Making* (Routledge 2004).

Joop Koppenjan is Professor of Public Administration at the Erasmus University Rotterdam, The Netherlands. Until recently he was Associate Professor at the Faculty of Technology, Policy and Management of Delft University of Technology. His research topics include policy networks, governance, project management, public private partnerships and public values. He is co-author with Erik-Hans Klijn of *Managing Complex*

Networks: Strategies for the Public Sector (Sage 1997), and *Managing Uncertainties in Networks: A Network Approach to Problem Solving and Decision Making* (Routledge 2004).

Vivien Lowndes is Professor of Public Policy, School of Politics and International Relations, University of Nottingham, having been previously Pro Vice-Chancellor (Research) at De Montfort University, Leicester, UK. She has conducted research projects on citizen participation, partnership governance, local political leadership and community cohesion for the ESRC and other UK and European bodies. She has undertaken work on faith engagement in public policy and is co-editor of *Faith in the Public Realm* (Policy Press 2009). Vivien Lowndes has also carried out a major piece of action research on 'preventing violent extremism' at the local level. She is a regular policy adviser to local and central government.

Richard Mulgan is Emeritus Professor in the Crawford School of Economics and Government, The Australian National University. He previously held chairs at the Universities of Otago (Classics, Political Studies) and Auckland (Political Studies) and at The Australian National University (Public Policy). His first book was *Aristotle's Political Theory* (Oxford University Press 1997) and his most recent book was *Holding Power to Account* (Palgrave Macmillan 2003).

R. A. W. Rhodes is Professor of Government in the School of Government at the University of Tasmania. He is also Professor Emeritus of Politics at the University of Newcastle (UK). Previously, he was the Director of the UK Economic and Social Research Council's 'Whitehall Programme' (1994–1999); Distinguished Professor of Political Science at The Australian National University (2005–7); and Director of the Research School of Social Sciences at The Australian National University (2007–8). He is the author or editor of some 30 books including recently: *The State as Cultural Practice* (joint author, Oxford University Press 2010); *ComparingWestminster* (joint author, Oxford University Press 2009); *Observing Government Elites* (joint editor, Palgrave Macmillan 2007); *The Oxford Handbook of Political Institutions* (joint editor, Oxford University Press 2006), and *Governance Stories* (joint author, Routledge 2006). He is Treasurer of the Australasian Political Studies Association, life Vice-President of the Political Studies Association of the United Kingdom, and a Fellow of the Australian Academy of Social Sciences. He has also been a Fellow of the Royal Society of Arts and an Academician of the Academy of Social Sciences (UK). He served as editor of *Public Administration* from 1986 to 2011.

Fritz W. Scharpf studied law and political science at Tübingen, Freiburg and Yale Universities: LL.M. Yale 1961; Dr. iur. Freiburg 1964. He was Visiting Assistant Professor, Yale and Chicago Law Schools (1964–66); Professor of Political Science, University of Konstanz (1968); Director at Wissenschaftszentrum, Berlin (1973); Director at the Max Planck Institute for the Study of Societies, Cologne (1986–2003). His Monographs in English are: *Crisis and Choice in European Social Democracy* (Cornell 1991), *Games Real Actors Play. Actor-Centred Institutionalism in Policy Research* (Westview 1997), *Governing in Europe. Effective and Legitimate?* (Oxford University Press 1999), *Community and Autonomy. Institutions, Policies and Legitimacy in Multilevel Europe* (Campus 2010).

Chris Skelcher is Professor of Public Governance at the Institute of Local Government Studies (INLOGOV), University of Birmingham, UK. His research examines the democratic performance and consequences of new forms of governance in comparative perspective as well as studies of European cities and US-UK business improvement districts.

John Stewart is an Emeritus Professor at the University of Birmingham. He was appointed to launch management courses for senior local government officers in the Institute of Local Government Studies at Birmingham. He later became Director of the Institute and Head of the School of Public Policy. He has written widely on the politics and management of local government and on public management generally. In 2007 the Society of Local Government Chief Executives gave him the inaugural Presidents Award for an outstanding contribution to local government. His books include *Modernising British Local Government* (Palgrave Macmillan 2003) and *The Nature of British Local Government* (Palgrave Macmillan 2001).

Katrien Termeer is Professor and Chair of the Public Administration and Policy Group at Wageningen University. She has worked at Erasmus University Rotterdam; the Technical University of Delft; the Ministry of Agriculture, Nature and Food; and at Sioo, the Inter-University Centre for Organizational Change and Learning. Her research and teaching activities focus on processes of societal change, public leadership, new modes of governance, and reflective action research. Her main fields of interests are adaptation to climate change, sustainable agriculture and revitalizing rural areas.

Jean-Claude Thoenig is a *directeur de recherche* (emeritus) at the French Centre national de la recherche scientifique (CNRS). He is affiliated with Dauphine Recherches en Management (DRM) (Université Paris-Dauphine). His contributions to social and management sciences are in the areas of sociology of organizations (public and profit) and political sociology (policy analysis and evaluation). He is a former Dean and Professor at INSEAD. He has been a consultant for the European Commission and for the French government. He has played a pioneering role in developing public management programmes for city and regional administrators, for the École Nationale d'Administration (Paris) and the European Institute for Public Administration (Maastricht). His recent books include *When Managers Rebel* (joint author, Palgrave Macmillan 2010).

Patrick Weller holds the Premier of Queensland Chair in Governance and Public Management and is the Director of the Centre for Governance and Public Policy at Griffith University, Australia, where he has held a chair of politics since 1984. His most recent books are *Comparing Westminster* (joint author, Oxford University Press 2009), *Inside the World Bank* (joint author, Palgrave Macmillan 2009), *Kevin Rudd: The Making of a Prime Minister* (Melbourne University Press 2010), and *Learning To Be a Minister* (joint author, Melbourne University Press 2010).

Paul Williams is Reader in Public Management and Collaboration, Cardiff School of Management, University of Wales Institute, Cardiff. Paul combines extensive experience of working as a public sector manager in Welsh local government for over 20 years with academic experience as a researcher, lecturer and consultant in public policy and management. He has undertaken research for a wide range of agencies at local and national government levels in Wales on equality, sustainable development, community strategies, the role of elected members, and collaborative working. He has a record of publications in these policy areas and his research interests are currently focused on collaboration between health and social care, leadership for collaboration, and the role of individual agents in the collaborative process.

Baron Wilson of Dinton GCB. Richard Wilson entered the Civil Service in 1966 and served in a number of departments including 12 years in the Department of Energy where his responsibilities included nuclear power policy and the privatization of Britoil. He worked in the Cabinet Office under Margaret Thatcher from 1987–90 and after two years in the Treasury was appointed Permanent Secretary of the Department of the Environment in 1992. He became Permanent Under Secretary of the Home Office in 1994 and Secretary of the Cabinet and Head of the Home Civil Service in January 1998. Since his retirement in September 2002 he has been Master of Emmanuel College, Cambridge.

Chapter 1

YESTERDAY WHEN I WAS YOUNG[1]

R. A. W. RHODES

INTRODUCTION

Before Bob Dylan and the explosion in the number of Anglo-Saxon singer-songwriters, the French had their *chanteurs à texte* and numbered among their post-war exemplars are Charles Aznavour, George Brassens, Jacques Brel, and Serge Gainsbourg. Their songs are avowedly poetic and often have a Gallic bitter-sweet quality. So, when a young Charles Aznavour sings of 'the thousand dreams I dreamed, the splendid things I planned', I think of the 1980s when, as joint editor of *Public Administration* and soon to be professor, opportunity was a vista spread before me. When an old Aznavour sorrowfully looks back and sings of 'yesterday when I was young', I think of the past 25 years and remember opportunities both missed and taken. My story of *Public Administration* is a story of a fall and a rise; of dashed hopes and new horizons.

This collection provides a portrait of the journal's work over the past 25 years and acts as a sourcebook of key articles in the field. This chapter tells the story of the journal up to my appointment as editor. I then describe the ways in which the journal changed over the past 25 years. I analyse the ways in which the subject matter of the journal has changed, updating the analysis in Rhodes *et al.* 1995 and Dargie and Rhodes 1996. However, this analysis does not tell us anything about broader changes affecting the journal. So I discuss the effects of professionalisation, corporatisation, marketisation, internationalisation, and digitization. I then describe the articles I have selected and discuss the criteria used to choose them. Finally, I speculate on the future of the discipline and the journal.

FROM ROYAL INSTITUTE OF PUBLIC ADMINISTRATION (RIPA) TO INTERNATIONAL JOURNAL

Public Administration was the journal of the RIPA. The Institute was born in May 1922.[2] It sought to combine professional development with the work of a learned society. The first issue of the *Journal of Public Administration* was published in January 1923. It changed its name to *Public Administration* in 1926 and it was published by Oxford University Press until 1930 when the Institute became its publisher. Up to the outbreak of the Second World War, the Institute never became a staff college for the civil service as some hoped. Rather, it was 'in essence a learned society' (Nottage and Stack 1972: 302). Its journal became one of the oldest and most prestigious in any subfield of political science.

The post-war years saw a great expansion of the Institute's work and heightened status; it became the *Royal* Institute in 1954. It introduced corporate membership for local authorities, nationalised industries and health authorities, all of which improved its finances. It expanded its training courses most notably for the UK's former colonies. Its staff increased to almost 100, and its income to over £400,000.

The RIPA's research and publications also grew. This work epitomised traditional public administration. It was institutional, analysing the history, structure, functions, powers and relationships of government organizations (Rhodes 1991 and 1996). Perhaps the exemplars are in *The New Whitehall Series* where retired permanent secretaries described their departments; skeletons without flesh let alone life. As a novitiate, I read Newsam (1954) on the Home Office, Bridges (1964) on the Treasury, and Sharp (1969) on housing and local government. There were 15 in the series. Somehow I never got around to reading Sir Harry Melville on the Department of Scientific and Industrial Research, or the other eleven in the series. Practitioners had no monopoly on turgid description. Chester and Willson's (1968 [1957]) account of *The Organization of British Central Government 1914–64* delivered boredom by the megaton. I still have my copies of these volumes. When writing this introduction, I took them off my bookshelves, probably for the last time, and smiled in fond recollection at these faded artefacts of a long gone era.

The journal was no exception to this dusty tradition. It typified the institutional tradition and a hostility to theory as it celebrated its 50th year. It is striking to see the differences between these articles and today's contributions. Articles were short, descriptive, historical, and concentrated on the formal-institutional aspects of government. They were often papers delivered at conferences, often organised by the RIPA. The articles had little theoretical content. They were not formally 'academic' in the sense that they had no abstract, introduction, argument, sub-headings, or conclusion. The topics were organised chronologically rather than by theme. There was little reference to the relevant academic literature. Occasionally there were footnotes which cited books and articles but there were no bibliographies. Authors did not engage with the academic literature.

Writing in 1972, its Director thought 'the Institute is better equipped than ever to take advantage of the opportunities that the times will doubtless present' (Nottage 1972: 443). Like most of us, he did not foresee the oil crisis, turbulent economic times, and the arrival of Margaret Thatcher. By 1992, the RIPA was in administrative receivership: it was broke. Its Director described 1976–89 as 'a volatile period' (Shelley 1993: 473). Shelley identifies several reasons for the RIPA's demise: the Institute overextending itself in leasing new premises; the slump in the overseas training market; auditing problems; and the cautious lending policy of the Bank. As editor of the journal, I was a bit player. I attended several executive council meetings, more as observer than participant. I spoke only on journal matters and then briefly. It seemed obvious to me the RIPA collapsed for two core reasons. It had too little capital to underpin its work and the civil service refused to provide core funding. At many points, the Cabinet Office could have intervened to save the Institute with a modest injection of capital. It chose not to do so, yet it was to spend millions in the 1990s and 2000s on the Civil Service College, the Centre for Management and Policy Studies, and the National School of Government. It seemed a wasted opportunity at the time. With 20/20 hindsight, it beggars belief.

I was a new boy among the great and good of Whitehall. My reputation was a tad 'unsound'. Christopher Pollitt encouraged me to apply for the job but, he explained, he also had to lobby for me because I was an outsider to the RIPA's world with a vocal commitment to theory and methods – guilty on both counts.[3] I was patronised. I remember Nevil Johnson, a former editor who became a member of the executive council of the RIPA, telling me how he ran the journal. I listened politely. Much as I found his Oakeshottian view of British government refreshingly eccentric, I knew we did not need a return to his editorial hand.

I was offered a six-year term as joint editor with Christopher Pollitt and, from 1988, I was sole editor. At the time, I thought six years was more than enough. Christopher reminds me regularly that I have served the longest six-years of any editor he knows.

He regularly warned me I was in danger of 'going stale'. He now needs to find another conversational gambit with which to upbraid me.

Before I became editor, I thought *Public Administration* was traditional and boring. It had a clear commitment to publishing practitioners and building bridges between academics and the worlds of British central and local government. After 1964, the journal became more professionalised with academics the main contributors. The subject matter remained diverse with the case study as the dominant method. There was little or no external research funding. The journal evolved cautiously rather than in leaps and bounds but it was beginning to change; to become a professional academic journal with little or no practitioner involvement.

Under Michael Lee and Christopher Pollitt's guiding hands there were major changes in the design and format of the journal.[4] They introduced systematic 'double blind' refereeing, and special 'theme issues'. These trappings of professionalism became the norm. Although it was unremarked in their editorial announcing the other changes, they also included a 'statement of purpose' for the journal. Crucially in my view, this statement announced the decision to reject 'manuscripts solely or primarily concerned with the detailed description of particular administrative practices or specific organizations' and to insist that case studies 'will be accepted only if they satisfy the two criteria of analytical rigour and a broad current interest' (Lee and Pollitt 1982: inside front cover). The statement was the death knell for the traditional article and a clear recognition of the impact of the social sciences on the subject. It was also a barrier to practitioners whose expertise lay in their detailed knowledge of administrative practices and specific organizations.

The journey to the academy had begun in earnest and I was happy to continue with these innovations. Indeed, I was sure the journal could change more with me as editor. But would I get the opportunity? I watched events at the RIPA unfold with a horror born of naked self-interest. I wanted to stay as editor because it was the top journal in my field. It now looked as if it would fold with the Institute. So, it had to be saved from receivers whose main concern was the value of the RIPA's assets rather than the academic integrity of its journal. Some horrendous names were broached and only the libel laws prevent me naming who might have happened to the journal. Enter Sue Corbett.

Sue Corbett was a distinguished member of the publishing profession, now retired. She was with Basil Blackwell publishers for 25 years and a member of Blackwell Publishing's management committee. Latterly, she became Managing Director of Medicine at Wiley-Blackwell. We met 'when I was a politics book editor and therefore pursuing you in the hope of getting you to write a book' (personal correspondence 12 May 2010). Like me, at the time she was a mere mortal. We kept bumping into each other because of the journal. Blackwell began to publish the journal for the RIPA from the summer of 1984 and Sue became journals' editor. She was the obvious person for me to talk to, especially as we got on; it was fun.

Sue persuaded Blackwell to buy the journal outright with me as the editor. There was only one problem. The print-run might have been some 10,000 copies but, with the demise of the RIPA, the corporate members, who accounted for most of those copies as a benefit of membership, were no more. We feared the worst, and we were right. Corporate members did not renew as individual subscribers. Almost literally, we had to start again to rebuild the subscription base. We also had to ensure a regular supply of copy. Back then, the journal was not made-up more than two issues ahead rather than the four to six of today. There could be no pretence the journal spoke to, or for, a professional public servant audience, and there was no longer a learned society. So, two of the normal sources of articles had dried up. We had to rely on academic colleagues. The journal had to survive in the fiercely competitive world of academic publishing without its practitioner membership base. It had to become a world-class *academic* journal selling to university and other libraries at home and abroad. And that is what Sue and I set out to do.

We had no magic formula but we knew the journal had to change and move beyond case studies of British government to attract a broader academic readership if we were to repair the subscription base. An editor is always victim of the material submitted; journals get typecast. Nonetheless, editors can, slowly, influence the direction a journal takes. I broadened its scope by publishing many more theory and comparative articles. To signal our new ambitions, for the Spring 1992 issue, we adopted a new name and became *Public Administration: an international quarterly*. I sought to create an international journal and Sue rode out the financial hard times and backed my judgement.

We were willing to experiment and learn. Christopher Pollitt had introduced 'Notes and Surveys'. This mutated into 'Currents' to encourage shorter practitioner pieces. In 1992, we introduced 'Public Management' and 'Comparative and International Administration'. In 1999, the latter became the 'European Forum' (Rhodes 1999). Judging by the volume of material they attracted, both 'Public Management' and the 'European Forum' were successes. Other experiments were less successful. We tried to expand reviews to include digital, web-based material. We encouraged review articles. Academic colleagues were reluctant to write them because they were not 'research' and did not count, therefore, for the research audit. Most recently (Rhodes 2008), we abolished all sections. It was a tribute to the success of the 'European Forum' that we no longer needed a separate section to attract non-UK material.

There are various crude measures of journal success. The number of submissions increased from some 120 a year in 1986 (including RIPA conference papers, public lectures and prizes) to over 300 new manuscripts a year in 2009. The number of articles published increased from 24 to 60 a year. On average, we rejected four out of every five papers submitted and, in theory at least, we published higher quality articles. The circulation grew steadily from some 1,300 in 1990s to over 3000 today. Despite the increase in the number of articles published, our impact factor remained firm.[5] In 2008, it increased to 1.269 and the journal was ranked 6th in the public administration category. *Public Administration* was always in the World 'Top 10'.

A PORTRAIT: FROM PRACTITIONERS' REFLECTIONS TO ACADEMIC SPECIALIZATION

Editors can become obsessive about their journals. I have already explored its changing subject matter from 1945–69 (Dargie and Rhodes 1996) and from 1970–94 (Rhodes *et al.* 1995). I might be fascinated by such exercises but I am reliably informed they have limited appeal to normal people. So, here I summarise the changing contents of the journal only briefly, providing a broad-sweep portrait of the major changes in content rather than a detailed analysis. I focus on the 1990s and 2000s but, first, I describe where I started.

Between 1970 and 1989, the dominant contributors to the journal became academics. Practitioner contributions dropped from an average of 68 a year between 1945 and 1969 to 23 between 1970 and 1994. The subject matter of the journal remained diverse. There was one significant trend between 1970 and 1989; the growth in articles focused on public policy-making. Rather surprising given that it was in fashion, there was almost no increase in the articles about public management in the 1980s. However, in 1990, when the journal introduced its 'Public Management' section, the proportion of articles on public management increased from an average of eight per cent over the period 1970–1989 to 32 per cent between 1990 and 1994. There was a significant change in research funding with 20 per cent of the articles based on funded research. Of the several sources, the ESRC accounted for nearly half, and was growing. Empirical analysis in all its forms became the dominant research method, and of the several empirical methods employed, the case study was the most important. Finally, there was an increase in the theoretical content of articles. Although the number of theoretical articles remained constant at some 4–6 per cent, as Dunsire (1995: 33) observes, 'most contributors to a journal such as this [*Public Administration*], including practitioners, are aware of theoretical writings on their topics'. Case studies were now topped and tailed with theory. The overall picture is that of a subject developing a stronger theoretical and empirical character by the mid-1990s.

TABLE 1 *Subject matter, 1990–2009*

SUBJECT	1990–1994		1995–1999		2000–2004		2005–2009	
	Numbers	%	Numbers	%	Numbers	%	Numbers	%
TRADITIONAL								
Theory	7	4.51	15	6.61	5	2.4	24	10.13
Public Management	50	32.26	36	15.86	38	18.27	24	10.13
Participation	1	0.65	8	3.52	2	0.96	4	1.69
Public policy-making and planning	20	12.9	14	6.17	9	4.32	4	1.69
Accountability	1	0.65	12	5.29	6	2.88	6	2.53
Personnel	2	1.29	4	1.76	0	0	2	0.84
Budgeting	3	1.94	15	6.61	5	2.4	3	1.27
Intergovernmental relations	4	2.6	12	5.29	2	0.96	2	0.84
Local government and other subcentral bodies	15	9.68	28	12.33	24	11.54	24	10.13
Central government	17	10.97	6	2.64	7	3.37	10	4.22
Law	0	0	3	1.32	3	1.42	3	1.27
Sub-total	120	77.42	153	67.4	101	48.56	106	44.72
INTERNATIONAL AND COMPARATIVE								
EU	3	1.94	11	4.84	19	9.13	19	8.01
Western Europe	11	7.1	25	11.01	43	20.7	58	24.47
Eastern Europe	0	0	3	1.32	1	0.48	2	0.84
USA	1	0.65	5	2.2	7	3.37	10	4.22
Australasia	0	0	9	3.96	10	4.81	13	5.49
Other	20	12.9	1	0.44	5	2.4	5	2.1
Sub-total	35	22.58	54	23.79	85	40.87	107	45.15
NEW								
Policy networks and governance	0	0	20	8.81	22	10.58	24	10.13
Sub-total	0	0	20	8.81	22	10.58	24	10.13
TOTAL	155	100	227	100	208	100	237	100

In the 1990s and the 2000s, much remained the same. Contributors remained overwhelmingly academic. In the 2000s, 94 per cent of the contributors were academics. Most articles had no research funding but of those that did, nearly all were funded by the ESRC. From 1990 to 2004, public management was the largest single category, although it tailed off in the late 2000s. Traditional public administration pottered along. Although some classical topics, such as administrative law, almost disappeared, others aged well. Local government and the National Health Service continued to attract much scholarly attention. Some topics, such as accountability, staged a mini-comeback. The contents remained diverse. The journal published articles on policy areas new to its pages (for example, sport, the police). However, there are three standout changes: theory; comparative public administration; and policy networks and governance. Theoretical articles became much more common, rising steadily to 10 per cent. The increase in comparative material from some 23 per cent to 45 per cent was gratifying but expected; it was editorial policy. The increase in the articles on networks, inter-organizational analysis and governance was not an editorial decision. It reflected changing academic interests. It was a rapid increase within the period. From nothing in the early 1990s, the number of articles increased to some 10 per cent throughout the 2000s. I sought to reflect the changing contents of the journal in my selection of articles for this collection (see below).

WHAT HAS CHANGED?

A content analysis of the journal tells us about the changing intellectual interests of the journal's contributors. There were also some broader changes affecting the journal; professionalisation, corporatisation, marketisation, internationalisation, and digitisation.

Professionalisation

The most obvious effects of professionalisation are the greater attention paid to theory and methods. An attendant outcome is specialisation. Younger colleagues cut their teeth on specific topics. I intend no criticism. I did the same; my early research interest of intergovernmental relations was nothing if not specialised. Such specialisation has long been a feature of a discipline that is technical and professional, rather than theoretical, and concerned with practical problems and their solutions. So, we master such subjects as human resource management, performance measurement, and budgeting within the micro-world of a local authority, a regional agency, or a non-governmental public body. It is a characteristic of professionalisation. Specialisation will become a problem, however, if it drives out an interest in broader issues such as the changing nature of the state or the role of bureaucracy in the post-bureaucratic era. The discursive essay is becoming a rarity, all the more welcome for its scarcity.

The research environment also changed. Young academics were trained to write academic articles for professional journals. The role model was American political science. So, they 'engaged with the literature', explained their methods, set out their research question and hypotheses, marshalled their data, and, even in the UK, employed statistical and deductive reasoning. They expected referees' reports. The commissioned piece was even rarer. The piece based on a practitioner's reflections was nigh extinct.

Corporatisation

Increasingly academics worked in a 'publish or perish' environment brought on by the audit explosion that engulfed the public sector, not just universities. 1986 saw the British government's first research assessment exercise (RAE), measuring the quality of academic research. Equivalent assessments followed roughly every five years. There were major consequences for the journal.

Departments shed their so-called 'tails' of colleagues who did not publish. More people wrote more articles on more and more specialised topics. Over the next two decades, refereed articles in international journals became the yardstick of excellence. *Public Administration* thrived, whether the measure is submission rate, circulation, or the impact factor. The effects were most pronounced in the two years before the RAE, when submissions escalated. There was a tailing off immediately after an RAE, so aspiring contributors take heed!

Marketisation

Professionalisation also affected marketing. In my first decade as editor, I paid no more than passing attention to the 'impact factors' produced by Thomson ISI (or the Institute for Scientific Information). This measure is flawed for the social sciences, yet it is reported on the journal's web site and every year I discuss with the publishers what we will do to improve the impact factor. All major publishers produce guides to improving your impact factor. For example, publishers devise strategies for 'optimising citations'.

- Court high impact academics and convince them to publish with you.
- Publish your best papers early in the year to make the most of the citation 'window'.
- Network wherever you can. Personal bonds can play a significant role in submissions.
- Ensure that your review process works efficiently and that turnaround times are short.
- Commission review and survey articles because they can attract up to twice as many cites as research papers in the same subject.
- Avoid short communications which count as research papers but attract few cites.
- Collect papers into thematic sets as either special issues or symposia in standard journal issues.
- Make your best papers available free online.

There are also 'cynical strategies' which, of course, no publisher would recommend and no editor would employ.

- Encourage authors to cite previous papers from your journal.
- Add highly cited articles in your journal to the list of references of papers under review.
- Agree mutual citation pacts with the editors of other journals in the same area.

Market considerations are not a UK phenomenon. Impact factors are ubiquitous. The Australian equivalent of the RAE is the Excellence in Research for Australia (ERA) Initiative. It is run by the Australian Research Council, which ranked journals A*, A, B or C depending on quality. A key predictor of that ranking was a journal's impact factor. There are no sour grapes here. The ERA ranked *Public Administration* A* (the top rank).[6] My aim is simply to describe the world journal editors live in, and to note the close relationship between professionalisation and marketing. Of course, publishers pay attention to impact factors. They would be foolish not to.

Internationalisation

The major change for *Public Administration* was its advance into Continental Europe. In 1986, the journal was the premier outlet for British public administration research. Now, it is an international journal, and we added 'an international quarterly' to its title as a signal of this change. Most of its content was from academics not based in the UK and about countries other than the UK. Credit must be given to Walter Kickert who did sterling work developing the 'European Forum'. *Public Administration* is no longer solely or even mainly a UK journal.

Internationalisation will be fostered by the twin trends of diversification and specialisation because they open opportunities for authors from many countries and disciplines. Public administration has ever broadening boundaries. In 1986, we may have published papers on public management but, with the coming of the new public management, there was a large increase in interest. The journal's terms of reference now cover public management and public policy. Moreover, even these broad areas are broadly conceived. It remains editorial policy to turn down case studies that do not address a theoretical or public policy issue of broad interest. We do not turn down any article because of its disciplinary or country origins.

Further internationalisation is inevitable. The journal has barely touched the huge Asian market, notably China. In 2009, we appointed the first Asian members of the Editorial Board. Our first Asian symposium will be published in 2012. Already Chinese authors submit regularly to the journal. They can struggle with the Western rules of the game. Their rejection rate is high. But many Chinese scholars are now trained in the USA, with PhDs from the best schools. The competitive advantage of the West will not last.

Digitisation

Digitisation was the key to the rebirth of *Public Administration* and it will be at the heart of its future academic and commercial success. Publishers now sell electronic access to bundles of journals. It is possibly the major marketing innovation of the 2000s.

We are all familiar with some degree of digitisation. *Public Administration* introduced its on-line manuscript management system in 2003. So, authors submit on-line and the editor's decision and the referees' reports are sent electronically. I used to have a journal secretary who wrote to authors on headed paper. Now I am my own secretary working through a web site in the USA. The offprint is gone. We now get the pdf. Articles still appear in hard copy but, thanks to *EarlyView*, the electronic version appears months before. I used to go the library to browse the journals' section. Now I get my e-mail announcement and download any article I want to my laptop. It is but the beginning. Digitisation already means I rarely look at the hard copy of any journal including the one I edited. Soon, the hard copy will only be printed on demand. Warehouse and distribution costs will be a thing of the past. What price a 'Kindle'™ for journals?

THE CHAPTERS

Over the past twenty-five years *Public Administration* has pioneered new approaches and published many leading articles. I could not possibly 'represent' the scope and coverage of the journal in 12 articles selected from the hundreds available. I don't try. Instead, I paint a personal picture of the journal and the selection reflects editorial policy and my interests. However, I looked for some 'objective' criteria both to support my preferences and to act as a counterweight to possible errors of judgement. There were two obvious starting points: citations, and the analysis of the journal's contents (above).

I know citation league tables can exert a perverse influence. For example, deans and other university managers use them to set inappropriate targets for 'staff' – are we still their colleagues? Nonetheless, we scour such rankings when they are published; they are often a source of malicious fun. Whether it is the ranking of universities or disciplines, we view them as confirmation of our relative standing. So, my first cut was a list of the most cited articles since 1986. There are several weaknesses with using citations. The longer an article has been published, the greater the number of citations. So, I also compiled a list of articles with the most citations in the 2000s, enabling me to balance old and new material. However, few articles published before 1990 are ever cited and none before 1986 made the top 100, yet I wanted some material from the earlier years. In addition, five authors accounted for one-third of all citations. I decided no author would have more than one article. That way the reader will hear more authorial voices. At best, the citations provide only a rough guide to the relative standing of articles. They did not determine the final selection.

I also wanted my selection to illustrate the changing contents of the journal. The content analysis suggests the main foci of the journal became theory, comparison, and public management. I use these broad categories to organise the book. So, Part I comprises theoretical articles from the 'Main articles' section, Part II contains comparative material from the 'European Forum', and Part III draws its material from the 'Public Management' section. That said, articles in the comparative section attracted fewer citations than articles in the rest of the journal. So, for this section, I had to exercise editorial privilege. For example, I always encouraged articles from Commonwealth countries and I insist the Commonwealth be present here. I also asked my European Editor, Walter Kickert, to nominate his favourite articles.

There was a particular problem when choosing the public management articles for this book. Articles about the practice of public administration are commonly about issues of the day and take the form of a case study in a particular country. Unfortunately, today's problems rapidly become tomorrow's antiquities and nobody cares any more. Even worse, the preoccupations of one country are not shared elsewhere. So, in Part III, I sought articles that addressed general issues of concern to practitioners which, I hope, will not date too quickly and are not specific to the UK.

I was also keen the journal should be an outlet for new approaches in public administration. Looking back over twenty-five years, it seems odd to describe the new public management, policy networks, and governance as 'new'; they are now so well-established. In 1986, they were not new; they were unknown. As the content analysis reveals, they are now an important and growing subset of articles in the journal.

Finally, this collection is more than a compilation of significant articles. It has a unique feature – the authorial afterword. Any article published in the 1990s, let alone the 1980s, will begin to show signs of wear and tear. So, everyone contributes an afterword of some 1,000 words reflecting on what they got right, and what they got wrong, and the continuing relevance of their findings.[7]

Part I focuses on theory and, in Chapter 2, Colin Hay reflects on the status of rational choice in public administration. In the USA, rational choice theory is probably the most influential approach in the study of politics. It is less influential in the UK and Continental Europe, but it is body of theory that public administration scholars need to engage with, if only to expound and clarify their own theoretical position. As the 'Afterword' emphasises, Colin invites us to reflect on the meaning of rationality beyond the narrow confines of utility-maximising behaviour and on the implications of assuming politicians and bureaucrats act only in their narrow, instrumental self interest. His argument that rational choice should be seen as a heuristic analytical strategy, not as an explanatory, predictive, theory, remains important and salient today. Colin Hay's article was an obvious choice because it was a winner of the United Kingdom Public Administration Consortium (UKPAC) Prize for best article of the year.

As the previous section shows, the study of networks and governance was a distinct and distinctive development in both the study of public administration and the pages of the journal. At its heart were two research programmes funded by the Economic and Social Research Council (ESRC); on local governance, and Whitehall. Chapter 3 by R. A. W. Rhodes surveys the findings of the Whitehall Programme and provides a summary of the first-wave theories of network governance. It tells the distinctive story of fragmentation, networks, unintended consequences and diplomacy in British government and challenges the managerial story of recent changes. The 'Afterword' reflects briefly on the limits of the first-wave and briefly outlines the successive waves of governance theory; on metagovernance, and decentred governance.

Chapter 3 offers a broad survey of network governance and its application to British government. Chapter 4 unpacks the idea by exploring multi-organisational partnerships in urban regeneration. Vivien Lowndes and Chris Skelcher identify a four-stage life cycle: pre-partnership collaboration, partnership creation, partnership programme delivery and partnership termination. They argue for separating such organisational forms from the modes of governance of networks, market and hierarchy to better manage the conflicts between them. As their 'Afterword' makes clear, partnerships are now institutionalised in UK public management and the research agenda has moved on to explore the mix of modes of governance and the role of individual actors in managing the mix.

Even editors can be surprised by the contents of their journal. I planned for and got more articles on public policy and public management. I did not expect the classical topics of traditional public administration to revive. Chapter 5 on accountability is a good example of revival. Richard Mulgan wrote a fine book on the topic: *Holding Power to Account: Accountability in Modern Democracies* (2003). His chapter rehearses many of the themes developed in that book, especially the argument that expanding the idea of accountability weakens its core idea of external scrutiny. As he stresses in his 'Afterword', the 'obligation of officials to answer to those they serve and to face sanctions from them' is a 'vital safeguard'. Whatever nuances, emphases or qualifications one might want to enter today, the core argument remains valid ten years later and explains why it is one of the more highly cited articles of the 2000s.

Part II comprises articles on comparative public administration. Chapter 6 is a genuinely comparative article, not a case study, of cabinet government in Westminster systems. Pat Weller points to the nigh endless confusions in the debate about cabinet government and identifies four meanings of the term: as the constitutional theory of ministerial and collective responsibility, as a set of rules and routines, as the forum for policy-making and coordination, as a political bargaining arena between central actors, and as a component of the core executive. Somewhat depressingly, in his 'Afterword', he concludes 'nothing has changed'. Examples abound whether it is the confusions of the House of Lords Select Committee on the Constitution's (2010) recent analysis of the Cabinet Office or the UK coalition government's view that collective responsibility still applies, except when it does not!

Fritz Scharpf's account of the joint decision trap in European Union (EU) policy-making in Chapter 7 is one of the classic articles of European public administration. He takes the idea of *'politikverflechtung'* in German federalism – an idea he pioneered – and applies it to EU policy-making. He points out that in both cases the affected governments participate in central decisions and the *de facto* requirement of unanimous decisions systematically generates sub-optimal policy. The result is, in Scharpf's neatly phrased paradox, 'frustration without disintegration and resilience without progress'. As he argues in his 'Afterword', this 'joint decision trap' is not the only mode of governance available in theory or practice, but it stands out because it has the potential for effective European solutions with some opportunities for democratic self-determination.

In Chapter 8, Erik-Hans Klijn, Joop Koppenjan and Katrien Termeer show that when case studies are linked with theory they can produce findings of general relevance. The case study is of renovating post-war housing in Groningen, The Netherlands. The theory is network theory. The outcome is a series of recommendations about creating win-win games, investing resources, limiting interaction costs, mobilizing commitment, political-administrative management, and open interaction. The article was one of the first to explore network management as part of the toolkit of government. As their 'Afterword' makes clear, the literature on network management has blossomed over the past 15 years. Subsequently, the authors wrote two important books on managing networks (Kickert, Klijn and Koppenjan 1997; Koppenjan and Klijn 2004). But for most readers, this is where it started. It attracts many citations, and it was nominated by the European editor as one of his favourite pieces from the 'European Forum'.

For Chapter 9, there is a personal tale. I am not sure that Jean-Claude Thoenig and I have ever had a face-to-face academic discussion. Our encounters have been fleeting, at official functions and the like. But early on in my career, his work with Michel Crozier on French public and territorial administration exercised an important influence on my work on British central-local relations (Crozier and Thoenig 1976). I do not even know if he is aware of his influence! However, when Walter Kickert acquired his article for the journal, I was delighted to renew our author-reader relationship. I was fascinated. The 1976 analysis had stood the test of time. French territorial administration was still polycentric, characterised by its honeycomb pattern of relations, the accumulation of political mandates, the cross-regulation of political and administration hierarchies, and centrifugal forces undermining state authority. When he describes the model as 'robust' in his 'Afterword', it is hard to disagree.

Part III focuses on public management. It is hard to find anything new to say about Chapter 10 by Christopher Hood on the new public management (NPM). It attracts massive citations and it is probably impossible to write on the topic without including it in the references. However, there is a story about it coming to *Public Administration*. In 1985, the Government and Law Committee of the ESRC funded a three-year research initiative on current changes in the system of government, with Nevil Johnson as its guiding hand. I asked Nevil to edit a special issue on the programme but he said no. I was puzzled. I was not sure why he did not want to draw attention to the findings of his programme. Perhaps editing the journal for a decade was enough for him. Anyway, I ignored him, and approached the several researchers on the programme personally, including Christopher Hood. They all thought it was a splendid idea and the journal published a special issue on *The new public management* (Volume 69 Number 1 1999). Since then, Christopher's article has made a major contribution to the journal's impact factor all by itself. As Christopher's 'Afterword' notes, it can be cited for the wrong reasons. He was not an advocate of NPM but a sceptical commentator. The research programme may be forgotten but his article is not and, if the fashion for NPM has subsided, many of its ideas and practices have become part of the mainstream.

The network literature now occurs in many guises from arcane theory to practical manuals. There is a large and growing literature on managing networks and this topic has expanded to encompass such topics as interorganisational analysis, collaboration, partnerships, and even coordination. It tends to focus on macro and structural factors in examining networks. From my youth at the Institute of Local Government Studies (INLOGOV), University of Birmingham, I remembered the work of John Friend on the idea of the 'reticulist' or 'network former' who activates decision networks (Friend, Power and Yewlett 1974: xxvii, 185, and 364–7). Chapter 11 by Paul Williams also looks at the individuals who manage the links between organisations – boundary spanners – and the ways in which they manage complexity and interdependence. He seeks to put the people back into networks and to reorientate the field. As his 'Afterword' suggests, now the challenge is to go into the field and watch boundary spanners 'in action'. The topic is as important, and neglected, today as it was when Williams wrote his article.

John Stewart was my boss at INLOGOV in my first lecturing job. Michael Clarke was the Director of the Local Government Training Board and one of John's regular co-authors. It is John Stewart I know best because he was an inspiration to this novitiate. He had a knack for communicating. He could hold an audience of local government officers under his spell even when they were sceptical. His work of corporate management and planning in local government commanded much attention among academics and practitioners alike in the 1970s. As I watched, it did not seem possible that, like him, I could write widely read books or command large audiences. I was not then, nor am I now, an advocate of his brand, or any other brand, of managerialism. However, Chapter 12 on the public service orientation is a remarkably prescient piece of work. Two decades later, the label may have gone but the basic ideas about service delivery and citizen choice and voice are at the heart of the managerial agenda for the 2000s. They were barely on the horizon when this chapter was written. Moreover, many of the issues it identifies remain to dog the service delivery agenda. The authors' 'Afterword' is slightly apologetic about their use of language and for underestimating the extent of change needed. Maybe, but being first excuses a lot.

Sir Richard Wilson, now Baron Wilson of Dinton, was Secretary to the Cabinet and Head of the Home Civil Service. Just before he retired, Sir Richard delivered a lecture on what had changed since his predecessor Lord Bridges wrote his *Portrait of a Profession* in 1950. Chapter 13 is one of the few pieces the journal published by a serving civil servant since 1992. I knew Sir Richard because he helped me with the ESRC's Whitehall Programme, smoothing access to central government departments. I was daunted by the demands the job made on him. I was impressed by his enthusiasm and willingness to look after an academic who simply could not have been a priority. I suspect his civility is a long-standing virtue of mandarins and his lecture is a tribute not only to the capacity of the civil service to respond to its political masters but also to its traditions and their ability to endure. As Baron Wilson emphasises in the 'Afterword', too often the role of the civil service as a 'shock absorber' is undervalued. Coping is not a history making activity but it is essential for all that (Rhodes 2011). It seems fitting that my picture of a journal that grew out of the ashes of the RIPA should end with the voice of a civil servant for whom, as for Lord Bridges, the learned society would have been a natural outlet for his thoughts.

CONCLUSIONS: WHERE TO NEXT?

In the early 1990s, I was pessimistic about the fate of the discipline in Britain in the 1980s (Rhodes 1991 and 1996) because of the impact of managerialism, the demise of the RIPA, and dependence on government funding. Hood (1999) compared this dodo or pessimistic view of the discipline with the phoenix or progressive view which stresses growing intellectual rigour and professionalisation. He itemised the advent of organisational analysis, policy analysis and a new generation of social science scholars. Hood demurred from judgements of decline or progress, however, inclining to a chameleon perspective that stresses an evolutionary view of the subject and its mainstreaming within political science. Boyne (1996) is also unsympathetic to the decline thesis, welcoming the shift to the new public management paradigm. In the 1980s, it was appropriate for the editor of the RIPA's *Public Administration* journal to reflect on the state of *British* (and perhaps Commonwealth) public administration. In 2010, such parochialism will not do. Instead, I must reflect on the state of *European* public administration; on its distinctive characteristics and on whether it is declining or prospering.

The discipline of public administration has shared problems no matter where it is studied. Mackenzie (1970: Chapter 2) defines disciplines not by their subject matter, methods or agreed paradigm but as social entities with shared traditions and supported by organisational forms such as departments or faculties in universities. In this sense, public administration was, and remains, a discipline. However, there can be no pretence to a disciplinary core. The first characteristic of the discipline is its profusion of contending theories and plurality of methods in both America and Europe. This shift from order to chaos, from traditional public administration to a range of contending approaches, has been noted so often, it does not require further elaboration here (see, for example, Henry 1999, Hood 1999, Lundquist 1985, Rhodes 1991). Second, its traditional subject matter of the history, structure, functions, powers and relationships of government organisations is also the happy hunting ground of many other disciplines. So, public administration competes for attention with economics departments and business schools among others. Many of the fears expressed about the future of public administration were about its disciplinary standing. The subject matter attracted ever more attention and was never in danger of disappearing from academic agendas.

Third, public administration is a practical subject, perhaps even a profession, which seeks to provide timely advice and train practitioners. It receives much financial support from government both in research grants, consultancies and other applied work. There are two ever-present dilemmas here. Academic fame and fortune lies in developing theory, in publication in international refereed journals, and standing with one's colleagues. The discipline survives, even thrives, in the 2000s because some of its leading players mastered the 'trick' of linking policy and academic relevance. It has a cadre of senior academics engaging with one another's work. We may specialise in central-local relationships, public service delivery or other topics of the day, but we locate such topics in the broader agendas of the social and human sciences. Yet the more successful we are in bridging theory and practice, the greater our dependence on government research support. We become too sensitive to the state's research agendas, courting the danger of becoming a slave social science of either mere technicians or loyal servants of power or, of course, both (Donovan 2005). Conversely, the more we seek to meet the academic criteria and focus on (say) theory, the less interesting our work to practitioners and the less inclined they are to fund research.

Fourth, public administration is all too often parochial, none more so than the world leader in the field, American public administration. As Kickert (1997: 28) points out, American public administration occupies a 'dominant position in the professional field' yet it is 'exceptionally unique'; for example it has no state tradition. The point about American parochialism is often conceded (Heady 2001, Stillman 1997). Indeed, Richard Stillman (2010), the editor of *Public Administration Review* (PAR), argues that the mission of his journal is to 'promulgate generalist administrative ideas' to forge a 'corporate identity of like-minded generalist professionals'. That mission is specific to a country with no such cadre of state officials. He talks as though American practitioners are the only relevant audience, since PAR is a local professional journal. On the other hand, European public administration is shaped by several distinct state traditions; for example, the consociational, Napoleonic, and *rechtsstaat* traditions (see Dyson 1980, Kickert 2007). We can pride ourselves that we have a plurality of parochialisms to go with our many theories and eclectic methods!

Finally, this parochialism sustains some distinctive research agendas. I give two examples; something old and something new. Most countries have a juridical tradition not found in America or Britain whether it is the French *droit adminstratif* or the German *rechtsstaat*. There is also the recent explosion of work on networks and governance It has had four main expressions; the 'Anglo-governance school' in the UK (Marinetto 2003, Rhodes 1997 and 2007), *steuerungtheorie* in Germany (Mayntz 1993 and 2003, Scharpf 1997), network management in The Netherlands (Kickert, Klijn and Koppenjan 1997, Koppenjan and Klein 2004), and a normative literature that raises the question of whether networks and governance increase participation (Sørensen and Torfing 2005).

These local traditions vie with the mighty American presence in the field. The size and prestige of the American profession mean that if American scholars develop a new intellectual fashion, it almost invariably becomes everybody else's fad. I consider such intellectual trends as reinventing government and public value as agendas heavily conditioned by their American constitutional and political context. They travel poorly, and probably should not travel at all (Rhodes and Wanna 2009), yet still they attract often uncritical disciples. The problem is compounded by the reluctance of American public administration to engage with the rest of the world. When the American's 'discovered' policy networks, they displayed limited awareness of the four schools of network governance in European public administration.

The consequences for *Public Administration* are unfortunate. American scholars offer little of their work to non-US journals, and the work they do offer is often too narrow for an international readership. To be blunt, we do not get their best work. We conspire to support American parochialism. We rank their journals as 'international' when the overwhelming proportion of that journal content is by Americans for Americans on America (Sharman and Weller 2009). So, America remains the Dark Continent for European public administration. The question is whether we should bother to adventure there as either editors or authors? Of course we will, and we should engage with interesting ideas and practices wherever we may find them, but the future does not lie in American parochialism. Rather, the future lies in developing our own parochialisms.

European public administration no longer has an agreed theoretical core. It grapples with but does not resolve the divide between pure and applied research. It is parochial, and challenged by American traditions of study. Yet it is a thriving area of research with a cadre of distinguished professors with distinctive research agendas. The journal has increasingly mirrored the diversity of the subject, and I hope it will continue to do so.

Colleagues will continue to bemoan the lack of a disciplinary core or our failure to engage with practitioners. Others will extol the virtues of the latest American intellectual fashion, and rail against European parochialism. I hope all of this comes to pass and the analysis and debate takes place in the pages of the journal. We may have moved from order to chaos but for the journal that translates into diversity and controversy; into a prospering discipline. What fun![8]

ENVOI

I empathise with Charles Aznavour's sadness when he sings 'there are so many songs in me that won't be sung', but I do not have his Gallic cast of mind. Late in his career Bob Dylan gave us a trio of CDs to rank with his best – 'Time Out of Mind', 'Love and Theft', and 'Modern Times'. So, I have more songs to sing and as Dylan reminds us, 'it's not dark yet' even if 'it's getting there'.

NOTES

[1] I would like to thank Eilidh St John for research assistance and Sue Corbett, Jenny Fleming, Christopher Pollitt, and Pat Weller for commenting on the first draft.

[2] This brief history of the RIPA is drawn from Nottage and Stack 1972; Nottage 1972; and Shelley 1993.

[3] The post-war editors of the journal were D. N. Chester (1946–1966); Nevil Johnson (1966–1981); Michael Lee (1981–1986); Christopher Pollitt (1981–1988); and R. A. W. Rhodes (1986–2011).

[4] All editors incur massive debts with their editorial team, editorial board and journal referees. After 25 years, it is just not possible to thank everyone by name but I would not like anyone to think I am ungrateful for their sterling support. There are the few who served beyond the call of duty. I mourn the passing of my 'Public Management' and latterly 'Reviews Editor', Bill Jenkins. He joined me in 1992 and we worked together for 17 years. Jean Frostick and Sally Crawford were magnificent journal managers and, best of all, fun colleagues. Walter Kickert's work in building the 'European Forum' was integral to the journal's success.

[5] The impact factor is calculated by dividing citations in the past two years by the total number of articles. So, the more articles you publish, the harder it is to maintain your impact factor, given that only a minority of articles ever attract significant attention.

[6] See: http://www.arc.gov.au/era/era_journal_list.htm; and Rhodes and Hamilton 2007. Both last accessed 31 May 2010.

[7] The authors have not changed their original texts and we have only edited the chapters for obvious spelling and other mistakes and to ensure a uniform design and layout.

[8] If European public administration prospers in its diversity, I must enter a qualification about British public administration. Its position is more precarious. It is a small discipline compared to that of The Netherlands let alone Germany, reliant on government especially research council support, with only a small postgraduate recruitment with which to replace its grand old men and women. In the era of the global financial crisis, it is vulnerable to changing government policy and legislative agendas and cuts in public expenditure (see Hood 2011).

REFERENCES

Boyne, G. 1996. 'The intellectual crisis in British public administration: is public management the problem or the solution?' *Public Administration*, 74, 3, 679–94.

Bridges, Sir Edward (later Lord) 1950. *Portrait of a Profession*. Cambridge: Cambridge University Press.

Bridges, Lord. 1964. *The Treasury*. London: Allen & Unwin.

Chester, D. N. and F. M. G. Willson. 1968 [1957]. *The organization of British central government 1914–1964*. 2nd edition. London: Allen & Unwin.

Crozier, M. and J. C. Thoenig. 1976. 'The Regulation of Complex Organised Systems', *Administrative Science Quarterly*, 21, 4, 547–70.

Dargie, C. and R. A. W. Rhodes. 1996. 'Public Administration 1945–1969', *Public Administration*, 74, 2, 325–332.

Donovan, C. 2005. 'The governance of social science and everyday epistemology', *Public Administration*, 83, 3, 597–615.

Dunsire, A., 1995. 'Administrative theory in the 1980s: a viewpoint', *Public Administration*, 73, 1, 17–40.

Dyson, K. H. F. 1980. *The state tradition in Western Europe: a study of an idea and institution*. Oxford: Martin Robertson.

Friend, J. K., J. Power and C. J. L. Yewlett. 1974. *Public planning: the inter-corporate dimension*. London: Tavistock.

Heady, F. 2001. 'Priorities for 2001 and beyond', *Public Administration Review*, 61, 4, 390–395.

Henry, N. 1999. *Public administration and public affairs*. 7th edn. Upper Saddle River, NJ: Prentice-Hall.

Hood, C. C. 1999. 'British public administration: dodo, phoenix or chameleon?' In J. Hayward, B. Barry and A. Brown (eds), *The British study of politics in the twentieth century*. Oxford: Oxford University Press for the British Academy: 287–311.

Hood, C. 2011. 'It's public administration, Rod, but maybe not as we know it. British Public Administration in the 2000s', *Public Administration*, 89, 1, 128–139.

House of Lords Select Committee on the Constitution. 2010. *The Cabinet Office and the centre of government*. 4th Report, Session 2009–10, HL 30. London: The Stationery Office.

Kickert, W. 1997. 'Public management in the United States and Europe'. In W. J. M. Kickert (ed.), *Public management and administrative reform in Western Europe*. Cheltenham: Edward Elgar: 15–38.

Kickert, W. (ed.). 2007. *The study of public management in Europe and the US. A competitive analysis of national distinctiveness.* Abingdon, Oxon: Routledge.

Kickert, W. J. M., E-H. Klijn and J. F. M. Koppenjan. (eds). 1997 *Managing complex networks: strategies for the public sector*. London: Sage.

Koppenjan, J. and E-H. Klijn. 2004. *Managing uncertainties in networks: a network approach to problem solving and decision making.* London: Routledge

Lee, J. M. and C. Pollitt. 1982. 'From the editors', *Public Administration*, 60, 1, 1–2.

Lundquist, L. 1985. 'From order to chaos: recent trends in the study of public administration'. In Jan-Erik Lane (ed.), *State and Market: The Politics of the Public and the Private*. London: Sage Publications: 201–30.

Marinetto, M. 2003. 'Governing beyond the centre: a critique of the Anglo-Governance School', *Political Studies*, 51, 3, 592–608.

Mayntz, R. 1993. 'Governing failure and the problem of governability: some comments on a theoretical paradigm'. In J. Kooiman (ed.), *Modern governance*. London: Sage: 9–20.

Mayntz, R. 2003. 'New challenges to governance theory'. In H. P. Bang (ed.), *Governance as social and political communication.* Manchester: Manchester University Press: 27–39.

Mackenzie, W. J. M. 1970. *The study of political science today*. London: Macmillan.

Mulgan, R. 2003. *Holding power to account: accountability in modern democracies*. Houndmills, Basingstoke: Palgrave Macmillan.

Newsam, Sir Frank 1954. *The Home Office*. London: Allen & Unwin.

Nottage, R. and F. Stack. 1972. 'The Royal Institute of Public Administration, 1922–1939', *Public Administration*, 50, 3, 281–304.

Nottage, R. 1972. 'The Royal Institute of Public Administration 1939–1972', *Public Administration*, 50, 4, 419–443.

Rhodes, R. A. W. 1991. 'Theory and methods in British public administration: the view from political science' *Political Studies*, 39, 3, 533–54.

Rhodes, R. A. W. 1996. 'From institutions to dogma: tradition, eclecticism and ideology in the study of British public administration', *Public Administration Review*, 56, 6, 1996: 507–16.

Rhodes, R. A. W. 1997. *Understanding governance*. Buckingham and Philadelphia: Open University Press.

Rhodes, R. A. W. 1999. 'Editorial: *Public Administration* in Europe', *Public Administration*, 77, 1, 1–6.

Rhodes, R. A. W. 2007. '*Understanding Governance*: ten years on', *Organization Studies*, 28, 8, 1243–1264.

Rhodes, R. A. W. 2008. 'Editorial: *Public Administration* in the digital era', *Public Administration*, 86, 1, 1–4.

Rhodes, R. A. W. 2011. *Everyday life at the top*. Oxford: Oxford University Press, forthcoming.

Rhodes, R. A. W., C. Dargie, A. Melville and B. Tutt. 1995. 'The state of public administration: a professional history, 1970–1995', *Public Administration*, 73, 1, 1–16.

Rhodes, R. A. W. and M. Hamilton. 2007. 'Australian political science: journal and publisher rankings' (http://www.auspsa.org.au/index.php?option=com_content&task=blogcategory&id=15&Itemid=33). Last accessed 31 May 2010.

Rhodes, R. A. W. and J. Wanna. 2009. 'Bringing the politics back in', *Public Administration*, 87, 2, 161–83.

Scharpf, F. W. 1997. *Games real actors play. Actor-centred institutionalism in policy research*. Boulder, Colorado, Westview Press.

Sharman, J. C. and P. Weller. 2009. 'Where is the quality? Political science scholarship in Australia', *Australian Journal of Political Science*, 44, 4, 597–612.

Sharpe, E. 1969. *The Ministry of Housing and Local Government*. London: Allen & Unwin.

Shelley, I. 1993. 'What happened to the RIPA?' *Public Administration*, 71, 4, 471–490.

Sorsensen, E. and J. Torfing. 2005. 'Democratic anchorage of governance networks', *Scandinavian Political Studies*, 28, 3, 195–218.

Stillman II, R. J. 1997. 'American vs. European public administration: does public administration make the modern state, or does the state make public administration?' *Public Administration Review*, 57, 4, 332–338.

Stillman II, R. J. 2010. 'Why PAR matters: reflecting on ASPA's flagship journal at 70', the 2010 Stone Lecture, American Society of Public Administration Annual Conference, San Jose Fairmont, San Jose, California, April 9–13.

PART I: THEORY

Chapter 2

THEORY, STYLIZED HEURISTIC OR SELF-FULFILLING PROPHECY? THE STATUS OF RATIONAL CHOICE THEORY IN PUBLIC ADMINISTRATION

COLIN HAY

The appeal of rational choice theory to scholars of public administration and political analysis more broadly undoubtedly lies in its promise to deliver a naturalist science of the political. Crucial to this is the assumption of rationality, which effectively serves to render (political) behaviour predictable in any given context. This it does by eliminating the indeterminacy otherwise injected into social systems by human agency. If individual conduct can be assumed rational, and an actor's utility function can be specified, then that actor's behaviour is rendered entirely predictable in any given political setting. The opportunity structure dictates the rational choice – or, conceivably, choices – for any agent in any context. The assumption that there is only one rational course of action in any given setting is a starting premise in many introductions to rational choice (see for instance Dunleavy 1991, pp. 3–4), but it is important to note that most non-trivial game theoretical models have multiple equilibria and are, therefore, indeterminate (to some extent). This is a point to which we return in more detail presently. Suffice it for now to note that such indeterminacy arises not from human agency *per se* but from the structure of the context itself. In short, rational choice's indeterminacy is not ontological but contingent upon the context in question. Moreover, it does not inhere in the human subject. Rational choice is, consequently, incapable of dealing with the inherent indeterminacy injected into social systems by *human agency*. It is, moreover, based upon a methodology which seeks (even when this may prove elusive) fully determinate predictions. Just as an object dropped from a tower cannot choose to ignore the theory of gravity, so too a political subject facing a strategic conundrum has no choice other than to select the rational course of action. As this suggests, if the 'choice' is rational it is not a choice at all.

The rationality assumption is, then, a convenient short-cut which makes possible a naturalist science of the political such as is capable of generating, through a process of deduction, testable and predictive hypotheses. Yet it comes at a price – a price which many rational choice theorists are prepared to concede – namely the implausibility of the very assumptions upon which such a process of deduction is predicated (see, most famously, Friedman 1953, pp. 14–15; North 1990, p. 17). There is, in short, a significant trade-off. This, I contend, should make us wary of the causal, explanatory or predictive inferences invariably drawn from rational choice modelling (see also Hollis and Nell 1975).

Indeed, I go further, arguing that rational choice is best seen not as a theory at all, but rather as a set of analytical strategies for the construction of stylized heuristics (cf. Ward 2002). Cast in such terms, rational choice may be liberated both from its naturalist and positivist connotations and deployed in the service of a great diversity of otherwise incompatible theoretical perspectives.

To be clear at the outset, although critical of the grand and totalizing theoretical pretensions of much rational choice theory and, by implication, many rational choice theorists, this paper does not present a critique of rational choice *per se*. Used judiciously and cautiously for a series of carefully specified purposes it is a potentially powerful weapon in the armoury of the critical political analyst. Yet offered – as it so often is – as a universal theory of (political) conduct, it prejudges the question of rationality, commits itself to assumptions whose implausibility many of its exponents freely admit, and renders redundant the crucial question of the conditions under which the rationality assumption is most likely to hold (Green and Shapiro 1994; Taylor 1995). As we shall see, there is a clear danger of the self-fulfilling prophecy in such a totalizing meta-narrative. For, arguably, rational choice models correspond most closely to the reality they purportedly represent where they 'describe' the behaviour of actors who have internalized rational choice assumptions. (And by extension, the same is true of realism in international relations theory and, indeed, much neo-classical economics.) As this suggests, behaviour consistent with such modelling cannot necessarily be taken as confirmation of the veracity of the model (far less, the theory more generally).

INTRODUCTION

Stated most simply, rational choice theory is the modelling of political behaviour on the simplifying assumption that political actors are instrumental, self-serving utility-maximizers. Its *raison d'être* is the construction of stylized (preferably, mathematical) models of political conduct. What makes such modelling possible is the assumption that individuals are rational and behave *as if* they engage in a cost-benefit analysis of each and every choice available to them before plumping for the option most likely to maximize a given utility function (generally, an expression of material self-interest). (It is now conventional for rational choice theorists to declare themselves agnostic about the specific utility function to be maximized in any given context, insisting that the term rationality refers only to the efficiency with which means are deployed in the service of given preferences. However, it is still the case that most rational choice inspired game theoretical modelling draws on a remarkably narrow set of utility functions which seem to correspond closely to a simple conception of material self-interest and to be preserved from one game to the next and from one author to the next. Capital maximizes profit, political parties the chance of their election or re-election, public servants the budgets of their bureaus, and so forth.) They behave rationally, maximizing personal utility net of cost while given little or no consideration to the consequences, for others, of their behaviour. Generally speaking, rational actors will only take account of the consequences of their action for others in so far as those consequence have (or are anticipated to have) knock-on implications for their own ability to maximize their personal utility in the future. In most cases, however, such complex feedback effects are discounted in rational choice models which tend to assume that actors are motivated solely by short-term personal gain, with longer-term consequences essentially discounted. Obvious exceptions are many, if not all, forms of rational choice which make use of evolutionary game theory. An alternative strategy, which does at least give the impression of bringing altruistic behaviour under the covering law of rational choice, is to suggest that vicarious pleasures (and hence utility) follow from altruistic behaviour or, as in Gary Becker's formulation, that it is rational to act altruistically since the 'beneficial indirect effects on the behaviour of others' may out-weigh 'the direct "disadvantages"' (1976, p. 287; cf. Elster 1979, pp. 141–6). This is an ingenious solution to the 'problem of altruism', but arguably one which, in dissolving altruism into rational self-interest, fails to capture the ethical/moral imperative which underpins all altruistic behaviour. If altruism is defined, as perhaps it should be, as behaviour in which considerations of self-interest are subordinated to a perceived ethical/moral imperative of care for others, then such a 'solution' will not suffice.

The purpose of rational choice theory is to produce a deductive and predictive science of the political, modelled on precisely the same assumptions that have proved so influential (and, arguably, so useful) in neo-classical economics (Mueller 1989, p. 1). Given their exceptional degree of influence, it is, in fact, very difficult to gauge the utility of neo-classical economic assumptions. That models predicated upon rational choice assumptions seem to have explanatory potential within economic systems, may reflect nothing other than the prevalence of rational choice assumptions in the mindsets of public policy-makers thoroughly immersed in neo-classical economics since their undergraduate days.

The contribution of rational choice to public administration and political science more broadly has been considerable. Indeed, any attempt to list the crowning achievements of the latter over the past 50 years would surely see rational choice very well represented. Especially significant has been its ability to reveal the often perverse and collectively irrational effects of individually rational action.

In public administration, such a logic is most clearly reflected in the expansive public choice literature which explores the collectively irrational consequences of budget-maximizing bureaucratic behaviour. From William Niskanen's pioneering *Bureaucracy and Representative Government* (1971) – indeed, arguably before (see, for instance, von Mises 1944; Tullock 1965; Downs 1967) – the defining feature of public choice theory has been its emphasis upon the political pathologies which are almost invariably seen to issue from the attempt of public authorities to correct market failures. This general theme has been variously explored, to reveal: (1) the (supposed) inexorable tendency for the over-supply of public goods which arises from the budget-maximizing behaviour of bureaucrats and their control over the release of budget-relevant information to elected officials (Niskanen 1971); (2) the (supposed) erosion of market discipline which follows from the rent-seeking behaviour of organized interests able to secure for themselves a quasi-monopoly status (Olson 1982); and (3) the (supposed) economic pathologies (principally instability and inflationary pressures) which arise from the translation of electoral self-interest into a politically-engendered business cycle (Nordhaus 1975; Alesina 1989). The affinities with the new right are clear and scarcely veiled (though for an important attempt to fashion a distinctly radical public choice alternative, see Dunleavy 1991).

In more general terms, it is rational choice theory's emphasis upon collective action and, in particular, its identification of the problem of 'free riding' that has perhaps proved most notable. Here, despite a situation in which cooperation will secure mutual advantage, (rational) actors (motivated solely by self-interest) have a perverse incentive to non-participation. The logic, given rational self-interest, is impeccable. For, in many situations in which collective action is required to achieve a given end, a rational actor will (rightly) discount the likelihood of her own behaviour influencing significantly the overall outcome. Moreover, if others cooperate she will reap the benefits of their cooperation regardless of her participation. So why incur personal costs by taking unilateral action? In such scenarios, the dependence of a favourable outcome upon coordinated or collective action is sufficient to create (perverse) incentives for actors to free ride on the (anticipated) conduct of others. Tragically, if all individuals behave rationally, no cooperation arises and an outcome which is both collectively and individually sub-optimal ensues.

A now classic example is the so-called 'tragedy of the commons', first identified by Garrett Hardin (1968). It provides an intuitively-plausible and all too compelling model of the seemingly intractable problem of environmental degradation in contemporary societies. The systematic exploitation and pollution of the environment, it is argued, is set to continue since individual corporations and states, despite a clear collective interest, choose not to impose upon themselves the costs of unilateral environmental action. Their logic is entirely rational (or, at least, entirely instrumental). They know that environmental regulation is costly and, particularly in an open international economy, a burden on competitiveness. Accordingly, in the absence of an international agency capable of enforcing the compliance of all states and all corporations, the anticipation of free-riding is sufficient to ensure that corporations and states do not burden themselves with additional costs and taxes. The long-term effects for the environment are all too obvious. Individual rationality translates into collective irrationality.

As this already serves to indicate, the assumption of rationality tends to be a pessimistic one. *Ceteris paribus*, self-serving, utility-maximizing behaviour in situations of perfect or near-perfect information translates into collectively irrational outcomes. Indeed, the almost natural affinity between public choice theory on the one hand and the new right's antipathy to the state on the other might plausibly be attributed to the projection of such pessimistic assumptions onto public officials. The story of rational choice theory is, then, frequently one in which collective goods are sacrificed on the altar of narrowly conceived material self-interest (and, indeed, long-term self-interest is sacrificed for short-term material gain). There are, of course, notable exceptions, such as the work of Charles Taylor on social revolutions – see Taylor 1976; see also Shubik 1970. For many this is an unduly pessimistic depiction of the human subject, a far from universal condition and a wild extrapolation from particular contexts and times in which the narrow pursuit of self-interest has (regrettably) become institutionalized as the dominant mode of conduct. In short, what is (thankfully) politically, institutionally and culturally contingent is presented as a trans-historical and universal necessity.

For these critics, however, the pathology of such totalizing rational choice theory which claims a universal applicability lies not in the assumption of rationality as such. Rather it is the consequent inability to consider the conditions (political, institutional, cultural) under which actors deploy exclusively goal-oriented instrumental rationalities and, by extension, the conditions under which the pursuit of collective goals and the provision of public goods might replace such logics of calculus (Green and Shapiro 1994, p. 97; Taylor 1995).

To be fair, many contemporary rational choice theorists are immune from such criticisms, having softened, qualified and/or contextualized strong rationality assumptions. Such authors tend to see actors as rational only in the sense that they are instrumental in their attempts to maximize a given utility function, declaring themselves agnostic in general terms about the specific utility function to be maximized (for instance Olson 1965, p. 65; Buchanan 1977; Tsebelis 1990, p. 18; Dowding 1991, p. 31). As Patrick Dunleavy explains, within such a framework, 'someone behaves "rationally" if they optimise their preferences in a consistent fashion, however ill-advised we may judge their preferences to be' (1991, p. 3).

This somewhat thinner conception of rationality is certainly preferable to universalizing attempts to derive a theory of human conduct from an assessment of narrow self-interest alone. Yet it is not unproblematic. It, too, leaves rational choice theorists unable to address the question of the conditions under which alternative logics of appropriateness (say) may substitute for logics of calculus as the dominant mode of conduct within a given institutional setting. It also leaves unanswered the question of how we might determine (inductively or deductively) the specific utility function informing rational conduct in any given setting. This fact has not gone unnoticed by a number of rational choice theorists, who have argued (rightly) that the exogenous nature of actors' utility functions to rational choice modelling demonstrates that rational choice cannot be viewed as a free-standing or universal theory. As Hugh Ward explains, 'it needs other perspectives to help explain why individuals have the interests they do, how they perceive those interests, and the distribution of rules, powers and social roles that determines the constraints on their actions' (2002, p. 65; see also Dunleavy 1991; Ferejohn 1991, p. 248; although cf. Klosko 1987; Riker 1990, p. 174). Finally, the dropping of any *a priori* assumptions about the utility functions that rational subjects maximize may become particularly problematic where rational choice theorists engage (as often they do) in the retroductive process of developing *post hoc* explanations of known facts (as described by Fiorina and Shepsle 1982, p. 63). The clear temptation, in such situations, is to fiddle with alternative specifications of the utility function until such time as a good predictive model is found (for outcomes we already know). As Peter C. Ordeshook notes, 'even if such models fit the data up to an acceptable level of statistical accuracy, we must contend with the fact that we can establish nearly any reasonable outcome as an equilibrium to some model, provided only that the model is sufficiently complex'. Once this is acknowledged, 'designing assumptions so that a model's predictions fit the data is, in fact, little more than an exercise in curve fitting' (1993, p. 95, cited in Green and Shapiro 1994, p. 35). Moreover, as Leibnitz demonstrated, for any finite number of observations there is an infinite number of algebraic models which adequately fit or describe the data. Consequently, that a rational choice model can be fitted to the data in this way says less about the theory's explanatory power than it does about the conviction of the theorist to model such behaviour in rational choice theoretical terms. As Green and Shapiro mischievously note, 'given the lack of specificity about what it means to be a rational actor, it is not obvious what sorts of behaviour in principle would fail to be explained by some variant of rational choice theory' (1994, p. 34). This having been said, if it is conceded that rational choice is not a stand alone theoretical paradigm and needs to be supplemented by other theories, then the possibility clearly exists to import *a priori* assumptions about the utility to be maximized in any given context from other theoretical perspectives. In this way, *post hoc* rationalization need not degenerate into *ad hoc* rationalization (Ward 2002). Such an approach is entirely consistent with the revised and more modest deployment of rational choice modelling within a post-naturalist political analysis proposed in the final section of this paper (see also Bates *et al.* 1998a and b).

In the pages that follow, I consider the extent to which these widely identified and much debated limitations of rational choice theory can be overcome. I argue that if recast less as of a universal theory of human conduct – or, indeed, a theory at all – and more as a set of analytical strategies for exploring the logical consequences of a given set of heuristic or imported assumptions, rational choice has a crucial role to play in critical political analysis (see also Lane 1995, pp. 123–4; Ward 2002, p. 88). Cast in this more modest and subsidiary role, it is a particularly potent analytical device in puncturing convenient myths, problematizing taken for granted assumptions and, above all, warning of the perverse consequences of institutional (and other) incentives to instrumentally rational action.

The argument is developed in three sections. In the first of these I consider the nature of rational choice theory itself, examining its deductive mode of reasoning and considering the two dominant defences that have been offered of the parsimonious simplicity of its analytical assumptions when set against the complexity of the (political) reality they purport to represent. I suggest: (1) that parsimony is the very condition of rational choice modelling and, indeed, of a deductive and predictive science of politics; (2) that in complex and open social systems, parsimony effectively guarantees implausible analytical assumptions; (3) that implausible analytical assumptions are incompatible with the deduction of genuinely causal/explanatory inferences; and, (4) that if this is conceded, the status of rational choice as an explanatory/predictive theory needs to be reassessed.

In the subsequent section I turn from the question of complexity to that of contingency, interrogating rational choice theory's ingenious, if ultimately problematic, attempt to preserve a predictive science of politics by effectively assuming away the indeterminacy injected into human affairs by agency. I suggest that despite its emphasis on choice, rational choice theory has an essentially hollow conception of the human subject whose (rational) conduct is, ultimately, determined and thereby rendered predictable (in many cases absolutely) by the context itself. In games with multiple equilibria, for instance, as already noted, though the outcome is not fully determinate, neither is it indeterminate. A strong prediction is made that whatever specific outcome arises will lie along the Pareto frontier of the actor's utility function.

In the final section I consider the role that rational choice might play in a post-positivist, post-naturalist critical political analysis that acknowledges precisely the complexity and contingency of political systems that renders rational choice theory's attempt to furnish a predictive science of politics ultimately futile.

PARSIMONY, COMPLEXITY AND THE ASSUMPTION OF RATIONALITY

Rational choice theory's approach to political analysis is both deductive and parsimonious. It values the simplicity of the assumptions upon which its modelling, and the deduction of predictive or explanatory inferences, is predicated. This, in itself, is unremarkable. For, the formal/mathematical modelling of political (or, indeed, economic) conduct is likely to prove impossible given more complex analytical assumptions.

Parsimony may well be valued in its own right and it can certainly be defended in its own terms; but for our purposes it is important to note that parsimony is a *necessary* condition of the type of formal analytical-deductive modelling which characterizes rational choice theory. Without it, rational choice is impossible. This immediately raises an interesting, and crucial, ontological issue, still rarely (though, in recent years, more frequently) discussed by contemporary political analysts – namely, the degree of complexity of the social and political reality rational choice modelling seeks to capture. As King, Keohane and Verba note, for parsimony to be adopted as a guiding principle of good political analysis implies 'a judgement, *or even assumption*, about the nature of the world: it is *assumed* to be simple' (1994, p. 20, emphasis added). Moreover, as they go on, 'the principle of choosing theories that imply a simple world is a rule that clearly applies in situations where there is a high degree of certainty that the world is indeed simple'. Consequently, 'we should never insist on parsimony as a general principle in designing theories, but it is useful in those situations where we have some knowledge of the simplicity of the world we are studying' (1994, p. 20).

Important though these remarks are, they beg a series of crucial questions. First, the degree of complexity of the social and political reality we seek to interrogate and/or model is an ontological not an epistemological matter and, as such, does not avail itself as readily as King *et al.* seem to assume, of empirical adjudication (King *et al.* 1994). What, after all, would count as definitive evidence of the 'simplicity of the world we are studying'? Second, to assume that analysts who prize parsimony do so because they presume (or presume to know) the world to be simple is to underestimate the complexity of the issues at stake here. Theories of complex adaptive systems, for instance, predict complexity within systems characterized by simple rules (I am indebted to Daniel Wincott for pointing this out to me). It is, moreover, to assume a necessary correspondence between the degree of complexity of one's analytical assumptions on the one hand and the (perceived) degree of complexity of the reality one seeks to interrogate with such assumptions on the other. This, as we shall see, very many rational choice theorists would categorically reject. Indeed, this is an issue on which they are clearly divided.

Rational choice theorists here find themselves confronted with a stark choice: do they follow the implicit path suggested by King *et al.* above by effectively denying the (onto-logical) complexity of political reality, defending parsimonious assumptions as effectively accurate representations of a relatively simply external reality which naturally lends itself to rational choice modelling; or do they acknowledge the ontological complexity of that political reality while defending (on the grounds of utility) the parsimonious assumptions which render such modelling possible? The potentially tautological qualities of the concept of utility should not, however, be overlooked. As Joan Robinson notes, 'utility is a metaphysical construct of impregnable circularity; utility is the quality in commodities that makes individuals want to buy them, and the fact that individuals want to buy the commodities show that they have utility' (1964, p. 46). As Donald P. Green and Ian Shapiro demonstrate with characteristic clarity and insight, rational choice theorists are divided in their answer to this challenge as much as by anything else (1994, 23 ff.). Arguably, of course, it is something of a simplification to suggest that the options available to rational choice theorists at this point fall only into these two categories. Nonetheless, those rational choice theorists who have responded to this challenge do seem to have organized themselves into two distinct camps (again, I am indebted to Dan Wincott for discussions on this point).

Both strategies have their appeal. The former, based upon a 'covering-law' conception of scientific development must staunchly refuse to concede the irrealism of rational choice assumptions or modify (in the direction of greater complexity) any offending assumption (see, for instance, Tsebelis 1990, p. 38; Ferejohn 1991; Noll and Weingast 1991). For it is only in this way that any explanatory/predictive inference can credibly be defended as having been derived from law-like generalizations (or covering laws). The problems with such a strategy are two-fold. First, modifying implausible assumptions can only be allowed to go so far, for ultimately it can only serve to render rational choice modelling impossible (computationally) by degrees. Parsimony, as we have established, is the very condition of existence of formal theory. Second, though theoretically consistent in its own terms, it is something of a blow that others defending similar (and in some cases identical) assumptions on the grounds of their analytical utility are quite happy to concede that such premises bear little or no relationship to an external political reality (for instance,

Moe 1979, pp. 215–16). In the light of such concessions, the 'covering law' defence appears both convenient and possibly somewhat disingenuous.

The leaves the latter strategy – to mount an instrumental defence of implausible assumptions on the grounds that they are the very condition of existence of the formal modelling to which rational choice theorists aspire. The approach is, at least, disarmingly candid, but it raises a series of issues about the status of rational choice models as theories in their own right and of rational choice as a theory more generally – issues to which we now turn.

The instrumental defence is most clearly and famously stated by Milton Friedman. For Friedman, the decisive test of a theory is its predictive or explanatory power, not the realism, accuracy or plausibility of its assumptions. Indeed, he goes further still, suggesting that 'truly important and significant hypotheses will be found to have "assumptions" that are wildly inaccurate as descriptive representations of reality, and, in general, the more significant the theory, the more unrealistic the assumptions' (1953, pp. 14–15). (The precise sense of the term 'significant' appealed to here is, of course, left unspecified.)

Putting to one side the suggested (and, presumably, weak) inverse correlation between the implausibility of one's theoretical assumptions and the significance of the theoretical contribution one makes – which is, after all, an empirical matter of sorts – Friedman's key point is that theories should be judged not in terms of their analytical content or internal structure, but their ability to generate testable hypotheses capable of enduring the rigours of sustained empirical verification/falsification. This may seem fair enough but, as we shall see, it is particularly important that we proceed with a certain degree of caution before falling for Friedman's alluring gambit.

Leaving aside the recent critique of Green and Shapiro (1994), which suggests that rational choice models within political science have simply been insufficiently tested to be regarded as having any demonstrable explanatory or predictive power, there are at least two (further) problems with this formulation.

First, and (as already suggested), within social and political systems, evidence consistent with the predictions of an influential theory should not always be taken as confirmation of the theory. For influential theories and/or the influential assumptions on which they are predicated may well already have been internalized by the subjects of the theory (market actors, party strategists, public officials, policy-makers and the like), leading them to act in a manner consistent with the theory's predictions, whether the thesis is accurate or not.

Moreover, even were we able to discount entirely the possibility of such 'double hermeneutic' effects (Giddens 1984, p. 374), in what sense, if any, can we legitimately claim to have explained (or even described) the generation of a given outcome by appealing to a stylized and formal model whose assumptions we freely admit are implausible or, worse still, demonstrably false? If we have to make assumptions about political and economic actors which we know to be inaccurate in order to construct a formal model which might adequately capture their observed conduct, how can we credibly claim to have explained that conduct? As George Tsebelis notes, 'a scientist who is willing to make the "wildly inaccurate" assumptions Friedman wants him (sic) to make admits that "wildly inaccurate" behaviour can be generated as a conclusion of his theory'. For, 'the assumptions of a theory are, in a trivial sense, also the conclusions of the theory' (1990, p. 32).

This is problematic enough when it comes to making retrospective predictions – in other words, constructing formal models which might 'predict' behaviour that has already been observed. It is altogether more problematic, and highly suspect normatively, when it comes to drawing genuinely predictive inferences, especially those which might either inform public policy or, as in much public choice theory, which are motivated precisely by that aim. The suggestion that similar models deploying identical, but similarly implausible, assumptions have led to 'significant' theoretical advances, 'useful' insights or even empirically-verified predictions in the past, cannot absolve us of responsibility for foisting our political desires upon witting or unwitting, willing or unwilling political actors in the name of science. As Green and Shapiro suggest,

> Too often, prescriptive conclusions . . . are floated on empirically dubious rational choice hypotheses. . . . When explanatory [and often retroductive] rational choice theorising is used to advance prescriptive claims . . . it takes on an ideological character that is exposed by a critique of the questionable empirical foundations on which it rests. (1994, pp. 11–12; see also Dunleavy 1991)

An example may serve to reinforce the point. Assumptions about rational expectations have proved highly influential in policy-making circles since the mid-1980s and have, arguably, led to a series of important insights into macroeconomic theory. However, to use such assumptions – which are known to approximate market expectations only poorly – to derive the need for central bank independence if inflation is credibly to be checked, without caveats and without examining the record of independent central banks in controlling inflation, seems both irresponsible and pseudo-scientific. Moreover, that record is hardly unambiguous, a point to which we return presently. Yet, this notwithstanding, it surely underpins the move to central bank independence in the 1980s and 1990s. Similar comments might just as easily be made of new right variants of public choice theory (for a more thoroughgoing empirical critique see Dunleavy 1991, pp. 210–48).

Where does this leave rational choice theory? At minimum, it suggests that neither the covering law nor the Friedman-instrumental defence will suffice. That having been said, there is much to commend in the candour of the latter in acknowledging the inherent implausibility of any set of assumptions consistent with the formal modelling of political behaviour. Yet ultimately something has to give. My suggestion – one which will not, I imagine, commend me to most rational choice theorists – is that the status of rational choice be downgraded from the theoretical to the heuristic and its pretensions to both naturalism and positivism be rejected. This has two clear advantages. First, the conditional character of rational choice's predictions (acknowledged, to be fair, by many, but very rarely where policy implications are being discussed) is brought to the fore. Second, and relatedly, the danger of rational choice becoming a self-fulfilling prophecy is significantly attenuated.

This proposed 'downgrading' of the status of rational choice is born of a (prior) onto-logical commitment (on my part) to a conception of political reality as being sufficiently complex to preclude the possibility of predictive modelling with plausible assumptions. Yet, less this be dismissed as precluding rational choice theory by ontological fiat, it is important to note that this is effectively the same ontological commitment declared by Friedman in the passage from 'The Methodology of Positive Economics' discussed above. Where I differ from Friedman is in rejecting the (epistemological) claim that genuinely causal/explanatory inferences can legitimately be drawn from assumptions in whose accuracy/plausibility the analyst has no confidence.

As this suggests, the problem lies less with the inability of rational choice theory to operationalize successfully a positivism appropriate to political analysis – as in the influential critique of Green and Shapiro (1994) – but in the nature of political reality itself (cf. Pierson 2000, p. 26). It is the promise of positivism, rather than the ability of rational choice to realise that promise, that may well be illusory. 'Reality' may simply not avail itself of the sort of parsimony on which rational choice (as a theory with universal pretensions) is predicated.

This is an important point and one which, I imagine, will mark for many my point of departure from rational choice theory. Yet, in pointing to the inherent limits (as I see it) of a universal theory of political (or, indeed, economic) behaviour in a world of acknowledged complexity and contingency, my aim is not to reject rational choice out of hand. Rather, as will become clear presently, I seek to encourage the heuristic deployment of rational choice assumptions by political analysts who reject the naturalist and positivist pretensions with which rational choice has been so closely allied – and who have tended to reject rationalism as a consequence.

Rational choice has contributed a great deal to contemporary public administration and there is much that it can contribute further. Yet if it is to realize fully that potential, it is important that we consider anew the necessity of the largely unquestioned link between rational choice on the one hand and both naturalism and positivism on the other. It is to these issues that we turn directly in the final section. Before doing so, however, it is first important that we consider the thorny question of structure and agency and, in particular, the paradoxical structuralism of rational choice. For, as I shall argue, it is agency – the capacity of actors to exercise genuine choice in a given context – that is the key to the complexity of social and political systems. It is this, I argue, that rational choice denies. However perverse it may seem, then, it is the often unacknowledged structuralism of rational choice theory that is the key to its defence of a naturalist science of politics.

WHEN IS A CHOICE NOT A CHOICE? WHEN IT'S A RATIONAL CHOICE

If there are inherent limits to a naturalist science of politics, these owe their origins to the indeterminacy injected into social and political systems by human agents. The (insurmountable) problem, for those in pursuit of a predictive science of politics, is the 'problem' of human agency. Agents are inherently unpredictable; indeed, without this indeterminacy there would be little need for politics (cf. Gamble 2000). Yet it is this which imposes non-negotiable limits upon the ability of political scientists to predict political outcomes. For how can the analyst predict the outcome of the next election if the electorate have yet to decide how (or, indeed, whether) to vote; and when those who have decided whether and how to vote can change their mind at any point?

Stated most bluntly, agency – the capacity of actors to exercise genuine choice in a given context such that their behaviour cannot be predicted (reliably) in advance – gives rise to the indeterminacy of social and political outcomes and hence to the complex and open-ended character of social and political systems. Rational choice, premised as it is upon the generation of predictive/explanatory models of human behaviour, denies agency, indeterminacy, and hence the complexity of social and political systems. Though convenient, and arguably the very condition of a predictive science of politics, this is problematic.

Cast in somewhat different terms, there is a qualitative difference between the subject matters of the physical and social sciences that places severe limits upon a naturalist social science. For while the latter must deal with conscious and reflective subjects, capable of acting differently under identical stimuli, the former's units of analysis can be assumed inanimate, unreflexive and hence entirely predictable in response to external stimuli. Of course it should be noted that to some extent Heisenberg's 'Uncertainty Principle' changes all this at least for the physics of small particles, suggesting that the velocity and position of an object (a sub-atomic particle, say) cannot both be known simultaneously. For to measure one accurately is to impose limits on the accuracy with which the other can be measured. Yet even Heisenberg's principle it should be noted takes the form of a 'law' which is assumed to be immutable, infinitely generalizable and trans-historical. Agency injects an inherent indeterminacy and contingency into human affairs for which there is simply no analogue in the physical sciences.

In itself, there is probably nothing terribly contentious about this claim. Yet, if accepted, it has important implications for what follows. For, if actors' behaviour is not given by the context in which they find themselves (in the same way that a particle's kinetic energy is given by the gravitational field within which it is situated) – indeed, if actors may refashion the context in which they find themselves and hence any regularities it may previously have given rise to – then what hope is there for a predictive science of the political? It is for precisely this reason that agency does indeed pose a 'problem' for aspiring political *scientists*. Thus the appeal of rational choice, as a universal theory of the social sciences, arguably lies in its characteristically ingenious attempt to sidestep the problem of agency, by appearing, simultaneously, to be both voluntarist and structuralist.

Rational choice theory is not, then, all that it might first appear. As a perspective which emphasizes the rationality exhibited by conscious and reflective actors in the process of making choices it could scarcely be better placed to deal with the 'problem' of agency. Or so one might be forgiven for thinking. Is it any wonder that an author of the stature of David Easton should describe rational choice theory as the predominant post-behavioural response to 'behaviouralism's neglect of the actor' (1997, p. 20)? In one sense, he is right to do so, for rationalism probably does owe its undoubted influence to its perceived ability to offer a solution to the problem of agency that behaviouralism left unresolved. Yet that solution, as I will argue, is almost entirely illusory and it is here that Easton surely gets it wrong. The rational actor model, he suggests,

> gained sway because it inadvertently fit into the voluntarist tendencies of the counter-cultural sentiments of the time. . . . The image of the individual was subtly changed by rational modelling. He or she was not just a subject reacting to external circumstances but was proactive – choosing, selecting, rejecting in terms of his or her prefer-ences or utility-maximising behaviour. The focus shifted decisively from the structure or constraints surrounding behaviour . . . to the actor and his or her strategies of choice in pursuit of individual volitions. (Easton 1997, pp. 21–2)

The extent to which voluntarism chimed with the 'countercultural sentiments of the time' need not concern us here. The point is that, all appearances to the contrary and such sentiments notwithstanding, rationalism is in fact about as far from voluntarism as one can get (see also Dowding 1991; Dunleavy 1991, p. 6).

For, within any rational choice model, we know one thing above all: that the actor will behave rationally, maximizing his or her personal utility. Consequently, *any rational actor in a given context will choose precisely the same (optimal) course of action*. Actors are interchangeable (Tsebelis 1990, p. 43). Moreover, where there is more than one optimal course of action (where, in short, there are multiple equilibria), we can expect actors' behaviour to be distributed predictably between – and only between – such optima.

What this implies is that the agent's 'choice' is rendered predictable (and, in many cases, entirely predictable) given the context. At this point it is perhaps important to explain why the possibility of multiple equilibria does not pose any serious impediment to the argument advanced here. Three points might here be made. First, though not fully determinate, a model which predicts multiple equilibria is not indeterminate either. As social scientific predictions go, to be able to eliminate all non optimal outcomes is not bad going. Second, the (partial) indeterminacy of game theoretical models which predict multiple equilibria is a product not of rational choice's conception of agency but of its conception of the structure of the context itself. Change the context while retaining the actors' utility functions (by repositioning the actors within a different institutional domain) and a fully determinate model/prediction may well follow. Third, if it is conceded that the possibility of multiple equilibria renders rational choice predictions indeterminate (however partially), then significant problems follow for any totalizing pretensions rational choice theorists may harbour. For, if variables exogenous to the model (such as ideas) must be invoked in order the explain the selection amongst multiple equilibria, then rational choice modelling is, in itself, contingent. If this is conceded, it is but a small step to acknowledging that rational choice is incapable of providing an integrated and self-sufficient theory of political, far less, social behaviour (for examples of the appeal to ideas as exogenous variable which might be conjured to resolve the indeterminate nature of rational choice models in situations of multiple equilibria, see Bates 1988; North 1990; Goldstein and Keohane 1993; for a perceptive commentary, see Blyth 2002, pp. 18–20). (I am indebted to Albert Weale, Daniel Wincott and Steven Lukes for various discussions on this important point.)

In the light of the remarks above, it is surely tempting to ask: 'When is a choice not a choice?' Answer: 'When it is a rational choice'. As George L. Shackle notes,

> Economic man (sic) obeys the *dictates of reason*. . . . To call this conduct choice is surely to misuse words, when we suppose that to him the ends among which he can select, and the criteria of selection are given, and the means to each end are known. . . . Choice in such a theory is empty. (1969, pp. 272–3, original emphasis)

If the actor is, indeed, 'the very model of a modern individual' (Hollis 1998, p. 16), then she or he will behave in any given situation is a manner determined (and thereby rendered predictable) by the context itself. The implications of this are clear. We need know nothing about the actor to predict the outcome of political behaviour. For it is independent of the actor in question. Indeed, it is precisely this which gives rational choice modes of explanation their (much cherished) predictive capacity.

While it may seem somewhat perverse to detect in rational choice theory a basic structuralism, this is by no means as contentious as it might at first seem. For one of its principal protagonists, George Tsebelis, notes precisely this paradox.

> That the rational-choice approach is unconcerned with individuals seems paradoxical. The reason for this paradox is simple: individual action is assumed to be an optimal adaptation to an institutional environment, and the interaction between individuals is assumed to be an optimal response to one another. Therefore, the prevailing institutions (rules of the game) *determine* the behaviour of the actors, which in turn produces political or social outcomes. (1990, p. 4, emphasis added)

Keith Dowding is no less clear in stating that 'rational choice theory ... produces a form of structural explanation in that the main explanatory component is the structure of the models ... applied to different situations' (1991, p. 23).

Yet this is not just any form of structuralism. For whereas, conventionally, structuralism is associated with the claim that the actor is a prisoner of her environment, in rational choice theory (as the name would perhaps imply), the actor is deemed autonomous and free to choose – if only to choose the sole 'rational' option in any given context. It is this, in the end, that is the genuine paradox. Yet, arguably, it is in the conflation of choice and structural determination which this paradox implies that rational choice theory's particular appeal resides. For it allows rational choice theorists to deal (ostensibly) with questions of choice and agency, which would normally entail some recognition of the indeterminacy of political outcomes, without ever having to concede the open-ended nature of political systems and the contingency of political dynamics. In short, it allows a naturalist notion of prediction to be retained despite the theoretical incorporation of human agency, for which there is no natural scientific analogue. In the end, however, this is a façade. For what sense does it make to speak of a rational actor's *choice* in a context which there may be only one rational choice and the actor is assumed to be rational? It should be noted that even in a situation of multiple equilibria, the 'choice' is unlikely to be considerable. Moreover, in such situations exogenous structural variables are invariably imported to resolve any seeming indeterminacy, thereby rendering the revised model fully determinate once again.

This brings us full circle. For it suggests that rational choice theory can deliver a naturalist science of politics only by virtue of the implausible assumptions it makes about the universally instrumental, self-serving and utility-maximizing character of human conduct. These serve, in effect, to empty agency of any content such that the actor becomes a mere relay for delivering a series of imperatives inherent in the context itself. In short, a naturalist science of politics is only possible if we assume what we know to be false – that all actors, in any given context, will act in a manner rendered predictable (in many cases fully determinate) by the context as agency is substituted for a utility function. Soften the assumptions, or even the universality of the assumptions, and the fragile edifice of naturalism crumbles. With it must go the universal pretensions of much rational choice theory and, indeed, the very possibility of a predictive science of the political. Yet if such a predictive science can only be constructed on the basis of assumptions we know to be implausible, even false, should such a loss be mourned?

What, then, of the alternatives? It is perhaps eventually time to consider the role of rational choice within a post-naturalist and non-positivist political analysis premised upon an ontology of contingency and complexity.

FROM RATIONAL CHOICE AS THEORY TO RATIONAL CHOICE AS HEURISTIC DEVICE

As the above discussion indicates, the role of theory in rational choice is the simplification of an external reality as a condition of the generation of predictive hypotheses. These are, at least in principle, capable of falsification. That having been said, the emphasis in rational choice theory tends to be on the deduction and derivation from initial assumptions of stylized models of political behaviour, rather than on the testing of the formal models thereby generated. Given the implausibility of the assumptions on which most of these models are predicated, this is perhaps not surprising. This is invariably seen as a weakness of contemporary rational choice. It is, for instance, the focus of attention of perhaps the most influential critique to date of rational choice (Green and Shapiro 1994). Yet, paradoxically perhaps, if we abandon the desire to produce formal models of political behaviour whose sole purpose is to represent accurately an external political reality and/or predict accurately political outcomes, then such potential weaknesses can be recast as an advantage. In this final section my aim is to expand upon and defend this crucial, if some what cryptic, observation.

Consider first the following passage from the introduction to Melvin J. Hinich and Michael C. Munger's influential text on the spatial theory of voting:

> Formal theories help social scientists explore 'what if?' questions by deducing the implications of a set of premises ... the particular 'what if' implications derived from abstract theory may have little to do with the world of directly observable phenomena. (1997, pp. 1, 4)

This is an important statement, for it suggests something of a tension, characteristic of much rational choice theory, between the practice of rational choice on the one hand and the positivism its exponents invariably espouse on the other. This, I will suggest, we should seek to resolve in favour of the former. The tension becomes somewhat clearer if we compare the above extract with the following passage, a little later in the same text:

> The external application, or 'testing', of formal theory is by *analogy*: the theory is tested by measuring relationships among observable phenomena, in the hope that the observable phenomena are 'like' the relationships the model focuses on. (1997, p. 5, original emphasis)

Well, which is it to be? Are rationalism's assumptions genuinely chosen for interest's sake or heuristic value alone as means to the end of conducting hypothetical thought experiments (along the lines, 'what if the world were like this?'). If so, it is a non-correspondence theory. Or are they intended to provide approximations, however rough, of an external reality against which they might be evaluated? If so, it is a correspondence theory. In the former case, the plausibility or implausibility of the assumptions is of no great consequence. For the purpose of the process of theoretical deduction is, presumably, to reveal the consequences of a world (unlike our own) in which the hypothecated assumptions *were* true. In Robert E. Lane's terms, rational choice understood in this way, is an 'aid to thought', not a predictive or explanatory theory (1995, pp. 123–4). While this might make rationalism sound like a rather fanciful and indulgent pursuit, the value of such hypothetical reasoning should not be so easily dismissed. Indeed, this strikes me as precisely the role that rational choice might play in the development of post-positivist, post-naturalist political analysis. This, I suggest, is a first way forward.

It is perhaps important at this point to note that although I here seek to offer a potential defence of rational choice as a non-correspondence theory, an alternative and rather more influential defence of rational choice is to recast it as a conditional correspondence theory – in other words, to argue that rational choice theory works only under certain conditions (where, for instance, the choices are simple, the stakes high and the opportunities for learning considerable). This is, in essence, the (partial) defence of an (albeit qualified) rational choice advanced by Green and Shapiro (1994, 1995). Yet, however tempting this alternative strategy may seem, it implies a profound ontological unevenness and inconsistency – some parts of the social universe are simple, some complex – that I reject.

A similar, precautionary, logic informs Robert E. Goodin's (1998) reflections on the design of institutions. *Ceteris paribus*, we should seek to design institutions capable of resisting subversion by purely self-interested 'knaves', whether or not we have good reasons for believing the political landscape to be populated by such actors. Yet, as he also notes, it may be that the kind of institutions we might design to protect us from such knaves are considerably worse in other respects than those we might otherwise design, and are, accordingly, best avoided. Here additional assumptions about the prevalence of 'knavishness' and the likelihood of knaves capturing public office become particularly important.

The positing of 'what if' questions, then, can be extremely useful. It has the potential, for instance to provide timely and powerful warnings about the likely consequences of existing political trajectories. If it appears as though political parties increasingly appeal to the electorate in much the same way as corporations appeal to consumers, then it might be useful to model formally the consequences, say, within a (stylized) two-party, first-past-the-post electoral system, of such a dynamic. The point, of course, would not be to seek to *explain* the conduct of the parties exhibiting such a logic, but rather to point to the positive and/or negative consequences of such a dynamic in the hope that it might either be encouraged or resisted. Such reflection might also draw attention to the conditions under which political parties come to exhibit this particular 'rationality'. Of course, rather than treating rationality as an invariant and unquestionable characteristic of all human behaviour, this more conditional mode of analysis relies on treating rationalities as variable and context dependent.

Similarly, were we concerned (as well we might be) with the seemingly growing power of capital with respect to the state under conditions of regional and/or global economic integration, we might usefully construct a formal model of an open and global/regional economy in which capital were freely mobile. Though hypothetical, this might allow us to examine the potential implications of further doses of capital liberalization. Again, the assumptions would be chosen not for their correspondence to the existing state of affairs but as a means of exploring, through extrapolation, potential future scenarios. The purpose would be not so much to produce predictive hypotheses (that the optimal rate of taxation of mobile capital in [today's] open economy is zero) so much as *conditional predictions* (that further capital liberalization may serve, by degrees, to compromise the financial underpinnings of the welfare state). As in the case of the free mobility of capital, these might take the form of precautionary political warnings of the potential consequences of the untempered unfolding of existing dynamics, made at a point at which such logics might still be checked.

A second way forward, revealing an alternative but no less promising strategy, is suggested by an important recent article on democratic transitions by Robert H. Bates and colleagues (1998a; see also 1998b) (I am indebted to Hugh Ward for drawing my attention to this significant contribution). Rather than using rational choice as an analytical device to explore hypothetical assumptions picked for their heuristic value, they use it to generate a formal model on the basis of *a priori* assumptions imported from an alternative theoretical perspective. In other words, rather than explore the conditional nature of rational choice modelling, they import (more plausible) assumptions about identities and interests from a very different theoretical tradition (namely, interpretivism). This serves to indicate how rational choice can potentially be deployed in the service of a disparate range of theoretical perspectives.

In their important contribution, the authors acknowledge what they see as the inherent limitations of rational choice (as a stand alone theoretical perspective) in dealing with situations characterized by instability, ethnic or religious tension and conflict, and/or path-breaking institutional change – in short, disequilibrium. As they note, 'several of the attributes that suggest possible limitations to the use of rational choice theory suggest possible strengths of a major alternative . . . interpretivist theory' (Bates *et al.* 1998a, p. 223). Bates *et al.* thus seek to explore what they see as 'complementarities' between these two theoretical traditions, exploring the potential for 'theoretical integration' (ibid.; see also Ferejohn 1991). In essence, the analysis they present deploys rational choice techniques to model the mobilization of both revolutionary consciousness and the translation of this into revolutionary practice. This it does by endogenizing interests and identities using interpretivist techniques to provide a 'political anthropology' of individuals' motivations, values and expectations. Such an approach, in keeping with its indebtedness to inter-pretivism (and in opposition to more conventional rational choice), stresses the political power of ideas (in effect, their independent causal role) and the centrality of the politics of interpretation to political dynamics.

This is a major contribution to the existing literature whose significance has perhaps yet to be fully appreciated. Yet, despite its many strengths, it is not totally unproblematic. The 'theoretical integration' proposed is not as easily achieved as Bates *et al.* seem to assume – it is not just a matter of exploring potential synergies and commonalities between cognate theoretical perspectives. For rational choice and interpretivism (as theoretical perspectives) are premised upon mutually incompatible ontological and epistemological assumptions (on the difficulties of inter-paradigm synthesis, see also Hay and Wincott 1998). The post-positivist epistemology and post-naturalist ontology of interpretivism cannot be easily reconciled with the positivist epistemology and naturalist ontology of rational choice theory. Again, something has to yield. Yet while Bates *et al.* do not explore this tension (which, to be fair to them, they do acknowledge) and continue to couch their contribution in the problematic language of 'synthesis' and 'integration', this should not detract from their contribution. Indeed, their seminal article might easily be recast in slightly different terms. In the spirit of the present paper, Bates *et al.* might more usefully be seen as deploying rational choice *techniques* and *analytical strategies* in the service of interpretivist *theory*. If read in this way, their work represents a significant (if, to some extent, unintended) contribution to the sort of post-positivist, post-naturalist political analysis that I have sought to defend in this paper.

Yet Bates *et al.*'s work is something of an exception. Sadly, few rational choice theorists have embraced this kind of rationale. And, scared off presumably by the epistemology, the ontology or the algebra, virtually no attempt has been made by, for instance, interpretivists to explore the utility of rational choice analytical techniques. This makes Bates *et al.*'s contribution all the more significant. Instead, speculative and implausible ('what if') assumptions are all too frequently adopted as if accurate representations of an external reality and used as the basis from which to construct formal models of the polity or economy. This is despite the acknowledgement, by some rational choice theorists, that all rational choice 'prediction' is conditional. The more applied and policy-oriented the rational choice modelling, however, the fewer the caveats of this sort that seem to be entered. Such models are then presented to, and frequently accepted by, policy-makers, as accurate representations of the systems they purport to reflect. The hypothetical nature of the initial assumptions is now forgotten, as open economy macroeconomic models are used to derive optimal taxation regimes (Tanzi and Schuknecht 1997; Tanzi and Zee 1997), as central banks are given independence on the basis of, frankly, fanciful assumptions about the 'rational expectations' of market actors (Lucas 1973; Sargent and Wallace 1975; Kydland and Prescott 1977; Sargent 1986), and as public bureaucracies are retrenched or marketized on the basis of equally implausible assumptions about the narrow self-interest of public officials (Tullock 1965; Niskanen 1971, 1975; Buchanan 1977; though, for a powerful corrective, Dunleavy 1991). In each case the overwhelming empirical evidence against both the assumptions and the inferences logically derived from them is simply overlooked.

Interestingly, though perhaps unremarkably, the empirical evidence on the effects of central bank independence fails to lend much support to the 'rational expectations' thesis, there being no statistically significant correlation between the granting of independence and improved anti-inflationary performance (Posen 1993). When it is considered that central bank independence tends to be seen as an institutional fix for administrations anxious to enhance their anti-inflationary credibility, this is all the more troubling for proponents of this, the latest, economic orthodoxy. For an excellent discussion of these issues, see Watson (2002). Similar observations might be made about capital mobility and corporate taxation regimes. For despite the prediction that the optimal rate of taxation on mobile capital in an open economy is zero, foreign direct investment continues to be associated positively with high rates of corporate taxation and the market access this tends to secure (see, for instance, Cooke and Noble 1998; Swank 2001).

All this is worrying enough in its own terms. But is it merely compounded by an additional factor which we have thus far mentioned only briefly and in passing. Rational choice models, accorded the status of scientific theories by analysts and policy-makers alike, may become self-fulfilling prophecies. For, the more their assumptions, premises, inferences and conclusions are received as unquestioned fact, the more their predictions appear confirmed by political practice. As John A. Vasquez perceptively notes,

> The extent to which rational choice analysis can become a rigorous science will depend very much on the extent to which people or leaders accept its rules to guide their behaviour. In doing so, they will not only create a reality but people who are 'rationally-calculating individuals'. Such a science succeeds in explaining (sic) more and more of the variance *not because it is able to uncover the 'causes' of behaviour, but because it produces them*. (1998, p. 219, emphasis added)

This is an extremely significant observation and applies not only to rational choice perspectives such as neo-classical economics and rational choice theory but, potentially, to all conduct-shaping social, political and economic theories. Its logic is impeccable and, in essence, very simple. If political actors internalize assumptions, for instance about the limited parameters of political choice in an era of globalization, they will act on the basis of such assumptions, however inaccurate they may be, to produce outcomes consistent with the theory's predictions (scaling their political ambitions accordingly). In so far, then, as the predictions of rational choice theory or neo-classical economics conform to political and economic practice, it may well be because political and economic actors have internalized precisely such theories, incorporating them within their modes of calculation and practice.

Such reflections are, again, chastening and may serve to remind political analysts – particularly those with a direct line to holders of public office and particularly those claiming a scientific licence for their insights – of their responsibilities to us all. If, as seems invariably the case, rational choice models are premised upon implausible and often false assumptions, chosen so as to render possible the deductive generation of predictive inferences, then it is imperative that they are either presented in such terms or exposed as such. Yet, as I have been at pains to suggest, while rational choice models may well be innately prone to implausible premises, there are ways of making a virtue of this. Rational choice models, as heuristic devices, offer us a neat, analytically precise and conceptually rigorous means of exploring hypothetical scenarios and, indeed, of discrediting accepted wisdoms and perceived inevitabilities. A rational choice, liberated from the largely self-imposed shackles of naturalism and positivism is, as I have sought to suggest, a potentially powerful weapon in the armoury of critical political analysis.

ACKNOWLEDGEMENT

An earlier version of this paper was presented in the seminar series, *Rationality in Question* at the Centre for Philosophy of Natural and Social Science at the London School of Economics, February 2003. The author would like to thank participants on that occasion, together with Robert E. Goodin, Steven Lukes, Eleonora Montuschi, Albert Weale, Dan Wincott and two anonymous referees for *Public Administration* for their insightful, incisive and encouraging comments. The usual disclaimers apply.

REFERENCES

Alesina, R. 1989. 'Politics and Business Cycles in Industrial Democracies', *Economic Policy*, 8, 1, 57–98.

Bates, R.H. 1988. 'Contra Contractarianism: Some Reflections on the New Institutionalism', *Politics and Society*, 16, 2/3, 387–401.

Bates, R.H., R.J.P. de Figueiredo and B.R. Weingast. 1998a. 'The Politics of Integration: Rationality, Culture and Transition', *Politics and Society*, 26, 2, 221–56.

Bates, R.H., A. Greif and M. Levi, *et al.* 1998b. *Analytic Narratives*. Princeton, NJ: Princeton University Press.

Becker, G. 1976. *The Economic Approach to Human Behaviour*. Chicago, IL: Chicago University Press.

Blyth, M.M. 2002. *The Great Transformations: Economic Ideas and Institutional Change in the Twentieth Century*. Cambridge: Cambridge University Press.

Buchanan, J.M. 1977. 'Why Does Government Grow?', in T.E. Borcherding (ed.), *Budgets and Bureaucrats: The Sources of Government Growth*. Durham, NC: Duke University Press.

Charlesworth, J.C. 1967. 'Identifiable Approaches to the Study of Politics and Government', in J.C. Charlesworth (ed.) *Contemporary Political Analysis*. New York, NY: Free Press.

Cooke, W.N. and D.S. Noble. 1998. 'Industrial Relations Systems and US Foreign Direct Investment Abroad', *British Journal of Industrial Relations*, 36, 4, 581–609.

Dowding, K. 1991. *Rational Choice and Political Power*. Cheltenham: Edward Elgar.

Downs, A. 1957. *An Economic Theory of Democracy*. London: Harper Collins.

Downs, A. 1967. *Inside Bureaucracy*. Boston, MA: Little, Brown.

Dunleavy, P. 1991. *Democracy, Bureaucracy and Public Choice*. Hemel Hempstead: Harvester Wheatsheaf.

Easton, D. 1997. 'The Future of the Postbehavioural Phase in Political Science', in K.R. Monroe (ed.), *Contemporary Empirical Political Theory*. Berkeley, CA: California University Press.

Elster, J. 1979. *Ulysses and the Sirens: Studies in Rationality and Irrationality*. Cambridge: Cambridge University Press.

Ferejohn, J. 1991. 'Rationality and Interpretation: Parliamentary Elections in Early Stuart England', in K.R. Monroe (ed.), *The Economic Approach to Politics: A Critical Reassessment of the Theory of Rational Action*. New York, NY: Harper Collins.

Fiorina, J. (ed.). 1996. *The Rational Choice Controversy*. New Haven, CT: Yale University Press.

Fiorina, M.P. and K.A. Shepsle. 1982. 'Equilibrium, Disequilibrium and the General Possibility of a Science of Politics', in P.C. Ordeshook and K.A. Shepsle (eds), *Political Equilibrium*. Boston, MA: Kluwer Academic.

Friedman, J. (ed.). 1996. *The Rational Choice Controversy*. New Haven, CT: Yale University Press.

Friedman, M. 1953. 'The Methodology of Positive Economics', in *Essays in Positive Economics*. Chicago, IL: University of Chicago Press.

Gamble, A. 2000. *Politics and Fate*. Cambridge: Polity.

Giddens, A. 1984. *The Constitution of Society*. Cambridge: Polity.

Goldstein, J. and R.O. Keohane (eds). 1993. *Ideas and Foreign Policy: Beliefs, Institutions and Political Change*. Ithaca, NY: Cornel University Press.

Goodin, R.E. 1998. 'Institutions and Their Design', in R.E. Goodin (ed.), *The Theory of Institutional Design*. Cambridge: Cambridge University Press.

Green, D.P. and I. Shapiro. 1994. *Pathologies of Rational Choice Theory*. New Haven, CT: Yale University Press.

Green, D.P. and I. Shapiro. 1995. 'Pathologies Revisited', *Critical Inquiry*, 9, 1/2, 235–76.

Hall, P.A. and R.C.R Taylor. 1996. 'Political Science and the Three New Institutionalisms', *Political Studies*, 44, 4, 936–57.

Hardin, G. 1968. 'The Tragedy of the Commons', *Science*, 162, 1243–8.

Hargreaves Heap, S., M. Hollis and B. Lyons, *et al.* 1992. *The Theory of Choice*. Oxford: Blackwell.

Hay, C. 1999. *The Political Economy of New Labour: Labouring Under False Pretences?* Manchester: Manchester University Press.

Hay, C. and D. Wincott. 1998. 'Structure, Agency and Historical Institutionalism', *Political Studies*, 46, 5, 951–7.

Hinich, M.J. and M.C. Munger. 1997. *Analytical Politics*. Cambridge: Cambridge University Press.

Hollis, M. 1998. *Trust Within Reason*. Cambridge: Cambridge University Press.

Hollis, M. and Nell, E. 1975. *Rational Economic Man*. Cambridge: Cambridge University Press.

Jeffreys, H. 1961. *Theory of Probability*. Oxford: Oxford University Press.

King, G., R.O. Keohane and S. Verba. 1994. *Designing Social Enquiry: Scientific Inference in Qualitative Research*. Princeton, NJ: Princeton University Press.

Klosko, G. 1987. 'Rebellious Collective Action Revisited', *American Political Science Review*, 81, 557–61.

Kydland, F.E. and E.C. Prescott. 1977. 'Rules Rather than Discretion: The Inconsistency of Optimal Plans', *Journal of Political Economy*, 85, 3, 473–92.

Lane, R.E. 1995. 'What Rational Choice Explains', *Critical Review*, 9, 1/2, 107–26.

Lucas, R.E. 1973. 'Some International Evidence on Output-Inflation Trade-Offs', *American Economic Review*, 63, 326–34.

Moe, T.M. 1979. 'On the Scientific Status of Rational Choice Theory', *Journal of Political Science*, 23, 213–43.

Mueller, D.C. 1989. *Public Choice II*. Cambridge: Cambridge University Press.

Niskanen, W.A. 1971. *Bureaucracy and Representative Government*. Chicago, IL: Aldine-Atherton.

Niskanen, W.A. 1975. 'Bureaucrats and Politicians', *Journal of Law and Economics*, 18, 4, 617–43.

Noll, R.G. and B.R. Weingast. 1991. 'Rational Actor Theory, Social Norms and Policy Implementation: Applications to Administrative Processes and Bureaucratic Culture', in K.R. Monroe (ed.), *The Economic Approach to Politics: A Critical Reassessment of the Theory of Rational Action*. New York, NY: Harper Collins.

Nordhaus, W.D. 1975. 'The Political Business Cycle', *Review of Economic Studies*, 42, 169–90.

North, D.C. 1990. *Institutions, Institutional Change and Economic Performance*. Cambridge: Cambridge University Press.

Olson, M. 1965. *The Logic of Collective Action*. Cambridge, MA: Harvard University Press.

Olson, M. 1982. *The Rise and Decline of Nations*. New Haven, CT: Yale University Press.

Ordeshook, P.C. 1993. 'The Development of Contemporary Political Theory', in W.A. Barnett, M.J. Hinich and N.J. Schofield (eds.), *Political Economy: Institutions, Competition and Representation*. Cambridge: Cambridge University Press.

Pierson, P. 2000. 'Increasing Returns, Path Dependence and the Study of Politics', *American Political Science Review*, 94, 2, 251–69.

Popper, K. 1969. 'Science, Conjecture and Refutation', in *Conjectures and Refutations*. London: Routledge and Kegan Paul.

Posen, A. 1993. 'Why Central Bank Independence Does Not Cause Low Inflation: There is No Institutional Fix for Politics', in R. O'Brien (ed.), *Finance and the International Economy 7*. Oxford: Oxford University Press.

Ragin, C.C. 1994. *Constructing Social Research: The Unity and Diversity of Method*. Newbury Park, CA: Pine Forge Press.

Riker, W.H. 1990. 'Political Science and Rational Choice', in J. Alt and K.A. Shepsle (eds.), *Perspectives on Positive Political Economy*. Cambridge: Cambridge University Press.

Robinson, J. 1964. *Economic Philosophy*. Harmondsworth: Penguin.

Sargent, T.J. 1986. *Rational Expectations and Inflation*. New York, NY: Harper and Row.

Sargent, T.J. and Wallace, N. 1975. 'Rational Expectations, the Optimal Monetary Instrument and the Optimal Money Supply Rule', *Journal of Political Economy*, 83, 2, 241–54.

Shackle, G.L. 1969. *Decision, Order and Time in Human Affairs*, 2nd edn. Cambridge: Cambridge University Press.

Shubik, M. 1970. 'Game Theory, Behaviour and the Paradox of the Prisoner's Dilemma', *Journal of Conflict Resolution*, 14, 181–202.

Swank, D. 2001. 'Political Institutions and Welfare State Restructuring: The Impact of Institutions on Social Policy Change in Developed Democracies', in P. Pierson (ed.), *The New Politics of the Welfare State*. Oxford: Oxford University Press.

Tanzi, V. and H.H. Zee. 1997. 'Fiscal Policy and Long-Run Growth', *International Monetary Fund Staff Papers*, 44, 2, 179–209.

Tanzi, V. and L. Schuknecht. 1997. 'Reconsidering the Fiscal Role of Government: The International Perspective', *American Economic Review*, 87, 2, 164–68.

Taylor, M. 1976. *Anarchy and Cooperation*. London: Wiley.

Taylor, M. 1995. 'When Rationality Fails', *Critical Review*, 9, 1/2, 223–34.

Tsebelis, G. 1990. *Nested Games: Rational Choice in Comparative Politics*. Berkeley, CA: University of California Press.

Tullock, G. 1965. *The Politics of Bureaucracy*. Washington, D.C.: Public Affairs Press.

Vasquez, J.A. 1998. *The Power of Power Politics: From Classical Realism to Neotraditionalism*. Cambridge: Cambridge University Press.

von Mises, L. 1944. *Bureaucracy*. New Haven, CT: Yale University Press.

Ward, H. 2002. 'Rational Choice' in D. Marsh and G. Stoker (eds.), *Theory and Methods in Political Science*, 2nd edn. Basingstoke: Palgrave.

Watson, M. 2002. 'The Institutional Paradoxes of Orthodox Economic Theory: Reflections on the Political Economy of Central Bank Independence', *Review of International Political Economy*, 9, 1, 183–96.

Zellner, A. 1984. *Basic Issues in Econometrics*. Chicago, IL: University of Chicago Press.

AFTERWORD: RATIONALITY AS RATIONALIZABILITY

It is both a rare honour and a great pleasure, on the occasion of the twenty-fifth anniversary of *Public Administration* no less, to be invited to revisit one of my own pieces after the passing of some time. Whilst authors are notoriously poor judges of their own work, I am particularly delighted that it is my article on the status of rational choice theory in public administration and, indeed, political science more broadly, that I am here invited to revisit. And I am no less delighted by the interest, debate and controversy that this piece has generated in the intervening years. The article itself was certainly intended as a provocation – though perhaps more for those too ready, in my view, to dismiss the rational choice perspective out of hand without first seeking to understand it than for those it is typically seen to critique. In fact I do not really see is at a critique of rational choice theory at all so much as a warning as to the dangers of some of the uses to which it has been put and still might be put. In that respect I am particularly pleased by the generally warm reception it has received amongst rational choice theorists themselves.

The article, like so much of what I would regard as my 'better' work, would not have been written without the influence of others – in this case the invitation from Steven Lukes to reflect out loud and in public on the concept of rationality in political science in a seminar series on 'Rationality in Question' at the London School of Economics in 2003. At the time that struck me as a rather daunting task, a task made no less daunting by both the source of that invitation (it is difficult to imagine a more accomplished authority on the concept of rationality) and the venue for the seminar. But it also struck me as a fantastic opportunity to work out more thoroughly and in greater depth a perspective on rational choice theory that I had started to develop in my book, *Political Analysis* (2002). Rational, or otherwise, it was not an invitation that I was going to refuse.

Reflecting on the piece today, a number of things strike me. First, its content and focus – however much I would continue to defend these - are somewhat narrower than the initial invitation. Indeed, there is a very important point here. To reflect on rational choice theory is, of course, to reflect on the concept of rationality; but to reflect on the concept of rationality in political analysis is not necessarily to confine oneself to rational choice theory. Indeed, far too often, it strikes me, rational choice is seen to hold a monopoly over the content and use of the concept of rationality. That is a shame. For whilst utility-maximising behaviour is, of course, a form of rational action, action need not be utility-maximising for it to be regarded as rational. For me rationality entails no more (and no less) than that an actor is capable of offering a rationale for their behaviour after the fact. In effect, rational action is perhaps better conceived of as 'rationalisable' action. Thus understood, there is more to rationality than utility-maximising behaviour and more to the analysis of rationality than rational choice theory. Such a reclamation of the concept of rationality is a theme I hope to return to in later work.

A second thing that strikes me about this piece with the benefit of some hindsight is the place that it occupies in the development of my own work. The paper, in effect, is a bridge, taking me from a nascent and developing view of rational choice theory (as initially set out in *Political Analysis*) towards the more substantive account of the sources of political disaffection and disengagement that would inform the analysis of *Why We*

Hate Politics (2007). The piece is not a critique of rational choice, but it is a warning as to the dangers of projecting narrowly self-interested motives onto political actors without reflecting on the status of such assumptions. In effect, I seek in it to remind us that rational choice theory presumes instrumental self-interested behaviour not because its exponents genuinely believe such behaviour to be ubiquitous – but, rather more prosaically, since it makes possible the kind of modelling that is the theory's very rationale. There is, if you like, a clear disjunction between rational choice theorists' declared ontology and the private ontologies they hold. As Milton Friedman (1953: 14–15) and Douglass North (1990: 17) both concede, the behavioural assumptions that neo-classical economists and rational choice theorists (like themselves) declare are not a reflection of deeply held convictions, but an analytical convenience. My paper is a reminder of that and a reflection on its implications.

In a political landscape now shaped so heavily by the influence of rational and public choice theoretical models and in which politicians and citizens alike seem invariably to treat as self-evident the incapacity of political elites to act in pursuit of anything other than their own self-interest, those implications are considerable. Here I draw attention merely to one – that, as analysts of politics, we need to be very careful about the ease with wish we fall back into simply assuming the worst of political actors (or, worst still, declaring – for analytical convenience – assumptions which have a similar effect). Far too much of our work is informed, without question or justification, by the projection of narrowly self-interested motives on to all political actors. I ask not that we desist from this, but that we are more aware of what we are doing, more capable of offering a justification, more willing to acknowledge other sources of political motivation and, above all, more aware of the need to consider the biases injected into the accounts of politics we provide by such analytically convenient assumptions. In the process we might ask ourselves whether we think Milton Friedman and Anna Schwartz's (1971) *A Monetary History of the United States* would have enjoyed the same influence over public policy had its cover contained a simple health warning – 'the authors of this work would like to remind you that they do not believe the behavioural assumption which make possible the analysis contained within it'.

REFERENCES

Friedman, M. 1953. *Essays in Positive Economics*. Chicago: University of Chicago Press.

Friedman, M. and A. J. Schwartz. 1971. *A Monetary History of the United States, 1867–1960*. Princeton, NJ: Princeton University Press.

Hay, C. 2002. *Political Analysis*. Basingstoke: Palgrave Macmillan.

Hay, C. 2007. *Why We Hate Politics*. Cambridge: Polity.

North, D. C. 1990. *Institutions, Institutional Change and Economic Performance*. Cambridge: Cambridge University Press.

Chapter 3

THE GOVERNANCE NARRATIVE: KEY FINDINGS AND LESSONS FROM THE ESRC'S WHITEHALL PROGRAMME

R. A. W. RHODES

INTRODUCTION

This article attempts the impossible – a summary of 23 research projects carried out over five years. So, to state the obvious, I provide a *personal* interpretation of the Economic and Social Research Council's (ESRC) Whitehall Programme's key findings and lessons. I tell the distinctive story of *governance*. This story, with its emphasis on networks, contrasts sharply both with the Westminster model and its story of a strong executive running a unitary state and with new public management (NPM) and its story of the search for efficiency through markets and contracts. I use the Whitehall Programme to provide a language for re-describing the world. With the Local Governance Programme (Rhodes 1999a), the Whitehall Programme played a part in challenging the dominant, managerial account of change in the 1980s and 1990s. Both supported a view of the world in which networks rival markets and bureaucracy as governing structures; that is, as ways of allocating resources and co-ordinating policy making and implementation.

I build my story of change over the past two decades around nine aphorisms.

- From government to governance.
- More control over less.
- The hollowing-out of the state.
- The weakness of the core executive.
- The sour laws of unintended consequences.
- The loss of trust.
- It's the mix that matters.
- Diplomacy and hands-off management
- From deconcentration to decentralization.

These aphorisms are not hypotheses or generalizations. They are narrative devices which I use to explain governance theory and to summarize findings. Similarly, I use boxes either to summarize relevant findings from projects on the Whitehall Programme or to illustrate arguments. Both devices help me to cover a lot of ground quickly and I hope clearly.

I have discussed governance theory at length elsewhere (Rhodes 1997a and 2000c) so here I limit myself to a definition. Governance refers to: *self-organizing, interorganizational networks* with the following characteristics.

(1) Interdependence between organizations. Governance is broader than govern- ment, covering non-state actors. Changing the boundaries of the state meant the

boundaries between public, private and voluntary sectors became shifting and opaque.

(2) Continuing interactions between network members, caused by the need to exchange resources and negotiate shared purposes.

(3) Game-like interactions, rooted in trust and regulated by rules of the game negotiated and agreed by network participants.

(4) A significant degree of autonomy from the state. Networks are not accountable to the state; they are self-organising. Although the state does not occupy a privileged, sovereign position, it can indirectly and imperfectly steer networks.

I use this notion and the aphorisms to describe the changes in British government and appraise critically the effects of recent reforms.

Finally, I paint a vainglorious picture of the Programme's achievement in challenging the language of the new public management (NPM) and putting governance on the agenda in the guise of joined-up government. The aphorisms address the question, 'what happened?' I also address the question 'so what?' I try to draw lessons relevant to the continuing search to modernize government from my aphorisms.

CONTEXT

I begin with the obvious – a dictionary definition of the Westminster model:

> The characteristics of the Westminster model ... include: strong cabinet government based on majority rule; the importance attached to constitutional conventions; a two-party system based on single member constituencies; the assumption that minorities can find expression in one of the major parties; the concept of Her Majesty's loyal opposition; and the doctrine of parliamentary supremacy, which takes precedence over popular sovereignty except during elections (Verney 1991, p. 637).

The model has been criticized and adapted and there are several variants (see Bevir and Rhodes 1999). But there is a clear baseline to any discussion of the Westminster model and there are strong family likenesses between the several varieties. The family lived happily under the roof of the Whitehall Programme (see box 1).

BOX 1 *Variations on the Westminster model**
The findings of several projects, for example on cabinet committees and permanent secretaries, provide critical variations on the central beliefs of the Westminster narrative.

Cabinet committees are effective when there is a clear relationship between the committee and the department carrying out the policy; and a clear sense of political direction about the committee's goals (Brady and Catterall, in Rhodes 2000a vol. 1, ch. 9).

The system of cabinet committees does not provide evidence of prime ministerial government but of the frequent failure of Prime Ministers to exercise leadership. The frequent attempts to strengthen co-ordination reflect the weakness of the Prime Minister in performing his or her key duties (Brady and Catterall, in Rhodes 2000a vol. 1, ch. 9).

Permanent secretaries are no longer anonymous 'Mr Fixits' for their minister or the locus of institutional scepticism but the conservators of their department and its public face (Theakston 1999).

Britain does not have prime ministerial or cabinet government but ministerial (or baronial) government (Jones 1998; Norton in Rhodes 2000a vol. 2 ch. 7).

'Britain did enjoy an exceptional degree of continuity and order but it contained two contradictions: between the limited role of the state in practice and the lack of constitutional checks on its unlimited theoretical power; and between the popular conception of the state's class neutrality and its partiality when it intervened (Lowe and Rollings, in Rhodes 2000a vol. 1 ch. 6).

*These illustrations are from the projects' summary reports in Rhodes 2000a. The author-date citations in parentheses are listed in the references at the end of the article.

BOX 2 *From Westminster model to New Public Management*
Several projects identify changes in the Westminster model under the impact of NPM.

The story of internal regulation is the story of a plural centre seeking to extend its control (Daintith and Page, in Rhodes 2000a vol. 1, ch. 4).

Regulating and auditing quasi-markets is expensive and costs are rarely identified clearly (Whiteside, in Rhodes 2000a vol. 2, ch. 9).

The Treasury has a clear set of views on social policy covering not only the levels of spending but also the content. The Treasury's approach is dominated by short-term spending decisions and it has lost the analytical capability to control the link between economic and social policy and to comment on policy content (Parry and Deakin in Rhodes 2000a, vol. 2, ch. 5).

The attempt to separate policy from service management has failed. Creating operational agencies increased their policy making role; policy migrated to the agency and policy making became an exercise in managing ambiguous boundaries (Elder and Page, in Rhodes 2000a vol. 1, ch. 12; Day and Klein, vol. 1, ch. 13).

Agencification and managerialism created two cultures – mandarins and managers (Day and Klein in Rhodes 2000a vol. 1, ch. 13).

The label NPM covers many varieties of public sector reform (Hood 1995; Rhodes 1998b), including: privatization, marketization, corporate management, regulation, and decentralization. It is perhaps the most popular account of recent changes (see box 2).

GOVERNANCE

If the Westminster model and NPM are familiar stories about British government, governance with its stress on the shackles on leaders, undermining the 'leaders know best' strand of the British governmental tradition is not so well known.

From government to governance

This aphorism summarizes the shift from line bureaucracies to fragmented service delivery. After 1979, function-based policy networks based on central departments (or sections of them) changed in two ways. First, the membership of networks became broader, incorporating both the private and voluntary sectors. Second, the government swapped direct for indirect controls. British government privatized the utilities. It contracted-out services to the private sector. It introduced quasi-markets through purchaser-provider splits when services could not be privatized. It bypassed local authorities for special-purpose bodies. It removed operational management from central departments and

---

BOX 3 *Fragmentation*

I live in North Yorkshire in a quiet rural area with a few small towns. It is not the cosmopolitan capital of the western world. There is night life, but it shuts at 11 p.m. The government requires health and local authorities to provide for AIDS sufferers. To plan the service, 19 organizations come together to form the planning team. An unbelievable 39 organizations are involved in delivering the service. There is no hierarchy among the organizations. No one organization can plan and command the others. And yet there are only 24 people who are HIV positive in the area. A tinge of black humour is unavoidable: there is only one clear policy choice – find a patient for each organization (Rhodes 1998c).

---

vested it in separate agencies (see Rhodes 1997a, chs 5–7). Fragmentation not only created new networks but it also increased the membership of existing networks (see box 3).

Central departments are no longer either necessarily or invariably the fulcrum, or focal organization, of a network. Power relations may remain unequal. The government can still set the boundaries to network actions. It funds the services. But it has also increased its dependence on multifarious networks. The policy of marketizing public services speeded up differentiation and multiplied networks. Such trends make steering more difficult, so the mechanisms for integration multiply. Governance has become the defining narrative of British government at the turn of the century, challenging the commonplace notion of Britain as a unitary state with a strong executive.

More control over less
Government policy now fragmented service delivery. It compensated for its loss of hands-on controls by reinforcing its control over resources.

Decentralizing service delivery was coupled with both centralized financial control and a massive extension of regulation (see box 4). The government adopted a strategy of 'more control over less'.

The reasons for these changes have been often rehearsed. For example, it can be argued that the drive to make government smaller had its roots in New Right party politics and poor economic performance (see Hood 1996, pp. 273–82; Wright 1994, pp. 104–8). Others stress the ways in which governmental traditions, or a set of beliefs about the institutions and history of government, led to different interpretations of public sector reform and its problems (Rhodes 1999c and citations). So, different countries have different reasons for implementing reforms which can have little in common with one another beyond the label new public management. The debate about the causes and consequences of reform will continue but one point seems clear, the pace of change in Britain was greater than

---

BOX 4 *The growth of internal regulation*

Christopher Hood and his colleagues (1998 and 1999) show that the loss of control, whether through privatization or deconcentrating managerial authority, has fuelled regulatory growth.

Between 1976–95 the number of regulatory bodies increased by 22% from 110 to 134. Staffing increased by 60% to about 14,000. Spending increased by 106% to about £766 million, a figure doubled by including compliance costs.

They conclude government devotes as many resources to regulating itself as it does to private utilities; this regulation has become more formal, intensive, complex and specialized; like Topsy it just grew; and the regulators are unregulated.

---

elsewhere in Western Europe. Three characteristics of the British governmental tradition eased public sector reform.

First, a defining characteristic of the British governmental tradition is its strong executive. Margaret Thatcher exercised strong, directive, and above all persistent, executive leadership to push through reform of the civil service. Riddell (1997) argues 'the Blair Presidency' continues the tradition.

Second, Britain's uncodified constitution does not entrench the rights of institutions or individuals. So, there are few constitutional constraints on executive leadership when the government has a majority in Parliament. Once the government decided on a change, it could force it through.

Finally, the Conservative government devised a clear set of political ideas to justify and 'sell' its various reform packages. It attacked big government and waste, used markets to create more individual choice and campaigned for the consumer.

One theme remains constant; containing public spending to provide more services for the same or less money. This imperative drove the search for management reform. Although a commonplace of the academic literature, it is worth stressing that administrative reform is always political. Since 1979 the reform of the civil service has been rooted in the political decision to cut government spending and to exert effective control over the administrative machine.

The hollowing out of the state

Governance is also the product of the hollowing-out of the state from above (for example, by international interdependencies), not just from below (by marketization and networks), and sideways (by agencies) (Rhodes 1994, pp. 138–9).

The European Union shows how transnational policy networks emerge when, for example, there is a high dependence in the policy sector; policy making is depoliticized and routinized; supra-national agencies are dependent on other agencies to deliver a service; and there is a need to aggregate interests. In the EU, multi-level governance links the Commission, national ministries and local and regional authorities It is a specific example of the impact of international interdependencies on the state (see box 5).

BOX 5 *The EU and hollowing-out*

Menon and Wright (1998) argue 'there is no doubt' the UK has 'forged an efficient policy making and co-ordinating machine' because the government speaks and acts with one voice. It has also been successful in its 'basic strategy of opening up and liberalising the EU's economy'. However, its 'unjustified reputation' for being at the margins of Europe is justified for EU constitution building and 'an effective and coherent policy making machine becomes ineffective when it is bypassed' for the history-making decisions.

Bulmer and Burch (1998, p. 624) conclude:
'At the levels of policy and political management, the impact of EC-EU on the activities of the British government has been profound. Membership has brought new issues on to the agenda, given whole areas of policy a European dimension, required the development of new expertise on the part of officials and ministers, involved intensive and extensive negotiations with EU partners and raised significant problems about policy presentation and party management' (see also Rhodes 2000a, vol. 1, ch. 3).

Three epigrams from Richard Rose (2000) (and in Rhodes 2000a, vol. 2, ch. 3) dramatize the external limits to independent action by the British core executive.
'All politics is international'.

'There are two kinds of countries: those that are small and know it and those that are small and don't'.
'What goes on outside the world of Westminster is more important to the peace and prosperity of the British people than what is done by Her Majesty's Government, including its first minister.'

So, the hollowing-out thesis suggests that not only external dependence but also internal fragmentation create many challenges to the capacity of core executives to steer. Two examples of the effects of internal fragmentation will suffice. Day and Klein (1997 and in Rhodes 2000a, vol. 1, ch. 13) argue the NHS Executive has hollowed out the Department of Health because policy as well as operational management has migrated from the core department to the agency. Similarly Norton (Rhodes 2000a, vol. 2, ch. 7) argues that decentralizing power to bodies outside government has further limited the capacity of ministers to have an independent impact on policy outcomes and is, therefore, evidence of hollowing out.

The weakness of the core executive
The strong executive strand of the Westminster model overstated the power of the British centre which was always embedded in complex sets of dependencies (see box 6).

BOX 6 *Power-dependence in the core executive*
The core executive refers to 'all those organizations and procedures which co-ordinate central government policies and act as arbiters of conflict between different parts of the government machine, not just prime minister and cabinet' (Rhodes and Dunleavy 1995, p. 12).

Martin Smith (1999, ch. 2) usefully links the notion of the core executive to power-dependence (Rhodes 1999b) to show the constraints on leadership in British government. Power-dependence means *all* actors within the core executive have resources and to achieve goals resources have to be exchanged. So, even actors with many resources, such as the Prime Minister, are dependent on other actors to achieve their goals. This distribution of resources, coupled with the strength of departments and their overlapping networks, mean the core executive is fragmented and central co-ordination is difficult (See also Smith in Rhodes 2000a, vol. 1, ch. 2).

Other projects discuss the weakness of the core executive rather than its dependency relationships

The core executive does not co-ordinate British government (Brady and Catterall in Rhodes 2000a, vol. 1, ch. 9), control is plural (Daintith and Page in Rhodes 2000a, vol. 1, ch. 4) and the core is fragmented (Parry and Deakin in Rhodes 2000a, vol. 2, ch. 5).

The core executive is 'elusive and fluid' and the notion needs to be 'widened' to include 'the strictly political dimension of policy making' and 'deepened' to cover 'the relatively low level at which ... key decisions are taken' (Lowe 1997).

Norton (Rhodes 2000a, vol. 2, ch. 7) describes the core executive as baronial: 'Ministers are like medieval barons in that they preside over their own, sometimes vast, policy territory. Within that territory they are largely supreme.... The ministers have their own policy space, their own castles – even some of the architecture of departments ... reinforces that perception – and their own courtiers. The ministers fight – or form alliances – with other barons in order to get what they want. They resent interference in their territory by other barons and will fight to defend it.
In sum, power-dependence characterizes the links between both barons and the barons and Prime Minister.

'It often feels like a very hostile world out there' said one former Prime Minister, 'and the fact was I could do very little about it' (quoted in Rhodes 2000a, vol. 2, ch. 4).

Referring to the 1960s, Lowe and Rollings (Rhodes 2000a vol. 1, ch. 6) conclude: 'political and administrative fragmentation may have sapped the ability of the core executive to co-ordinate a strong central policy, but the fundamental impediment to modernization remained the power of vested interests within the broader governance'.

NPM created a greater need for co-ordination while reducing governmental ability to co-ordinate. Concern for this decline in central capability was voiced by Sir Robin Butler (1993, p. 404), former Head of the Home Civil Service, when he wrote: 'it is essential that it does not reach the point where individual Departments and their Agencies become simply different unconnected elements in the overall public sector, with . . . *no real working mechanisms for policy co-ordination*' (emphasis added).

The Conservative government did not strengthen strategic capacity with the other changes. This search for co-ordination lies at the heart of New Labour's reforms. As Kavanagh and Seldon (in Rhodes 2000a, vol. 2, ch. 4) point out we have seen prime ministerial centralization in the guises of: institutional innovation and more resources for No. 10 and the Cabinet Office; and strong political and policy direction as No. 10 seeks a firm grip on the government machine. The pendulum swings yet again as the centre promotes co-ordination and strategic oversight to combat Whitehall's departmentalism. They argue such 'power grabs' are 'a reaction to felt weakness, a frustration with the inability to pull effective levers'.

However, in spite of the strong pressures for more and pro-active co-ordination throughout Western Europe:

> the co-ordination activities of the core remain in practice modest in scope: most internal co-ordination takes place at lower levels of the state hierarchy; is rarely strategic or even directive, but selective, issue oriented and reactive; is negative in the sense that it is characterised by the toleration of heavily compartmentalised units pursuing mutual avoidance strategies to reduce tensions'. . . . All governments have resorted to a variety of measures to reduce the burden of co-ordination, . . . but with only limited success and . . . many of the measures adopted have served only to complicate and even increase co-ordination requirements (Hayward and Wright in Rhodes 2000a, vol. 2, ch. 2).

The sour laws of unintended consequences
Unintended consequences are not the result of Sod's law that 'if it can go wrong, it will go wrong'. They are not just the result of poor design or wayward implementation by other agencies. They are unavoidable because new knowledge does not increase control of the social world but alters that world and sets it off in new directions. Policies are theories about how to change the social world. Implementation provides findings of how that world is both changing and in so doing changes the policies. The impact of knowledge on political institutions is like a crash involving a heavy lorry.

Governance understood as steering networks is a prime example of unintended consequences because it is an unintended consequence of marketization. To recap briefly, marketizing public services fragmented the institutional structure delivering those services. Because service users and their problems do not fit neatly into institutional boxes, organizations have to co-operate to deliver their services effectively. Such sets of organizations, or networks, do not work through competition but by co-operating with one another. So co-operation vies with competition as the organizing principle of service delivery. Marketization encourages an ironic stance. The Conservative government's policy of marketization set out to break up what it saw as producer networks. But the competition-based fragmentation which undermined existing networks created pressures to form new networks which, in turn, undermined the competitive rationale of marketization. Truly there are no simple solutions to complex problems.

The loss of trust
Networks are a distinctive way of co-ordinating and, therefore, a separate governing structure from markets and hierarchies (or bureaucracies). Trust is their central co-ordinating mechanism in the same way that commands and price competition are the key mechanisms for hierarchies and markets respectively. The loss of trust is a general argument about marketization and its effects. It is also a specific argument about eroding public service ethics.

On trust and marketization, Newman *et al.* (1998, 105) conclude:

> Relational contracts involve a degree of trust between client and contractor. The client must be prepared to trust the contractor to behave within the spirit of the agreement on the assumption that the reputation and future business growth of the contractor depend on it. The contractor must be prepared to trust that the client understands the realities of the new situation, i.e. that the private sector needs to make a return on investment (See also Rhodes 2000a, vol. 2, ch. 10)

In other words, as it evolved, contracting-out by central government departments laid less emphasis on price and competition and paid more attention to building long-term relationships characterized by trust and co-operation. Contracts acquired the characteristics of networks.

On public service ethics, such reforms as managerialism and open competition for civil service jobs can be seen as diluting standards. Box 7 provides an example of behaviour ostensibly modelled on the new mangerialism which violates such ethics (see also Committee of Public Accounts 1994).

BOX 7 *Marketization and declining standards in public life*

Yorkshire RHA awarded a contract to Yorkshire Water for clinical waste incineration worth £7.2 million of capital and £2 million a year in revenue. It was not let competitively. It was for *fifteen* years. The authority did not get NHS Executive approval. The Committee of Public Accounts (1997) was 'concerned' about a further eight instances of 'unacceptable' behaviour which they noted 'with surprise' and 'serious concern', including on one occasion, an 'appalled'.

The Regional General Manager defended his actions claiming he brought a more commercial attitude and a willingness to embrace risk to health services management. He embraced 'the rhetoric of the day (in summary the ministerial encouragement to break away from the bureaucratic stranglehold).' The point is of sufficient importance to warrant a lengthy quote from the former chief executive of Yorkshire RHA, Keith McLean.

'The culture of the day in the NHS should be recognised as a real factor. In the 1988–93 period, senior managers were encouraged *from the highest levels* to focus on the achievement of nationally desired results. The service was in the throes of radical structural change with the introduction of a market approach and, . . ., it felt to me and perhaps others that the regulatory framework of the pre-reform era was relaxed to give local managers the space to achieve change quickly through the exercise of managerial discretion. The advent of the Chief Executive . . . was a signal of the changing culture. Several of the regulations which are said to have been transgressed in Yorkshire have since been modified in the direction of greater flexibility . . . and the coming changes were, inevitably, 'in the air' before they actually came about' (Committee of Public Accounts 1997, p. 40 emphasis added).

Mr McLean accepted that he embraced 'the culture of the day too enthusiastically and uncritically in pursuit of successful outcomes' but insisted that his decisions must be placed in the broader context. His point about encouragement from the highest level is accurate. The impact of marketization and the decline in standards could not be clearer.

BOX 8 *The limits to networks*

Networks are effective when for example:

- actors need reliable, 'thicker' information;
- quality cannot be specified or is difficult to define and measure;
- commodities are difficult to price;
- professional discretion and expertise are core values;
- flexibility to meet localized, varied service demands is needed;
- cross-sector, multi-agency co-operation and production is needed;
- monitoring and evaluation incur high political and administrative costs; and
- implementation involves haggling.

The costs of networks include:

- closed to outsiders and unrepresentative;
- unaccountable for their actions;
- serve private interests, not the public interest (at both local and national levels of government);
- difficult to steer;
- inefficient because co-operation causes delay;
- immobilized by conflicts of interest; and
- difficult to combine with other governing structures (see Rhodes 1997a, 1997b and 1998b).

It's the mix that matters

No governing structure works for all services in all conditions. The issue, therefore, is not the superiority of markets over hierarchies but the conditions under which each works best. The limits to markets and hierachies are well documented. The limits to networks are less well known. So box 8 lists the costs and benefits of networks. The central advantage of networks is that they give professionals the freedom to use their expertise and tailor services to clients. Instead of costly monitoring and evaluation of service quality, and haggling with staff about their performance, networks trust professionals to follow high standards. The guarantees for those standards comes through training, accreditation and policing by the national professional association, not the employer. The main disadvantage of networks is that they are difficult to hold to account, witness the long-standing struggle for managerial control of doctors in the NHS.

Network negotiation and co-ordination can also be confounded by the political context in which they are embedded. Rapid rates of change, endemic social conflicts and short-term political, especially party political, interests can all undermine negotiations and the search for an agreed course of action. So, whatever the governing structure, there is a high probability that it will produce unintended consequences because of the political context, inappropriate conditions, and the unpredictable impact of social knowledge. Or, to be succinct, as Harold Macmillan would have it: 'events, dear boy, events'.

Diplomacy and hands-off management

I use 'diplomacy' to refer to management by negotiation. As Sir Douglas Wass said 'finesse and diplomacy are an essential ingredient in public service' (cited in Hennessy 1989, p. 150). Such skills lie at the heart of steering networks.

The idea is not new but it has been temporarily misplaced. Nicholson (1950, p. 15) identifies seven diplomatic virtues: truthfulness; precision; calm; good temper; patience; modesty; and loyalty (to the government one serves). There is a charming quality to Nicholson's account. The budding diplomat is advised that: 'above everything, do not allow yourself to become excited about your work' (p. 116). He then adds: "But", the reader may object, "you have forgotten intelligence, knowledge, discernment, prudence, hospitality, charm, industry, courage and even tact". I have not forgotten them. I have taken them for granted' (p. 126). For all its slightly old-fashioned, even quaint, air Nicholson signals an important shift in style to a language which stresses sitting where the other person sits and helping other people to realize their objectives. If this shift seems prosaic, if the style seems obvious, then the following story suggests there is still some way to be travelled before management by diplomacy becomes prominent.

The scene is the annual conference of the Queensland Division of the Institute of Public Administration Australia. The event is a public lecture in which I contrast the style of the 'head kicker' – Australian for macho-manager – with that of the diplomat. As I mingled after the address, three female public servants working for the Queensland government approached me, congratulated me on my talk, 'but', they commented, 'they won't listen to you. That diplomacy is *girlie talk*'. My instant response was to laugh. On reflection, I realized that language about sitting where the other person sits and helping other people to realize their objectives was seen as 'soft'. It would not seem too harsh to conclude that the tool kit of the public service manager is overly restricted.

The new style of hands-off management involves setting the framework in which networks work but keeping an arm's length relationship. For example, a central department can: provide the policy framework and policy guidance; prod the network into action by systematic review and scrutiny of its work; use patronage to put 'one of its own' in key positions; mobilize resources and skills across sectors; regulate the network and its members; and provide advice and assistance (Cm 2811, 1995; Rhodes 1997b and citations). Such steering may be imperfect but just as there are limits to central command, there are limits to independent action by self-organizing networks.

The new style also employs a colourful language. For example, civil servants in the Department of Health confronted with the challenge of instilling financial discipline in doctors liken their task to 'herding cats' and their management tools to 'rubber levers' which when pulled bend in the middle but effect little change on the ground.

From deconcentration to devolution

Decentralization encompasses both deconcentration and devolution. Deconcentration refers to the redistribution of administrative responsibilities in central government. Devolution refers to the exercise of political authority by lay, elected, institutions within territorial areas. In the UK, most of the reforms of the 1980s and 1990s sought to deconcentrate managerial authority; for example to agencies. Devolution was a feature of public sector reform elsewhere in Europe. With the advent of the Labour government, devolution became a political priority in Britain.

The British unitary state was always a differentiated polity – a maze of divided functional authority. Government Offices for the Regions (GOs) were an embryo reform of that system. The aim was to improve the coordination between the regional offices of Whitehall departments to meet the demand for a single point of contact and to simplify the government machine and improve value for money. Mawson and Spencer (1997, pp. 81–3; Rhodes 2000a vol. 2, ch. 12) conclude that the decision to set up GOs was 'a radical departure from the centralised and compartmentalised traditions of the civil service'. They have led to greater co-ordination in the regions. Although 'much remains to be done in developing the skills of civil servants in networking partnership development', none the less GOs are a key mechanism for developing holistic governance. Potentially, they are also 'the building blocks of a devolved democratically elected regional structure' but their misfortune was to be created by the Conservative government and abandoned by the Labour government which favoured Regional Development Agencies (RDAs) to fuel regional economic regeneration. The RDAs both supplanted, and in the eyes of some 'undermined', GOs when they were on the verge of success.

Devolution reinforces functional decentralization with divided political authority. Devolution to the English regions will not take place in the life of this Parliament. But RDAs have not stilled the clamour of regional voices for devolution. So, political decentralization remains on the political agenda and the civil service may soon confront a patchwork quilt of regional assembles and directly elected mayors in England (as well as Scotland, Wales and Northern Ireland) with new machinery of government to manage intergovernmental relations both for domestic matters and the EU. Diplomatic skill in intergovernmental bargaining will become a prominent part of a civil servant's repertoire. Britain will get a taste of the federal-provincial diplomacy so characteristic of other Westminster systems such as Australia and Canada. In the words of the Head of the Home Civil Service, Sir Richard Wilson (1998), the civil service 'are going to have to learn skills that we haven't learned before'. In short, the networking skills increasingly required to manage service delivery will also be at a premium in managing the intergovernmental relations of devolved Britain. The task is to manage packages, packages of services, of organizations generally and of governments in particular.

CONCLUSIONS

Box 9 summarizes the shift from hierarchy to networks. What lessons can we draw from a view of the world in which networks rival markets and bureaucracy as a means for delivering services?

Too often academics seek to play the role of *ersatz* public servant. We try to provide data, even solutions, to present-day problems. But the social sciences offer only provisional knowledge. Prediction is probably an impossibility, only hindsight is a realistic goal. An awareness of our limits does not make the social sciences useless. If we cannot offer solutions, we can define and redefine problems in novel ways. We can tell the policy makers and administrators distinctive stories about their world and how it is governed. The new public management told a story of economy, efficiency and effectiveness which contrasted sharply with the story of the local government officer as professional with clients and the permanent secretary as policy adviser and fire-fighter for the minister.

The governance narrative stresses differentiation, networks, hollowing-out, trust and diplomacy. Its language contrasts sharply with that of managerialism, markets and contracts. The ESRC's 'Local Governance' and 'Whitehall' Programmes helped to change the language of the 1980s from managerialism to networks. If there is a simple lesson, it

---

BOX 9 *Characterizing governance*

Following Martin Smith (1999) changes can be described as a shift from bureaucracy or hierarchy to networks.

Hierarchy
A high degree of state control, the result of policies such as nationalization.
A large bureaucratic machine.
Legitimacy to undertake large-scale intervention in society.
The incorporation of key economic groups into the policy process.
A high degree of consensus between officials and politicians over their role in governing and decision making.

Networks
A shift from bureaucratic management to decentralized and delayered management.
A tendency to set overall direction of policy rather than detail of policy – a lack of detailed intervention.
Control over a smaller public sector.
The exclusion of economic groups from the policy process.
Loss of consensus between officials and politicians.
Concern with managing networks rather than directing state bureaucracies (see also Rhodes 2000a vol. 1, ch. 2).

However, this trend is not specific to the post-war period. Thus, Lowe and Rollings (Rhodes 2000a, vol. 1, ch. 6) caution against the argument there was a unilinear increase in state intervention after 1900 and a hollowing-out after 1945. They record the rise and fall of governance (as networks) in the twentieth century, arguing it was pre-eminent at the turn of the century, obsolete in the 1960s and reinvented in the 1980s.

---

is that in the complex world of diplomacy in governance there are no simple solutions based on markets or bureaucracies or networks.

This lesson is broad. In fact, it is unpacked by each aphorism. The lessons in box 10 parallel the earlier sections of the paper.

The maxim 'for every complex problem there is a simple solution and it is always wrong' may not be literally correct but it should instil a modicum of caution in the breast of the would-be reformer.

BOX 10 *The lessons of governance*
- Fragmentation limits the centre's ability to command.

- Regulation substitutes for control but who regulates the regulators?

- External dependence further erodes the ability of the core executive to act.

- Fragmentation confounds centralization, undermining the ability of the core executive to co-ordinate.

- Knowledge, or policy learning, changes problems as policies seek to solve them.

- Marketization corrodes trust, co-operation and shared professional values, undermining the networks it only partially replaces.

- All governing structures – markets, bureaucracies and networks – fail, so 'if it ain't broke don't fix it'.

- Steering networks needs diplomacy, so hands-off management is the only effective operating code.

- Decentralization is a key mechanism for developing holistic governance.

These lessons are directly relevant to many reforms under New Labour. Thus, the White Paper on *Modernising Government* (Cm 4310, 1999) aspires to 'joined-up' or 'holistic' government. Both phrases are synonyms for steering networks and the White Paper is a response to felt weakness: 'in general too little effort has gone into making sure that policies are devised and delivered in a consistent and effective way across institutional boundaries – for example between different Government departments and between central and local government'. It describes the challenge as 'to get different parts of government to work together' by, for example: 'designing policy around shared goals'; 'involving others in policy making'; 'integrating the European Union and international dimension in our policy making'; and regarding 'policy making as a continuous learning process'. Specific proposals include: organizing work around cross-cutting issues; pooled budgets; cross-cutting performance measures; and appraisal systems which reward team working.

The government's approach will have to confront the lessons in box 10. The search for co-ordination lies at the heart of New Labour's reforms and yet Hayward and Wright (2000) show that horizontal co-ordination is the philosopher's stone of modern government, ever sought, but always just beyond reach. Ministers, the barons at the heart of British government, defend their fiefdoms; it was ever thus. Equally, action zones show the limits to vertical co-ordination. There is an epidemic of zones, to the point where the solution (to fragmentation) becomes part of the problem (by adding to the bodies to be co-ordinated). For example, John Denham (1999), a junior minister in the Department of Health, concedes that 'zones can sometimes make government look more, rather than less complicated to the citizen' and there is the danger of 'initiative overload' because the zones do not join-up.

Zones show the government adopting an instrumental approach to network management which assumes the centre can devise and impose tools to foster integration in and between networks and realize central government's objectives. It is an example of imposed consensual technocracy which will not solve the problem of co-ordination. The reforms have a centralizing thrust. They seek to co-ordinate departments and local authorities by imposing a new style of management on other agencies. So, they 'do not want to run local services from the centre' but '[T]he Government is not afraid to take action where standards slip'; an obvious instance of a command operating code (Cm 4310 1999, pp. 35, 37, 45, 53, 55). Zones are owned by the centre and local agendas are recognized in as far as they facilitate the central agenda. Such a code, no matter how well disguised, runs the ever-present risk of recalcitrance from key actors and a loss of flexibility in dealing with localized problems. Gentle pressure relentlessly applied is still a command operating code in a velvet glove. When you are sat at the top of a pyramid and you cannot see the bottom, control deficits are an ever-present unintended consequence. Network structures are characterized by a decentralized negotiating style which trades off control for agreement. Management by negotiation means agreeing with the objectives of others, not just persuading them that you were right all along or resorting to sanctions when they disagree.

All governing structures fail. Bureaucracy and red tape is an old litany. We also become increasingly conscious of the limits to marketization. If contracting-out remains, the purchaser-provider split has gone and the private finance initiative stores up problems. The Treasury may avoid capital spending but there is an 'affordability gap' because hospital trusts do not have the resources to pay the private sector. As with the previous government, the full costs of this policy emerge slowly. Similarly there are limits to networks and box 8 lists them. I do not suggest that joined-up government and networks are unworkable, it is important to remember that *all* governing structures fail. Networks have distinct advantages. First, markets and hierarchies fail. Networks work in conditions where they do not. The list of conditions in box 8 are conditions under which markets fail; for example, where it is difficult to specify the price of a good or service! Second, networks bring together policy makers and the implementing agencies, and by so doing increase the available expertise and information. Third, networks bring together many actors to negotiate about a policy, increasing the acceptability of that policy and improving the likelihood of compliance. Fourth, networks increase the resources available for policy making by drawing together the public, private and voluntary sectors.

New Labour rejects the command bureaucracy model of Old Labour with its emphasis on hierarchy, authority and rules. At first sight, it accepts the Conservative government's policy of marketizing public services but it pragmatically accepts such reforms as the Citizen's Charter while rejecting others. Distinctively, it advocates joined-up government or delivering public services by steering networks of organizations where the currency is not authority (bureaucracy) or price competition (markets) but trust. In the parlance of the chattering classes it is the 'Third Way' in action. It exemplifies the shift from the providing state of Old Labour and the minimal state of Thatcherism to the enabling state.

There is much to welcome in New Labour's modernizing programme for central, local and devolved government. But the government lacks the trust it seeks to inspire. It fears the independence it bestows. So, the White Paper on *Modernising Government* recognizes the need to manage networks but fails to recognize the limits both to central intervention as it tries to balance independence with central control and to networks as a fallible governing structure.

My story stresses muddling through based on provisional knowledge and diverse, local policy responses to contested definitions of problems. There is no tool kit for the central steering of decentralized networks. 'Hands off' is the hardest lesson of all to learn.

REFERENCES

Bevir, M. and R.A.W. Rhodes. 1999. 'Studying British government: reconstructing the research agenda', *British Journal of Politics and International Relations* 1, 2, 215–39.

Brady, C. and P. Catterall. 1997. 'Managing the core executive', *Public Administration* 75, 3, 509–29.

Bulmer, S. and M. Burch. 1998. 'Organising for Europe: Whitehall, the British State and European Union', *Public Administration* 76, 4, 601–28.

Butler, Sir Robin. 1993. 'The evolution of the civil service', *Public Administration* 71, 395–406.

Catterall, P. and C. Brady. 1998. 'Cabinet committees in British governance', *Public Policy and Administration* 13, 4, 67–84.

Cm 2748. 1995. *The civil service. Taking forward continuity and change.* London: HMSO.

Cm 2811. 1995. *Department of National Heritage Annual Report 1995.* London: HMSO.

Cm 4310. 1999. *Modernising government.* London: Stationery Office.

Committee of Public Accounts. 1994. *The proper conduct of public business.* London: HMSO.

———. 1997. *The former Yorkshire Regional Health Authority: the inquiry commissioned by the NHS chief executive.* HC 432 Session 1996–97. London: The Stationery Office.

Day, P. and R. Klein. 1997. *Steering but not rowing? The Transformation of the Department of Health: a case study.* Bristol: The Policy Press.

Denham, J. 1999. Speech to the CIPFA/Public Management and Policy Association Conference on an 'An Epidemic of Zones: Illness or Cure?'. International Conference Centre, Birmingham.

Hayward, J.E.S. and V. Wright. 2000. 'Governing from the Centre: policy co-ordination in six European core executives', in R.A.W. Rhodes (ed.), *Transforming British government. Volume 2. Changing roles and relationships.* London: Macmillan.

Hennessy, P. 1989. *Whitehall.* London: Secker & Warburg.

Hood, C. 1995. 'Contemporary public management: a new global paradigm?', *Public Policy and Administration*, 10, 2, 104–17.

———. 1996. 'Exploring variations in public management reforms of the 1980s', in H.A.G.M. Bekke, J.L. Perry and T.A.J. Toonen (eds.), *Civil service systems in comparative perspective.* Bloomington: Indiana University Press.

Hood, C., O. James, G. Jones, C. Scott and T. Travers. 1998. 'Regulation inside government': where new public management meets the audit explosion', *Public Money and Management* 18, 2, 61–8.

Hood, C., C. Scott, O. James, G. Jones and T. Travers 1999. *Regulation inside government: waste-watchers, quality police and sleaze busters*. Oxford: Oxford University Press.

Jones, G.W. 1998. 'Reforming No. 10', *Talking Politics* 11, 1, 21–7.

Lowe, R. 1997. 'The core executive, modernization and the creation of PESC, 1960–64', *Public Administration* 75, 4, 601–15.

Mawson, J. and K. Spencer. 1997. 'The Government Offices for the English Regions: towards regional governance?', *Policy and Politics* 25, 1, 71–84.

Menon, A. and V. Wright. 1998. 'The paradoxes of "failure": British EU policy making in comparative perspective', *Public Policy and Administration* 13, 4, 46–66.

Newman, J., S. Richards and P. Smith. 1998. 'Market testing and institutional change in the UK civil service: compliance, non-compliance and engagement', *Public Policy and Administration* 13, 4, 96–110.

Nicholson, H. 1950. *Diplomacy*. Oxford: Oxford University Press.

Norton, P. 1997. 'Leaders or led? Senior ministers in British Government', *Talking Politics* 10, 2, 78–85.

Rhodes, R.A.W. 1994. 'The hollowing out of the state', *Political Quarterly* 65, 138–51.

———. 1997a. *Understanding governance: policy networks, governance, reflexivity and accountability*. Buckingham: Open University Press.

———. 1997b. 'It's the mix that matters: from marketization to diplomacy', *Australian Journal of Public Administration* 56, 40–53.

———. 1998a. 'The changing nature of central government in Britain: the ESRC's Whitehall Programme', *Public Policy and Administration* 13, 4, 1–11.

———. 1998b. 'Different roads to unfamiliar places: UK experience in comparative perspective', *Australian Journal of Public Administration* 57, 19–31.

———. 1998c. 'Diplomacy in Governance', *Politics Today* 7, 3, 24–7.

———. 1999a. 'Foreword: governance and networks', in G. Stoker (ed.), *The new management of British local governance*. London: Macmillan.

———. 1999b, 1981. *Control and power in central-local government relationships*. Farnborough: Gower. Reprinted with a new Preface and three extra chapters.

———. 1999c. 'Traditions and public sector reform; comparing Britain and Denmark', *Scandinavian Political Studies* 22, 4, 341–70.

———. (ed.) 2000a. *Transforming British government*. 2 vols. London: Macmillan.

———. 2000b. 'A guide to the ESRC Whitehall Programme, 1994–1999', *Public Administration* 78, 2, 251–82.

———. 2000c. 'Governance and public administration', in J. Pierre (ed.), *Debating governance*. Oxford: Oxford University Press.

Rhodes, R.A.W. and P. Dunleavy (eds.). 1995. *Prime minister, cabinet and core executive*. London: Macmillan.

Richards, S., P. Smith and J. Newman. 1996. 'Shaping and reshaping market testing policy', *Public Policy and Administration* 11, 2, 19–34.

Riddell, P. 1997. 'Advising the Prime Minister'. Paper to the ESRC Conference on 'Future Whitehall'. Church House, London.

Rose, R. 2000. *The paradox of Downing Street: the Prime Minister in a shrinking world*. London: Macmillan.

Smith, M.J. 1998. 'Theoretical and empirical challenges to British central government', *Public Administration* 76, 3, 45–72.

Smith, M. 1999. *The core executive in Britain*. London: Macmillan.

Theakston, K. 1999. *Leadership in Whitehall*. London: Macmillan.

———. (ed.). 1999. *Bureaucrats and leadership*. London: Macmillan.

———. 1997. 'Comparative biography and leadership in Whitehall', *Public Administration* 75, 651–67.

———. 1997. 'New Labour, New Whitehall?', *Public Policy and Administration* 13, 1, 13–34.

Verney, D. 1991. 'Westminster model', in V. Bogdanor (ed.), *The Blackwell encyclopaedia of political science*. Corrected paperback edition. Oxford: Blackwell.

Wilson, Sir Richard. 1998. 'Modernising government: the role of the senior civil service'. Speech, Senior Civil Service Conference, Oct.

Wright, V. 1994. 'Reshaping the state: implications for public administration', *West European Politics* 17, 102–34.

AFTERWORD: WAVES OF GOVERNANCE

The argument in this article that recent changes in the pattern and exercise of state authority took the form of a shift from government to governance; from a hierarchic or bureaucratic state to markets and then to governance in and by networks, produced extensive and vigorous debate (for a summary, see Rhodes 2007). Ten years later, it has produced three waves of governance literature: network governance, metagovernance, and decentred governance. Of course, each approach persists. They overlap and interweave. However, separating the waves highlights important differences in approaches to the study of governance.

The network governance literature of the 1990s argued that the changing nature of the state followed from the public sector reforms of the 1980s. The reforms are said to have precipitated a shift from a hierarchic bureaucracy toward a greater use of markets, quasi-markets, and networks, especially in the delivery of public services. The effects of the reforms were intensified by global changes, including an increase in transnational economic activity and the rise of regional institutions such as the European Union. The resulting complexity and fragmentation are such that the state increasingly depends on other organisations to secure its intentions and deliver its policies. Network governance evokes a world in which state power is dispersed among a vast array of spatially and functionally distinct networks composed of all kinds of public, voluntary, and private organisations with which the centre now interacts (for a critique and reply see Marinetto 2003; Rhodes 2007). The network governance literature offers a compelling picture of the state; indeed Marsh (2008: 738) is concerned it 'may be becoming the new orthodoxy'.

In the 2000s, the second-wave of network governance accepted the shift from bureaucracy to markets to networks but disputed it led to any significant dispersal of state authority. For example, Pierre and Peters (2000, 78, 104–5 and 111) argue the shift to network governance could 'increase public control over society' because governments 'rethink the mix of policy instruments'. As a result 'coercive or regulatory instruments become less important and . . . "softer" instruments gain importance'; steering not rowing. In short, the state was not hollowed-out but reasserted its capacity to govern by regulating the mix of governing structures such as bureaucracy, markets and networks and deploying indirect instruments of control (see Rhodes 1997). The term 'metagovernance' or 'the governance of government and governance' (Jessop 2000: 23) is the umbrella concept that describes this redefined role of the state and its characteristic indirect policy instruments for managing network governance. Given that governing is distributed among various private, voluntary, and public actors, and that power and authority are more decentralised and fragmented among a plurality of networks, the role of the state has shifted from the direct governance of society to the 'metagovernance' of the several modes of intervention. There has been a shift from command and control through bureaucracy to the indirect steering of relatively autonomous stakeholders. In sum, the metagovernance story is about 'bringing the state back in (yet again)' (Jessop 2007: 54).

Most recently, the third-wave narrative of 'decentred governance' challenges the idea there are inexorable, impersonal forces driving a shift from government to network governance. To decentre is to focus on the social construction of a practice through the ability of individuals to create, and act on, meanings. It is to unpack a practice into the disparate and contingent beliefs and actions of individuals (Bevir and Rhodes 2003: Chapter 4). Governance is constructed differently by many actors working against the background of diverse traditions. In effect, the decentred governance approach pronounces the death of the Anglo-governance school, of metagovernance, and of the state. Instead, the approach focuses on the various traditions that have informed the diverse policies and practices by which elite and other actors have sought to remake the state (Bevir and Rhodes 2010).

This shift to a narrative of decentred governance challenges a craving for generality that characterises the earlier waves of governance by defining governance as a series of family resemblances, none of which need be always present. There is no list of general features or essential properties that are supposed to characterise governance in every instance. Rather, there are diverse practices composed of multiple individuals acting on changing webs of beliefs rooted in overlapping traditions. Patterns of governance or state authority arise as the contingent products of diverse actions and political struggles informed by the beliefs of agents as they arise against a backcloth of traditions.

This conception of the stateless state leads to a new research agenda; to the 3Rs' of rule, rationalities and resistance. Thus, a decentred approach suggests that political scientists ask whether different sections of the elite draw on different traditions to construct different narratives about ruling (see Rhodes 2011). The approach also draws attention to the varied rationalities that inform policies. Rationalities refer here to the scientific beliefs and associated technologies that govern conduct. The term captures the ways in which governments and other social actors draw on knowledge to construct policies and practices to regulate and create subjectivities (see McKinlay and Starkey 1998). Finally a decentred approach draws attention to the diverse traditions and narratives that inspire street level bureaucrats and citizens. Subordinate actors can resist the intentions and policies of elites by consuming them in ways that draw on their local traditions and their local reasoning (see Maynard-Moody and Musheno 2003).

The study of governance remains a lively and contested area. One obvious indicator is the increase in the articles on this topic in the pages of *Public Administration*. The journal played a part in sustaining the debate. Another indicator is the growth in textbooks, handbooks, and encyclopaedia of governance (see Kjaer 2004; Bevir 2007). For some, it is a weasel word and its opacity may even fuel its popularity. But for all the criticisms, the concept remains important because it directs our attention to the changing role of the state, its relationship to civil society, and how we understand both.

REFERENCES

Bevir, M. (ed.). 2007. *Public Governance*. 4 volumes. London: Sage.

Bevir, M. and Rhodes, R. A. W. 2003. *Interpreting British Governance*. London: Routledge.

Bevir, M. and Rhodes, R. A. W. 2010. *The State as Cultural Practice*. Oxford: Oxford University Press.

Jessop, B. 2000. 'Governance failure'. In G. Stoker (ed.). *The New Politics of British Local Governance*. Houndmills, Basingstoke: Macmillan, pp. 11–32.

Jessop, B. 2007. *State Power*. Cambridge: Polity.

Kjær, A. M. 2004. *Governance*. Cambridge: Polity.

Marinetto, M. 2003. 'Governing beyond the centre: a critique of the Anglo-Governance School', *Political Studies*, 51, 3, 592–608.

Marsh, D. 2008. 'What is at stake? A response to Bevir and Rhodes', *British Journal of Politics and International Relations*, 10, 4, 735–739.

Maynard-Moody, S. and M. Musheno. 2003. *Cops, Teachers, Counsellors: Stories from the Front Lines of Public Service.* Ann Arbor, Michigan: The University of Michigan Press.

McKinlay, A. and K. P. Starkey (eds). 1998. *Foucault, Management and Organization Theory: From Panopticon to Technologies of Self.* London: Sage.

Pierre, J. and B. G. Peters. 2000. *Governance, Politics and the State.* Houndmills, Basingstoke: Macmillan.

Rhodes, R. A. W. 1997. 'It's the mix that matters: from marketization to diplomacy', *Australian Journal of Public Administration,* 56, 2, 40–53.

Rhodes, R. A. W. 2007. 'Understanding Governance: ten years on', *Organization Studies,* 28, 8, 1243–1264.

Rhodes, R. A. W. 2011. *Everyday Life in British Government.* Oxford: Oxford University Press, forthcoming.

Chapter 4

THE DYNAMICS OF MULTI-ORGANIZATIONAL PARTNERSHIPS: AN ANALYSIS OF CHANGING MODES OF GOVERNANCE[1]

VIVIEN LOWNDES AND CHRIS SKELCHER

INTRODUCTION

Debates in the academic and public management worlds are currently emphasizing the benefits that collaborative, inter-agency partnerships can offer as a means of achieving public policy goals. The idea of 'collaborative advantage' (Huxham 1996) presents an attractive alternative to the market, quasi-market and contractualized relationships that have dominated the public management reform movement internationally in the past decade. It also encourages further progress away from the large-scale, bureaucratic and paternalistic public service organizations which developed to deliver welfare state programmes in the third quarter of this century.

There has been recent and sustained growth in the number and types of partnerships created to realize public policy intentions. Governmental bodies in the UK, particularly at the local level, have been active in establishing formalized collaborative relationships with businesses, voluntary (or non-governmental) organizations and community associations. Such partnerships are particularly pronounced in the fields of urban and rural regeneration, where local authorities have created working arrangements with a range of other agencies to promote the economic, social and political revitalization of communities, but are also found in social care, education, environmental and other policy sectors. These relationships are formalized by an agreement between the parties which is given concrete expression through the creation of an organizational structure – a partnership board or forum. Here, strategy is developed and decisions are made which may have implications for the policies, resources and actions of the individual agencies involved.

The argument put forward in this article, however, is that *partnership* as an organizational structure is analytically distinct from *network* as a mode of governance – the means by which social co-ordination is achieved. The creation of a partnership board does not imply that relations between actors are conducted on the basis of mutual benefit, trust and reciprocity – the characteristics of the network mode of governance. Rather, partnerships are associated with a variety of forms of social co-ordination – including network, hierarchy and market. The failure to distinguish between partnerships as organizational manifestations and the modes of social co-ordination that accompany them has constrained theoretical development and empirical investigation of this important field. Drawing on our studies of UK urban regeneration partnerships, we argue that market and hierarchical arrangements as well as networking are apparent in partnerships. Indeed, we propose that partnerships pass through a life cycle in which different modes of governance assume a particular importance at different points in time and in relation to particular partnership tasks. Strategies to develop effective partnerships thus involve combining different modes of governance in an environment where the power relations between various partners will be shifting and the resulting dynamics will at one point stimulate co-operation and at another competition.

We begin by identifying the factors behind the growth of partnerships in local governance, and urban regeneration in particular. We then explore the concept of modes of governance, examining the characteristics of market, hierarchy and network. This leads to the formulation of a model which shows how different modes of governance are combined within the life cycle of urban regeneration partnerships, illustrated from our recent empirical research. The article concludes by discussing the implications for theory and practice of the notion of plural modes of governance within multi-organizational partnerships.

MOTIVATIONS FOR MULTI-ORGANIZATIONAL PARTNERSHIPS

Resource dependency issues have been an important motivator in the development of partnerships by UK public service agencies. The impact of continued constraint on public resources since the mid-1970s has stimulated governmental bodies to search out new sources of finance and to examine whether the creation of multi-agency partnerships involving public, private, voluntary and community organizations could offer ways of delivering more with less. Partnerships have the potential to increase resource efficiency, making better use of existing resources by reducing duplication and sharing overheads. They can add value by bringing together complementary services and fostering innovation and synergy. Finally, partnerships enable the levering-in of new resources – either by enabling access to grant regimes requiring financial and in-kind contributions from the private and voluntary/community sectors or using private sector partners to overcome public sector constraints on access to capital markets (Mackintosh 1992).

There is more to the emergence of the new orthodoxy of partnerships than overcoming resource dependencies. Multi-agency partnerships arise from the search by public bodies for integration within an increasingly fragmented organizational landscape. Local authorities, for example, are now commonly composed of a federation of different units – purchasers and providers, devolved budget centres, localized service outlets and other structures – all with varying degrees of autonomy from the centre of the organization which was, in the earlier era of large public bureaucracies, the locus of power and authority. Simultaneously, the range of different agencies involved in shaping and delivering public policy has increased dramatically. Non-elected governmental bodies, private firms and voluntary and community organizations all have new roles in the fragmented and quasi-market environment arising from the new public management. Yet unlike the simple ideal-type market, these actors are necessarily connected through a complex web of interdependencies in which collaboration is required to achieve singular and common purposes. As Kickert et al. (1997, p. 3) argue: 'One of the major challenges with which public management is confronted is to deal with network-like situations, that is, situations of interdependencies'. Partnerships provide a means of developing strategic direction and co-ordination within this 'polycentric' terrain (Rhodes 1997a, p. xii).

The growth of partnerships also reflects the complexity and intransigence of the 'wicked issues' (Stewart 1996) facing government – issues that can only be tackled by bringing together the resources of a range of different providers and interest groups. As Rhodes (1997a, p. xv) notes: 'Messy problems demand messy solutions', and so the apparently tidy hierarchy of the public bureaucracy is reshaped to establish lateral, diagonal and vertical relationships with other bodies operating at different tiers and in associated policy fields. Kickert (1993, p. 201) views these issues not so much as 'problems and difficulties which have to be mastered, but as sources of innovation'. The innovation has come in the form of strategies to develop interrelationships, trust and collaboration in an environment of resource scarcity where organizations would typically be oriented to defence and self-protection behind their bureaucratic ramparts. Consequently, at the local level, the growth of multi-agency partnerships is associated both with the changing agenda of local government and with a desire to address in innovative ways those issues that cross organizational boundaries. As Tony Blair has argued:

> If local people are to enjoy a sound economy and a better quality of life and if communities are to deal with cross-cutting issues like youth justice, drug abuse and social exclusion, we have to harness the contribution of businesses, public agencies, voluntary organizations and community groups and get them working to a common agenda (1998, p.10).

Finally, the growth of multi-agency partnerships forms part of a strategy to open up local decision-making processes. This arises in the context of demands from interest groups and community bodies for more voice in decisions affecting their lives, together with the significant disenchantment with formal political processes exemplified by low turnouts in local elections, particularly among young people and excluded communities (Stoker 1997). As their role moves away from that of monopolistic service provider, many local authorities are embracing a vision of community governance in which they orchestrate and facilitate partnerships involving a range of local stakeholders (Stewart 1995). This developing politics of partnership may be seen as complementing formal democratic processes or, more radically, as empowering traditionally excluded social groups (Wheeler 1996). On the other hand, partnerships may be criticized as reflecting a broader democratic deficit in which non-elected bodies and self-selected representatives gain power at the expense of elected politicians (Skelcher 1998).

The growth of multi-organizational partnerships in urban regeneration reflects the four factors outlined above. In resource terms, emphasis has been placed firmly upon ideas of flexibility, synergy, added value and leverage. The existence of a local partnership involving public, private, voluntary and community interests is a precondition of application to most British government and European Union funding regimes for regeneration. Organizational fragmentation makes partnership a necessary integrative mechanism. Activities central to the regeneration agenda which were previously carried out within the boundary of a local authority are now dispersed to government departments and a range of other agencies – for example housing associations, housing action trusts, training and enterprise councils, urban development corporations and further education corporations. Urban regeneration is a wicked issue *par excellence*, the complexity and breadth of its concerns providing a powerful argument for partnership working in the context of plural politics.

CONCEPTUALIZING MULTI-ORGANIZATIONAL PARTNERSHIPS

Interagency relationships: competition and collaboration

Understandings of the interactions between organizations have broadly originated from two organizing principles: competition and collaboration. Resource dependency theory is concerned with examining patterns of contest, power and domination in an environment characterized by the struggle over scarce resources (Klijn 1997; Alter and Hage 1993). Here, alliances between organizations arise in response to current or potential threats from competitors or the perceived opportunity to expand domains and, in the process, extend influence and secure new resources. As Alter and Hage (1993, p. 109) explain: 'Organizational decision makers' primary focus is on finding and defending an adequate supply of resources'. The policy networks literature has developed a rather more sophisticated version of resource dependency theory which recognizes the role of norms and values (appreciative systems) in sustaining inter-organizational relationships over time (Rhodes 1997b).

In contrast to the competitive imperatives implicit in the resource dependency approach, collaboration theory is characterized by a notion of synergistic gain and programme enhancement from sharing resources, risks and rewards and the prioritizing of *collaborative* rather than *competitive* advantage (Huxham 1996). Emerging from the corporate strategy literature, the concept of synergy refers to 'the additional benefits of companies acting together rather than severally' (Mackintosh 1992, p. 212). Working together offers organizations the possibility for improved delivery of individual objectives and the creation of new opportunities (Huxham 1996; Carley 1991). In this sense collaboration moves beyond the purely instrumental relationships suggested by classic resource dependency theory. Crucially, collaborative advantage is seen as involving a broad range of benefits, some of which will not be definable at the start of the relationship.

Urban regeneration partnerships are an expression of the desire for, and utility of, collaboration. However, their experience also demonstrates the tensions involved in seeking collaboration in a severely constrained resource environment. The collaborative model of inter-agency relationships is challenged by resource dependency issues – contest, domain invasion and temporary alliances to achieve competitive advantage in the context of self-interest. Agencies and localities are competing fiercely for government and European monies at the same time as the criteria for funding regimes stress co-operation and partnership building (Stewart 1994). Co-operative partnership relationships do emerge and operate effectively, but there is a tension between the harsh realities of the resource environment and the need to collaborate (Lowndes *et al.* 1996). The imperative to collaborate is driven by more than programmatic needs. There is also a moral dimension that distinguishes urban regeneration partnerships from business collaboration in the market place. This is the aspiration to further public interests rather than private gain. Such public or community service motivation is expressed in different ways by those involved in urban regeneration partnerships, whether in terms of business leaders' paternalism, councillors' party politics, community activists' demand for empowerment or the professionals' language of sustainability and capacity building.

Inter-agency relationships as modes of governance

Although the competition/collaboration dichotomy is helpful in understanding the changes currently taking place in the public service, the reality is more complex and subtle. Essentially, our focus is on forms of social coordination – in other words with *governance* – and the way this is achieved through multi-organizational partnerships. Kooiman (1993) sees *governance* as the emerging pattern arising from *governing* – the purposive means of guiding and steering a society or community. Different patterns or *modes* of governance are the outcome of social processes but also provide the medium through which actors interpret and act to shape their reality. Governance is not an exclusively political concept. It can refer to ways in which co-ordination is achieved and sustained within economic and social life, as in discussions of corporate governance (Cadbury Report 1992; Rhodes 1997b; CIPFA 1994). Mayntz (1993, p. 11) reflects this wider view when she refers to governance as 'a mode of social co-ordination or order'.

Attempts to differentiate modes of governance owe an intellectual debt to Williamson's analysis of markets and hierarchies as distinct governance structures associated with particular transaction costs on actors (Williamson 1985). Subsequent debates have added a third category to Williamson's formulation. Different triads of terms result: markets, hierarchies and networks (Thompson *et al.* 1991); markets, politics and solidarity (Mayntz 1993); markets, bureaucracies and clans (Ouchi 1991); price, authority and trust (Bradach and Eccles 1991); community, market and state (Streek and Schmitter 1985). Although there are differences of emphases in these analyses, three ideal types emerge (figure 1).

A *market* mode of governance revolves around contractual relationships over property rights. Price mechanisms are the means by which these relationships are mediated and where conflicts emerge there may be haggling or a recourse to law in order to determine the liabilities of the parties involved. Markets provide a high degree of flexibility to actors in determining their willingness to form alliances, although the competitive nature of the environment and the parties' underlying suspicion may limit the degree of commitment to any collaborative venture. Essentially, actors prefer to be independent and will choose to collaborate only when they see particular advantages to themselves. The *hierarchical* mode of governance overcomes, in theory at least, the problems of co-ordination and collaboration found in the market place. The imposition of an authoritative integrating and supervisory structure enables bureaucratic routines to be established. Coordination can be undertaken by administrative fiat, and the employment relationships pertaining within the organization encourage at least a certain level of commitment by staff. The cost, however, is a reduction in flexibility and innovation because of a tendency to formalization and routinization. The *network* mode of governance arises from a view that actors are able to

	MARKET	HIERARCHY	NETWORK
Normative basis	Contract – Property rights	Employment relationship	Complementary strengths
Means of communication	Prices	Routines	Relational
Methods of conflict resolution	Haggling – Resort to courts	Administrative fiat – supervision	Norm of reciprocity – reputational concerns
Degree of flexibility	High	Low	Medium
Amount of commitment among the parties	Low	Medium	High
Tone or climate	Precision and/or suspicion	Formal, bureaucratic	Open-ended, mutual benefits
Actor preferences or choices	Independent	Dependent	Interdependent

(Adapted from Powell 1991, p. 269)

FIGURE 1 *Modes of governance: market, hierarchy and network*

identify complementary interests. The development of interdependent relationships based on trust, loyalty and reciprocity enables collaborative activity to be developed and maintained. Being voluntary, networks maintain the loyalty of members over the longer term. Conflicts are resolved within the network on the basis of members' reputational concerns.

Partnerships and plural modes of governance

In reality, however, a particular set of organizational arrangements may be associated with a variety of modes of governance. As Bradach and Eccles (1991, p. 289) observe: 'The ideal types ... serve as a useful starting point. ... The assumption that these mechanisms are mutually exclusive, however, obscures rather than clarifies our understanding. ... Price, authority and trust are combined with each other in assorted ways in the empirical world'. They point to such examples as the hierarchical nature of contract relationships, the market-like features found within modern bureaucracies (for example profit centres and internal trading), the importance of status hierarchies within networks and the significance of trust and personal networks in market transactions.

Consequently the analytical categories employed in the governance literature should not be taken as being identical to those in the organizational studies and public management fields. The multi-organizational partnership as an organizational form should not be confused with the network as a mode of governance. Neither is there a necessary correspondence between the two. The loyalty, trust and reciprocity which characterize the ideal-typical network mode of governance may not always be appropriate for the variety of tasks required of a multi-organizational partnership. As Rhodes (1997a, p. xii) explains, selecting between modes of governance 'is a matter of practicality; that is, under what conditions does each governing structure work effectively?' Our research demonstrates that partnerships are organizational arrangements associated with a variety of modes of governance. The research shows that multi-organizational partnerships have a particular affinity with network modes of governance, but that – at different stages of the partnership life cycle – hierarchical and market relationships also assume importance.

PARTNERSHIP LIFE CYCLES AND MODES OF GOVERNANCE

Our starting point in the analysis of multi-organizational partnerships is to identify a life cycle through which they pass. This typically has four stages, each having key features in terms of the predominant mode of governance and relationship between stakeholders (figure 2). In brief, our argument is as follows:

- *Pre-partnership collaboration* is characterized by a network mode of governance based upon informality, trust and a sense of common purpose.
- *Partnership creation and consolidation* is characterized by hierarchy based upon an assertion of status and authority differentials and the formalization of procedures.
- *Partnership programme delivery* is characterized by market (or quasi-market) mechanisms of tendering and contract, with low levels of co-operation between providers.
- *Partnership termination or succession* is characterized by a re-assertion of a network governance mode as a means to maintain agency commitment, community involvement and staff employment.

These different modes of governance overlap and coexist throughout a partnership's life cycle. The balance and tensions between different modes shift as the agenda for

STAGE IN THE LIFECYCLE	MODE OF GOVERNANCE	RELATIONSHIP BETWEEN STAKEHOLDER
Pre-partnership collaboration	Networking between individuals/organizations.	Informality, trust and co-operation. Willingness to work together to achieve collective purpose. Differential resources result in emergence of inner and outer networks, with some actors becoming marginalized.
Partnership creation and consolidation	Hierarchy incorporating some organizations. Formalization of authority in partnership board and associated staff.	Negotiation and contest over definition of membership and allocation of board seats. Disruption of network as informal balance of power codified. Informal systems and agreements are replaced by hierarchical structure with formalized procedures and decisions.
Partnership programme delivery	Market mechanisms of tendering and contractual agreements. Regulation and supervision of contractors. Networking assists in production of bids and management of expenditure programme.	Low co-operation between providers. Purchasers' suspicion of over-selling by potential providers. Distinction between inner and outer network sharpens as partnership determines agreed bids and/or fund allocation. Reliance on informal agreements within network to negotiate complexities of contracts. Emergence of trust-based contracting with some organizations.
Partnership termination and succession	Networking between individuals/organizations as means to maintain agency commitment, community involvement and staff employment.	Uncertainty as network stability afforded by partnership comes to an end. Potential for new openness/expansion of links. Trust and informality, with negotiation and contest concerning strategic role of partnership.

FIGURE 2 *Networks, markets and hierarchies in a partnership life cycle*

action and the relationship between partners change. However, as we illustrate below, the network mode of governance has a continuing importance as the sub-structure of successful partnerships. We now consider each of the life-cycle stages in turn, illustrating the analysis with reference to our empirical research on urban regeneration partnerships. The data are drawn from two studies: an analysis of urban regeneration partnerships in three metropolitan areas in England (Skelcher *et al*. 1996) and succession strategies for a City Challenge board (Sullivan and Lowndes 1996).[2]

Pre-partnership collaboration

We found most evidence of ideal-type network relationships in the phase of pre-partnership collaboration. Interactions between potential partners were characterized by informality and a stress on personal relationships. A civil servant from one of the government offices of the regions painted this picture of how partnerships are put together:

> I have meetings with X on bridges and pavements in the city – he says what the council can do and I say what we can do, then we put it together. Individuals not institutions is what it's all about – individuals can work together and understand what it's all about.

A local authority respondent noted that:

> When things work and when they don't is patchy, but personalities are important, particularly a capacity to be positive even when under stress, and not to be threatened by other agencies. It sounds trite but it helps when people like each other!

The quality of relationships was linked to the level of trust between actors and the extent to which interaction was seen as leading to mutual benefit. One interviewee observed that where there was little trust between agencies, only chief executives or senior officers ('the heavies') attended inter-agency meetings. When there was greater trust, a wider group of individuals tended to be involved, allowing for a greater variety of inputs, a more efficient use of resources, and a broader sense of ownership. Another interviewee explained that relationships were built out of a combination of 'vision' and 'cost-benefit analysis': vision was important in gaining the commitment of partners while cost benefit analysis determined whether relationships would be maintained over time. The expectation of mutual benefit was seen as crucial in pre-partnership collaboration: 'You need to create a situation in which everyone is putting in *and* getting out – then you avoid the institutional difficulties of "what's in it for me?" People want something for their money, although it might not be a formal output. Once common interest falters, the partnership's done'.

The importance of informality, personal relationships and trust in pre-partnership collaboration was regarded negatively by some of our informants. Network-style relationships were viewed by those who felt excluded or marginalized as 'cosy', 'cliquey' or 'sewn-up'. The reliance on social contact, friendship and personal trust made it hard for new actors to 'break in' to networks. Information was seen as passing between those 'in the know' with little consideration for new groups, those outside established relationships (often women's and minority ethnic groups), or for small or poorly resourced organizations with little opportunity to 'play the networks'. A worker in a small Asian women's advice centre, reflecting on her ability to find out about new funding opportunities and partnership initiatives, commented: 'Whether we get the information or not . . . whether it comes in time, seems to be a matter of chance . . . You have to be seen around, otherwise you miss out on what's going to happen'.

Getting to know key individuals and building relationships took time and could distract organizations from their 'core business'. As one informant noted: 'You could pack your week with inter-agency meetings, but what would you drop then?' Networking was seen as having costs as well as benefits: agencies sought to balance the possible costs of involvement against uncertain long-term gain, and their own organization's interests against wider service or policy concerns. Certain well-resourced organizations were perceived as all too keen to take advantage of the fragility of network relationships in order to shape 'common purpose' to suit their own priorities. A member of a residents' association noted that:

> Some of the organizations you're involved with, you don't invite them to certain meetings because they'll take over. And in particular I'm thinking of X because however little they are involved – even if it's only 5 per cent funding from them – they want it to comply with their rules, they want to vet the adverts – and to take the credit!

Stereotypes about particular agencies, or sectors, presented an obstacle to building relationships and trust. A training and enterprise council officer noted the suspicion among private sector board members that the voluntary sector was 'left wing' and difficult to work with, and their surprise at 'the balanced perspective' that a new voluntary sector representative had brought to the board. A voluntary sector interviewee expressed his cynicism about private sector motives, complaining that business interests were trying to 'colonize' the urban regeneration agenda. Both the private and the voluntary sector complained about local authorities' 'political' outlook.

Our research pointed to the value of brokerage or facilitation both to stimulate pre-partnership collaboration and to reduce some of the misunderstandings and inequities inherent in 'organic' network relationships. A former city action team project officer described her experience thus:

> We acted like a kind of dating agency – bringing people together. We helped form partnerships that wouldn't necessarily have come together unless someone pushed them together. We took the bottle to the party! We had a Heineken budget – it refreshed the parts other budgets didn't reach! The main outcome for us was not what the partnership produced, but getting it started.

Our research showed that pre-partnership collaboration was characterized by network forms of social co-ordination, although other modes of governance were important too. Hierarchies based on resource, information and status differentials were superimposed on network relationships, leading to the formation of inner and outer networks and the exclusion or marginalization of some potential partners. Market-like cost-benefit calculations were also important for individual agencies in deciding whether or not to invest in potential partnership opportunities.

Partnership creation and consolidation

We observed a clear trend towards formalization as pre-partnership collaboration gave way to more focused activity. The stimulus for informal relationships to evolve into formal partnerships varied: in some cases it was a project requirement (as in Business Link), in other cases it was necessary in order to bid for funding (as with the Single Regeneration Budget), or it came out of the 'natural' development of inter-agency work. One interviewee noted how joint training activities had led to the emergence of an informal network of individuals, who later acted to formalize their relationship. Another group had held a public event that led to further interest in 'their' issue and a demand for a more formal partnership structure. There was a clear contrast between those networks that evolved towards greater formality (in response to changing circumstances and priorities) and those which had formality forced upon them, typically in order to access government or European regeneration funding regimes.

Interviewees varied in how they valued formality and informality. A voluntary sector respondent explained that while networks often developed informally and 'by accident', it was important to formalize relationships in order to ensure that they constituted more than a set of personalized contacts. Formalization was linked to increased transparency and clearer accountability by some, particularly those who highlighted the 'exclusive' tendencies of informal relationships. Formalization was also seen as necessary 'to get things done' in terms both of accessing funds, but also of ensuring probity and effective implementation structures. The setting up of some kind of bureaucracy – with clear roles, responsibilities and reporting lines – was seen as a stage in the partnership's life cycle, as it moved from a concern with exchanging information and ideas to a focus on project or policy implementation.

On the other hand, a local authority respondent pointed out that formal arrangements did not guarantee meaningful relationships and could, in fact, limit a partnership's capacity for flexibility and innovation:

> Informal relationships are important – not necessarily detrimental. They can work better than overarching formal partnerships. It doesn't necessarily mean that if you have a piece of paper that says you're a partnership then you are. You've got to get on with the reality of partnership. In a rapidly changing world, if you get too wrapped up in procedure, you can never change anything.

Some of the partnerships we studied succeeded in maintaining informal network-style relationships alongside more formal ways of working. Many of those we talked to saw networks as the life-blood of the partnership, pointing to the importance of sustaining these 'beneath the surface' of increasingly bureaucratic and hierarchical arrangements – for instance by adopting relatively informal approaches to meetings and decision-making and valuing social and personal interactions among partners.

Partnership creation involved negotiation and contest over 'who's in and who's out', a significant shift to hierarchical structures compared with the relatively fluid memberships and indistinct boundaries in pre-partnership collaborations. This was sometimes focused on a particular issue like the allocation of seats to a board or management committee; at other points it was played out in terms of debates about leadership, remit and priorities. We observed the tensions that arose in the context of a lack of 'common currency' among agencies and interests of different types. Different representatives within a partnership drew their legitimacy from different sources – from election, appointment, common experience, professional expertise, leadership skills – but these various mandates were not mutually recognized and there was a lack of clarity about their relative value (Lowndes 1997). As noted above, some partners mistrusted the 'political' approach of councillors, some councillors did not want to work with non-elected government agencies, and there was repeated questioning of the representativeness of community leaders, user groups and voluntary organizations. It was common for the local authority and the training and enterprise council to vie with each other for leadership roles. At the same time, there was a clear perception from the voluntary sector that the 'big agencies' collectively 'wrote the rules', often to the detriment of community interests.

Hierarchies that had been relatively hidden or unimportant in pre-partnership collaboration became more visible and formalized in the creation phase. In the process, the voluntary and community sectors were often relegated to the periphery:

> In all the work I've been involved in, it's always us that have had to put the effort in to reach the council's level. We've always had to come up to their level. They've never come down to ours! (resident group chair).

> I think a lot of time is wasted ... in saying 'Well, exactly who do you represent?' For the voluntary and community sector it's one of the biggest time-wasters, trying to pin down people and make them responsible for a certain section of society rather than just recognizing that they are entitled to their own particular opinion and that it's how you build the network that's important (community worker).

> I think it's a fallacy that the Black networks are not necessarily there – I think that they're very much there but they quite possibly operate on a different basis. And if they don't conform to the local authority or the City Challenge view then they (the agencies) are not going to see them and they are going to lose out on that potential to support regeneration (project officer in small voluntary organization).

Our research showed that partnership creation and consolidation was characterized by the increased importance of hierarchy as a mode of governance. However, informal network relationships continued to be of considerable significance and the nature of the hierarchy was essentially contested and problematic. Rules for partnership needed to be negotiated across organizational boundaries and cultures. A local authority officer captured the challenge thus:

> We have to work around the dates of key meetings of the different organizations, and we need approvals at different levels. It's like an irregular heartbeat, not faster or slower but we have to be able to spot the right moment – things are no longer based on the regular committee cycle.

Partnership programme delivery

Terms like *partnership* and *network* imply consensus and collaboration, yet our research underlined the fact that inter-agency working involves a high degree of competition among organizations. Competition exists between partnerships (and localities) in the bidding processes for central government schemes like City Challenge and Single Regeneration Budget (SRB), and European funds like URBAN. The aim of such competition is to stimulate partnerships to develop innovative and cost-effective programmes of work, and to ensure the funder receives value for money and maximum programme effectiveness. The downside of these competitive regimes includes:

- the simultaneous fragmentation of resources and duplication of effort involved in expecting neighbouring localities to bid against each other (and the damage done to broader inter-agency relationships);
- the aggregate costs of the bidding process for all involved (losers as well as winners);
- the tendency for bids to stress quantifiable output measures over qualitative outcomes (and to 'talk these up'); and
- the injustice and inefficiency inherent in allocating resources on the basis of the entrepreneurial skills of partnerships rather than the assessment of relative need.

The research also pointed to the significance of competition *within* localities and partnerships. As alluded to above, there is competition to join and remain a member of partnerships likely to make successful bids. In the context of the organizational fragmentation that characterizes the urban regeneration field, agencies compete with one another for recognition of their role in any proposed initiative and their right to represent a particular community or interest group. This competition for status is accentuated because of each agency's need to demonstrate its performance and achievement to current or potential funders.

Our research showed that the network-style relationships often associated with partnership working – resting on trust and mutuality – are threatened, or undermined, by the imperative to compete. Each agency has to judge whether those bodies they work with are best regarded as friend or foe – potential competitor or a potential partner. Such judgements are particularly important for smaller agencies and voluntary or community bodies whose survival may literally depend upon gaining access to a winning partnership. Despite the official insistence on community involvement in partnership bids, the competition inherent in the SRB process has often excluded voluntary and community organizations; as an officer from one of the government offices of the regions explained:

> Unless you're cute and big, the voluntary sector could get squeezed out. Small and specialized voluntary organizations haven't got the clout or understanding or strategic overview required by the SRB process. These organizations are valuable because they bring enormous energy and commitment, but . . . you need political clout and strategic nouse to get into partnerships to bid for SRB.

Once established and in receipt of grant funding, partnerships face the challenge of distributing funds for programme implementation. It is at this stage that competitive pressures congeal into market-style relationships based upon tendering and contractual agreements. Our research showed that trust between agencies often reached an all-time low in the bidding process as potential providers refused to co-operate with each other and those involved in allocating contracts became increasingly suspicious of potential providers' claims. Many interviewees pointed to the fact that different agencies were 'all after the same money' and 'at each other's throats' as a result. Agencies were seen as jostling to 'take credit' for past achievements and assert 'ownership' of joint projects. The allocation of funds for programme implementation sharpened the distinction between an inner and an outer network. In one of the City Challenge areas we studied, the term 'partner' became a euphemism for 'failed bidder', referring to the outer circle of interested parties, as distinct from the core organizations involved in 'delivering the programme'.

There was some recognition, however, that market-style relationships could undermine the potential gains from partnership – in terms of added value, flexibility and innovation. People told us that while money (or the possibility of money) could bring agencies together, it could not keep them round the table. As one local authority officer put it: 'There's a vast difference between a package of money and real inter-agency working. You can have the first with outright enemies!' A partnership might succeed in spending money without reaping the potential gains of collaborative working. Some interviewees pointed to the detrimental impact on partnership working of funding relationships. A training and enterprise council board member felt that his agency's initial focus on seeking funding bids from 'partners' had limited its appreciation of the need to build relationships of quality and depth. There had been an assumption that funding would secure and cement relationships, while in fact it had acted as a brake on the building of trust and a sense of interdependence. In another research site, interviewees felt that City Challenge boards had encountered difficulties in building meaningful relationships because of the stress placed on the rapid disbursement of funds. A City Challenge director explored this issue with reference to the sustainability of partnership relationships: 'There is an issue about the robustness of activity once the money's gone. . . . We mustn't get obsessed with money.

Money is not a strategic issue but a tactical one. The strategic issues are about people, will, networks and structures'.

Our research affirmed the coexistence of collaboration and competition in the context of multi-organizational partnerships. It highlighted the significance of market-style modes of governance in the programme implementation phase of urban regeneration partnerships. The tensions between market and network modes of operation were clear, particularly the potential for market-style relationships to undermine – or impede the development of – trust, mutuality and co-operation between partners. It was clear that many of those involved in partnerships recognized the importance of nurturing initial network relationships into the implementation phase, seeing them as an important resource for 'getting things done' as well as exchanging ideas. Where mixed modes of governance had developed (like trust-based or 'relational' contracting), interviewees tended to explain this with relation to 'culture' and 'traditions' specific to their partnership and locality.

Partnership termination and succession

Many of the urban regeneration partnerships we looked at were time-limited, or at least their funding was. Debate about 'exit' or 'succession' strategies was lively – what should happen after City Challenge, for instance, had spent its budget and come to the end of its five-year life? Partners' tended to take one of three stances (Sullivan and Lowndes 1996):

'*Keep the partnership going*'. Those who wished to keep a formal partnership in place after funding ceased were driven by a belief that either (a) valuable relationships had been built and might perish without a formal framework; or (b) specific partnership outputs (both social and infrastructural) needed managing and developing beyond the life of the funded partnership; or (c) the locality continued to have pressing social and economic needs despite the funded intervention and that a continued partnership would help to keep attention focused on the area. One statutory sector interviewee argued that:

> There are networks in this city that operate on the basis of people like us (City Challenge board members) and it would be a great pity if the capital investment and investment in effort – both by people who live there and people who take an interest in it – gets lost. There is an important interest group which will provide a channel of communication that residents don't have.

'*Let it die peacefully*'. Those who were happy to see the partnership terminated stressed the futility of trying to keep a structure and a programme going without a dedicated budget. They also suggested that being prepared to 'close up shop' was a mark of the partnership's success: the goal of regeneration work was to build capacity in the local community and not to perpetuate dependency on the benevolence of an 'official' body. There was a suspicion that those who argued for the continuation of the partnership were engaged in organizational self-justification. As one interviewee put it: 'If the primary aim is to empower people who live there, continued patronage might not help. We should be aiming for self-sufficiency'. Some interviewees were happy to see the partnership wound-up because of the burden that involvement placed on local bodies and key individuals, particularly from the community and voluntary sector. Despite 'capacity building' activities, a sense of 'network fatigue' was obvious in localities coming to the end of a significant regeneration programme – people 'needed a break'. One interviewee remarked, with an air of desperation: 'There has to be a limit . . . you just cannot keep on creating networks'. A community director from City Challenge explained that:

I don't care if I'm elected again because there's a lot of hard work – meeting after meeting and sometimes you think 'Is it worth it?'. The flak is unbelievable. And you think 'What the hell's it all about?' And even after City Challenge goes we're going to get it – because we're living here!

'Support what lasts'. This cluster of views represented something of a middle way. It recognized the importance of sustaining momentum in the wake of a major regeneration programme but saw the problems inherent in seeking to continue formal partnership arrangements in the absence of dedicated budgets, and in the context of 'network fatigue'. The stress here was on seeking support from mainstream local budgets (for example from the local authority, TEC, health or police) for focal points of activity in the locality, allowing co-ordination to arise from informal networks. For community-based activity such networking might be facilitated by an umbrella voluntary organization; service-based activity could draw on existing professional and user networks. As an interviewee argued:

You need to start with functions – like law and order – and ask 'What does the community want to do about it?' . . . . You shouldn't look for one structure . . . and stick it all under there. You should start with people's needs and build up from that. People stand more of a chance of having their voice heard if it's done organically.

Despite the diversity of views outlined above, it was clear that debates about succession strategies focused upon the importance of sustaining network-style relationships in the governance of urban regeneration. Those who favoured a continuation of formal partnership arrangements did so because they saw these as protecting existing and emergent networks. Those who were content to see the end of formal arrangements still recognized the centrality of networking to the future of urban regeneration in their locality, but thought that formal partnerships put undue pressure on networkers and that other forms of support were more appropriate in the long term.

While market and hierarchical modes of governance had played key roles in the earlier stages of formal partnerships, these were less significant as time-limited regeneration initiatives came to an end. In the absence of external funding, there were fewer tangible resources to 'trade' in a regeneration market-place, although there was competition between agencies both for control of partnership outputs and to 'take credit' for partnership achievements (thus gaining a 'reputational' resource). As funded programmes came to an end, the impetus to maintain a formal hierarchy receded. In the absence of formal programme objectives and resources to support a board structure and secretariat, the tensions inherent in keeping together a bureaucracy comprised of different agencies and interests were likely to become keener. The 'irregular heartbeat' of a partnership organization, referred to earlier, was likely to become more irregular and harder to manage.

CONCLUSION

Multi-organizational partnerships are organizational structures that are not synonymous with the network mode of governance. Such conceptual differentiation provides the basis for a richer understanding of inter-agency activity, avoiding the easy assumptions about trust and pluralism that can so easily be transferred from discussions of ideal-type networks into discussions of partnerships. Our work highlights that partnerships involve several different modes of governance – market, hierarchy and network. It also illustrates how different modes of governance predominate at different points in the life cycle of a multi-organizational partnership. This introduces a dynamic to the analysis of partnerships that has often been absent in empirical research. Questions of power and advantage and of exclusion and inclusion, for example, are seen in a new light if they are considered in terms of the changing imperatives faced by partnerships and the transition from one governance mode to another.

Wider implications arise from this exploration of meanings. There has been a tendency for analyses of UK public management in general and urban policy in particular to discuss recent developments in terms of epochs. The 1970s are presented as dominated by a hierarchical mode of governance based on large monopolistic public agencies, local authorities and government departments. The 1980s are characterized by the internal reorganization of the public sector along quasi-market lines and the emergence of new roles for private business as a supplier of public services. The 1990s are seen as the 'Age of the Network' (Lipnack and Stamps 1994), characterized by modes of governance that link public, private, community and voluntary sector actors; Tony Blair (1998, p. 13) uses the phrase 'a third way' to promote the network principle as the hallmark of the 1990s. Such periodization can be helpful but also risks oversimplification. As Rhodes (1997c, p. 42) explains: 'British government is searching for a new 'operating code'. This search involves choosing not only between governing structures but also the mix of structures and strategies for managing them'.

A crude periodization of modes of governance can also carry with it the myth of progress – bureaucracy as all-bad, markets as a necessary evil, and networks as the 'new Jerusalem'. The co-operation and mutuality implied by the ideal-typical network mode of governance can too easily be read on to actually existing partnership organizations, fostering assumptions of pluralism and benign state action. It is as though, in their discomfort with the introduction of markets, public managers have seized upon the network model, seeing it as more in tune with the underlying values of collective public purpose and welfare which the New Right agenda threatened. What remains unanswered – and, to some extent, unasked – are the conventional questions of the pluralist debate: who has power, who gains and who loses as the policy makers' obsession with networks and partnerships grows? Distinguishing organizational structure from mode of governance facilitates a more critical analysis of multi-organizational collaboration and offers a route by which the implicit assumptions can be challenged.

The lessons go wider than the academic world. The design of partnerships and their management over time has been little informed by theory. The development of effective partnerships requires that attention is paid to the tensions generated by their development over time as their primary tasks change from formation into delivery and then to closure or succession. The central challenge for co-operative strategy lies in managing the interaction of different modes of governance. As Rhodes (1997c, p. 47) has said of the governance conundrum: 'It's the mix that matters'.

Yet the key to sustaining collaboration seems to involve the underlying presence of a network mode of governance even when market or bureaucracy predominate. Such relationships cannot be forced and will survive only where there is perceived need and collective will among participants. In our research sites, the networks likely to survive the termination of official partnership activity included some which predated the partnership, some which had been born through it, and others which were evolving just as the partnership came to a close. In governance terms, the legacy of time-limited partnerships lies in a capacity for networking and an understanding of how 'mixed' modes of co-ordination operate. As Cropper (1996, p. 89) argues:

> Where specific collaborative arrangements are disbanded, traces of organization are ... likely to remain, more loosely formed than before, but potentially capable of generating and pursuing collective strategies. Professional, role and social networks and networking practices, reusable learning about effective procedures and management methods and enhanced understanding of the interests and capacities of others are examples of such traces.

That these traces remain and are capable of stimulating new partnerships is an indication that – whatever the conflicts, mistrust and tensions generated by market and hierarchy – there exists a continued potential for collaborative activity in pursuit of public purpose. As Lipnack and Stamps (1994, p. 199) put it: 'boundary-crossing networks expand social capital'.

NOTES

[1] This article is a revised version of a paper presented to the Fourth International Conference on Multi-Organisational Partnerships and Co-operative Strategy, Balliol College, Oxford, UK, 8–10 July 1997.

[2] The research on urban regeneration partnerships was funded by the Joseph Rowntree Foundation (Skelcher *et al.* 1996). The project studied urban regeneration initiatives in three contrasting metropolitan districts, involving City Challenge boards, further education corporations, community organizations, voluntary sector agencies, training and enterprise councils, task forces, urban development corporations, regional offices of government, chambers of commerce and local authorities. Interviews were held with 60 individuals from this range of agencies. Three informants in each district kept diaries recording network activity within and between agencies for one week each month over a four-month period. Practitioner workshops were held in each of the three sites at the mid-point of the research to explore interim findings and gather further data. Focus groups developed case study materials on key issues. The article also draws upon a study of City Challenge succession strategies which involved interviews, focus groups and observation (Sullivan and Lowndes 1996). Thanks are due to the other researchers involved in the two projects: Angus McCabe, Philip Nanton and Helen Sullivan.

REFERENCES

Alter, C. and J. Hage. 1993. *Organizations working together*. Newbury Park, Ca.: Sage.

Blair, T. 1998. *Leading the way: a new vision for local government*. London; Institute for Public Policy Research.

Bradach, J. and R. Eccles. 1991. 'Price, authority and trust: from ideal types to plural forms' in G. Thompson, J. Frances, R. Levacic and J. Mitchell (eds.), *Markets, hierarchies and networks: the co-ordination of social life*. London: Sage.

Cadbury Report. 1992. *The report of the Committee on the Financial Aspects of Corporate Governance*. London: Gee & Co.

Carley, M. 1991. 'Business in urban regeneration partnerships', *Local Economy* 6, 2.

CIPFA. 1994. *Corporate governance in the public services*. London: CIPFA.

Cropper, S. 1996. 'Collaborative working and the issue of sustainability', in C. Huxham (ed.), *Creating collaborative advantage*. London: Sage.

Huxham, C. (ed.). 1996. *Creating collaborative advantage*. London: Sage.

Kickert, W. 1993. 'Complexity, governance and dynamics: conceptual explorations of public network management', in J. Kooiman (ed.), *Modern governance*. London: Sage.

Kickert, W., E.-H. Klijn and J. Koppenjan. 1997. 'Introduction: a management perspective on policy networks', in W. Kickert, E.-H. Klijn and J. Koppenjan (eds.), *Managing complex networks: strategies for the public sector*. London: Sage.

Klijn, E.-H. 1997. 'Policy networks: an overview', in W. Kickert,E.-H. Klijn and J. Koppenjan (eds.), *Managing complex networks: strategies for the public sector*. London: Sage.

Kooiman, J. 1993. 'Findings, speculations and recommendations' in J. Kooiman (ed.), *Modern governance*. London: Sage.

Lipnack, J. and J. Stamps. 1994. *The age of the network: organizing principles for the 21st century*. New York: John Wiley.

Lowndes, V. 1997. 'Management change in local governance', in G. Stoker (ed.), *The new management of local governance*. London: Macmillan (forthcoming).

Lowndes, V., A. McCabe and C. Skelcher. 1996. 'Networks, partnerships and urban regeneration', *Local Economy* 11, 4.

Mackintosh, M. 1992. 'Partnership: issues of policy and negotiation', *Local Economy* 7, 3.

Mayntz, R. 1993. 'Governing failures and the problems of governability: some comments on a theoretical paradigm', in J. Kooiman (ed.), 1993. *Modern governance*. London: Sage.

Ouchi, W. 1991. 'Markets, bureaucracies and clans', in G. Thompson, J. Frances, R. Levacic and J. Mitchell (eds.), *Markets, hierarchies and networks: the co-ordination of social life*. London: Sage.

Powell, W. 1991. 'Neither market nor hierarchy: network forms of organisation', in G. Thompson, J. Frances, R. Levacic and J. Mitchell (eds.), *Markets, hierarchies and networks: the co-ordination of social life*. London: Sage.

Rhodes, R. 1997a. *Foreword* in W. Kickert, E.-H. Klijn and J. Koppenjan (eds.), *Managing complex networks: strategies for the public sector*. London: Sage.

———. 1997b. *Understanding governance*. Buckingham: Open University Press.

———. 1997c. 'From marketization to diplomacy: it's the mix that matters', *Public Policy and Administration* 12, 2.

Skelcher, C. 1998. *The appointed state: quasi-governmental organisations and democracy*. Buckingham: The Open University Press.

Skelcher, C., A. McCabe and V. Lowndes. 1996. *Community networks in urban regeneration*. Bristol: Policy Press.

Stewart, J. 1995. 'A future for local authorities as community government' in J. Stewart and G. Stoker (eds.), *Local government in the 1990s*. London: Macmillan.

———. 1996. *Local government today*. London: Local Government Management Board.

Stewart, M. 1994. 'Between Whitehall and townhall: the realignment of urban regeneration policy in England', *Policy and Politics* 22.

Stoker, G. 1997. 'Local political participation', in R. Hambleton and associates, *New perspectives on local governance*. York: York Publishing Services.

Streek, W. and P. Schmitter (eds.). 1985. *Private interest government*. London: Sage.

Sullivan, H. and V. Lowndes. 1996. *City challenge succession strategies: governance through partnership*. Birmingham: INLOGOV (unpublished consultancy report).

Thompson, G., J. Frances, R. Levacic and J. Mitchell (eds.). 1991. *Markets, hierarchies and networks: the coordination of social life*. London: Sage.

Wheeler, R. (ed.). 1996. 'Special issue on 'Empowerment'', *Local Government Policy Making* 22, 4.

Williamson, O. 1985. *The economic institutions of capitalism*. New York: Free Press.

AFTERWORD: MANAGING MIXED MODES
OF GOVERNANCE

The continuing importance of multi-organisational partnerships in public administration is beyond doubt. Our article studied the British urban regeneration partnerships of the mid 1990s. These were the forerunners of a new paradigm for UK governance in which the process of domestic policy formulation and delivery was relocated from mainstream bureaucracies to arm's-length arenas composed of public agencies (usually represented by managers rather than politicians), businesses and NGOs (Sullivan and Skelcher 2002). While the New Labour governments of 1997–2010 vigorously promoted the partnership paradigm, the article shows that they didn't invent it. Today the partnership approach has cross-party support and, more importantly, has become institutionalised in the day-to-day practices of thousands of UK public managers.

Internationally, the picture is more varied. Forms of collaborative management, public-private partnerships and network governance have been adopted to differing extents in different countries, reflecting their particular political mandates and constitutional regimes. Nevertheless, the underlying theoretical and practical problems described in the article remain highly relevant in the current era of public austerity in the wake of the global financial crisis.

Multi-agency collaboration reflects a search for efficiency and effectiveness within an organisationally fragmented and fiscally constrained government landscape. It also reflects a search for new responses to 'wicked issues' – complex and intransigent problems that cannot be tackled by one profession or agency alone. Borrowing a phrase from Weber, there appears to be an 'elective affinity' between network institutions and the contemporary challenges faced by public policy and administration. However, the significance of the article lies in its insistence that partnerships *are not the same as* networks. We cannot 'read off' network attributes – relations of trust, mutuality and interdependence – from organisational arrangements called partnerships. Such arrangements do not guarantee innovative governance relationships. For us as authors, two interesting lines of enquiry have developed from this insight.

First, it is important to understand the disconnect that often exists between formal institutional rules and informal practices, with the latter operating as a parallel regime 'beneath the radar', or even existing in direct contradiction to formal rules. The gap between formal and informal rules (and the iteration between them) may actually be productive in the sense of providing space for 'institutional entrepreneurs' to develop new hybrids, perhaps suited to particular local contexts or as a creative response to fast-changing policy environments (Lowndes 2005). The article highlights the disjunctures between the operating procedures of different partners ('the irregular heartbeat') and explores the different settlements that emerge over time as partnerships confront new challenges (including their own winding-up). As such it anticipates theoretical work on evolutionary institutional change (Mahoney and Thelen 2010) and on emergent institutional design in local governance (Leach and Lowndes 2007).

Second, the article hints at, but does not develop, the importance of partnership discourses that may have only a loose attachment to practice 'on the ground', yet are 'actively deployed as part of political projects' (Levitas 2005, 3). Subsequent research has developed a clearer understanding of the multiple discourses of 'partnership' – as community empowerment, managerial coordination, and credible commitment – and the way in which these reshape the position of public managers as nodal actors operating as intermediaries between civil society and politicians (Skelcher, Mathur and Smith 2005; Munro, Roberts and Skelcher 2008).

The significance of our article lies in elaborating the network mode of governance as an ideal type which, in reality, exists alongside and often in combination with other modes of governance – notably hierarchies and markets. Partnership working involves a mix of modes of governance, in a dynamic relationship that evolves over time. The specific 'life cycle' model is of less importance than the light it sheds on the increasingly diverse ways in which governance is institutionalised.

As such, the analysis provides an important counterweight to the fashionable claim of a transition from 'government to governance'. While the phrase provides a nice rhetorical flourish, it rather misses the point. The process of governance is not new, it has just become progressively de-linked from representative and bureaucratic institutions. Empirical changes in the *institutional framework* of governance have served to direct our attention towards governance-as-process and away from government-as-organisation (Lowndes 2001). Studying the way in which governance is differently institutionalised over time, and across space, is a central concern of public administration. Research on multi-agency and multi-level partnerships is just the latest iteration of this task.

It is clear that a rich research agenda remains. Elements of our original critique remain to be developed and tested in the field. For instance, further research is required on the role of agency within different modes of governance. The article draws attention to the pivotal role of 'individuals' in making partnerships work. But we still know very little about the role of the 'reticulist' or partnership broker, and how it contributes to changing concepts of good public management or democratic governance. We don't know enough about how individual actors – politicians, partners, professionals and, indeed, citizens – triangulate between the demands of multiple modes of governance, and negotiate their boundaries. To borrow a term from Ostrom (2005), we need to 'animate' the study of multi-organisational partnerships. Linked to this are the enduring questions about power raised at the end of the article: 'who has the power, who gains and who loses as the policymakers' obsession with networks and partnerships grows'. There is a continuing need to examine the interaction of partnerships with formal democratic institutions – both on the ground and in a normative sense (Justice and Skelcher 2009).

A final comment. Reading the article more than ten years on, we are struck by the form of presentation – a parsimonious conceptual framework with evidence clearly marshalled around the propositions. The method is dealt with in a brief footnote. The article does not show the hallmarks of repeated rounds of aggressive reviewing and defensive response – theoretical arabesques, weighty referencing, risk-free datasets, and methodological post-hockery. Would it be published today?

REFERENCES

Justice, J. and C. Skelcher. 2009. 'Analyzing democracy in third party government: business improvement districts in the US and UK', *International Journal of Urban and Regional Research*, 33, 3, 738–753.

Leach, S. and V. Lowndes. 2007. 'Of roles and rules: Analysing the changing relationship between political leaders and chief executives in local government', *Public Policy and Administration*, 22, 2, 183–200.

Levitas, R. 2005. *The inclusive society? Social exclusion and new Labour*, Basingstoke: Palgrave Macmillan (second edition).

Lowndes, V. 2001. 'Rescuing Aunt Sally: taking new institutionalism seriously in urban politics', *Urban Studies*, 38, 11, 1953–1971.

Lowndes, V. 2005. 'Something old, something new, something borrowed. . . How institutions change (and stay the same) in local governance', *Policy Studies*, 26, 3, 291–309.

Mahoney, J. and K. Thelen (eds). 2010. *Explaining Institutional Change: Ambiguity, Agency and Power*, Cambridge: Cambridge University Press.

Munro, H., M. Roberts and C. Skelcher. 2008. 'Partnership governance and democratic effectiveness: community leaders and public managers as dual intermediaries', *Public Policy and Administration*, 23, 1, 61–79.

Ostrom, E. 2005. *Understanding Institutional Diversity*, Princeton, NJ: Princeton University Press.

Skelcher, C., N. Mathur and M. Smith. 2005. 'The public governance of collaborative spaces: discourse, design and democracy', *Public Administration*, 83, 3, 573–596.

Sullivan, H. and C. Skelcher. 2001. *Working Across Boundaries*, Basingstoke: Palgrave.

Chapter 5

'ACCOUNTABILITY': AN EVER-EXPANDING CONCEPT?

RICHARD MULGAN

That 'accountability' is a complex and chameleon-like term is now a commonplace of the public administration literature. A word which a few decades or so ago was used only rarely and with relatively restricted meaning (and which, interestingly, has no obvious equivalent in other European languages (Dubnick 1998, pp. 69–70)) now crops up everywhere performing all manner of analytical and rhetorical tasks and carrying most of the major burdens of democratic 'governance' (itself another conceptual newcomer). In the process, the concept of 'accountability' has lost some of its former straightforwardness and has come to require constant clarification and increasingly complex categorization (Day and Klein 1987; Sinclair 1995).

One sense of 'accountability', on which all are agreed, is that associated with the process of being called 'to account' to some authority for one's actions (Jones 1992, p. 73). Indeed, this sense may fairly be designated the original or core sense of 'accountability' because it is the sense with the longest pedigree in the relevant literature and in the understanding of practitioners (Finer 1941, p. 338; Thynne and Goldring 1987, p. 8; Caiden 1988, p. 25). Such accountability has a number of features: it is *external*, in that the account is given to some other person or body outside the person or body being held accountable; it involves *social interaction and exchange*, in that one side, that calling for the account, seeks answers and rectification while the other side, that being held accountable, responds and accepts sanctions; it implies *rights of authority*, in that those calling for an account are asserting rights of superior authority over those who are accountable, including the rights to demand answers and to impose sanctions. (The inclusion of sanctions in the core of accountability is contestable on the grounds that it may appear to go beyond the notion of 'giving an account'. On the other hand, *'calling* to account', as commonly understood, appears incomplete without a process of rectification.)

In the context of a democratic state, the key accountability relationships in this core sense are those between the citizens and the holders of public office and, within the ranks of office holders, between elected politicians and bureaucrats. Core accountability has thus commonly covered issues such as how voters can make elected representatives answer for their policies and accept electoral retribution, how legislators can scrutinize the actions of public servants and make them answerable for their mistakes, and how members of the public can seek redress from government agencies and officials. It leads to questions about different channels of accountability and their relative merits, about the balance between accountability and efficiency, and about distinctions between political and managerial accountability.

But more recently, in academic usage at least, 'accountability' has increasingly been extended beyond these central concerns and into areas where the various features of core 'accountability' no longer apply. For instance, 'accountability' now commonly refers to the sense of individual responsibility and concern for the public interest expected from public servants ('professional' and 'personal' accountability), an 'internal' sense which goes beyond the core external focus of the term. Secondly, 'accountability' is also said to be a feature of the various institutional checks and balances by which democracies seek to control the actions of the governments (accountability as 'control') even when there is no interaction or exchange between governments and the institutions that control them. Thirdly, 'accountability' is linked with the extent to which governments pursue the wishes or needs of their citizens (accountability as 'responsiveness') regardless of whether they are induced to do so through processes of authoritative exchange and control. Fourthly, 'accountability' is applied to the public discussion between citizens on which democracies depend (accountability as 'dialogue'), even when there is no suggestion of any authority or subordination between the parties involved in the accountability relationship.

Linguistic development is not necessarily unhealthy and unbending resistance to new meanings is generally futile. The main purpose of this article is to analyse the relentless ramification of 'accountability', rather than to deplore it. Each of the extensions in meaning will be discussed in turn, with an indication of how it has grown out of the core meaning and can still be distinguished from that meaning. However, no analysis of accountability can pretend to be wholly without ulterior purpose. While many of the new analyses of accountability have added significantly to the understanding of public institutions (Day and Klein 1987; Romzek and Dubnick 1987), others, it will be suggested, by extending the concept of 'accountability' beyond its accustomed contexts, may involve a degree of unnecessary academic complication. They may also imply a questionable shift of focus away from the central importance of external scrutiny. The original core of accountability, signifying external scrutiny, justification, sanctions and control, is sufficiently distinct and important to warrant separate identification.

'ACCOUNTABILITY' AND 'RESPONSIBILITY'

One indication of how far the concept of 'accountability' has come to dominate its academic territory is provided by the changing terms used to discuss two seminal debates in public administration. In the United States, academic analysis of the relationships between bureaucrats and the public is grounded in the classic exchanges between Carl Friedrich and Herman Finer over how far public servants should rely on their professionalism and sense of personal morality and how far they should simply be following instructions from their political masters (Friedrich 1940; Finer 1941). This debate was originally couched in terms of different senses of 'responsibility', with Friedrich emphasizing the inward responsibility of public servants to their professional standards and values and Finer reasserting the primacy of responsibility to external political direction. Finer, the advocate of external control, used 'accountability' to define his preferred sense of 'responsibility': 'First, responsibility may mean that X is accountable for Y to Z. Second, responsibility may mean an inward sense of moral obligation' (Finer 1941, p. 338). But, significantly, the argument is expressed as a preference for a particular type of 'responsibility' rather than a type of 'accountability'. Half a century later, however, this same debate is now naturally described as an argument over the relative merits of different types of 'accountability', external or internal (Harmon and Mayer 1986, pp. 47–9; Romzek and Dubnick 1987, p. 229, Dubnick 1998, p. 73; March and Olsen 1995, pp. 165–7; Peters 1995, p. 318). Thus, 'accountability' has been extended beyond its core meaning of external scrutiny, as used by Finer, and now also includes Friedrich's inner responsibility of the individual to his or her conscience or moral values.

On the other side of the Atlantic and in Westminster jurisdictions generally, the traditional starting point for discussing such issues has been the role of ministers in answering to Parliament for the actions of their departments. Here the classic formulation has been in terms of 'ministerial responsibility'. The problems that arise from attempting to hold ministers solely responsible for all departmental behaviour have traditionally been explored by analysing the different senses of responsibility (Hart 1968; Thynne and Goldring 1987, ch. 1). 'Accountability' might be brought in, as it was by Finer, to identify one of the senses or aspects of responsibility (Marshall and Moodie 1959, p. 68) but accountability was certainly not expected to cover the whole range of activities and processes covered by responsibility. Today, however, the same issues are most naturally canvassed in terms of different approaches to the problem of government 'accountability' (Marshall 1991; O'Toole and Chapman 1995; Pyper 1996; Rhodes 1997, pp. 101–3). 'Ministerial responsibility' still remains in currency but more as a technical, constitutional term to be explained in terms of the history of Westminster conventions rather than as a readily understandable concept.

The expansion of 'accountability' has thus been accompanied by a corresponding contraction in 'responsibility'. Sometimes the two terms are used interchangeably, but 'responsibility' is now increasingly confined to its more accustomed ethical territory of personal liability, freedom of action and discretion, that is to the more internal aspects of official activity (Harmon and Mayer 1986, pp. 48–50; Uhr 1993). Whereas formerly 'accountability' was usually seen as a part of 'responsibility' (the external aspect), the position is now often reversed with 'responsibility' taken to be a part of 'accountability' (the internal aspect).

A more promising development in the territorial jousting between 'accountability' and 'responsibility' is the emergence of a half-way position in which the field is divided between the two. 'Accountability' can then denote one set of responsibility/accountability issues, those concerned with the 'external' functions of scrutiny, such as calling to account, requiring justifications and imposing sanctions (i.e. the original, core senses of accountability), while 'responsibility' is left to cover the 'internal' functions of personal culpability, morality and professional ethics (Uhr 1993; Bovens 1998). Such a distinction allows 'accountability' to stand on its own, no longer under the wing of 'responsibility', and thus recognizes its growing salience, while still confining it to its original, and still most widely accepted, sense.

'INTERNAL' ACCOUNTABILITY

The redescription of the Friedrich/Finer debate, whereby 'accountability' now covers the area of administrative discretion championed by Friedrich against an undue concentration on external scrutiny, indicates the most significant extension of 'accountability'. This area of supposed 'internal' accountability is variously described, in whole or in part, as 'professional' (Romzek and Dubnick 1987, p. 228; Sinclair 1995, p. 223), 'personal' (Sinclair 1995, pp. 223, 230–1), 'inward' (Corbett 1996, pp. 201–2) or 'subjective' (Kernaghan and Siegel 1987, p. 298; Gagne 1996).

We may begin with 'professional accountability' which is itself a term of some ambiguity and straddles the line between external and internal aspects of accountability, thus helping to facilitate the extension of 'accountability' to a more internal focus. In the first place, the accountability of professionals can refer straightforwardly to a species of external scrutiny specifically designed to match the complexities of professional knowledge. Romzek and

Dubnick, for instance, in their influential typology of accountability systems (Romzek and Dubnick 1987), describe 'professional accountability' as a system marked by deference to expertise where reliance must be placed on the technical knowledge of experts and where close control from outside the organization is inappropriate. However, though broad scope must be granted to the discretion of professionals, the accountability of the professionals still lies in their ultimate answerability to their administrative and political superiors.

> ... public officials must rely on skilled and expert employees to provide appropriate solutions. Those employees expect to be held fully accountable for their actions and insist that agency leaders trust them to do the best job possible. If they fail to meet job performance expectations, it is assumed that they can be reprimanded or fired (Romzek and Dubnick 1987, p. 229).

The authors identify accountability with the 'management of expectations' by public servants and note that these expectations can be generated both internally and externally (p. 228). But even where the source of accountability expectations are internal, they are internal to the organization not to the individual. From the point of view of the particular officials, all accountability involves control from someone else and in that sense is external. This deference to superiors is a familiar feature of accountability within bureaucracies and other hierarchical organizations (sometimes referred to as 'managerial' accountability (Day and Klein 1987, p. 26)) and clearly falls within the purview of core accountability (Stewart 1986, pp. 126–31). Moreover, in spite of their emphasis on the point of view of public servants, Romzek and Dubnick leave no doubt that the driving force behind all systems of accountability, including professional accountability, is the democratic imperative for government organizations to respond to demands from politicians and the wider public (Romzek and Dubnick 1994, pp. 263, 269).

'Professional' accountability is also evident in systems of professional peer review. Because professionals, virtually by definition, lay claim to expert knowledge beyond the full understanding of non-professionals, their actions can be fully assessed only by fellow-professionals (Deleon 1998, pp. 548–51). External scrutiny, if it is to be reliable and effective, requires the establishment of review boards or disciplinary committees containing members of the profession. Standard examples of such peer review mechanisms are the disciplinary boards operated by the medical and legal professions.

The accountability of professionals to their peers raises potential difficulties in the context of the broader democratic accountability of publicly employed officials to the public. Particularly in relation to highly specialized and independent professions, such as doctors, there may be conflict between the practitioners' accountability to professional bodies and their accountability to the 'lay' representatives of the public they are supposed to serve (Day and Klein 1987, ch. 3). But such difficulties stem from the need to satisfy multiple channels of external accountability, a familiar problem for many public officials. For instance, similar conflicts occur for bureaucrats dealing with legislative committees where there may be a clash between the officials' duty to their superiors in the executive and their accountability to the legislature. This type of professional accountability, however, need not involve any extension of the core meaning of accountability. It still requires external accountability to superiors.

Professional accountability, however, does sometimes extend beyond purely external scrutiny to cover adherence to professional norms or 'standards'. A fully qualified professional is someone who has acquired the techniques and values of the particular profession and is required to exercise professional judgment, typically in an unsupervised context (Friedrich 1940; Romzek and Dubnick 1987, p. 229). Such independent action in accordance with professional standards is now being described in the academic literature as involving the exercise of accountability (Sinclair 1995, p. 223). In one sense, such a usage does not go beyond the core sense of external scrutiny. The concept of 'account-*ability*' includes an implication of potentiality, literally an 'ability' to be called to 'account'. It may thus refer to the potential for external scrutiny under which most expert professionals work, however independent they may be in their day-to-day decisions. Every medical doctor, for instance, knows that any action he or she takes (or does not take) could potentially become the object of disciplinary investigation or a legal action. In this respect, professionals are literally accoun*table* in their professional actions because they are *able* to be called to account later for any of their actions. But, in this case, the accountability they potentially face in all their actions is still conceived of as an external accountability, in the core sense.

However, professional accountability for independent discretionary acts is also being used to refer to the purely personal exercise of judgment and adherence to internalized standards, regardless of any external scrutiny or sanction, actual or potential. In this sense, accountability is being clearly identified with the sense of personal responsibility which covers the conscientious performance of duties, sometimes referred to as 'role-responsibility' (Hart 1968, pp. 212–4; Lucas 1993, pp. 193–4; Harmon and Mayer 1986, p. 49). Here, the sole source of obligation is internal, in the professional's personally endorsed values. The sanction, if any, is also internal, in the individual's own sense of professional guilt or malfeasance. In this respect, internalized professional accountability shades into what is known as 'personal' (Sinclair 1995, p. 223) or 'inward' accountability (Corbett 1996, pp. 201–2) where the basis for action is not so much the individual's professionalism as his or her own personal sense of morality involving general moral values such as honesty, integrity and fairness. Indeed, personal and professional values are hard to separate, as is clearly evident from the way in which codes of professional ethics typically refer to general values such as honesty, fairness and justice, as well as to standards specific to the profession in question. If there is any 'other' to whom one is accountable for maintaining such personal and professional standards it is a hypothesized inner self or personal conscience (Corbett 1996, p. 201).

Day and Klein note a similar internalization of accountability in their study of lay members of the public placed in supervisory roles over expert providers of public services in health, police, water, education and social work. Their main focus was on how the non-expert board members could hold expert professionals to account. However, as well as being asked about the accountability of professionals under their supervision, board members were also asked about their own accountability, to whom, if anyone, they themselves were accountable (Day and Klein 1987, pp. 100–01, 128–30, 152–3, 183–5, 217–19). Because most of those interviewed were appointed rather than elected in their own right to represent the public, this question posed a potential problem which some respondents obviously had difficulty in answering. Many opted for accountability to the general public while others mentioned accountability to the authority that had appointed them (and a few who had been appointed by partisan local authorities preferred accountability to a political party (p. 184)). A substantial number accepted that there was no clear accountability at all. In the face of this impasse, some followed the suggestion that they were ultimately accountable to themselves or their consciences (pp. 101, 218). As the authors summarize their findings:

Lastly, many members tended to define accountability in terms of their responsibility, either to the community being served or to their own sense of what was sensible or proper: they internalised accountability, as it were, as a general duty to pursue the public good according to their own criteria of what was right (p. 229).

Such extension of 'accountability' from external reckoning to internal agonizing involves an easy transition. External accountability seeks to investigate and assess actions taken (or not taken) by agents or subordinates and to impose sanctions. The extent to which individual agents or subordinates can fairly be held accountable for particular actions, particularly when it comes to the matter of sanctions, depends on whether they can be said to have been genuinely involved in deciding those actions. Thus, external accountability and blame inevitably raise issues of individual choice and personal responsibility (Bovens 1998). Individual choice and responsibility, in turn, lead to questions of professional morality and personal values. After all, the term 'responsibility' itself has travelled a similar route from the external to the internal, from the capacity to 'respond' or answer to someone else, to the capacity to act freely and 'responsibly'. Indeed, in the case of 'responsibility', the transition is so firmly established that, as already noted, the secondary, internal sense has now come to predominate over the original, external sense. If 'responsibility' can make this change, why should not 'accountability' follow suit, at least part of the way?

On the other hand, the internalization of accountability, though understandable, is not logically inevitable. Granted the complexities involved in separating the internal from the external aspects of human action, a sufficiently robust distinction can still be maintained between having to account to someone else for one's actions and not having to do so. It make sense to say that particular public servants are accountable to certain other people and bodies through certain mechanisms for the performance of certain tasks. These processes of external accountability can be said to have a particular impact on the decisions and behaviour of public servants. However, a full explanation of why public servants decide and behave as they do will also require reference to other 'internal' factors such as their personal and professional values which, as Friedrich recognized, can be identified separately from the requirements of external accountability. The growing use of 'accountability' and 'responsibility' to refer to the external and internal aspects of behaviour respectively helps to mark this important distinction.

The internalization of 'accountability', though finding currency among academics, does not appear to be widely accepted among actual practitioners themselves. For instance, in her research into the views on accountability of senior public servants in the Australian state of Victoria, Sinclair endorses a wide-ranging view of accountability. She includes 'professional' and 'personal' accountability as forms of accountability (along with 'political', 'public' and 'managerial') and quotes Day and Klein as evidence for an internalized sense of accountability. However, it is notable that her discussion of these inner forms of accountability in open-ended conversations with her respondents (Sinclair 1995, pp. 229–31) is conducted in terms of concepts other than accountability. 'Professional' accountability is largely a matter of probity and being business-like while 'personal' accountability raises issues of honesty and the public interest. Whereas the external forms of accountability ('political', 'public' and 'managerial') were volunteered by the respondents themselves in answer to questions about their accountability, the two internal forms are the researcher's own labels. In this respect, her supposed 'chameleon' of accountability is, at least in part, an invented animal.

Though Day and Klein themselves identify an internalized sense of accountability, their reported research shows that their respondents embraced such a concept with reluctance. In their interviews, internalized accountability was proffered as a solution to the dilemma facing board members who felt they ought to be publicly accountable but could not say to whom. But not all respondents took this route. Others were prepared to face the consequence that they were actually unaccountable (Day and Klein 1987, p. 183). Moreover, even those who did opt for inner accountability appear to have done so only under probing questioning. It was not a species of accountability which came immediately to mind like external accountability. That is, the notion of internalized accountability may sometimes be seized on as a last resort by those who feel that they ought to be accountable to someone but cannot identify to whom. Though the notion has sufficient logical plausibility to be intelligible and acceptable, it should not be represented as common usage.

'ACCOUNTABILITY' AND 'CONTROL'

Another extension of accountability is its application to various methods of imposing control over public organizations. The core sense of accountability is clearly grounded in the general purpose of making agents or subordinates act in accordance with the wishes of their superiors. Subordinates are called to account and, if necessary, penalized as means of bringing them under control. In a democracy, it is because the people wish to control the actions of public officials that they (or their representatives) make these officials answer, explain and accept sanctions. Indeed, the auditing of government agencies was identified with an earlier, more specific sense of 'control' (as in government 'controllers' or 'comptrollers' (Gregory 1990). Understanding 'control' in the broadest sense of making public agencies do what the public and their representatives want, accountability and control are intimately linked because accountability is a vital mechanism of control (Uhr 1993, p. 6).

However, accountability is sometimes taken to be more than just a mechanism of control; it becomes identified with control itself. The problem of accountability thus becomes: 'How do political leaders and the public persuade, cajole and force administrative agencies to do their bidding' (Peters 1995, p. 289). Constructing an appropriate structure of accountability amounts to constructing institutions which will guarantee that public officials are appropriately constrained. Indeed, if the central issue of democracy is to control the government so that it complies with the people's preferences, then the entire complex edifice of a modern democratic political system becomes in effect a system for securing government accountability (Day and Klein 1987, ch. 1).

From this perspective, institutions of accountability include all institutions that are aimed at controlling or constraining government power, for instance legislatures, statutory authorities, and courts. Devices of accountability then include the separation of powers, federalism, constitutionalism, judicial review, the rule of law, public service codes of conduct and so on, all of which have an effect on the control of public power. Also to be added are the key extra-governmental institutions of a democratically effective civil society which help to constrain governments, for instance competitive markets, interest groups and the mass media (Peters 1995, 300–1). In this way, accountability threatens to extend its reach over the entire field of institutional design.

On the other hand, such an extension, though understandable, is not logically inevitable. If 'accountability' is kept to its central sense of external scrutiny, it refers to only one type of institutional mechanism for controlling governments and government officials, where governments and officials are actually called to account, made to answer for their actions and to accept sanctions. In this case, there are other important types of control mechanism, besides accountability mechanisms. For instance, constitutional constraints or legal regulations control governments by restricting their freedom of action, requiring them to pursue certain purposes or to follow certain procedures. Public officials usually have full knowledge of these legal constraints and frame their policies and decisions so that they stay within the legal limits imposed upon them. For the most part, their compliance is unquestioning and unquestioned and issues of formal accountability do not arise.

Certainly, if agencies or officials step outside constitutional or legal limits they face the prospect of sanctions and will thus be held accountable, in the core sense, for their improper actions. But being accountable for alleged breaches of the law does not mean that compliance with the law is also an act of accountability or that the law itself is an accountability mechanism, again in the core sense. In this core sense, the legal accountability mechanism is confined to that part of the law which lays down enforcement procedures. The main body of the law, which most public servants follow as a matter of normal practice, is an instrument for controlling their behaviour but not for holding them accountable.

Within the bureaucracy itself, accountability can also be seen as merely one means whereby external agencies and the public control government policy. Government departments and other agencies are subject to different types and degrees of policy control, whether from executive politicians, legal mandates or their own internal leadership (Romzek and Dubnick 1987). Bureaucrats will normally be held accountable for their performance of given policies, both internally within the organization and often also to outside agencies. Such accountability, however, would usually be considered as only one mechanism by which the policy process is shaped to satisfy the demands of superiors. In the 'policy-cycle' literature, for instance (Parsons 1995, pp. 78–9), accountability occurs as part of later stages of 'evaluation' and 'correction'. During the prior stages of the cycle, such as 'issue definition' or 'options analysis', control is more likely to be exerted through policy makers attending to explicit instructions or being sensitive to political pressures. Admittedly, such analyses of the policy process are notoriously artificial and over-schematic and, no doubt, issues of external evaluation and accountability impinge at all stages of actual policy making through the 'law of anticipated reactions'. The need eventually to answer to supervisors casts a long and influential shadow over the behaviour of public servants. Again, we should remember the element of potentiality in accountability, the implication that an official *may* be called to account for anything at any time. None the less, the point remains that accountability, in the core sense of answering to external scrutiny, is only one aspect of how government agencies are subjected to public control. From this perspective, bureaucratic agencies are not primarily structures of accountability. They involve accountability but are equally structures of policy development and policy implementation.

On such a more restrictive view of accountability, only a few institutions, such as audit offices, ombudsmen and administrative tribunals, are properly described as 'institutions of accountability' because their primary function is to call public officials to account. Other institutions may adopt an accountability role, though it is far from their primary purpose. For instance, legislatures have a variety of functions – legislative, financial, investigative and so on – among which holding the executive publicly accountable is merely one, albeit extremely important, function. Within the overall operations of a modern legislature, accountability is particularly associated with certain procedures, such as committee inquiries or (in systems of parliamentary government) the formal questioning of ministers. But it may occur at any point, in legislative debate or financial authorization, where members of the government are required to explain their actions and take the consequences. Thus legislatures are vital institutions for securing public accountability but accountability is only one among a number of their purposes.

Similarly, the legal system, whose overall function is to enforce the community's laws, is primarily concerned with regulating the behaviour of private organizations and individual citizens. In most political systems, the courts also play an important part in upholding the constitution and restraining government power. In so far as the courts offer members of the public the opportunity of holding public government officials to account for their actions, they can be said to act as institutions of public accountability. Again, accountability, in its core sense, can be seen as an important, but not necessarily defining, role for the legal system and the courts.

Similar distinctions can be applied within the private sector and civil society. Some non-governmental institutions may be said to have primarily an accountability function, for instance watchdog groups set up with the prime purpose of monitoring and scrutinizing particular areas of government activity. Other organizations, such as sectional interest groups or the media, have a more partial or incidental (though no less important) accountability focus. The dominant function of most interest groups, for example, is to lobby for their members' interests, a goal which sometimes involves active investigation of government policies and the interrogation of government officials. As recognized stakeholders, they may lay claim to a right to question and be informed and thus enforce accountability on governments. The media, too, though in the business of entertaining and informing (usually for profit), also assist the accountability of governments by their capacity to make politicians and officials face public scrutiny.

Thus, a broader, institutional and organizational approach to accountability may encourage a tendency to equate accountability with the general democratic issue of how to design public institutions so that they are amenable to public control. The reason for this expansion of its meaning is clear.

The need to hold the government to account is itself critical to all effective attempts to control public power. Without mechanisms for demanding explanation, applying judgment and imposing sanctions, institutions that are designed to control will fail to achieve their purpose. So central is accountability as a means of achieving control that it can easily be taken to stand for control itself. Thus mechanisms designed to control, such as legal regulations or political instructions, can be taken for mechanisms of accountability even when they do not directly involve any actual accounting or scrutiny.

On the other hand, such an extension of meaning is not irresistible. A reasonably clear distinction may still be maintained between accountability and control by which accountability remains merely one means, or set of means, for enforcing control, through the demand for explanation and the imposition of sanctions. An institutional emphasis in the study of accountability, as in the typology of accountability systems constructed by Romzek and Dubnick (1987), is very much to be welcomed. No one type of institutional structure can be guaranteed to deliver effective accountability for all types of public activity. Designing public institutions in order to maximize the accountability of their officials requires a careful matching of appropriate institutional structures to the differing types of issues and skills involved (Deleon 1998). However, such an emphasis can still make sense within a more restrictive understanding of 'accountability' itself.

'ACCOUNTABILITY' AND 'RESPONSIVENESS'

A third extension of 'accountability' is to equate it with the responsiveness of public agencies and officials to their political masters and the public. 'Responsiveness', like 'control', refers to the aim of making governments accord with the preferences of the people. However, whereas 'control' stresses the coercive role of external pressure, 'responsiveness' points more widely to the public servants' general compliance with popular demands, for whatever motive. Just as accountability is such a powerful means of imposing control that is has sometimes been identified with control, it has also been seen as so important in encouraging responsiveness that the two concepts have on occasion been merged.

'Responsiveness' has been applied to two distinct relationships between officials and the wider public. In the first place, public agencies are expected to be responsive to other actors within the political system, particularly to elected politicians aiming to control their activities. They need to follow and anticipate the directions of their political masters (Saltzstein 1992; Romzek and Dubnick 1994, p. 266). Secondly, agencies providing services to members of the public are called on to be responsive to the needs of their clients in a way analogous to private sector firms being sensitive to consumer demands (Hughes 1994, pp. 236–7). In this case, the responsiveness of government officials is directly to the public rather than indirectly via the public's representatives.

The former avenue of responsiveness, that through the people's representatives, is a longstanding concern of democratic public administration. How to make the appointed bureaucracy comply with the wishes of the elected branches of government has been one of the recurrent themes of the responsibility/accountability literature. It is at the heart of the Friedrich/Finer debate and is also a key assumption of ministerial responsibility. If officials can be made compliant to their political superiors then the main objective of accountability will have been achieved. Indeed, according to some analysts, accountability is to be identified in terms of responsiveness. Thus O' Loughlin, in response to Romzek and Dubnik and their emphasis on managing expectations within agencies, seeks to reaffirm 'responsiveness to outside actors as the central spirit of accountability' (O'Loughlin 1990, p. 283). He develops measures of accountability which include the extent to which officials anticipate the wishes of their superiors and the quality of communications systems which exist between agencies and their superiors. The effectiveness of the accountability system is then assessed in terms of the extent to which the actions of officials are aligned with their political masters.

The identification of accountability with this type of responsiveness is, once again, readily understandable. It draws attention to the importance of anticipated reactions by officials as part of the effect of scrutiny mechanisms. That is, the effectiveness of accountability mechanisms is to be observed not simply in the occasions when officials are actually brought to account. Much more important in securing compliance is the ever-present threat of being called to account, the potential implicit in account*ability*. In addition, the emphasis on communications systems points to an important ingredient in successful accountability structures. Accountability depends on the free flow of appropriate information and on effective forums for discussion and cross-examination. Unless those calling subordinates to account have full access to the relevant people and the relevant information their investigations and assessments will be frustrated.

Once again, however, the identification is not inevitable. Instead of equating 'account-ability' and 'responsiveness', one can restrict 'accountability' to its core sense, in which case it becomes just one among a number of different motives that induce officials to follow and anticipate the wishes of their superiors. The fear of being called to account, of facing scrutiny and possible penalty, is undoubtedly a pervasive motive among public officials. On the other hand, other motives are not insignificant. For instance, professional public servants may accept the superior legitimacy of elected representatives and agree to defer to their political masters out of democratic conviction. More cynically, ambitious public servants may wish to ingratiate themselves with their superiors not through fear of accountability but in the hope of personal advancement. In such cases, it is not the fear of being called to account but rather personal values or career advantage that motivate responsiveness.

The other avenue of responsiveness, that of officials directly to members of the public, has figured prominently in the managerial literature on public sector reform (OECD 1987; Osborne and Gaebler 1992, ch. 6). One of the main aims of the managerial reform movement has been to make public agencies as responsive to their clients as private sector companies are to their customers. Public officials have been encouraged to be more directly approachable and accommodating to members of the public and less concerned with following set procedures or deferring to the instructions of their bureaucratic superiors. 'Client focus' is the major catch phrase and citizens' charters, agencification and competitive provision are some of the key mechanisms (Stewart 1992). This change in emphasis is sometimes described as an extension of 'accountability' (Hughes 1998, pp. 236–7). As well as being accountable 'upwards' through the hierarchical chain of managerial command, public servants, particularly those engaged in service delivery, are now also seen as accountable 'outwards', immediately to the public, through the requirement that they respond directly to their clients' expressed needs (Corbett 1996, pp. 198–200). Managerialist manifestos (OECD 1987, pp. 29, 126; World Bank 1998, p. 111) use 'responsiveness' and 'accountability' to citizens as interchangeable synonyms. Market-style relationships are said to provide an alternative channel of accountability because they provide incentives for providers to take the wishes of consumers 'into account' (Stone 1995, p. 521).

On the other hand, the identification can be challenged. If 'accountability' implies rights of scrutiny and possible sanction, then much of the client focus urged on the public sector does not imply accountability but more a general political imperative to provide better service to the public. Some of the client focus mechanisms certainly involve accountability procedures in the core sense, for instance where there is scope to complain about unsatisfactory service and seek redress. Charters with complaints procedures, ombudsmen and administrative tribunals are all institutions of accountability designed to make public servants more responsive to the public's needs. But where public providers have been induced to be more 'customer friendly' through other means, such as management incentives or changes in corporate culture, they have certainly been made more 'responsive' but not necessarily more 'accountable'.

Similarly, the private sector's focus on service to consumers, which provides much of the impetus for increased client responsiveness on the part of public agencies, need not be seen as due to any superior accountability in the private sector. While a customer may hold a private sector provider accountable in the case of a faulty individual purchase or contract, he or she has no general right to demand that the private provider offer services that meet his or her perceived needs. In a competitive market, the main mechanism of responsiveness is consumer choice, the capacity of the consumer to 'exit' to an alternative provider. Accountability, on the other hand, as usually understood, is a 'voice' not an 'exit' option in which subordinates are required to account and to accept direction. In the private sector, accountability applies more to owners and shareholders, who have rights to call the company's managers to account for the company's performance, than to customers whose main right is to refuse to purchase.

'ACCOUNTABILITY' AND 'DIALOGUE'

A final extension of 'accountability' is where the term is used to stand for the public dialogue which is seen as an essential part of democracy. Here it is the language-based nature of accountability that is stressed, rather than its institutional or motivational aspects. Accountability is seen to be a dialectical activity, requiring officials to answer, explain and justify, while those holding them to account engage in questioning, assessing and criticizing. It thus involves open discussion and debate about matters of public interest and so becomes equated with the principles of deliberative democracy. Day and Klein, for instance, ground their analysis of accountability in the assumption that it is a social activity requiring a 'shared set of expectations and a common currency of justifications' including 'agreement about the language of justification' (Day and Klein 1987, p. 5). In their conclusion they are drawn to the importance of dialogue between the various actors involved and assert that 'political deliberation . . . is at the heart of accountability' (p. 244).

March and Olson begin their treatment of accountability (March and Olsen 1995, ch. 5) with the notion of an 'account' itself which they understand as providing an interpretation or explanation. They thus place explanation and justification at the core of accountability. Calling people to account means inviting them to explain and justify their actions within two competing logics, that of consequences and that of appropriateness (p. 154). The accountability required of democratic governments produces contestable political 'accounts' within a context of shared beliefs and values (pp. 167–8) and thus helps to build the autonomous public sphere and civil society sought by Habermas and others (pp. 180–1). Harmon, too, in his critique of rationalism in public administration, sees the accountability of public servants as lying, at least in part, in a form of continuous, openended dialogue between themselves and their publics (Harmon 1995, pp. 191–97). Again, in effect, accountability is being linked to explanation and justification which implies a dialectical exchange between officials and those to whom they are accountable.

Certainly, the requirement that rulers and officials publicly account for their actions, whether to legislatures, the courts, in the media or on the hustings, does force them to engage in a form of dialogue with their public. Such dialogue may be seen as a critical element in modern deliberative democracy. Moreover, the activities of questioning and answering implicit in such accountability undoubtedly entail a key role for explanation and justification. Being called to account for one's actions often requires one to explain and justify what was done. Even where apparently 'bare' information is sought, such as in financial accounting, the information will only make sense within an explanatory and justificatory framework assumed by the questioner and accepted, or contested, by the respondent. The various discourses of accountability, including assumptions of institutional and personal responsibility, are an important aspect of accountability and worth careful academic investigation (Sinclair 1995; Bovens 1998).

However, it is one thing to recognize that accountability involves public explanation and justification and another to identify it with the dialogue between citizens found (or at least hoped for) in a deliberative democracy. The key difference is that the accountability of public officials, at least in its core sense, implies an unequal relationship of superior and subordinate in which the latter is required to take directions from the former and to accept sanctions, if necessary, for unsatisfactory performance. The dialogue of accountability occurs between parties in an authority relationship and can only be understood in the context of that relationship. This relationship is crucially different from that presupposed by democratic debate which takes place in a public space between citizens conceived of as equals. To be fair, the various theorists who have advanced the concept of accountability as dialogue have not been blind to the need for sanctions to enforce accountability (Day and Klein 1987, pp. 247–8; March and Olsen 1995, pp. 165–7; Harmon 1995, pp. 194–5) and have thereby recognized the tension that such enforcement may create with a more idealized form of democratic dialogue. None the less, to merge accountability with the general dialogue of democratic citizens is to extend it beyond its normal context of authority and control.

CONCLUSION

The scope and meaning of 'accountability' has been extended in a number of directions well beyond its core sense of being called to account for one's actions. It has been applied to internal aspects of official behaviour, beyond the external focus implied by being called to account; to institutions that control official behaviour other than through calling officials to account; to means of making officials responsive to public wishes other than through calling them to account; and to democratic dialogue between citizens where no one is being called to account. In each case the extension is readily intelligible because it is into an area of activity closely relevant to the analysis and assessment of accountability. The question of whom to hold to account for what raises immediate issues of personal responsibility and 'internal' values. The effectiveness of accountability mechanisms must be examined in the context of how bureaucracies are to be controlled and how bureaucrats can be made responsive to the wishes of elected politicians and the public. The public explanation and justification involved in accountability make it an important component of deliberative democracy. On the other hand, as already demonstrated, these connections may be recognized without necessarily extending the meaning of 'accountability' to include the areas and activities with which it is so closely related.

In some respects, the issue of definition is not just about terminology but also about institutional and administrative policy, about the relative emphasis to be placed on external scrutiny and sanctions compared with other means of securing the compliance of officials in a complex democracy. Given the current potency of 'accountability' as a political value, restricting it to its original meaning of external scrutiny is a means of siding with Finer and others in their resolute warning about the dangers of elevating administrative discretion beyond the reach of political direction. Conversely, embracing the extension of accountability to cover the pursuit of personal and professional values is sometimes linked with a recommendation to reduce the ever-increasing demands of political and managerial accountability and to place more trust in the independent judgment of public servants (Sinclair 1995, p. 233).

Similarly, in the case of responsiveness to members of the public, those accepting the equation of 'accountability' with a generalized 'client focus' are more likely to place faith in private-sector, market-style management mechanisms as a way of reducing the insensitivity of bureaucrats and to be relatively unconcerned about any possible erosion of traditional political accountability (Hughes 1998). On the other hand, those who insist on a clear distinction between 'accountability' and 'responsiveness' may do so because they wish to reassert the value of citizens' rights to call public servants to account and to enforce sanctions through political processes (Rhodes 1997, pp. 101–3).

The present author, it will be apparent, is more sympathetic to the linguistically conservative end of this spectrum which restricts 'accountability' to its assumed core and places particular emphasis on holding the powerful to account through political and legal channels of external scrutiny and sanctions. Some additional support for this stance has been found in the usage of actual practitioners, reported above, who did not volunteer the internalization of 'accountability' until pressed by researchers. The other extensions in meaning also appear to be more the creations of academics pursing their own intellectual agendas rather than the results of shifts in everyday usage. In the absence of further research, the suspicion must remain that the extension of accountability beyond its traditional, external focus, has little general support outside the academic community.

Refusal to accept the extensions of meaning proposed for 'accountability' does not, of course, solve the many complex issues that have been associated with accountability. The problem of the congruence between external scrutiny and internal discretion still remains, whether it is described as a clash between 'accountability' and 'responsibility' or between two aspects of 'accountability'. So too does the issue of the relative merits of citizens' rights of redress compared with competitive provision as means of ensuring satisfactory delivery of public services, whether it is a comparison of 'accountability' and market 'responsiveness' or of two types of provider 'accountability'. Within the purview of accountability in its restricted sense, there are still important distinctions to be made, for instance between political and managerial accountability (Day and Klein 1987, ch. 1; Hughes 1998, ch. 11), between ministerial and other avenues of public accountability (Uhr 1993; Finn 1993; Stone 1995; Pyper 1996; Thomas 1998), between the different accountability systems suited to different types of issue (Romzek and Dubnick 1987, 1994; Deleon 1998), and between the various processes of accountability (Mulgan 1997). However, in these continuing discussions, the interests of both analytical clarity and citizens' rights may be better served by keeping the concept of 'accountability' itself within limits.

ACKNOWLEDGEMENT

The author acknowledges many very helpful suggestions from the journal's anonymous reviewers.

REFERENCES

Bovens, M. 1998. *The quest for responsibility – accountability and citizenship in complex organisations*. Cambridge: Cambridge University Press.

Caiden, G.E. 1988. 'The problem of ensuring the public accountability of public officials', pp. 17–38 in J.G. Jabbra and O.P. Dwivedi (eds.), *Public service accountability*. West Hartford: Kumarian.

Corbett, D. 1996. *Australian public sector management*. 2nd edn. Sydney: Allen and Unwin.

Day, P. and R. Klein. 1987. *Accountabilities: five public services*. London: Tavistock.

Deleon, L. 1998. 'Accountability in a "reinvented" government', *Public Administration* 76, 539–58.

Dubnick, M. 1998. 'Clarifying accountability an ethical theory framework', pp. 68–81 in C. Sampford and N. Preston (eds.), *Public sector ethics*. London: Routledge.

Finer, H. 1941. 'Administrative responsibility and democratic government', *Public Administration Review* 1, 335–50.

Finn, P. 1993. 'Public trust and public accountability', *Australian Quarterly* 65 (winter), 50–59.

Friedrich, C.J. 1940. 'Public policy and the nature of administrative responsibility' pp. 3–24 in C.J. Friedrich and E.S. Mason (eds.), *Public policy*. Cambridge: Harvard University Press.

Gagne, R.L. 1996. 'Accountability and public administration', *Canadian Public Administration* 39, 213–25.

Gregory, R. 1990. 'Parliamentary control and the use of English', *Parliamentary Affairs* 43, 59–76.

Harmon, M.M. 1995. *Responsibility as paradox*. Thousand Oaks: Sage.

Harmon, M.M. and R.T. Mayer. 1986. *Organization theory for public administration*. Boston: Little, Brown.

Hart, H.L.A. 1968. *Punishment and responsibility*. Oxford: Oxford University Press.

Hughes, O.E. 1998. *Public management and administration*. 2nd edn. London: Macmillan.

Jabbra, J.G. and O.P. Dwivedi. eds. 1988. *Public service accountability: a comparative study*. West Hartford, Connecticut: Kumarian Press.

Jones, G.W. 1992. 'The search for local accountability', pp. 49–78 in S. Leach (ed.), *Strengthening local government in the 1990s*. London: Longman.

Kernaghan, K. and D. Siegel. 1987. *Public administration in Canada*. Toronto: Methuen.

Kinley, D. 1995. 'Governmental accountability in Australia and the United Kingdom', *University of New South Wales Law Journal* 18, 409–27.

Lucas, J.R. 1993. *Responsibility*. Oxford: Clarendon Press.

March, J.G. and J.P. Olsen. 1995. *Democratic governance*. New York: Free Press.

Marshall, G. 1991. 'The evolving practice of parliamentary accountability; writing down the rules', *Parliamentary Affairs* 44, 460–9.

Marshall, G. and G.C. Moodie. 1959. *Some problems of the constitution*. London: Hutchinson.

Mulgan, R. 1997. 'Processes of accountability', *Australian Journal of Public Administration* 56, 1, 25–36.

OECD. 1987. *Administration as service: the public as client*. Paris: Organisation for Economic Co-operation and Development.

O'Loughlin, M.G. 1990. 'What is bureaucratic accountability and how can we measure it?', *Administration and Society* 22, 275–302.

Osborne, D. and T. Gaebler. 1992. *Reinventing government*. Reading, MA: Addison-Wesley.

O'Toole, B.J. and R.A. Chapman. 1995. 'Parliamentary accountability', pp. 118–41 in B.J. O' Toole and G. Jordan (eds.), *Next Steps. Improving management in government*? Aldershot: Dartmouth.

Parsons, W. 1995. *Public policy*. Cheltenham: Edward Elgar.

Peters, B.G. 1995. *The politics of bureaucracy*. 4th edn. White Plains: Longman.

Pyper, R. (ed.) 1996. *Aspects of accountability in the British system of government*. Eastham: Tudor Business.

Rhodes, R.A.W. 1997. *Understanding governance. Public networks, governance, reflexivity and accountability*. Buckingham: Open University Press.

Romzek, B.S. and M.J. Dubnick. 1987. 'Accountability in the public sector: lessons from the Challenger tragedy', *Public Administration Review* 47, 227–38.

————. 1994. 'Issues of accountability in flexible personnel systems' in P.W. Ingraham and B.S. Romzek (eds.), *New paradigms for government*. San Francisco: Jossey-Bass.

Saltzstein, G.H. 1992. 'Explorations in bureaucratic responsiveness', pp. 171–89 in L.B. Hill (ed.), *The state of public bureaucracy*. M.E. Sharpe: Armonk.

Sinclair, A. 1995. 'The chameleon of accountability', *Accounting Organizations and Society* 20, 219–37.

Stewart, J. D. 1986. *The new management of local government*. London: Allen and Unwin.

Stewart, J. 1992. 'The rebuilding of public accountability' in N. Flynn (ed.), *Change in the civil service*. London: Chartered Institute of Public Finance and Accountancy.

Stone, B. 1995. 'Administrative accountability in the "Westminster" democracies: towards a new conceptual framework', *Governance* 8, 505–26.

Thomas, P.G. 1998. 'The changing nature of accountability', pp. 348–93 in B.G. Peters and D.J. Savoie (eds.), *Taking stock: assessing public sector reforms*. Montreal: McGill-Queen's University Press.

Thynne, I. and J. Goldring. 1987. *Accountability and control: government officials and the exercise of power*. Sydney: Law Book Company.

Uhr, J. 1993. 'Redesigning accountability', *Australian Quarterly* 65 (winter), 1–16.

World Bank. 1998. *World development report 1997*. Oxford: Oxford University Press.

AFTERWORD: STILL EXPANDING

The article was part of larger study of accountability which was eventually published in book form. It covered some of the initial, conceptual ground-clearing concerning the meaning of 'accountability' itself which was (and still is) a matter of dispute. The aim of the article was to demonstrate the proliferating uses of the term, which had shot from relative obscurity to fashionable, even faddish, ubiquity in little more than a decade. This expansion was explained in terms of understandable extensions from a core sense of being called to account for one's actions. The article also had a subsidiary purpose of arguing in favour of the core sense and rejecting the extended senses. The obligation of officials to answer to those they serve, and to face sanctions from them, was a vital safeguard which should not be r watered down by reliance on other, less robust motivations, such as professional norms of voluntary responsiveness.

Ten years later, the central argument still appears sound, though hindsight would naturally add different emphases to deal with trends which are much clearer now than then. First, some of the reasons for the persistent academic disagreement over the meaning of accountability are now becoming more apparent. Being a relatively new concept, accountability lacks the standard canonical treatment that helps to anchor academic discussion of other popular value-laden terms such as 'democracy' or 'liberty'. 'Accountability' has no Schumpeter, Dahl or Berlin to which everyone could refer.

Moreover, the increasing balkanisation of modern political science into different sub-disciplines militates against the emergence of any common linguistic currency. There are at least five separate branches of English-language political science, broadly understood, in which accountability is currently being analysed with almost no cross-fertilisation – Westminster-Dutch-Scandinavian public administration, United States public administration, democratic theory, comparative politics and international relations. The inevitable consequence of such over-specialisation is much wheel-reinvention as scholars in one sub-discipline labour to conclusions already well-established elsewhere. The present article attempted to bridge the two English-speaking branches of public administration on either side of the Atlantic, which were first in the field in the analysis of accountability, with a brief nod to democratic theory. But its currency has remained firmly isolated on the European side, within the Westminster-Dutch-Scandinavian tradition.

Another major deficiency, in retrospect, is that the article does not give enough attention to problems of accountability outside hierarchical government structures. The proposed core sense assumes a paradigmatic principal/agent relationship in which the person or institution holding to account (the principal) has authority over the person or institution being held to account (the agent). Without such authority, the principal cannot demand information or impose sanctions for poor performance. Relationships where compliance remains a matter of grace and favour or self-interested calculation, it is argued, are not true accountability relationships.

Such a paradigm fits well with the standard model of representative democracy whereby voters elect leaders who then direct a hierarchical bureaucracy, a chain of controlling principals and agents with a matching chain of accountability relationships. During the last decade, however, the relevance of the vertical model of government has been seriously questioned. Advocates of an alternative, governance model have emphasised the role played by loosely-linked networks of independent organisations, both public and private, where no one organisation is clearly in charge but coordination depends more on shared values, mutual benefit and trust. By definition, such relationships appear to rule out full accountability in the core sense because no one party to the relationship has the authority to direct the other.

One approach to this dilemmas has been to relax the definitional demands of 'accountability'. For instance, the right to demand an account may be said rest on a structure of mutual rights and obligations, such as those that link members of a partnership. No partner is in charge but each must answer to the other. The core of accountability thus becomes the right to ask for an account and the corresponding obligation to provide one. The final stage of accountability, the imposition of sanctions, is either removed from the requirements for accountability or softened into 'consequences' which may follow from the account but not necessarily through the direct authority of one of the parties. The article does mention in passing that the inclusion of sanctions in accountability is a contestable issue. But the inter-related questions of sanctions and authority would now require more detailed analysis and more allowance would need to be made for non-hierarchical accountability.

However, any further argument over an agreed sense of accountability appears increasingly futile. The article's central argument about proliferation of meanings ('an ever-expanding concept') remains its most enduring element. Accountability is a contested political concept, replete with positive connotations, which all players in the policy game think they must have in their rhetorical armoury. As such, any agreement on its meaning is as unlikely as a final consensus on political values.

PART II: COMPARISON

Chapter 6

CABINET GOVERNMENT: AN ELUSIVE IDEAL?

PATRICK WELLER

Cabinet government is apparently dead. That seems to be a common diagnosis of the state of government in Britain and Canada. The [then] incumbent prime ministers, Jean Chrétien and Tony Blair, have virtually dispensed with the support of cabinet and rule with fewer constraints than their predecessors. Cabinet has become little more than a cipher, held briefly each week more for the purposes of show than as a decision-making forum. Cabinet has been described as a focus group in Canada or as a reversion to a meeting of politicians discussing the political situation (in Britain). These two leaders can be seen as the epitome of prime ministerial power.

In Canada in 2001 Jeffrey Simpson published a book called *The Friendly Dictatorship*. He argued that Chrétien was merely the last, and most obvious, manifestation of dominant prime ministers able to govern in Canada with few limitations on their ability to get their own way. Cabinet had become little more than a focus group in which some ideas might be considered, but it did not meet for long and was not a deliberative or decision-making institution. Cabinet committees could decide on new policy initiatives, but they were not funded at that time. Rather they were put into a basket of new initiatives and the prime minister and the minister of Finance would determine at budget time which would be taken up. Within their portfolios ministers were left to their own devices, but wherever the prime minister wanted to become involved, he determined the direction and content of policy. Simpson argued that 'cabinet government presupposes collective decision making and responsibility, a collection of equals, with some inevitably being more equal than others because of the importance of their portfolios' (2001, p. 62). But the prime minister has become far too powerful for such a description to be applicable now. Simpson's polemic builds on the work of Donald Savoie, whose magisterial work, *Governing from the Centre: The Concentration of Power in Canadian Politics* (1999a), provides a detailed account of the growth in the power of the central agencies in Canada, and the significance of the Prime Minister and his office. Cabinet has a series of set agenda items: discussion, presentations, nominations and then the endorsement of committee decisions which are rarely disputed (Savoie 1999, p. 647). But it did no more. Savoie builds a case that these changes mean the prime minister is *'Primus*: there is no longer any *Inter* or *Pares'*.

A similar debate can be found in Britain, where Blair's cabinet still meets weekly but for shorter periods and with a more limited agenda than in earlier regimes. There are a number of standing items for cabinet but few policy issues brought there for decision. Cabinet government, say the observers, has declined under Blair. The prime minister makes the crucial decisions and the concept of collective debate has gone. Blair's biographer John Rentoul comments:

> Blair's management style ushered in a new low in the history of cabinet government in Britain. That style was 'hub and spoke' rather than collegiate, reducing most meetings of cabinet to just forty minutes of approving decisions taken elsewhere, parish notices

and short speeches either delivered by the Prime Minister or vetted by him in advance. (Rentoul 2001, p. 540)

Similar comments were made about the imperial style of Mrs Thatcher who did not welcome debate, but wanted decisions. Peter Hennessy claimed that 'she has put Cabinet government temporarily on ice'. (1986, p. 122)

But then there is the suggestion in many of these accounts that this state of affairs is an aberration. Hennessy goes on: 'the old model could be restored in the few minutes it takes for a new prime minister to travel from Buckingham Palace to Downing Street' (1986, p. 122). Rentoul too seems to believe that:

> Cabinet government was not dead of course; it was only sleeping. It could clearly reassert itself if the Prime Minister's authority or popularity slipped, as it did over Thatcher. (Rentoul 2001, p. 640)

It was just that cabinet government did not operate under Thatcher and Blair, the two most dominant leaders their parties had seen in a century.

Thus this debate is not unique to any one country, even if each analysis tends to be; it cuts across nations. It raises questions of the degree to which it can happen in other countries with similar parliamentary and cabinet governments. By contrast, similar concerns are not so often expressed in Australia. That the prime minister is powerful and dominant is not in doubt (see, for example, Weller 1989), but there is little suggestion there that cabinet has been supplanted and little angst about the excessive power of prime ministers. The interesting comparative question is: why not?

There is nothing new in these analyses, in the sense that, even if the prime ministers seem to be dominating to an even greater extent than before, they reflect the continuing debate about the power of prime ministers and the degree to which they can call the tune. All the observers are able to give a number of cases when prime ministers have chosen to become involved and where they have imposed their will. The capacity and power of prime ministers is not open to debate.

Most of these discussions then come to the core conclusion: that cabinet government is in decline, abeyance, sleeping or dead. Whether the prognosis is temporary or terminal is not settled. But they all also have an implicit assumption: that there is something identifiable called 'cabinet government' that can be identified and restored. Famously, George Jones described cabinet government in Britain as an elastic band; it could be stretched, but, as Thatcher's fall showed, 'the elastic will snap back on her' (cited in Foley 1993, p. 16). Like Hennessy and Rentoul, he implies a state of normalcy (to which the system snaps back) where cabinet government once again exists.

But what is cabinet government? It is difficult to describe any recognizable circumstance where it worked in a form that these critics would approve of. Nor are there working and historically accurate models against which performance can be judged. It can stretch from a set of arrangements within which almost anything goes to an ideal state that can never be achieved. Nostalgia for bygone systems may play a part. One account argued cabinet before 1916 was indeed 'a genuinely collective body' but at the same time 'cabinet was almost comically inefficient in its conduct of business'; such a system could not be maintained in the face of the demands of war and certainly could not run on that basis in the next century (Burch and Holliday 1996, pp. 12–13).

Cabinet government is often taken as given; even if not satisfactorily described, it is somehow recognizable when it exists. Analysis concentrates on the cabinet system, the cabinet environment, the core executive or some similar group of institutions. Definitions of cabinet government are often by default. A failure to allow cabinet to debate an issue or an independent decision taken by the prime minister without recourse to cabinet is interpreted as a decline of cabinet government. But the reverse is not derived from that: that cabinet government means that cabinet must discuss everything, or that no decisions can be made independently by the prime ministers.

This article explores the ways that cabinet government has been analysed by both academics and practitioners, and assesses whether these descriptions have an implicit model of normalcy. In particular it asks whether there have been trends in the decline of cabinet government or whether, in different ways determined in part by changing circumstances, prime ministers have always been able to determine how cabinet is run and usually got their own way whenever they chose to exert their influence. Then it asks how better to interpret the debate on the decline of cabinet government. We need to avoid the assumption that there is a zero sum game, that if prime ministers are powerful then cabinet has 'lost' influence. Prime ministerial influence and cabinet government are not polar alternatives. Prime ministers like Trudeau or Fraser both liked to debate and test arguments and to work through the cabinet as much as around it. But both still managed to get their own way.

We should not be overwhelmed by recent events, by being surprised by the management and practices of recent prime ministers. The argument that prime ministers are powerful and the cabinet has been relegated to become one of the 'dignified' parts of the constitution is scarcely recent, even if it is constantly rediscovered. The explicit theoretical debate began with John Mackintosh (1962; 3rd edn 1977) who emphasized that 'the country is governed by the Prime Minister who leads, coordinates and maintains a series of ministers'. The prime ministers on whose experience he drew were those who held office in the 1940s and the 1950s or earlier; Lloyd George and Chamberlain are described as dominant figures who almost did away with cabinet decision making. The thesis thus predates the 1960s and 1970s, yet often these are the very times to which commentators now look as a period when cabinet government flourished; that is, some years after cabinet had been declared comatose by Mackintosh and Crossman. Indeed arguments about dominant prime ministers can be found in descriptions of the governments of Gladstone and Peel. There are, it seems, various degrees of death and, at the least, a series of variations in practice over the decades. So can we find a suitable agreement on what cabinet government may be and hence take further the analysis of the way that we are governed?

THE ACADEMIC DEBATE

It is difficult to extract any obvious approach to cabinet government from the available literature, primarily because the analysis of cabinet comes from several different angles at once. Each of the five identified below starts from a different set of assumptions about the significant features of cabinet, and derives the analysis from there and then makes judgements about its performance from its own criteria.

Cabinet government as the focus for discussion of responsibility and accountability: a constitutional theory or legal approach

Cabinet is seen as the focus for the application of two basic constitutional doctrines: collective and ministerial responsibility to parliament and the electorate. These doctrines may be described in normative terms, proposing what ministers should do, or in pragmatic terms, explaining how these ideas are applied. They are central to any analysis of the relationship between the executive and the legislature. This relationship has been a focal point for debate in Britain with its unwritten constitution (see, for example, Woodhouse 1994) but is as uncertain in Australia where neither the prime minister nor the cabinet is mentioned in the Constitution, and ministerial power is derived from section 64 (for a discussion, see Forrest and Reid 1989). In practice much of the debate is derivative and needs to be tightened (for an attempt, see Weller 1999). Mackintosh spends some time considering the links between the cabinet, the parliament and the crown. Encel (1974) is almost entirely concerned with party links and the meaning and practice of ministerial or collective responsibility; the actual proceedings of cabinet are a black box, beyond scrutiny. French (1979) called these analysts 'theorists', interested in how governing ought to work (in contrast to the 'pragmatists' who were concerned to see that government worked better). The basic questions are: what is the meaning of constitutional and ministerial responsibility and how are they applied to cabinet? What impact do they have on the workings of cabinet? How is the executive held accountable to the legislature?

Cabinet as a formal administrative institution, based on rules and routines: a public administration or positional approach

Cabinet began as an informal meeting of ministers, but over the years the pressure of business and the demands on the time of ministers required that proceedings become more formal (Baker 2000; Weller 2001). The circulation and coordination of submissions, the development of cabinet handbooks that include the rules and conventions of cabinet have burgeoned, particularly after the establishment of a cabinet secretariat in wartime (the 1914–18 war in Britain; the 1939–45 war for Canada and Australia). Consequently promotion to cabinet brings expectations and duties for a new minister. Membership of cabinet shapes the roles and choices of ministers; expectations have been created by the historical development of cabinet rules. Prime ministers initially devised those rules and they can alter and adjust them, but do so with care. This approach is the traditional institutional study of the structure and organization of an established body. It leads to some fundamental questions. To what extent has the routinization and bureaucratization changed the way that cabinet works? Has it changed the manner and location of decisions? What impact do rules and routines have on outcomes?

An additional aspect is an analysis of the supporting departments or agencies that provide advice to the cabinet as a collectivity or to the prime minister. Does the prime minister need a department? Should the central agencies support the cabinet as a collectivity. The institutional arrangements vary from nation to nation; it is not significant (except in terms of political presentation) whether the supporting agency is called a Department (as in Australia) or an Office (Canada and Britain) (Weller 1983). The vital fact is what services they provide and to whom. There is no doubt that the support at the centre has grown, in both non-partisan officials and political appointees who have personal connections to the prime ministers. It is easy to assume that institutional existence means as a matter of course that the prime ministers have been strengthened (Savoie 1999a; Holliday 2000); but it is also possible to conclude there is still a hole at the centre, and that prime ministers often need more advice (Kavanagh and Seldon 1999). Solutions to the balance of power are invariably posed in institutional terms because they provide clear steps that can be taken. It is easier to propose institutional change than to exhort prime ministers to limit themselves or to play particular roles that are somehow seen as proper. Institutions provide potential and guidelines for how to act; they still need to be used.

Cabinet as a forum for making policy decisions which require the best available information and coordination to ensure those decisions are well-informed: a public policy or functional approach

Those who provide this emphasis are French's 'pragmatists'. Amid the furore of politics, cabinets are also the principal decision-making body in the polity, raising questions about their ability to collect and synthesize the necessary data, to determine priorities, allocate expenditure or work effectively in other areas. There is a concern about how to prevent fragmentation or excessive segmentation. Dell (1980) has questioned the notion of collective decision making, suggesting it is largely a fraud as most ministers have neither the knowledge nor the inclination to become actively involved in subjects beyond their portfolio. In response, Sir John Hunt argued that the inefficiencies were counterbalanced by the value of discussion as a means of ensuring support, with cabinet acting as the cement that held the government together (cited in Hennessy 1995). When central agencies seek to assist (Davis 1995) they are often accused of being over-powerful. Cabinet procedures will always in part reflect the working style of prime ministers, but the reflections of those who work for them are constantly thinking about ways they might be done better (Donoughue 1987; Blackstone and Plowden 1988; Hogg and Hill 1995). Lindquist and White suggest that in Canada too little attention has been given to the organization and running of cabinet as a complex organization, if it is to work more strategically (1997, p. 129). There are no Australian equivalents, but Weller (1989) seeks to explain how cabinet worked under Fraser, while Mills (1993) for Hawke, and Edwards (1996) for Keating, provide other insights. The questions arising from this body of literature are therefore: how is support for decision making organized? What advice is provided? To whom? How have those systems for advising cabinet as a collectivity been managed and to what effect?

Cabinet as a political battleground, as a contest for position, power, policy and reputation and in which incentives and resources are the best means for explaining action: a political science approach

This general area is where much of the debate on cabinet government takes place. One debate referred to the issue of prime ministerial government (Crossman 1963; Macintosh 1977; Weller 1985; Foley 1993, 2000). It examined the degree to which prime ministers increased their authority and usurped the influence of individual ministers. In Australia, Bunting (1988) proposes that as early as the 1960s cabinet had displaced ministers as the principal locus of decision-making. Others either assert that the proper term is 'ministerial government', at least in Britain (Jones 1979, p. 1) or that cabinet government is reasserted after the demise of a dominant prime minister such as Thatcher (Hennessy 1986). The organization of cabinet, the impact of federalism, access to ministerial positions, the use of cabinet committees (Mackie and Hogwood 1985), the provision of advice to the leaders or to the cabinet as a collectivity are all therefore weapons in the pursuit of influence and advantage. Laver and Shepsle (1993) try to identify in schematic ways the forces that help set a cabinet agenda. The crucial questions are therefore: how has the balance of power in cabinets changed? Has the position of prime minister been strengthened? What are the resources and incentives that can be applied by the different actors?

The most sophisticated addition to the debate has been the two books by Michael Foley (1993, 2000) on the British presidency. Foley explores the 'stretching of the leadership' and the consequential relations between prime ministers and their colleagues. But it is, as his subtitle notes, a study of the politics of public leadership and elections. He is less concerned with the balance of the internal decision-making or the continuing functions of the cabinet system.

Cabinet as a system of government

Rhodes (1995) developed the concept of the core executive to explain how cabinet decisions are made, drawing into the analysis those key advisers and civil servants who are often more important than junior ministers. He argues that: 'The label "cabinet government" was the overarching term for (some of) these institutions and practices but it is inadequate and confusing because it does not describe accurately the effective mechanisms for achieving coordination. At best it is contentious, and at worst seriously misleading, to assert the primacy of cabinet among all organisations and mechanisms at the heart of government' (1995, p. 12; see also Dunleavy and Rhodes 1990 for the first exposition of the core executive). Burch and Holliday (1996) too regard the cabinet as part of a set of interlocking institutions that need to be understood as a whole. They discuss the broader notion of the cabinet system as a set of arenas over which ministers and others fight for authority and influence. Here the cabinet is just part of, even if sometimes the key feature, that determines what happens in the system of governing. Decisions or, as Rhodes argues, the resolution of conflict may be undertaken in any part of that system, though Andeweg (1997) questions why the resolution of conflict, rather than, say, representation should be the primary function given precedence here. The principal questions in this approach are how the cabinet fits within the broader framework and what contribution it makes to decisions: that is, who coordinates and resolves conflict?

As an analytical device for understanding the centre of government, the concept of the core executive has value. But by incorporating the cabinet in the wider scenery as just one component, it ignores that fact that in many ways cabinet *is* different. Appointment to cabinet is the sign of success for ministers, particularly in Britain and Australia where there are tiers of ministers and only the senior sit in cabinet. It is the target of ambitions. Cabinet decisions, however they are made, have weight and legitimacy within the bureaucracy, greater than decisions emerging from other forums; they are the currency of government. If cabinet meetings had no practical or useful function they would be discontinued. But they are held, frequently and without question. Why? Even if cabinet may now serve different functions from those of the 19th and 20th centuries –and what they may be is an empirical question –its existence remains important.

The different criteria may lead to different judgements about whether the cabinet is working well, and hence different conclusions about what is required for it to be improved. The constitutional theorists will explore the relations between cabinet and other parts of the political system: cabinet government in their view works to the extent the cabinet is responsible to and responsive to the needs of the broader political system. The public administration school will ask whether the rules are being applied, whether the institutional and supporting arrangements are adequate or effective. The public policy advocates will question whether the cabinet, as it is working, has the capacity to fulfil a range of functions that require a broader outlook; they may argue it should have a strategic or priority-setting capacity. The power realists will look at the political outcomes and ask whether the balance of power may be, or should be, altered. So 'solutions' to a cabinet that does not live up to expectations may be better rules, more sophisticated co-ordination and more effective accountability.

IMPLICIT ASSUMPTIONS

The problems in determining what cabinet government is or what effective cabinet government would look like lie in the divergent expectations. There are times when there are hints at what might be entailed and some assumptions that can be derived from the accounts. Taking a couple of the categories can make the point.

The public administration approach suggests that cabinet government is alive when the rules of cabinet are being observed, when the items and policies are dealt with according to due process, whether it be in cabinet or around cabinet in committee. Cabinet procedures are provided in the Australian *Cabinet Handbook* or the British *Questions of Procedure for Ministers*; the distribution of responsibilities to cabinet committees determines which are the correct forums for debate. These handbooks establish the proper rules of engagement and should be honoured. Even though the rules are written and composed by the prime ministers, they create the framework for proper and conventional procedure and should be adhered to. But of course the rules have a primary purpose: they are composed by prime ministers and their officials so that cabinet can be organised the way they want it run (Baker 2000; Weller 2001). In June 2002, Chrétien published *A Guide for Ministers and Secretaries of State* (Canada 2002). Under the guise of a set of rules he clearly set out what the prerogatives and powers of the prime minister were. It is by no means a neutral document. In all countries the rules provide a base, but the prime ministers determine when they will be applied or relaxed. Their application can be as flexible as they like.

Those who see cabinet as an arena for power often see prime ministers as too powerful and imply that cabinet government requires the fulfillment of particular conditions. Some of the possible conditions can be explored here.

'Cabinet government is the *full* cabinet at work'. This condition is perhaps most common. Peter Hennessy often implies that it could be done better. His assumption seems to be that cabinet government requires a discussion of the vital issues in a meeting of 'full cabinet'. In his discussion of the Suez crisis he asks 'if the full cabinet had balked' would events have been different (2000, p. 238). But the full cabinet was not asked. Callaghan was 'the practitioner of traditional Cabinet collegiality' (2000, p. 395). There is in his view something good and proper in the 'full cabinet' being involved: a greater store of wisdom, broader discussion or some other benefit. Savoie hints at the same idea for Canada. He notes that with the existing system of two cabinet committees 'about half the Cabinet has to accept what has been decided by a committee of which they are not members and based on discussions in which they did not take part' (1999a, p. 649). Talking of Britain, Rose argues that in the past, 'the full cabinet met once and often twice a week' and that 'it is politically significant that their frequency and length has been decreasing' (2001, p. 167). On these criteria the health of cabinet government can be tested by the frequency and comprehensiveness of 'full' cabinet meetings as they are the symbol of collective decision.

A second implicit condition is that, as 'ministers have the statutory responsibility' to make decisions, then it must be theirs to make, not the prime minister's. This view argues that, in a proper system of cabinet government, prime ministers hold the ring rather than become directly involved. Thus Jones notes the prime ministers' role 'is to help forge politically acceptable solutions and to relate policies together in an order of priorities by providing a coherent theme, tone or philosophy. His contribution is not to be a substitute for his ministers but a supplement.... A prime minister cannot help cabinet colleagues arrive at a unified decision if he is a protagonist of a particular line' (1981, p. 219). So if prime ministers are driving the policy, perhaps with the ministers playing a secondary role, then cabinet government is in decline because prime ministers are taking over the proper ministerial responsibility. The best description of British government for Jones is ministerial government.

Yet none of these conditions applied consistently in any of the countries in the last century. No trend suggests that prime ministers have in the early decades been more likely to be restricted by their cabinet colleagues in battles they wanted to win. Their tactics may have differed but not the results. Not all prime ministers have been concerned to determine outcomes across the whole range of government activities; some are more intrusive and involved than others. But they usually know when they can win. Circumstances have changed: there is more direct media attention; more issues cut across individual portfolios; there are more international commitments as travel is easier. Further, styles will change from individual to individual. But if we ask whether cabinet government restricts and defeats prime ministers on a regular basis, then it is difficult to find examples where that might have occurred.

Looking at the prime ministers in several countries from the first half of the century can illustrate the point. In Canada Robert Borden could recall in 1917: 'The discussion was lengthy and eventually became so wearisome that I interposed, informing my colleagues that they had made me sufficiently acquainted with their views, that the duty of decision rested with me, and that I would subsequently make them acquainted with my conclusion' (Bliss 1994, p. 80). With R.B. Bennett, prime minister in the 1930s, 'the story went round that when Bennett was seen mumbling to himself, he was holding a cabinet meeting. "He was not above asking the opinions of others... he was only above accepting them"' (Bliss 1994, p. 113). Gordon Robertson, later clerk of the Privy Council Office in Canada, says that Mackenzie King lost interest in cabinet in his later years:

> More than once he left his ministers arguing over some point in a cabinet meeting while he went around the corner to his office in the East Block to have tea. Both he and his colleagues knew that they could reach no conclusion without him. (2001, p. 62)

At the least the prime minister's approval and consent was needed. King was always determined to get his own way. Later Robertson cited the view of Jack Pickersgill on Louis St Laurent:

> As St Laurent hated to waste time, cabinet meetings were exceedingly business-like.... No minister was restrained from presenting his views for fear St Laurent might take offence, but I believe some ministers were restrained by the fear of appearing to be ill-informed or ineffective. More than any prime minister I have known, St Laurent dominated his cabinet, not by imposing his authority, but by his sheer intellect, his wide knowledge, and his unequalled persuasiveness. (cited in Robertson 2001, p. 100)

And this was a time when there were powerful regional ministers. Prime ministers could still determine what happened when they cared.

In Australia, Billy Hughes paid little attention to the views of his colleagues and in 1919 spent months overseas at the Versailles conference, where he spoke on behalf of his country, without regular reference to the ministers back in Australia. At the same time he wanted to know everything that went on there and suggested that no cabinet decision should be regarded as final until they had been run past him on the other side of the world. Later Menzies ran his cabinet with a degree of imperiousness perhaps typical of one who ruled for 17 years and was never challenged in that time; the verdict of Sir Paul Hasluck was similar to that of Pickersgill on St Laurent: he dominated his cabinet intellectually because he was the best informed person in cabinet (Hasluck 1980, p. 9).

In Britain, Lloyd George created the Garden Suburb to give him greater control over his government. Chamberlain brooked no opposition within the cabinet and by one account almost dispensed with cabinet meetings. Churchill was capable of turning cabinet meetings into monologues when it suited him. Macmillan 'was a great one for bringing these broad themes to cabinet and for thinking aloud on them before his assembled colleagues. For him the full cabinet was a sounding board' (Hennessy 2000, p. 260). When Macmillan said that 'the cabinet left the whole management of this affair to me' we can be certain that he proposed that it should do so (Hennessy 2000, p. 255). Heath was said to have exercised 'overwhelming personal dominance' over his ministers (Hennessy 2000, p. 336). And so on.

To take one obvious implication: none of these leaders would have agreed that cabinet government required meetings all the time of the full cabinet. Full cabinets are essentially conveniences as cabinet serves many political and representational functions. In Canada its numbers once rose as high as 40 and cabinet has rarely been a decision-making forum; committees always did much of the work (Bakvis 2000). In Australia all ministers may have been members of cabinet before 1956 but since then (with the exception of 1972–75) cabinet has been in two tiers and varied in size. In Britain there are several tiers of ministers. Every prime minister in every country has chosen a number of subjects – war, security, nuclear policy, devaluations, budgets – which are discussed in a closed environment that will include crucial ministers and perhaps other advisers. None would regard such a tactic as a derogation of cabinet government.

Cabinet government has never been a synonym for *primus inter pares*. Prime ministers have always been able to win. Where they choose to exercise their authority depends on what they want. Savoie gives a concession in his analysis of Chrétien:

> To be sure prime ministers do not always bypass their cabinets or only consult them after the fact. They pick and choose issues they want to direct and, in some circumstances, may decide to let the Cabinet's collective decision-making run its course. . . . These are the issues on which a prime minister may hold no firm view, and decide that it is best to keep one's political capital in reserve for another day and another issue. (1999a, p. 650)

It was ever thus. Prime ministers with great political standing and extensive interests (say, one that has won three elections in a row (Chrétien) or the party's two biggest ever electoral wins (Blair)) have a store of capital that is vast if they choose to use it. These debates reflect the obvious reality that the influence of prime ministers has varied over the decades. There have been powerful and weak prime ministers.

Other sets of implicit assumptions may readily be discovered. Some writers may wish one or all of these conditions to be met. But none is satisfactory. To explain cabinet government in these terms, implying there is a normatively correct way for it to work, has severe limitations because it sets practical standards for an organization whose existence is conventional and ever-changing.

Further, implicit in most assumptions is the belief that cabinet can and should limit prime ministers whenever they become too ambitious or authoritarian and that powerful and dominant prime ministers are incompatible with cabinet government. Yet there is a problem with this argument. The occasions in Britain which are usually given as the high points of cabinet government coincide with examples of prime ministers whose governments are in disarray, even near paralysis: the principal examples are the debates on *In Place of Strife*, the 1976 IMF intervention and much of the debate on the EC in the Major cabinet. In each case the prime minister was using the debate to maintain party cohesion. It is odd to laud such circumstances as those in which some ideal of cabinet prevails.

A CHOICE OF TACTICS

Prime ministers' tactics change to suit circumstance and personality. The tactics can include:

- Control by debate at length. Trudeau and Fraser were both comfortable in cabinet debate; they liked issues to be thrashed out there and could be cutting in their questioning of ministers. But neither was prepared to let decisions run that they thought wrong. Cabinet debate did not mean that the prime ministers' views did not prevail, even where the numbers were against them. Even Major let 'people talk first, listening intently all the while and then expects everyone to agree with him (Foley 1993, p. 211). There is a difference between letting ministers talk it out as a means of keeping the party together and using cabinet as a seminar to discuss policy options before asserting their own decision determined beforehand; the former is an indication of weakness, the latter of style.
- Control by announcing the preferred outcome. Prime ministers can announce where they stand and let the ministers argue where they felt inclined, which might not be too often. Thatcher and Keating are examples in the modern era. They may not have had views on everything, but where they did their cabinets had no doubt where they stood. Whitlam chose to dominate some areas of policy and largely ignored others.
- Decision making by segmentation. Faced with a number of antagonistic and strong personalities, Attlee drove different policies through groups of ministers. As Hennessy has shown, nuclear policy was never divulged to all the cabinet. They did not need to know. War cabinets fit the same mould, whether Suez, Falklands or the Gulf. A full cabinet is not efficient.
- Control by intellect. Where the prime ministers were the best informed, the most experienced and the most intelligent, they could win arguments, or at least reduce the opposition to consent by silence (and fear) (St Laurent, Fraser, Trudeau, Menzies).
- Setting the tone. Some prime ministers may have vision, others want a cautious approach. Keating and Thatcher often fitted the former image; Chrétien the latter. These general approaches may be taken as given in the choices that ministers take.
- Bi-lateral discussion. Mulroney and Chrétien like to talk to ministers one on one, particularly foreign affairs and the economy where they have a particular interest. Policy may be thrashed out in camera. Blair and Thatcher preferred to use 'groups which do not qualify as cabinet committees' (Hennessy 2000, p. 79). 'As a project-orientated prime minister he [Blair] is more inclined to create teams and units than set up a Cabinet Committee . . . more co-ordination is done outside the Cabinet system' (Kavanagh and Seldon 2000, p. 321). Decisions were made by ministers and officials in and around cabinet.

Again it would be possible to add to this list of strategic and tactical choices. All prime ministers in the last 100 years have used some or all of them to gain their way. Almost no prime minister has sat back to allow others to dictate; they are after all the leaders of the government. They are expected to set the terms of debate and in summing up to define the decisions. Indeed cabinet will often look for a lead. Winners are trusted, their political instincts admired as long as events and polls are going well. A prime minister who will not give a lead is likely to be weaker than one who lays down the law and then wins again.

There is nothing inherently superior or proper about any one of these tactics; they depend on personality and circumstance. Nor can they be classified as exclusively modern. Budgets were always determined by the prime ministers and their chancellor/treasurer/finance minister, with the level of cabinet participation limited at best. Foreign policy was always shared, with prime ministers being involved where they chose and representing their countries at conferences abroad. Cabinet never was intended to be democratic. As Graham White so colourfully has put it:

> At first blush the idea that Canadian cabinets should be in the least democratic is as improbable as the notion that after ministering to the downtrodden of Calcutta, Mother Teresa spent her leisure hours on a supercharged Harley-Davidson riding with the local Hell's Angels chapter for a little mayhem and debauchery. (White 2001, p. 1)

Nor has the most recent *Guide For Ministers and Secretaries of State* (Canada 2002), released by Chrétien left any doubt about his perception of the powers and prerogatives of the prime minister.

What determines those tactical choices will, in part, be a matter of personality. The interests of prime ministers vary. Some care about a few things; others have broader agenda. Some concentrate on the big picture, the key initiatives and delegate the rest; others want to be constantly involved in detail. So will their approach to governing. But it will also depend on the lessons, both positive and negative, that people have learnt from the past. To take just two incumbents as examples: Chrétien is an instinctive and pugnacious politician; he has vast experience; he was first sworn in as a minister on the same day as Trudeau and Turner, two of his predecessors, in 1967 (Martin 1995). But he is not comfortable having rambling policy discussions, reminiscent of a university seminar, which was the way Trudeau liked to run the cabinet. He prefers an efficient and speedy process and is less inclined to reflect on the possible outcomes, rather than the results.

Blair had never been in government, but he had immediate past models from which to select: the collegiate approach of two weak prime ministers in Callaghan and Major; or the directive lead given by Thatcher. Given those models, what leader would not look at the lessons and longevity of Thatcher and assume that here was a well-charted path to pursue?

These examples can readily be extended. Keating, believing that Hawke had become too cautious, wanted to lead from the front on those issues he cared about (and almost ignored those he did not). Indeed as Britain went from a directive to a more consensual leader in 1990, Australia went the other way in 1991. What mattered was that the new leader was not like the old, not that one method was proper cabinet government and the other not. Circumstances have changed. In each case prime ministers will learn to avoid any recent lessons that led to electoral defeat and see where the advantage lies.

The party and parliamentary circumstances will be crucial. Every prime minister in the last fifty years who relied heavily on cabinet has been in a parlous political situation, either in parliament or in the polls. Lester Pearson never headed a majority government. By contrast Chrétien has led his Liberal party to three consecutive majority governments, an achievement not performed since Mackenzie King in the 1930s and 1940s. His ministers give him immense latitude because his political instincts and fighting spirit has proved so successful. Winners are powerful. Similarly Blair has given Labour its two largest majorities. Callaghan and Major could be challenged from within the cabinet and party because they had little electoral standing and their governments were drifting.

There is indeed a danger of arguing that cabinet government is discovered to be at its most powerful only when the government and the leader seems to be heading for defeat. If so, that is a dire prognostication for the success of cabinet government and it is not a state to which any prime minister would aspire. Nor for purposes of analysis is it a useful default mode for a normative notion of cabinet government. Again, to espouse cabinet government is not to describe which tactic should be used; advocating the application of 'true' cabinet government does not tell a prime minister how to govern.

Consequently the argument that cabinet is dead carries little weight because it lacks any precision. Cabinet, as evidence over the century shows, has been in a constant state of revision and evolution under different prime ministers and in all countries. But the debate raises a more interesting question: in what directions is cabinet evolving and with what effect? Has it retained some functions while developing others?

CABINET GOVERNMENT AS A SET OF ARRANGEMENTS

The concept of cabinet government is too central to our form of government to be defined out of existence. What is required is a concept that can incorporates the different academic approaches, with their emphasis on accountability, rules, policy and power, and at the same time allows a degree of flexibility and evolution. It cannot be described institutionally or procedurally; there are too many variations in practice and no acceptable normative models against which to assess performance. It cannot refer to the level of collegial decision. Nor simply to the fact that power is shared, in some degree, between prime ministers and ministers. It should usefully be able to be applied comparatively.

Two definitions of cabinet government, provided in interviews with officials in Canada and Britain, provided a different emphasis:

- Cabinet government is the arrangements the prime minister makes to ensure that decisions are made in the interests of the general, rather than the individual minister, with a view to presenting a unified program for legislation and supply (Canada);
- Cabinet government is a shorthand term for the process by which government determines its policy and ensures the political will to implement it (Britain).

A former Australian secretary to the Department of Prime Minister and Cabinet argues that the cabinet has two main functions: policy coherence and political support (Keating and Weller 2000). Again all these definitions are process neutral. They accept the need for political support and for coherent policy, but appreciate the mix will change from time to time. How the prime ministers use cabinets to achieve these objectives will differ from person to person. Some take individual initiatives, others work through the cabinet. Some discuss in a meeting of ministers; others work in and around the cabinet itself.

The essence of the definitions is prime ministers always need support and policy coherence and must work to achieve it. They need ministers to take over the day-to-day running of departments. That sharing of power is the core element of a cabinet system. But again there is no prescription for the way and extent to which power and decisions must be shared. They always do so to some extent. For a long time Chrétien gives a degree of influence to his minister of finance, Paul Martin. Blair has given chancellor Gordon Brown extensive autonomy. For a time in Australia Hawke and Keating made a powerful duo. Howard must now work closely with Peter Costello. Martin, Brown and Costello are all seen as possible successors to the incumbents and have their own power base in the party. They held crucial economic portfolios that reflect their significance and have to be treated with care. Relations between the prime ministers and these colleagues are sometimes strained, but they can never be consistently ignored.

To what extent power is shared with other ministers depends on the interests of the prime ministers and the quality and standing of those other key ministers. In most cases ministers are required to get on with the job for which they have statutory responsibility. Sometimes, indeed, far from complaining about excessive interference, they complain of the difficulty of attracting the prime ministers' interest when they want to take an initiative. Some regard it as a sign of competence that they do not involve the prime ministers on day to day business. But they know that where the prime ministers share an interest they will be required to work in cooperation with them and they usually relish the opportunity to do so. But in each case the initiative will lie with the prime minister, not the minister.

Maintaining collective support is an end that can be achieved by a variety of means, of which debate and information exchange in cabinet has always been but one. Powerful leaders achieve it through their authority, of which there may be few public signs. There is too much activity for prime ministers to know all that is going on; they can take support for granted, for a time at least. But there is a need to avoid a problem of equating weakness with collective weight: often the times when cabinet government is regarded at its strongest, are when governments are in crisis and when prime ministers have limited political power because of internal or external constraints. It does appear to be perverse to advocate normatively a form of collective decision making that signifies a government under siege.

Cabinet remains a useful forum for maintaining that collective support; indeed that still seems the most persuasive reason for the regular meetings of cabinet, whether they are seen as a focus group or a political forum. Indeed these traditional political functions of cabinet – exchanging information, taking the political temperature, geeing up ministers, providing a sense of solidarity, setting the tone, emphasising the current issues and their resolution – can be undertaken almost independently of policy functions. Hence the fact that often when big issues came to cabinet, the intent was as much to solidify support as determine any direction. Every government seems to still use cabinet for these political purposes, as insurance and to lock in support.

But the pressure and complexity of modern government means that a weekly meeting of busy ministers no longer seems the best way to make timely and sophisticated policy. So prime ministers choose to work with the principal players in and around those regular meetings. The weaknesses of cabinet are, as Kavanagh and Seldon (2000, p. 321) note, well established: too much information, too little time, too many busy people. Modern practices take this pressure into account by segmenting and organizing the decision-making. The process may, *de facto*, now be closer to Dell's image of collective purpose, with crucial policy decisions made around the cabinet. Cabinet itself is used to forge unity and collective purpose, rather than decide on a course of action.

If that is an accurate diagnosis, then cabinet is simply evolving as it did a century ago. If it is a political forum, not a decision-making one, then there is a logic in the regularity of meetings and the generality of the discussions. If decisions are taken elsewhere, in and around the system, in the prime ministers' offices, in the committees, that is a matter of efficiency and convenience. Cabinet is a working institution.

WHAT DETERMINES THE VARIATIONS IN PRACTICE?

The variations cannot be explained by constitutional theory. Certainly observers make comments on what prime minister should do. 'The self-restraint of co-operative government . . . is part of the job description' (Rose 1980, p. 340). Prime ministers should not pursue their own polices; their role is to hold the ring. These prescriptions may suit some ideal of a prime minister, or fit a model of practice for cabinet governments. But prime ministers do what they can, consistent with the ability to maintain collective support. If they can take extensive power, they will as long as it is consistent with continuing support. In institutions that are constantly evolving it can only be expected. Noticeably even in countries that have a constitution, cabinet is not mentioned; it remains a conventional part of the political scenery.

But again there is a *caveat*. In the last decades prime ministers may have appeared to gain power, but it may be greater influence over less. The move to reliance on markets has been a bi-partisan shift, as governments deliver less, even while they commission and pay for more. Central banks have been given greater independence, currencies float, governments are signatories to international trade agreements or join free trade blocs, appeals to the European Union or the World Trade Organisation take some decisions out of the hands of national governments. Globalization changes the role that cabinets and leaders play.

In federal states there is recognition that cabinet may have a representational role and that many policies have to be negotiated with leaders at other levels of government. In Canada and Australia the premiers of provinces and states are significant figures in their own right. In time the leaders of Scottish and Welsh assemblies too will gain in status and become players with whom prime ministers must negotiate.

We need to be careful about assuming that all countries start from the same position. According to one comparative study (Andeweg 1997), Britain's cabinet system is already more segmented and less collective than those of Australia, Canada, Germany or The Netherlands. In those places the pressures on cabinet are often representational, whether of coalition or regions. In Britain the main interests are departmental.

But the crucial factors are the national political traditions and the way they affect the position of the prime ministers. In Canada cabinet has fulfilled a variety of functions, primarily that of representation of the provinces. With numbers rising to 40 at times, and with political objections to a division of the cabinet into cabinet and non-cabinet members, it has never acted as a decision-making forum (Bakvis 2000). Indeed it is often not expected to be one. In the PCO the culture requires that most issues be negotiated outside the cabinet room. Bitter argument between ministers in cabinet is a sign that the PCO has failed. Ministers are not used to being directed by cabinet within their own portfolios. In the program review exercise in 1995, ministers fought to protect their departments from cuts; Ralph Goodale, Minister for Agriculture, asked the program review committee: 'What gives you the right to act as judges on what generations of other people have created? From what divine right do you derive the power to decide that 50 of my scientists will be without work tomorrow?' (Savoie 1999a, p. 180).

Ministers in Australia or Britain would not challenge the decision of a budget committee so passionately because their experience of a cost-cutting committee review is more regular; besides, the prime ministers give the committees that divine right (as Chrétien had done this time in Canada). So in that sense cabinet has never been the centre of decisions in Canada and the prime ministers have for decades, from John Macdonald onwards, shown both a detailed interest in the decisions of ministers and arranged the processes of government around the cabinet system. They have used different vehicles for decision as the issue and circumstances required.

Besides, the Canadian prime minister is invulnerable from internal revolt. Elected by convention delegates among whom MPs are a small minority, the prime minister does not owe his position to the parliamentary caucus. Ministers may wonder who the successor might be, but they can do nothing to influence the timing of that election, even if the prime minister is, according to the opinion polls, massively unpopular and leading the party to ruin. Both Trudeau and Mulroney decided when they would leave and both in effect handed a poisoned chalice to their successors. If a prime minister is constantly successful, as Chrétien has been, his position is much safer.

As both British parties move to leadership elections that are broader than just the parliamentary party, so they too will consolidate the position of the party leader. Those that do not elect can hardly remove. Even when it could, Thatcher's cabinet revolted only after the electoral college had required her to go to a second ballot. So prime ministers are becoming safer from internal revolt and their position is thus strengthened. But even without that change the conventions and practice of cabinet have always been in the hands of the prime ministers who exercised the power in ways that they saw best for the future of their government and for their own position. All the evidence suggests that cabinet government is a malleable institution and has been for a long time.

The exceptional case may be Australia. Again, like the Canadian leader, Australian prime ministers must deal with state premiers with an independent power base and different interests. They must negotiate with a Senate that has equal powers to the House of Representatives and in which no government has had a majority for over 20 years. The culture is different. Cabinet is a forum where rugged debate is expected. Central agencies are required to isolate the hard issues that need cabinet decision by determining the facts and letting cabinet decide on the direction. Australian cabinet ministers know that cabinet committees have the support of the prime minister.

But more important Australian prime ministers still depend for their futures on the support of the parliamentary party and can be removed by a vote at any time in the party room (Weller 1993). As long as they win elections, or seem likely to win, they are secure. But there is a record of successful and unsuccessful challenges, even to prime ministers who have won three elections. Prime ministers must therefore be even more conscious of the opinions and standing of their cabinet colleagues. The rules of engagement are thus different.

CAN CABINET GOVERNMENT BE RECOGNIZED?

These are variations to cabinet government; we cannot say that cabinet government exists in one place and not in another. Cabinet government can come in a number of forms, most of which are consistent with the circumstances we find in the countries under review. Cabinet government evolves to meet the challenges that emerge. Collective cabinet government might have been 'real' in the aristocratic clique of the late nineteenth century but that style could not survive war and the modern media. In each country the system has developed, become more bureaucratized, more fragmented, more managed, as much by necessity as by choice.

The idea of cabinet collectivity remains significant. Cabinet may be an ideal, or in the phrase of Seymour-Ure (1971), a principle; but its existence creates expectations for maintaining a minimum collective support. Meetings are still held because prime ministers see value, politically and organizationally, in such exercises. The ideal may be elusive, incapable of precise definition, let alone giving satisfaction, but it still stands as the core of the way that people perceive their system of government. All the accounts of cabinet government have in common is a sense of change in the face of the brute demands of decision-making. Under what circumstances could we really define cabinet government to be dead? To see the answer we can look either at countries where the language of collective cabinet is retained but dictatorship prevail and where there is no need to maintain the collectivity, or at the other extreme places where there is no collective input and where ministers make all the decisions. On this spectrum, none of the countries under review gets close to either extreme.

If then critics wish to declare cabinet government dead, it behoves them to identify the criteria they regard as essential to the proper working of cabinet government and the conditions to be satisfied before cabinet government can thrive. They should also explain why, under these conditions, government might be better and perhaps show by example when those conditions applied and with what results. That exercise would create normative criteria for good and effective government. But that they have failed to do. To state that prime ministers are as powerful as their ministers allow them to be is a truism that tells us little about the way government is, or should, operate; it merely notes the need to maintain collective support. The death of cabinet government is assumed by an analysis of the activities of prime ministers. But ministers exert authority within their portfolios and there is no consistent trend to suggest that prime ministers determine everything; they are influential in those areas where they care to act, as they always were. The oft-cited ideals of cabinet government, under Pearson, Callaghan and Major, are often governments under stress with politically or personally weak prime ministers. The most frequently cited examples of cabinet government in action are often examples of prime ministers allowing lengthy debate as a means of sustaining collective support. The strategy had been determined in advance; cabinet was used to bring the dissidents to heel and lock them in. Until some defensible normative criteria to define cabinet government are developed, it is premature to describe as dead an institution that was never more than an elusive ideal and indeed may never have existed in the forms its advocates proclaim as desirable.

If cabinet government is more usefully interpreted as a set of arrangements in which the ministers hold the statutory power and prime ministers, with greater or lesser intervention, determine how the individual is fitted into the collective will, then cabinet government remains, consistent with the past in intent and outcome, but different in form. Prime ministers need to gain that collective support from ministers who have statutory authority and for that the cabinet and its environs remain a vital forum. Cabinet meetings are not always effective ways of determining policy, so those policy decisions have been hived off into more effective processes. Cabinet government is a working set of arrangements, not a set of rules or a given distribution of power. Just as it was unrealistic to expect the style of the 19th century to survive war and economic development, so the modern cabinet too has to evolve to meet the pressures on it.

ACKNOWLEDGEMENT

I would like to thank Rod Rhodes, John Wanna, Ian Holliday and the anonymous referees for the Journal for their comments on an earlier draft. Versions of this paper were presented in public lectures at St Francis Xavier University in Nova Scotia and the University of Exeter. I would like to thank those universities for their invitations.

REFERENCES

Andeweg, R. 1997. 'Collegiality and collectivity: cabinets, cabinet committees and cabinet ministers' in P. Weller *et al.* (eds). *The hollow crown*. Basingstoke: Macmillan.
Baker, A. 2000. *Prime ministers and the rule book*. London: Politico's.
Bakvis, H. 2000. 'Prime minister and cabinet in Canada: an autocracy in need of reform', *Journal of Canadian Studies*, 35, 4, 60–79.
Bliss, M. 1994. *Right honourable men*. Toronto: HarperCollins.
Blackstone, T. and W. Plowden. 1988. *Inside the think tank: Advising the cabinet 1971–1983*. London: William Heinemann.
Bunting, J. 1988. *R. G. Menzies: a portrait*. Sydney: Allen and Unwin.
Burch, M. and I. Holliday. 1996. *The British cabinet system*. Hemel Hempstead: Prentice Hall.
Canada. 2002. *A guide for ministers and secretaries of state*. Ottawa: Privy Council Office.
Crossman, R. 1963. 'Introduction' to W. Bagehot *The English Constitution*. London: Fontana.
Davis, G. 1995. *A government of routines*. Macmillan, Melbourne.
Dell, E. 1980. 'Collective responsibility: fact, fiction or façade?', *Policy and practice: the experience of government*. London: RIPA.
Donoughue, B. 1987. *Prime minister*. London: Jonathan Cape.
Dunleavy, P. and R.A.W. Rhodes. 1990. 'Core executive studies in Britain', *Public Administration*, 68, 3–28.
Edwards, J. 1996. *Keating: the inside story*. Ringwood: Viking.
Encel, S. 1974. *Cabinet government in Australia*, 2nd edn, Melbourne: Melbourne University Press.
Foley, M. 1993. *The rise of the British presidency*. Manchester: Manchester University Press.
Foley, M. 2000. *The British presidency*. Manchester: Manchester University Press.
Forrest, J. and G, Reid. 1989. *The commonwealth parliament*. Melbourne: Melbourne University Press.
French, R. 1979. 'The privy council office: support for cabinet decision making', in R. Schultz *et al.* (eds), *The Canadian political process* 3rd edn. Toronto: Holt and Rinehart.
Hasluck, P. 1980. *Sir Robert Menzies*. Melbourne: Melbourne University Press.
Hennessy, P. 1986. *Cabinet*. London: Fontana.
Hennessy, P. 1995. *The hidden wiring*. London: Indigo.
Hennessy, P. 2000. *The prime minister*. London: Penguin.
Hogg, S. and J. Hill. 1995. *Too close to call: power and politics – John Major in No. 10*. London: Little Brown.
Holliday, I. 2000. 'Is the British state hollowing out?' *The Political Quarterly*, 71, 2, 167–76.
Jones, G. 1979. 'The prime minister's aides', *Hull Papers in Politics*, 6.
Jones, G. 1981. Review of Rose and Suleiman in *Public Administration* 57, 2, 219–20.
Kavanagh, D. and A. Seldon. 1999. *The powers behind the prime minister*. London: Harper Collins.
Keating, M. and P. Weller. 2001. 'Cabinet government: an institution under pressure', in M. Keating, J. Wanna and P. Weller (eds), *Institutions on the edge*. Sydney: Allen and Unwin Australia.
Laver, M. and K. Shepsle. 1993. 'Agenda formation and cabinet government', in *Agenda Formation* (W.H. Riker, ed.), Ann Arbor, MI: University of Michigan Press.
Lindquist, E. and G. White. 1997. 'Analysing Canadian cabinets: past, present and future', in M. Charih and A. Daniels (eds), *New public management and public administration in Canada*. Toronto: Institute of Public Administration of Canada.
Mackintosh, J.P. 1977. *The British cabinet*, 3rd edn. London: Stevens.
Mackie, J. and B. Hogwood (eds). 1985. *Unlocking the cabinet*. London: Sage.
Martin, L. 1995. *Chrétien: the will to win*. Toronto: Lester Publishing.
Mills, S. 1993. *The Hawke years*. Ringwood: Viking.
Rentoul, J. 2001. *Tony Blair prime minister*. London: Warner Books.
Rhodes, R. 1995. 'From prime ministerial power to core executive', in. R. Rhodes and P. Dunleavy (eds), *Prime minister, cabinet and core executives*. London: Macmillan.
Robertson, G. 2001. *Memoirs of a very civil servant*. Toronto: University of Toronto Press.
Rose, R. 1980. 'British government: the job at the top', in R. Rose and E. Suleiman (eds). *Presidents and prime ministers*. Washington, DC: American Enterprise Institute.
Rose, R. 2001. *The prime minister in a shrinking world*. Cambridge: Polity Press.
Savoie, D. 1999. 'The rise of court government in Canada', *Canadian Journal of Political Science*, 32, 4, 635–64.

Savoie D. 1999a. *Governing from the center*. Toronto: University of Toronto Press.

Seymour-Ure, C. 1971. 'The disintegration of the cabinet system and the neglected question of cabinet reform', *Parliamentary Affairs*, 24, 3, 196–207.

Simpson, J. 2001. *The friendly dictatorship*. McClelland and Stewart, Toronto.

Weller, P. 1983. 'Do prime minister's departments really create problems?', *Public Administration*, 61, 1, 59–78.

Weller, P. 1985. *First among equals: prime ministers in Westminster systems*. Sydney: Allen and Unwin.

Weller, P. 1989. *Malcolm Fraser prime minister*. Ringwood: Penguin.

Weller, P. 1991. 'Prime ministers, political leadership and cabinet government', *Australian Journal of Public Administration* 50, 3, 137–44.

Weller, P. 1993. 'Party rules and the dismissal of leaders', *Parliamentary Affairs*, 47, 1, 133–43.

Weller, P. 1999. 'Disentangling ministerial responsibility', *Australian Journal of Public Administration*, 58, 1, 62–4.

Weller, P. 2001. 'Ministerial codes, cabinet rules and the power of prime ministers', in J. Fleming and I. Holland (eds). *Motivating ministers to morality*. Aldershot: Ashgate.

White, G. 2001. 'Mother Teresa's biker gang, or cabinet democracy in Canada', paper presented at the 'Canada Today: a Democratic Audit' conference, Ottawa.

Woodhouse, D. 1994. *Ministers and parliament: accountability in theory and practice*. Oxford: The Clarendon Press.

AFTERWORD: NOTHING HAS CHANGED

In *Cabinet Government: An Elusive Ideal?* I sought to identify the different ways that the idea of cabinet government was conceptualised and consequently the difficulty of determining when cabinet government could be described as functioning well. There were, I argued, four different approaches based on constitutional theory, public administration, public policy and poetical science. The different perspectives determined what academics explored and what criteria they regarded as important for success. I also suggested that the appeal to the 'golden era' of cabinet government was a myth, always pushed somewhere in the past and derived more from lack of detailed knowledge than careful research.

Nothing has changed. For evidence, we can appeal to the House of Lords report on *The Cabinet Office and the Centre of Government*, issued in 2010. In the transcripts of evidence from academics and practitioners, all these different ideas are presented once again.

There is nostalgia for the days when cabinet government really existed. 'I think we should announce ourselves as representatives of the golden age', said Lord McNally of the Callaghan government (The House of Lords 2010: Evidence p. 46). The apex of cabinet government was the long meetings over the acceptance of the IMF terms in 1976–77. 'We served under the last Prime Minister who conducted Cabinet Government. I think the IMF crisis of 1976/1977 is regarded as a classic, whereby a whole Cabinet had to be brought in line with a particular line of policy', said Lord Lipsey. Note that cabinet was used to bring cabinet into line, not to make the decision. Channelling Bagehot, Lipsey argues that 'I think the Cabinet has come perilously close to moving from an efficient part of the constitution to a dignified part of the constitution'(p. 46). Others are more sceptical; former civil servant Richard Mottram proposed: 'The 1970s were certainly a golden age for cabinet government, compared to more recent times. They were, of course, also a time of serious failure for the United Kingdom as a country and for its system of government'. (p. 34). He went on: 'I am very nervous about golden ages.... I am cautious about the trappings of cabinet government and the likelihood that you can turn the Cabinet into an effective decision making machine' (pp. 44, 50). Of course Richard Crossman and John Macintosh had consigned cabinet government to the dustbin of history a decade *before* these events.

There are romantics who see cabinet government as a panacea. Peter Hennessy wishes it still worked better:

> New Labour created the most supine Cabinet since the war... Cabinet ministers are there to say 'Wait a minute'. The only sprinkler system the British system of government has – because for all the laws that we have there are no laws that cover the proper conduct in the cabinet room – if the Cabinet collectively or a sufficient of them is not prepared to say 'Oh, come off it' or 'Are you sure?', you cannot do anything about it (pp. 4, 9).

But when did this really occur? If the prime minister and leading ministers are agreed before the meeting, will their more junior colleagues challenge their decision and overturn it?

Most commentators agreed that collective government was dead (even while they opposed the idea that the Cabinet Office should support the prime minister lest that undermine the collective government they have just interred). They often wished it were not so. Andrew Blick and George Jones predictably argue that 'any support premiers receive from the cabinet office should only be in their role as chair of cabinet' (p. 175). Prime ministers should not be driving policy. Here is the normative interpretation of constitutional propriety, of the role that prime minister should play: making the collective system work, not taking the lead. It is never certain who will break the news to modern prime ministers that they are constitutionally out of order much of the time!

The civil servants are more relaxed. The changes have been evolutionary. A typical comment was; 'I am doubtful whether 1997 was a real watershed. There is a longer term trend. . .it is not a consistent trend' (Robin Mountfield, p. 75). The systems have adapted. The concern for them, as cabinet secretary Sir Gus O'Donnell stated, is what works. "Are we producing better outcomes?" (p. 146)

The political view is that modern demands have simply changed the approaches of prime ministers. One academic reports an early comment from Blair that 'Ministers have to understand they are the agents of the centre. They have been sent to the departments to carry out a strategy'. He added: 'I cannot imagine many other Prime Ministers saying that' (Kavanagh p. 22).

The realist version wants to describe what is and then make it work better. Blair adviser Jonathan Powell suggested that: 'Rather than arguing about the death of Cabinet government, when it in fact died a long time ago, we should spend more effort reinforcing the cabinet committees and their supporting infrastructure as a key part of government decision making' (p. 180).

A civil servant summarised the argument that was at the core of my article:

> I think it partly depends on whether you mean Cabinet government as a meeting once a week or Cabinet government as a set of principles. . . . Every single decision coming through one meeting a week at which there are 20–25 people is not a test of whether Cabinet government is dead' (Jeremy Heywood, p. 158).

He suggests that civil servants try to ensure that 'all the Cabinet departments and Cabinet Ministers with a responsibility have every opportunity to debate, discuss, disagree, agree and we do not announce a policy unless everyone with an interest is signed off and then everyone is bound by the principle of collective responsibility [that is] alive and well in Whitehall' (p. 158).

If further evidence was needed of the infinite flexibility of cabinet, it can be found in the way that cabinet procedures can be so readily adapted to meet new political circumstances. A coalition government in Britain created new demands. In May 2010 the Cabinet Office released its new description of cabinet. It notes:

> 'All government ministers are bound by the collective decisions of Cabinet and Cabinet Committees, **save when it is explicitly set aside**.' (bold type in the original)

So collective responsibility still applies, except when it does not!

Each cabinet committee has a chair and deputy chair, one from each party. Each has 'the right to remit an issue to the Coalition Committee if it affects the operation of the coalition and cannot be resolved by the originating committee'. It is an appeal, not to the cabinet but to the Coalition Committee (technically a cabinet committee, even if a committee for politics). The Cabinet Secretariat reports to 'the Prime Minister, the Deputy

Prime Minister and Ministers who chair Cabinet Committees'. Good luck: but who has the principal loyalty of the Cabinet Secretary in a time of crisis or tension? Are these constitutional principles being just or just operational rules *pro tem*?

All these provisions are necessary amendments. It is a coalition, after all, and novel modes of decision making and convention have to be worked out. Practices are presented in terms of constitutionality and good practice, and with a straight face suggesting that normal service continues. But they play havoc with normative 'constitutional' views of cabinet government and emphasise yet again that cabinet procedures are designed to make the politics work, not to fit some ideal version of what prime minister *should* or *should not* do, or how cabinet *should* work.

So the meaning and practices of cabinet government are still open to interpretation and re-engineering. What is manifestly true here of the United Kingdom is also true of Canada and Australia. There are debates on the workings of cabinet, and assertions that they have been undermined, all made with little historical knowledge or an appreciation that to practitioners, what works is more important than some notion of what cabinet government should be.

REFERENCE

House of Lords Select Committee on the Constitution. 2010. *The Cabinet Office and the centre of government*. 4th Report, Session 2009–10, HL 30. London: The Stationery Office.

Chapter 7

THE JOINT-DECISION TRAP: LESSONS FROM GERMAN FEDERALISM AND EUROPEAN INTEGRATION

FRITZ W. SCHARPF

INTRODUCTION

In political philosophy government is justified, in comparison to anarchy, as an arrangement for improving the chances of purposive fate control through the *collective* achievement of goals (including protection against threats) which would be beyond the reach
of *individual* action. The same logic of effectiveness would justify enlarging the scale of
government whenever the achievement of goals, or the defence against threats, would be
aided by the larger action space and resources of larger units. The countervailing logic
of democratic legitimacy, however, would favour smaller units of government in which
a greater homogeneity of preferences would allow collective choices to approximate
aggregate individual choices. It is also claimed that a world of small government units
would not, in the first place, produce most of the threats to security that large units of
government are needed to provide protection against (Kohr 1978).

The search for the optimal scale of government, in the light of apparent trade-offs
between the greater effectiveness of larger and the greater legitimacy of smaller units,
is the subject of sophisticated speculation in the fields of public choice, fiscal federalism
and political science (Breton and Scott 1978; Kirsch 1977; Mueller 1979; Oates 1972; Olson
1969; E. Ostrom 1984; Rothenberg 1970; Tullock 1969; Ylvisaker 1959). Historically, of
course, it was the nation state which, during the nineteenth and early twentieth centuries,
seemed to provide the most attractive balance: sufficiently large and resource-rich to
cope with most external threats, it was also internally homogeneous enough to facilitate
the acceptance of collective choices. Indeed, the history of national unification in the
nineteenth century, as well as of the disintegration of multi-national empires in the
twentieth century, suggest that national 'identity' was a more powerful determinant of
the prevailing scale of government authority than either the greater internal homogeneity
of sub-national communities or the greater power resources of supra-national political
units (Sharpe 1985).

In the post-1945 period, however, political authority on the scale of the nation state
seemed to have lost much of its claim to optimality. Having been rescued from military
disaster by the United States for the second time, most European nation states chose to
renounce their claims to military self-sufficiency in favour of an American-led alliance. At
the same time, European recovery, not only from war damages but also from the pre-war
disintegration of the international economy, seemed to require the creation of a larger
'common market' at least within Western Europe. For the committed 'Europeanists', of
course, this was only a beginning. They hoped, and worked, for a politically united
Western Europe which would again be able to hold its own in a world dominated by
military and economic 'super powers'. In these hopes they were encouraged by integration
theories in the social sciences, expecting closer communications among member countries,

and the 'forward spill overs' of functionally specific European institutions, to generate the political momentum for an ever deeper and wider social and political integration (Deutsch 1957; Haas 1958). Thus, NATO and the EEC were seen as only the first steps on the road to 'a more complete union' modelled after the federal system of the United States of America.

Thirty years later, NATO is still no more than a defence alliance under the undisputed hegemony of the United States, but as such it has been remarkably successful by its own standards. The European Community, on the other hand, has increased its territorial scale from the original six to twelve member states, and it has also broadened its functional responsibilities beyond the specific mandates of the original treaty. Indeed, there is considerable pressure for further functional expansion in such areas as industrial policy, technology policy, communications policy and monetary policy, where the Community is urged to assume governing responsibilities for which the nation state has become too small.

Nevertheless it is fair to say that the Community, unlike NATO, is not characterized by the self-satisfaction of secure accomplishments but, rather, by a pervasive sense of disappointment, frustration and general malaise. The 'Common Market', to be sure, is functioning more or less effectively as a customs union in the industrial sector, constraining the protectionist tendencies of member countries in exchange for the growing protectionism of the Community itself. In industrial policy, however, the relative success of common ventures in aerospace resulted mainly from collaboration outside of Community institutions, while Community efforts to cushion the decline of old industries are severely criticized as economically inefficient. Some beneficial programmes, such as the Regional Fund and the Social Fund, are ridiculously under-financed in relation to the problems they are supposed to attack, while in other areas the transfer of regulatory powers to the European level has mainly had the effect of frustrating more aggressive initiatives for pollution control or consumer protection at the national level. Most important, however, the centrepiece of European economic integration, Common Agricultural Policy, is now almost universally considered a grandiose failure. CAP has managed to generate huge agricultural surpluses, at the expense of European consumers and taxpayers who have to pay twice, for food prices far above the world-market level as well as for enormous subsidies for the purchase, storage and disposal of surplus production. And in spite of it all, CAP has neither been able to assure acceptable family incomes for small European peasants, nor has it maintained its major original achievement of common prices in a common European market for agricultural goods.

Thus, if there should be any 'spill overs' at all from functional integration, they are more likely to be negative. Indeed, the controversies over British contributions, which almost wrecked the Community in 1984, were closely related to the perversities of CAP, and so are the budgetary conflicts with the European Parliament. Open conflict, it is true, might help to politicize European issues and thus, ultimately, further political integration (Schmitter 1969). But it is hard to believe that extremely low voter participation at European elections should be understood as the expression of vigorous political demands for more integration, rather than as a vote of non-confidence for the Community.

At the same time, however, the European Community is not only just 'hanging on'. Direct elections for the European Parliament, which were finally accepted in the 1970s, may not have achieved the political mobilization that had been hoped for, but they are still a symbol of institutional consolidation. In spite of acute conflicts of interest, Britain is still within the Community, and Spain and Portugal have finally been admitted. The European

Monetary System did not only survive against many odds, but it is now promoted as the nucleus of a future European Monetary Union with a common currency and a unified monetary policy.

In short, the history of the European Community has not confirmed the hopes, of 'Europeanist' politicians and 'neo-functional' theorists alike, for dynamic processes of deepening and widening functional integration, culminating in the creation of a full-fledged federal state; but the European enterprise has proven much more resilient than the 'realist' school of international relations and the political and scholarly promoters of an *Europe des patries* would have predicted. Paradoxically, the European Community seems to have become just that 'stable middle ground between the cooperation of existing nations and the breaking in of a new one' which Stanley Hoffmann (1966, p. 910) thought impossible.

It is tempting to ascribe the paradox of European integration – frustration without dis-integration and resilience without progress – to historical accidents or to the interventions of certain powerful individuals. Instead, I will try to argue in this paper that the European malaise may be systematically explained as the consequence of a characteristic pattern of policy choices under certain institutional conditions. This pattern, the 'joint-decision trap', was first identified in the institutional setting of federal-*Länder* relations in West Germany. It can be shown that similar institutional conditions are producing similar decision patterns in the European Community.

TWO MODELS OF FEDERALISM

When 'Europeanist' politicians and social scientists were considering processes of inte-gration that might lead to a 'United Europe', what they had in mind was a federal system fashioned after the American model. What was created, however, were institutional arrangements corresponding more closely to the tradition of German federalism. The fun-damental difference between the two models is often misunderstood in Anglo-American treatises on federalism which tend to dismiss the German variant as little more than a camouflage for *de facto* centralization (Wheare 1960). Even William Riker (1964, p. 123), who recognized the unique characteristics of the German model, finds it hard to fit into his conceptual scheme which classifies federal systems according to the relative weights of the spheres of *independent* authority of central and constituent governments, respectively. What is missed is the possibility that authority might not be allocated, in zero-sum fashion, to either one or the other level of government, but that it might be *shared* by both (Johnson 1973). This is what distinguishes the German model from American federalism. Of course, a good deal of sharing, 'marble-cake' or 'picket-fence' like, is going on in the United States as well (Riker 1975), but differences at the constitutional level are nevertheless important.

In both models, the powers of the central government are limited, and constituent governments (the 'states' or the *Länder*) continue to exercise original governing pow-ers legitimated by democratic elections. In the American model, however, the central government's authority is derived entirely from direct elections of the President and of both houses of Congress, and the federal government is able to rely upon its own administrative infrastructure at regional and local levels whenever it so chooses. In other words, the exercise of federal government functions is formally independent of the gov-ernments of the American states, and those functions that have been taken over by the federal government are effectively nationalized. Whatever sharing of functions is going on, is voluntarily granted, and may be withdrawn again by the federal government, as is illustrated by successive waves of the 'New Federalism'.

In the German model, by contrast, only one house of the federal legislature (the *Bundestag*) is based upon direct, popular elections, while the other one (the *Bundesrat*) provides for the representation of *Länder* governments. In practice, all important federal legislation does require concurrent majorities in the *Bundestag* and the *Bundesrat* and does depend, therefore, upon the agreement of *Länder* governments. In addition, the federal government is severely limited in its executive powers, having to rely upon the administrative services of the *Länder* for the implementation of most federal legislation. On the other hand, the revenue of both, the federal government and the *Länder*, is generally determined by federal tax legislation which imposes severe constraints upon the financial freedom of action of *Länder* and local governments. In short: the exercise of most governing functions is shared between the federal government and the *Länder* governments in West Germany. More specifically, for my present purposes, *Länder* governments have a significant share in the exercise of many of the important functions of the federal government. It is in this regard that German federalism is most comparable to the European Community.

It is probably fair to say that, even in the heyday of political enthusiasm for European integration in the 1950s, a European union along the lines of the American model of federalism was never a realistic possibility. The Community was created by the action of national governments at a time when their own continuing viability was no longer considered precarious (as it had been immediately after the war). The potentially most powerful motive for federation, common defence, was satisfied by the separate organization of the NATO alliance under US hegemony. What remained was the opportunity pull of economic integration (Scitovsky 1958; Balassa 1962) whose attraction was certainly not sufficient to persuade national governments of the need to commit institutional suicide. While recognizing the advantages of a common European market, they also had every interest in retaining as much control as possible over the substance, direction and speed of future steps towards political integration.

The primacy of national control is reflected in the limited authority of the European Parliament, even though it is now elected directly, and in the fact that the European Commission, the executive body of the Community, does not derive its authority from either the Parliament or from direct elections. Instead, the centre of power has remained in the Council of Ministers, representing national governments, and in the periodic summit meetings of the European Council. In both bodies, the principle of unanimous agreement has prevailed in important matters, providing each member government with an effective veto over European policy decisions affecting its own vital interests. Furthermore, the European Community is without administrative agencies of its own at the regional and local level; it must rely entirely upon member governments to execute its policies. And, of course, the Community has not been invested with its own powers of taxation, depending primarily upon import levies and upon contributions from the revenues of the member states (v.d. Groeben and Mestmäcker 1974; Wallace, Wallace and Webb 1977).

This is not to suggest that there are no significant differences between European institutions and German federalism. In fact, the European Community is much weaker in relation to its member governments than the German federal government is in relation to the *Länder*. Nevertheless, institutional arrangements are sufficiently similar to suggest that the difficulties of European integration might be illuminated by reference to some of the problems of German federalism which have been studied more systematically.

The parallelism between European and German institutions appears to be particularly close in those areas of joint policy making which were added rather late (in 1969) to the existing structure of the German federal constitution. In these areas, which have been the subject of empirical and theoretical studies under the label of 'Politikverflechtung' (Scharpf, Reissert and Schnabel 1976, 1977, 1978; Hesse 1978; Schultze 1982; Benz 1985) federal policy making is operating under the same requirement of unanimous consent which prevails at the European level. It is here that the 'joint-decision trap' was first identified.

JOINT POLICY MAKING IN WEST GERMANY

Under the original scheme of the German federal constitution, most important legislative functions are exercised at the federal level (with the agreement of the Bundesrat), while administrative functions are, with few exceptions, reserved to the Länder. Similarly, in the area of public finance, taxation is almost entirely governed by federal legislation, but tax revenues are shared by Länder and local governments. Even more significantly, the federal share of total public investment expenditures has always remained below 20 per cent.

In the early post-war period, political pressures focusing upon fiscal inequalities between rich and poor Länder gave rise to a formalized system of horizontal and vertical fiscal equalization payments and to a number of extra-constitutional federal grant programmes in such areas as housing and subsidies to agriculture and industry in depressed areas. In the 1960s, these programmes were increased in scope and volume even though their immediate post-war justifications had become less compelling. Instead, it had become clear that some of the important responsibilities of the modern state depended more upon the planning and financing of public infrastructure and public services than upon legislation. To that extent, the relative importance of the governing functions reserved to the Länder was seen to increase, while the legislative powers of the federal government appeared to lose some of their political salience.

At the same time, however, it was widely felt that the action space, and the action perspectives, of Länder governments were too narrowly circumscribed to deal effectively with some of the problems that had become major political issues in the 'reformist' political climate of the mid-1960s. Foremost among these was the perceived need to deal with the 'education gap' (or, even more dramatically, the Bildungskatastrophe) when participation rates in secondary and university-level education were seen to be far lower in West Germany than in other modern countries. Similar needs were perceived in some areas of large-scale public infrastructure, such as urban and inter-urban mass transport, urban renewal or the modernization of the hospital system. Furthermore, German peasants were about to be exposed to the direct competition of their European neighbours which they could only survive, or so it was thought, if the modernization of their farms and of agricultural infrastructure was heavily subsidized. By the same token, it seemed necessary to accelerate and subsidize industrial development in those rural and peripheral areas where agricultural employment was about to decline. In addition, the late conversion of German economic policy makers to the Keynesian philosophy of anti-cyclical demand management emphasized the importance, for economic stabilization, of national controls over the volume and the timing of public-infrastructure expenditures.

What is important is that these were all policy areas under the dominant influence of the Länder, but that 'enlightened public opinion' was highly sceptical of their willingness, or ability, to provide acceptable solutions. Such scepticism was sometimes, as in education, based upon a preference for nationally uniform solutions over the ideological and religious pluralism of *Länder* policies. In other areas, such as university or hospital construction, it was thought that the positive externalities of large, central institutions might be ignored by the policy choices of smaller *Länder*, or that their resource base would be inadequate for projects that could take advantage of important economies of scale. The resource constraints of small or relatively poor *Länder* were also regarded as obstacles for efficient policy solutions in urban mass transportation, urban renewal and in agriculture (where the problems of small peasant holdings are concentrated regionally). In regional industrial policy, finally, criticism focused mainly upon the undesirable consequences of 'ruinous competition' between *Länder* which were forced to attract new industrial settlements through ever larger offers of subsidies. What was needed, in short, were joint federal-*Länder* efforts to mobilize the common resource base, and to exploit the combined action space, of both levels of government for the achievement of common, national goals.

The federal government had, of course, tried to deal with some of these problems through its grant programmes which attempted to provide a degree of co-ordination between *Länder* policies, to impose some uniform standards, and to equalize some disparities of *Länder* resources. It was constrained, however, by unresolved doubts about the constitutionality of conditional federal grants in areas within *Länder* jurisdiction. The whole range of issues was, therefore, entrusted to an expert commission whose final report recommended far-reaching changes in the constitutional arrangements of fiscal federalism (Kommission für die Finanzreform 1966). In the general spirit of 'reform politics' and under the aspects of a 'Grand Coalition', such changes had indeed become politically feasible.

But constitutional change under the West German 'Basic Law' does require two-thirds majorities in the *Bundesrat* as well as in the *Bundestag*. As a consequence, the constitutional reforms of 1969 had all the characteristics of a negotiated settlement among independent, sovereign parties. To that extent, they represent an even closer approximation to the decision structures of the European Community than does the original constitution of the Federal Republic. Briefly, agreement was reached on three new areas of joint policy making, each involving the federal government and all the *Länder*:

— 'Community tasks' requiring joint planning and joint financing in the areas of university construction, regional industrial policy, and agricultural structural policy (Article 91a, Basic Law);
— federal subsidies to *Länder* investment programmes in such policy areas as housing, urban renewal, urban transportation or hospitals, and in short-term economic stabilization (Article 104a IV, Basic Law); and
— federal-*Länder* agreements to collaborate in the planning of primary and secondary education and in research financing (Article 91b, Basic Law).

Of these, primary and secondary education turned out to be the ideologically most controversial policy area. As there was very little federal money at stake (apart from federally financed 'model experiments'), 'progressive' and 'conservative' *Länder* felt free to engage in all-out conflict over their educational philosophies. For once, the Social-Liberal federal government was also willing to take a clear cut partisan position, so that the first drafts of the 'integrated education plan' turned out to be remarkably progressive documents. Unfortunately, however, they could not be adopted at the level of the heads of government, where the agreement of nine (out of eleven) *Länder* prime ministers was formally required. As a consequence, existing educational policies remained unchanged while efforts continued to reach agreement over ever more watered-down versions of the educational plan. In the meantime, public enthusiasm and political support for educational reforms began to erode, and so did financial resources for education at the onset of the economic and fiscal crisis after 1974. Predictably, the difficulties of reaching agreement in the face of acute political conflicts led to outcomes which frustrated not only the qualitative goals of progressive educational reformers, but also the quantitative goals shared by both the progressive and the conservative members of the education establishment (see Heidenheimer, Heclo and Teich-Adams 1975, 1983). In the end, the whole enterprise was abandoned in 1982 (BMBW 1982).

The lesson was not lost on others, and the internecine ideological battles of the educationists were not repeated elsewhere. Realizing the importance of presenting a united front toward an outside world of political 'generalists' in chancelleries, finance ministries and parliamentary budget committees, agreement became the primary goal itself. Thus, the specialist ministries responsible for federal-*Länder* negotiations at both levels developed decision rules approaching unanimity even in areas where, by law, majority decisions would have been possible. Perhaps still more important was a perception of common interest which prevented even those *Länder* that would have benefited in the particular case, from voting with the federal government as long as there was no nearly unanimous agreement among all of them.

Länder solidarity thus prevented the federal government from playing off the interests of some *Länder* against others in forming the 'minimum winning coalitions' which coalition theory would have predicted under such circumstances (Riker 1962). In fact, the 'cartelization' of *Länder* interests has been observed even in the field of research policy, where independent action by the federal government and individual *Länder* would have been entirely feasible and probably more effective (Bentele 1979), or in the planning of federal highways, where the federal government is legally empowered to decide unilaterally, but is in fact dependent upon the expertise of highway administrations at the *Land* level (Garlichs 1980). If even such weak linkages could bring about the application of *de facto* unanimity rules, the underlying mechanisms must be powerful indeed, and they have been operative long before the federal constitutional court did write the unanimity requirement into law for some of the joint-programme areas (BVerfGE 1975, p. 96). Perhaps this might give pause to those who tend to regard unanimity in the European Community as a merely technical problem which could be solved by a more authentic interpretation of the Treaty of Rome.

The substantive outcomes of joint decision making in West Germany may be roughly described as follows. During the early 1970s, joint programmes were remarkably successful in increasing the financial resources available for their respective policy areas, and in defending their expenditure levels even after 1975, when many other programmes were severely curtailed in response to the fiscal crisis arising from the economic recession. As a matter of fact, the share of joint programmes among total federal expenditures increased from 6.8 per cent in 1970 to 9.5 per cent in 1974 and 11.2 per cent in 1977 (BMF 1985, tables 1 and 6). In the following years, however, the hopes associating joint decisions with new opportunities for more effective public policy making gave way to a growing sense of disappointment and frustration, first among political and bureaucratic insiders (Scharpf, Reissert and Schnabel 1977), but then among the wider public as well. Instead of utilizing the joint action spaces of the federal government and the *Länder* for the purpose of more active and creative problem solving, joint programmes were increasingly seen as being either inefficient, or inflexible, or unnecessary and, in any case, quite undemocratic.

On the basis of our detailed studies of decision processes and outcomes in the various joint-policy areas, we tend to agree with these criticisms and, indeed, we may have contributed something to their overall thrust and credibility. Obviously, a satisfactory restatement of our findings would be beyond the scope of this article, but the gist of our analyses might still be conveyed through a few illustrative examples.

As far as the alleged *inefficiency* is concerned, it is claimed that joint programmes tend toward 'overspending' even by their own narrow criteria of optimality, and that the inter-regional distribution of funds tends to violate even their own criteria of allocative efficiency. The first claim is, perhaps, best illustrated by the joint programme to finance capital investments in the hospital sector. As German health insurance regulations allow hospitals to charge their full operating costs to the insurance system, hospitals had every incentive to increase their capital expenditures, once the joint programme provided for the full reimbursement of investment costs. The *Länder*, on their part, did not wish to forfeit their allotted share (determined by a per capita formula) of the available federal funds – with the predictable outcome of rapidly increasing investments even in areas where hospital services were fully adequate. As a result, there are now considerable excess capacities in the hospial sector (and rapidly escalating deficits of the health insurance system). Apparently, the joint programme had eliminated existing financial constraints without being able to introduce functionally equivalent mechanisms of rational planning and efficient allocation (Schnabel 1980).

The per-capita formula for distributing federal funds among the *Länder*, which prevails not only in hospital finance but in most other joint-programme areas as well, is obviously also a source of allocative inefficiency whenever there should be significant inter-regional differences in the need for, or the existing supply of, particular public services. A glaring example was agricultural investment subsidies. There the established distribution of federal funds, favouring the big-farm regions of Northern Germany, was found to be grossly unresponsive to criteria of actual need and programme effectiveness by a programme planning and evaluation group set up by the ministers of agriculture themselves. Nevertheless, redistribution in favour of the disadvantaged small-farm and hill regions in Southern Germany proved impossible under the conditions of joint decision making.

The example of agricultural subsidies might also be used to illustrate the alleged *inflexibility* of joint decision making. Even more to the point, however, would be the case of regional industrial policy. Evolving from a tradition of *ad hoc* federal subsidies to depressed areas in the early post-war period, this had become the joint-policy area with the greatest claim to substantive and procedural rationality by the early 1970s. Far from distributing federal funds evenly among the *Länder*, or according to some arbitrary or traditional formula, regional policy managed to achieve agreement on economic criteria for subsidization and on the use of sophisticated econometric analyses for the designation of assistance areas. In the main, these were located along the eastern boundaries of the Federal Republic and in certain under-industrialized areas throughout the country.

The reputation for allocative efficiency suffered a severe blow, however, when regional industrial policy was unable to respond to the economic recession after 1974. Its impact was most severe in some of the old industrial regions, which in the past had been too prosperous to be included among the assistance areas. Now that their unemployment rates became much worse than those of many rural areas which were traditionally subsidized, agreement on an inter-regional redistribution of funds could not be reached. The best that the federal government could achieve was acquiescence of the beneficiaries of the status quo when *additional* federal funds were temporarily made available to some regions dominated by the newly depressed automobile industry. In the following years, similar *ad hoc* programmes were introduced for the Saar region, for regions dominated by the steel industry generally, and for the Bremen area suffering from the simultaneous decline of steel and ship building. Thus, regional policy is still aimed at under-industrialized peripheral areas while a growing number of special assistance programmes are used to subsidize declining industrial regions without curbing subsidies to peripheral regions. Instead of the necessary reorientation of assistance criteria in response to fundamentally changing economic circumstances, the result has been a cumulation of conceptually contradictory assistance programmes, reintroducing just that pattern of inter-regional competition for the subsidization of mobile firms which the original programme had been designed to eliminate.

The claim that some joint programmes may in fact be, or have become, *unnecessary*, is derived from a normative analysis of the type of problems that might justify joint federal-*Länder* action in the first place. Some of these justifications, such as the existence of significant inter-jurisdictional externalities, of economies of scale, or of redistributive goals (Oates and Wallace 1972; Breton and Scott 1978) seem to be as applicable now as they were when federal grant programmes originated in the early post-war period. In other areas, however, such as housing or urban renewal or, perhaps, local road construction, we have argued that the objective need for any federal involvement had disappeared over time. At least after the mid-1960s, aggregate disparities between the *Länder* had been sufficiently equalized to eliminate the need for federal intervention (and the fact that in these areas federal money is allocated to the *Länder* on a per-capita basis tends to confirm our judgement). At the same time, some of the joint programmes, in such areas as university construction, hospital investments and urban mass transport, seem to have achieved most of their original goals, so that the remaining externalities and economies of scale could be handled within *Länder* jurisdictions. In many areas, therefore, it has become difficult to identify any purposes of federal involvement which could not be equally well pursued at the *Länder* level. On the other hand, the degree of red tape generated by the cumulation of regulations in jointly financed programmes seems to be so high that the costs of delays and inefficiencies of programme implementation have themselves become a major source of irritation (Lehner 1979, 1979a; Zeh 1979; Borell 1981).

In addition to being allegedly inefficient, inflexible and, sometimes, unnecessary, joint programmes are also often criticized for their *undemocratic* character, confronting parliaments with the *faits accomplis* of bureaucratic negotiations between the two levels of government (Klatt 1979). To some extent, this criticism seems trivial, as some loss of parliamentary control is necessarily involved in all forms of intergovernmental bargaining. Parliaments may ratify or reject the outcome, but they will rarely be able to exercise direct control over the negotiation process itself – except by Carl Friedrich's 'rule of anticipated reaction'. To some extent, it may also express unhappiness with the political conditions of German federalism, combining party-political confrontation in the *Bundestag* with the need to reach all-party agreement in the *Bundesrat*, at least until 1982 (Lehmbruch 1976). But the criticism may also cut deeper. The fact that certain programmes are jointly financed by two (or sometimes three) levels of government reduces their opportunity costs at each level. In comparison to competing programmes which would have to be financed entirely from one source, joint programmes thus seem to have an 'unfair' advantage at each level. One of the consequences is the tendency to 'over-spend' on joint programmes, which was discussed above as one of the sources of inefficiency. Another is the distortion of 'real' political preferences at the local and *Land* levels whenever some programmes, but not all, are heavily subsidized by the federal government. Under such conditions, joint programmes may indeed become offers which a *Land* or a city 'cannot afford to reject', and, thus, a serious constraint upon local and regional democratic control (Späth *et al.* 1979). Finally, the role of *Länder* governments in federal legislation has tended to increase the salience of 'federal' issues in Länder elections at the expense of regional issues (Heidenheimer 1958; Hesse 1962; Lehmbruch 1976; Fabritius 1978; Abromeit 1982).

Taken together, these four lines of critical attack have seriously weakened the political attractiveness of joint programmes in West Germany since the mid-1970s (Schmidt 1980; BMF 1982). In addition, there have been specific reasons for disenchantment at each level. The federal government, for instance, found itself frustrated by the inflexibility of joint programmes when it tried to respond to the economic recession through fiscal redistribution. Instead of adjusting existing programmes as needed, it was forced to pay for additional programmes in regional industrial policy as well as in the field of public infrastructure investments (Nöllig 1977, p. 391). Furthermore, empirical research has demonstrated that increases in the volume of joint programmes were relatively ineffective as an instrument of anti-cyclical fiscal policy (Knott 1981). The *Länder* and, even more so local governments, tended to shift expenditures from one sector to another rather than to increase the overall level of their own spending as the federal government increased the volume of its grants (Reissert 1984). Thus, the federal government has again reduced its financial commitment to joint programmes from 11.2 per cent of total expenditure in 1977 to 8.2 per cent in 1980 and 7.4 per cent in 1983 (BMF 1985). One area, hospital finance, was even taken out of joint-finance arrangements altogether in 1984 (BMF 1985, pp. 43–4).

Resistance of the *Länder* against such cutbacks has been remarkably muted. It seems that some of the 'rich' *Länder* have by now concluded that joint programmes had been a bad idea to begin with, and that they would be better off regaining their freedom of independent action. Poor *Länder*, on the other hand, have been disappointed by the absence of significant redistributive effects (because of the per capita allocation of federal funds in most programmes). Furthermore, the standard of equal treatment in all programmes implied that rich and poor *Länder* had to comply with the same matching requirements, which meant that some of the poorest *Länder* were in fact unable to claim their allotted share of federal funds during the recession. They, surely, would have been better off if the earlier practice of bilaterally negotiated federal grants would have continued.

What has been described is, however, mainly the response of 'policy generalists' in the federal and *Länder* chancellories, ministries of finance and parliamentary budget committees. They seem now committed to resist all suggestions for establishing new joint programmes. But such suggestions are still forthcoming from the vertical alliances of 'policy specialists' who are pushed toward federal-*Länder* arrangements by the original logic of a constitution under which the fragmentation of functions can only be overcome through the sharing of responsibilities. In a period of general disenchantment with activist philosophies of state intervention, such pressures may be resisted. But the underlying logic is still powerful enough to prevent the wholesale dismantling of existing joint programmes.

JOINT POLICY MAKING IN THE EUROPEAN COMMUNITY

In some areas, the similarities between European policy making and joint policy making in Germany are so obvious as to be trivial. When small European programmes are simply 'tacked on' to ongoing national programmes, they will add to the bureaucratic and political costs of vertical co-ordination (Hrbek 1979) without being able to change national policy priorities very much. The only interesting question is whether European funds will add to, or substitute for, national expenditures, but the ability of national dogs to wag the European tail is not really in doubt. Thus, it is not at all surprising that decision patterns corresponding closely to the model of joint programmes in Germany have been identified in studies of the European Regional Fund (Bruder 1983; Noé 1983; Martins and Mawson 1982) and of the Social Fund (Laffan 1983), and that they also seem to govern the regional allocation of European R&D funds (Steinle and Stroetmann 1983).

The more interesting question is whether such similarities can also be found in Common Agricultural Policy which, by common consent, is the one area in which the European Community is approaching the full powers of a federal government. At least in the field of market and price regulations, CAP is not 'add on' but has replaced national programmes altogether, and its financial volume of 16.5 billion ECU in 1984 (amounting to 65 per cent of Community expenditure) is anything but trivial. Here, if nowhere else, we surely have a genuine European dog.

At the same time, CAP is formulated in a decision structure that is strikingly similar to that of joint programmes in West Germany. In both cases, important policy functions were moved up to the next-higher level of government, while their exercise remained dependent upon the unanimous agreement of member governments (Feld 1980). As in the German case, CAP was originally praised as a successful solution to the obvious co-ordination problems of national agricultural policies in an internationalized market for agricultural products, and it is now increasingly criticized for being outrageously wasteful as well as ineffective in terms of its own original goals. Most of the criticism is levelled at agricultural market policy (as distinguished from agricultural structure policy): it has burdened European consumers with food prices far above the world market; it has burdened European tax payers with a rapidly rising volume of subsidies; it is responsible for growing surpluses of agricultural production in Europe which must either be destroyed or dumped on the world market at enormous losses; and despite all these exertions, CAP was not successful in achieving its primary goals, a truly common market for agricultural products in Europe and adequate standards of living for low-income farmers (Body 1982; Rodemer 1980).

The alleged failures of CAP are directly related to its basic policy choices. At bottom, they can all be derived from the decision to protect and raise the income of European farmers through a system of price supports, rather than through direct income transfers. Once this choice had been made (which was probably inevitable in the light of the traditional agricultural protectionism of the founding members of the community), the further characteristics of CAP could be derived from the underlying structure of national interests (German and French, in particular) within the logic of unanimous decision making.

Compared to Germany, France had a much larger and, on average, more productive agricultural sector and significantly lower food prices. As a food-exporting country, France was vitally interested in free access to the larger European market, especially as she was likely to suffer from the German strength in industrial exports. German peasants, on the other hand, had little to gain and much to fear from a common European market for agricultural products, unless it was possible to maintain the high price levels prevailing in Germany for the typical products of German agriculture (mainly dairy products, meat, grains and sugar). The compromises which were reached after protracted negotiations, and dramatic Franco-German confrontations, predictably managed to accommodate both positions: the European market was to be opened to French producers (which precluded the general introduction of a system of production quotas), but prices were to be maintained at levels close to those prevailing in West Germany through a system of import levies and minimum prices (at which the 'European Agricultural Guidance and Guarantee Fund' has to purchase farm products that cannot be sold on the open market). As these 'intervention prices' were fixed far above the world market, and also far above production costs in the more productive agricultural regions in Europe, increasing agricultural surpluses were inevitable. The results were escalating guarantee payments which rapidly exceeded the revenue obtained through import levies. Far from being self-financing, the guarantee fund did require enormous subsidies, rising to more than 6 billion ECU (or about 75 per cent of the total community budget) by 1976, to almost 12 billion ECU in 1980 and to 16.5 billion ECU in 1984 (DIW 1984).

But even at that price, an effectively unified agricultural market could not be realized because of divergent national interests in the face of continuing variations in the exchange values of national currencies. When the French franc was devalued by 11 per cent in 1968, France was not willing to let food prices rise accordingly. Instead, food imports were subsidized and French agricultural exports penalized at the border. And when Germany revalued the Deutschmark later in the same year, the precedent was invoked to avoid price reductions for German farmers. A similar pattern was followed on many later occasions. The border levies on imports from low-value currency countries, and the border subsidies paid to exports from high-value currency countries, produced a 'green exchange rate' differing more and more from the official exchange rates among the currencies of member countries. As a consequence, the internal price level for agricultural products was relatively higher in the high-value currency countries such as Germany or the Netherlands, and so was the amount of EC subsidies flowing into these countries. Thus, the incentives for agricultural overproduction, which originally were the largest in France, have later tended to favour German and Dutch producers (Feld 1980).

At the same time, CAP was also unable to achieve the income goals for which it had been instituted. Price support for agricultural products meant that fewer people were leaving the farms than had been expected, so that per capita farm incomes still were not able to catch up with average earnings. Furthermore, while large and productive farms did extremely well at CAP prices, price support alone could not significantly reduce the economic plight of small peasants in agriculturally disadvantaged areas where industrial jobs are also scarce (Balz et al., 1982). A special subsidy programme for hill farmers does provide some income support, but its volume is minimal compared to the expenditures on price support.

As in the German example, the growing disappointment and frustration over CAP is beginning to have an effect. The United Kingdom and, to a lesser extent, the Federal Republic, as the two large net contributors to the Community budget, have been trying to apply financial brakes to the vicious cycle of agricultural subsidies and surpluses. The formal opportunity to do so was provided by the growing budget deficit of the Community requiring an increase of the VAT levy (which also required unanimous agreement). For several years, CAP barely managed to squeeze by without re-examination because rising prices in the world market for agricultural products had unexpectedly reduced the need for subsidies. But in the spring of 1984, some adjustment had become inevitable. It took the form of a relatively permissive quota system for milk production and a more decisive effort to eliminate border equalization subsidies and levies in order to bring the 'green exchange rate' more into line with official exchange rates (Jürgensen and Schmitz 1984). Obviously, this last measure would hurt producers in high-value currency countries, such as West Germany, and it is perhaps not surprising that the immediate German response (accepted by the Community) was to provide national subsidies to make up for these losses (DIW 1984a). Thus, the Community had eased its budgetary problems somewhat, but at the sacrifice of one of the most cherished principles of European integration – the elimination of national farm subsidies and their replacement by what should have been a *common* agricultural policy.

But even with the 1984 compromise, the future of CAP is far from assured. Incentives for overproduction have not been eliminated, quota systems have not worked well in other areas, and the spill-overs from exchange rate fluctuations are likely to disturb the regulated markets for agricultural products in the future again. Furthermore, the entry of Spain and Portugal, with large agricultural surpluses of their own, will upset the precarious equilibrium of the Community budget even though their major products are not as heavily subsidized as the 'Northern' products that were the subject of the original Franco-German compromise.

Nevertheless, judging by the past record as well as by the current 'revealed preferences' of national governments, it is more likely that CAP will hang on, even if its original logic and purpose should be distorted beyond recognition, rather than that it will be either scrapped or reorganized into a more defensible policy system. In the following sections, I will attempt to develop an analytical argument that might explain both the substantive deficiencies and the persistence of joint policy making in the Federal Republic and in the European Community.

JOINT DECISIONS AND THE PATHOLOGY OF PUBLIC POLICY

The contribution of institutional arrangements to the substantive deficiencies of joint policy making in West Germany and in the European Community are related to two simple and powerful conditions:

— that central government decisions are directly dependent upon the agreement of constituent governments; and
— that the agreement of constituent governments must be unanimous or nearly unanimous.

The German experience further suggests that the first condition may imply the second one, and that unanimity will evolve even in the absence of formal requirements. This might not be so if the number of constituent governments were very large (raising the transaction costs of unanimous agreement) or if the central government were allowed to negotiate bilateral agreements with each of the member governments separately. But in multilateral negotiations among a small group of governments over uniform regulations which will apply to all of them, unanimity seems a rational rule to follow for risk-averse participants even if they might benefit from majority decisions in the individual case (Everling 1980, p. 221). Nevertheless, it is useful to distinguish between the two aspects of 'joint decisions', their intergovernmental character, and the unanimity rule.

The importance of the *inter-governmental* aspect becomes clear when one compares the representation or regional interests in the US Senate and in the German *Bundesrat*. In both cases, the territorial distribution of societal interests is emphasized at the expense of other dimensions of multi-dimensional interests (and at the expense of the Rousseauean ideal of the 'general interest'). But while US Senators, ideally, represent only the interests of their constituents (mediated through their own interest in re-election), the *Bundesrat* also (or, rather, primarily) represents the institutional self-interests of *Länder* governments. Thus, Claus Offe's *'Interesse des Staates an sich selbst'* (1975, p. 13) will be introduced twice, as 'withinput' and as 'input' in Eastonian language (Easton 1965, p. 54), into the political processes of the central government. One might expect, therefore, that the policy output of joint decision systems, when compared with unitary governments or the American model of federalism, will be less responsive to constituency interests and more oriented toward the institutional self-interests of governments and their 'bureaucratic convenience' (Tullock 1965; Niskanen 1971). More important, however, is the fact that these governmental interests are not, in the strict sense, 'represented' at all. Instead, they are direct participants in central decision processes. In that regard, what we have is a system of direct, 'participatory' democracy without any of the safeguards for detached reflection on the general interest, by non-instructed delegates, which has been emphasized by theorists of representative government ever since Edmund Burke (Scharpf 1970). Also, as far as member states are concerned, there is none of the 'generalization of support' which Talcott Parsons (1967, pp. 231–4) thought necessary for the maintenance of effective government in a democracy. In joint-decision systems, the central government is not free to respond creatively to external demands, or to anticipate future consensus; its actions are determined directly by the immediate self-interests of member governments.

Nevertheless, differences are important. While decisions of the European Community are completely determined by the outcome of negotiations among member governments, the German federal government has a political identity, resources and strategic and tactical capabilities of its own. It cannot adopt and implement effective public policy without *Länder* agreement, but it can design and pursue bargaining strategies against the *Bundesrat* which the European Commission cannot similarly pursue against the Council of Ministers or the European Council.

But the German federal government is also paying a price for its greater strategic autonomy: being able to bargain with the *Länder* over policies which it considers essential to the national interest (or to its own political survival), it still must obtain their agreement. Sometimes it may be possible to design 'win-win solutions' which are intrinsically attractive to the *Länder* as well. More often, its original policy proposals were watered down in substantive compromises. And if the federal government insisted upon its objectives, it often had to buy support for national policies at the expense of permanent improvements of the institutional and financial position of the *Länder*. Thus, just as the emperors of the Holy Roman Empire were forced to expend their dynastic possessions and, finally, the imperial prerogatives, in order to maintain the loyalty of their vassal princes, so the German federal government has seen its share of total revenue reduced from 53 per cent in 1970 to 48 per cent in 1983 (BMF 1985, Table 2). As there was, of course no corresponding reduction of federal responsibilities, the total volume of the federal debt increased from 54 per cent of expenditures in 1970 to 105 per cent in 1980, while *Länder* debts increased only from 62 per cent to 76 per cent of expenditure during the same period (Simmert and Wagner 1981, p. 455). Being entirely the creature of member governments, the European Community could not, of course, be similarly exploited by them.

But what are the implications of inter-governmentalism for the substance of public policy? The most clear-cut connection seems to exist with the alleged tendency of joint programmes to increase expenditures beyond the level that would be politically acceptable within a unitary government. This tendency seems to follow directly from 'rational' calculations of financial costs and political benefits at each level of government. If we assume that elected officials are sensitive to interest group pressure at all levels of government, and that interest groups are capable of presenting demands and exerting pressure at each level as well, then the political benefits associated with positive responses to interest group demands will be fully realized at each level, even if the response is delivered by a joint programme. On the other hand, if the joint programme is also jointly financed, its costs will be reduced accordingly for each level of government. Compared to single-government decisions, therefore, joint decisions have politically more attractive cost-benefit ratios. To put it crudely, more votes can be bought for less money at each level.

The conditions assumed in this model are closely approximated in West Germany, where governments at the local, regional and federal levels are dependent upon direct elections, where interest groups are active at all levels, and where joint programmes have matching requirements involving at least two, and usually three, levels of government in their financing. Under such conditions, the separate calculation of costs and benefits at each level will indeed suggest a relative increase of expenditures on joint programmes at the expense of programmes which have to be financed entirely by a single level of government. Our interviews in Germany have shown that active participants in policy processes are fully aware of these mechanisms – which explains why the vertical coalitions of interest groups, politicians and bureaucrats specialized in a certain field, are completely unanimous, in spite of all other internal disagreements, in defending the privileged status of their policy field as one of the joint programmes. But what about CAP, where at least two of the conditions assumed above seem to be missing? First, there are no matching requirements in the core areas of price subsidies, so that expenditures are all on the European level. Second, even though there are now direct elections to the European Parliament, it is obviously impossible to interpret CAP as the response of vote-maximizing politicians at the European level. By contrast to the German model, where all levels of government are profiting from joint programmes, it seems that the European Community has to bear the full costs without capturing any of the political benefits associated with CAP.

But, of course, it is national, rather than European, politicians who are determining CAP choices. And their cost-benefit calculations are obviously quite different. If we differentiate, for the sake of clarification, between the calculations of policy specialists and of generalists (say, national ministers of agriculture and national ministers of finance), the former must see CAP as an entirely free good whose production they have every incentive to maximize. For the finance ministers, on the other hand, a self-interested response would seem to depend mainly on the net position of their country with regard to the EC budget. Net beneficiaries would surely have less reason to object to the cancerous growth of CAP than net contributors. Thus it must be the acquiescence, or resistance, of net-contributing countries, the Federal Republic and the United Kingdom in particular, which explains the growth of the CAP.

For most of the period since the commencement of CAP in the middle of the 1960s, it has been acquiescence. The Germans were, and are still (Höhnen 1984) aware of the fact that they had to buy CAP in exchange for the common market for industrial products which favoured German exports. And they also know that the high price levels prevailing under CAP, which are the cause of overproduction and, hence, of rising subsidies, were adopted at their own insistence to protect the prevailing income levels of German farmers. Thus, the one country that should have had a financial interest in limiting CAP was among its original supporters for reasons unrelated to the specific incentives and constraints of its decision structure.

Of course it is true that the Germans, like everybody else, had vastly underestimated the dynamics of price support, overproduction and escalating subsidies in European agriculture – but when they found out, they were already caught in the rigidities of an ongoing decision system based upon the principle of unanimous agreement. *Unanimity* is generally considered as the decision rule which is most in conformity with the methodological individualism of public choice theory. If collective decisions depend upon the voluntary agreement of all members of the community, they are also likely to meet the welfare-theoretical criterion of Pareto optimality (Buchanan and Tullock 1962). Difficulties are likely to arise from increasing transaction costs in large communities and from the disruptive consequences of 'strategic voting', when members are tempted to conceal their true preferences for public goods in order to exact concessions in the allocation of costs (Buchanan 1975, p. 41). Given the small number of member governments, and the transparency of their (institutional and constituency) interests, neither problem should be of great importance in German federalism or in the European community.

What public-choice theorists have generally neglected, however, is the importance of the 'default condition' or 'reversion rule', which was recently pointed out by Elinor Ostrom (1984). The implications of unanimity (or of any other decision rule) are crucially dependent upon what will be the case if agreement is not achieved. The implicit assumption is usually that in the absence of an agreed decision there will be no collective rule at all, and that individuals will remain free to pursue their own goals with their own means. Unfortunately, these benign assumptions are applicable to joint decision systems only at the formative stage of the 'constitutional contract', when the system is first established. Here, indeed, agreement is unlikely unless each of the parties involved expects joint solutions to be more advantageous than the status quo of separate decisions. Parties with no interest in joint decisons will either opt out or will have to be bribed with side payments. Thus, the original agreement is indeed likely to be in everybody's interest, which may explain the general sense of satisfaction, enthusiasm and optimism associated with the early years of both European integration and joint policy-making in West Germany.

The 'default condition' changes, however, when we move from single-shot decisions to an ongoing joint-decision system in which the exit option is foreclosed. Now non-agreement is likely to assure the *continuation* of existing common policies, rather than reversion to the 'zero base' of individual action. In a dynamic environment, the implications for the substantive quality of public policy are obvious: when circumstances change, existing policies are likely to become sub-optimal even by their own original criteria. Under the unanimity rule, however, they cannot be abolished or changed as long as they are still preferred by even a single member. Thus, the association of unanimity and Pareto optimality emphasized by public-choice theorists seems to be restricted to single-shot decisions. In ongoing decision systems, by contrast, unanimity is likely to be associated with a systematic deterioration of the 'goodness of fit' between public policy and the relevant policy environment – unless there should be very powerful mechanisms of consensus formation.

The problem is even more serious when the freedom of individual action is entirely eliminated even in areas where there is no prior agreed-on policy at all. Obviously, this is not a necessary characteristic of joint-decision systems: federal constitutions usually allow for the 'concurrent jurisdiction' of member governments as long as federal legislation has not 'pre-empted the field'. But if joint-decision systems are specifically set up to regulate externalities of member-government policies, or to establish a truly common market, then the field must be pre-empted (Weiler 1982). That also means, however, that member governments will be precluded from dealing individually with pressing problems even if the Community cannot agree on an effective solution.

In short, joint-decision systems are doubly vulnerable to the consequences of non-agreement: they may be incapable of reaching effective agreement, and they may lose the independent capabilities for action of their member governments. As a consequence, their overall problem-solving capacity may decline – certainly in comparison to a unitary state of similar size and resources, but possibly also in comparison to smaller states, with less resources but an unfettered ability to act individually. Everything depends, therefore, upon the capacity of ongoing joint-decision systems to generate, maintain and adjust agreement on joint policies in the face of inevitably differing interests, goals and perceptions, and in the face of inevitably changing circumstances.

'PROBLEM SOLVING' AND 'BARGAINING' IN JOINT DECISIONS

Obviously, effective agreement is problematical under all conditions (even Robinson Crusoe had difficulty in making up his mind). But in decision theory it is increasingly recognized that the nature of the problem, and its inherent difficulty, varies systematically with the modalities under which effective agreement must be achieved. One dimension of these modalities is defined by the applicable decision rules (unanimous, majority or unilateral/hierarchical decisions). The other dimension is defined by the prevailing orientation of participants, and by the strategies which they are expected to employ in order to influence the outcome. There is, as yet, no agreement on terminology: March and Simon (1958) discuss different 'processes of conflict resolution', Richardson (1982) refers to different 'styles of decision-making', while Boboma (1976) proposes to distinguish among different 'power systems'. But substantive agreement on the distinctions actually subsumed under these different labels seems to be remarkably high: March and Simon's (1958, p. 129) four-fold classification of 'problem-solving', 'persuasion', 'bargaining' and 'politics' is overlapping with Olsen's 'problem solving', 'bargaining', 'mobilization' and 'confrontation' (Olsen et al. 1982). And it also seems possible to relate Bonoma's (1976) discussion of 'bilateral', 'mixed' and 'unilateral power systems' and Bühl's (1984) emphasis upon dominant orientations toward 'values', 'interests' or 'power' to these more process-oriented classifications of decision making.

For present purposes I will adopt Richardson's generic label of 'decision styles' and a three-fold distinction between 'problem solving', 'bargaining' and 'confrontation'. At the most general level, each of these 'styles' may be characterized by specific value orientations and sanctioning strategies: 'problem solving' by the appeal to common ('solidaristic') values and by resort to ostracism and exclusion as the ultimate collective sanction; 'bargaining' by the appeal to the individual self-interests of all (necessary) participants and by resort to incentives; and 'confrontation' by the appeal to the interests of the dominant individual or coalition and by resort to power and coercion as the ultimate sanction. While these definitions are logically independent from the applicable rules of decision (prescribing 'unanimous', 'majority' or 'unilateral/hierarchical' assent for effective decisions), that does not preclude substantive interdependence. Obviously, 'confrontation' under majority rules means something different from 'confrontation' under the unanimity rule. In each case, therefore, it is the specific combination of a decision style with a decision rule which will determine the characteristic capacity of the decision system to reach effective agreement on collective policy choices.

Returning, after this exercise in conceptual clarification, to the problems of conflict resolution and consensus formation in joint-decision systems operating under the unanimity rule, one might consider 'confrontation' as the least promising style of decision. As German education reformers had to learn the hard way, there is no sense in trying to push people around if you are dependent upon their agreement in the end. Indeed, Gerhard Lehmbruch (1976) has based his incisive analysis of the political dynamics of German federalism during the period of the Social-Liberal coalition squarely upon the idea that there was a fundamental contradiction between the confrontation politics staged by the federal government against the parliamentary opposition, and the manifest need to obtain all-party agreement in the *Bundesrat* for all major policy initiatives. But, of course, confrontation under the unanimity rule is a highly asymmetric game, and there is no reason to assume that the opposition parties should have been equally unhappy about its outcomes.

More generally, 'confrontation' under the unanimity rule seems highly serviceable for participants interested in preserving the status quo (or in exacting maximum concessions for their agreement to policy changes). It is the proponents of policy change who depend upon agreement, and who are likely to suffer defeat when a confrontational decision style prevails. And even here there are differences, depending upon whether the exit option is available, and whether it can be employed as a credible threat. In German federalism, exit is generally foreclosed in regulatory programmes, but individual *Länder* might opt out of matching-grants programmes. In the European Community, however, 'secession' also continues to be a live political option which may be invoked in confrontation strategies. Both Charles de Gaulle and Margaret Thatcher have been able to achieve significant policy changes in this fashion. But, of course, secession might not have quite the same threat value for all member countries, and its credibility might be quite low in the case of countries whose economic stake in, and political attachment to, the Community is known to be very high. On the whole, therefore 'confrontation' is indeed the least promising decision style for policy changes and institutional reforms in joint-decision systems. If progress is to be achieved at all, it must be achieved within a 'bargaining' or 'problem-solving' framework in which it is not possible to short-circuit the requirement of unanimous agreement, and to impose solutions unilaterally.

Of these 'bargaining' seems to be the less demanding and, hence, more robust decision style. It is premised upon the assumption that participants will pursue their individual self-interest, and that agreement can only be obtained if its anticipated utility is at least as high for each participant as the anticipated utility of no co-operation (Nash 1950). 'Problem solving' in its pure form, on the other hand, is premised upon the existence of a common utility function and the irrelevance of individual self-interest for the decision at hand – either because individual interests are submerged in the common interest, or because they are effectively neutralized through institutional arrangements separating the pursuit of common goals from the distribution of costs and benefits. Furthermore, while disagreement may be an entirely acceptable outcome in 'bargaining', it is not so in 'problem solving', where the common commitment to the common goal would delegitimate open non-co-operation. But that does not mean that agreement should be more easily obtained: battles over the proper definition of the common goal, or over appropriate strategies, might indeed be more bitter and divisive than the search for mutually agreeable compromises at the 'bargaining' table (Bonoma 1976).

Two further points need to be emphasized. First, the distinction between 'bargaining' and 'problem solving' is not logically related to the difference between zero-sum and non-zero-sum games. Indeed, in the prototypical exchange situation analysed by Nash (1950), bargains will only be struck if individual valuations of tradeable goods are sufficiently different to allow *both* parties to increase their respective utilities. Conversely, zero-sum conflicts over the distribution of limited resources are perhaps better resolved in the 'problem-solving' style by recourse to common norms and values and, perhaps, to adjudication, rather than by pure 'bargaining', where the have-nots are without recourse against the distribution of original 'endowments'.

Second, just as 'mixed-motive games', combining elements of zero-sum and positive-sum situations, are more important in real-world situations than either of the pure game forms (Bacharach and Lawler 1980), so is there also a wide overlap between 'bargaining' and 'problem solving' in real decision processes. The empirical distribution may be highly asymmetrical, however. While pure 'bargaining' seems to be quite frequent in practice, it is unlikely that there will be many 'problem-solving' interactions without an admixture of 'bargaining' behaviour. Thus, decision styles may evolve and change over time in real-world decision systems, but it is possible that their dynamics will have only one stable resting point at the 'bargaining' end of the continuum.

In discussing this hypothesis, it seems useful to distinguish the pursuit of common interests from that of a class of individual interests whose realization does depend upon co-operation. In the case of jointly produced private goods it is indeed likely that purely self-interested exchange relationships may develop into stable networks of mutual dependence in which participants will anticipate, and respect, the self-interest of their partners (Scharpf 1978). But that will not, by itself, move interactions out of the 'bargaining' mode. The same is true of that 'cooperation among egoists' which Axelrod (1981) discovered in computer-simulated iterations of the Prisoners' Dilemma and in similarly structured real-world situations (Axelrod 1984). The Prisoners' Dilemma is, after all, one of the 'paradoxes of rationality' (Howard 1971) in which narrowly selfish calculations will lead to sub-optimal outcomes in terms of individual self-interest. What has been discovered, following theoretical work in biological evolution (Trivers 1971; Dawkins 1976), is a certain strategy ('Tit-for-Tat') which is co-operative but non-exploitable, and which does so well in long iterations of the game that it tends to drive other strategies out of competition. Thus, co-operation eliminates the 'paradox' and allows participants to return to the rational pursuit of their individual self-interests.

By contrast, what is necessary for the 'problem-solving' style to emerge is an orientation towards *common* interests, values or norms which are distinct from the individual self-interest of participants (Bonoma 1976, p. 507) and which, therefore, may facilitate voluntary agreement even when sacrifices in terms of individual self-interest are necessary and cannot be immediately compensated through 'side payments' or 'package deals'. Only when this is possible is there a good chance that ongoing decision systems operating under the unanimity rule might be able to avoid the 'joint-decision trap'.

The emergence of such common orientations may be rooted in genuine altruism – a human motive whose possibility is certainly not ruled out by methodological individualism (Sen 1970; Elster 1979, p. 141) but which, nevertheless, is unlikely to play much of a role in interactions among governments, rather than among individuals. More pertinent may be the perception of a common 'identity' defined in terms of an ethnic or cultural homogeneity or a 'community of fate' derived from shared perceptions of a common history, of a common 'manifest destiny' (or common ideological goals), or of a common vulnerability. As Peter Katzenstein (1984, 1985) has pointed out, it is the latter characteristic which helps to explain the greater ability to achieve policy consensus of the smaller European states, as compared to the larger ones. And it is worth emphasizing that the perception of a common vulnerability may be derived not only from the exposure to external military or economic threats, but also from the living memory of fratricidal internal conflicts, as in the cases of Austria and Finland – which may also explain the rapid evolution of neo-corporatist arrangements in post-Franco Spain (Pérez-Diaz 1985).

Unfortunately, neither German federalism nor the European Community have been able to profit much from such perceptions of common identity or common fate during the last decade or so. In Germany, the post-war ideology of 'social partnership' is eroding under the impact of the world-wide recession (Vobruba 1983) and party-political confrontation during the period of the Social-Liberal coalition did reinforce ideological divisions in the political arena. Europe, on the other hand, has certainly profited from the traumatic memories of two world wars. But once the European Defence Community had failed, the overriding problems of common European vulnerability, protection against Germany and protection against the Soviet Union, were institutionally entrusted to NATO (and substantively to the United States), rather than to the Community. In most other regards, of course, the present European condition is one which tends to emphasize historic, ethnic, cultural, ideological and economic diversity, rather than identity, at least when compared to the smaller European states which, in some cases, are doing very well under the near-unanimity rules of consociational democracies (Lehmbruch 1967; Lijphart 1975; Katzenstein 1984).

The question is, therefore, whether 'problem solving' does have any chance at all in joint-decision systems which do not have the benefit of a traditional sense of common identity or an overriding perception of common vulnerability? There is a certain parallel here to early sociological discussions of *Gemeinschaft* and *Gesellschaft*, and to the pessimistic hypothesis, entertained by Tönnies (1963) and Freyer (1964, p. 182), of an unidirectional erosion of the traditional motivational resources of *Gemeinschaft*. But, of course, at the interpersonal level, *Gemeinschaften* are newly created all the time, and the same is true in modern industries, where they have been rediscovered under the new label of 'clans' or the old one of 'communities' (Ouchi 1980; Streeck and Schmitter 1984; Hollingsworth and Lindberg 1985). But it is also true that the evolution of 'communal' or 'solidaristic' norms among egotistic actors (who are not part of a traditional community, or shocked into solidarity by the awareness of their fatal vulnerability to internal conflict) must be a fragile process which is easily reversed.

This is true even under the best of circumstances, when the non-negative-sum character of the common enterprise is fully recognized by all participants. The willingness to accept unilateral sacrifices, on the understanding that they will not be exploited but reciprocated by others when the occasion arises, presupposes a high degree of mutual trust. If that is not yet established, but needs to be built into the process itself, the most fatal risk is bona fide disagreement over the purpose and direction of the common enterprise, which is easily misinterpreted as defection from the common endeavour. When that happens, any unilateral retaliation is likely to provoke more suspicion and even harder retaliation, setting in motion that downward spiral of 'sacrilege' and 'just retribution' which Victor Pérez-Diaz (1985) found in the Basque conflict. Thus, the absence of any strong moral, ideological or idealistic commitment on all sides is almost a necessary precondition for the *gradual* evolution of communal norms. But in the absence of such non-egotistic commitments it is also hard to see how community interactions might rise above the calculus of individual self-interest.

The best hope of avoiding this 'double bind' exists, of course, under conditions of continuous economic growth, when the common enterprise is clearly a positive-sum game from which all are profiting. And if it is possible to establish agreement on common criteria for the distribution of benefits and contributions under these benign circumstances, there is at least a chance that the agreement might hold even when the nature of the game changes to zero-sum or negative-sum.

On theoretical grounds, there is indeed reason to assume that commonly accepted 'rules of fairness' may evolve from the interaction of purely egotistical participants (Baumol 1982; Runge 1984). Similar processes of rule generation must have been going on in German federalism and in the European Community as well, or else even the limited degree of mutual accommodation and adaptation to changing circumstances, which they have in fact achieved, would have been impossible. But given the absence of a more fundamental ideological agreement on common values, purposes and strategies, one would also expect such rules to be relatively simple and 'obvious' in the sense defined by Schelling (1960) and, hence, quite rigid in the face of changing circumstances.

In our studies of joint decisions in German federalism, we have indeed discovered a number of such rules which all seem to follow from a common logic of conflict avoidance or conflict minimization under conditions of continuing goal dissensus (Scharp, Reissert and Schnabel 1976, pp. 62, 218–35; 1978). The most important one, governing institutional change, will be discussed in the next section. More pertinent to the present discussion are two rules governing the distribution of federal funds among the *Länder*. According to the first, all *Länder* must be allowed to benefit *equally*, according to some simple and straightforward formula, such as the number of inhabitants or, perhaps, the number of registered automobiles for the allocation of road-building funds. But if equality cannot be maintained, the fall-back rule seems to require that the losers in relative terms must at least receive their past share in absolute terms.

The fall-back rule is, of course, what one would expect from individualistic bargaining, with status quo policy as the base line for everyone, while the first rule has some claims to greater dignity. In jurisprudence and philosophy, formal equality is justified as the measure of distributive justice which should be applied in the absence of more compelling criteria based upon either unequal needs or unequal contributions (Noll 1984; Rawls 1971). As it is difficult, under conditions of party-political competition, ideological heterogeneity and significant differences in size, wealth and economic conditions, for the German *Länder* to agree upon substantive criteria of unequal need and merit, it is perhaps not surprising that formal equality, in the form of uniform conditions and per capita formulas, prevailed in most of the joint programmes in West Germany. But the rule obviously does not explain the highly unequal allocation of contributions and benefits among the member countries of the European Community, or in German regional assistance.

In both cases there was, at least originally, a rough agreement on the recognition of unequal needs and deserts which, in the EC, was presumably based upon the perception of a fundamental asymmetry of interests between West Germany and the rest of the Community. If the Germans were seen as the major beneficiaries of a common market for industrial goods, it was only fair that they should bear the major burden of EC financial contributions, and that they should benefit less from Community programmes. A slightly different justification could point out that the Community lacks the mechanism of horizontal transfer payments which were used to reduce fiscal inequalities among the German *Länder* long before the invention of joint programmes (Franzmeyer and Seidel 1976). Some EC programmes, such as the Regional Fund and the Social Fund, should thus be regarded as functional equivalents to fiscal equalization (Reissert 1979) which, of course, would preclude reference to formal equality as the relevant criterion of justice.

When the same contribution rules were applied to the United Kingdom, however (or now to Portugal), they had distributive consequences which certainly the British did not consider fair. Yet, under the unanimity requirement, the Community was unable to agree on new rules which would have redefined the criterion of fairness in the light of the new situation. Instead, the decision style changed from a search for just solutions to 'bloody-minded' bargaining and even confrontation, and it took the combined threats of British exit and of the bankruptcy of CAP to achieve even the *ad hoc* adjustments of 1984. Apparently, rules of fairness that depart from formal equality are less 'obvious' in the sense defined by Schelling (1960) and, therefore, more difficult to redefine consensually in the face of changing circumstances. If they are challenged, the joint-decision system is more likely to revert to the calculus of pure individual self-interest than to adjust its standards of fairness.

This does not mean that consensus is now impossible, and that joint-decision systems will necessarily destroy themselves through self-blockage. In an ongoing system without exit, and with 'pre-emption', pressures to reach some kind of agreement are very powerful, indeed (Weiler 1982, p. 49). But the terms of agreement are likely to be defined by a 'bargaining' logic in which the benefits received under the present policy become the base line below which nobody will settle. In the case of regional assistance in Germany, additional federal funds were required for add-on programmes dealing with the new problems of declining industrial areas. In the absence of a federal government with independent resources, or of an 'hegemony' that could be exploited (Olson and Zeckhauser 1966), 'log rolling', 'package deals' and 'side payments' are the typical modes of conflict resolution in decision systems confronted with a plurality of veto positions (Taylor 1980).

Given the claims to a substantive 'intelligence of democracy' associated with seemingly similar patterns of bargaining in American pluralism (Lindblom 1965; Dahl 1967), it is perhaps necessary to spell out more precisely what I consider the deficiencies of 'bargaining' in joint-decision systems. They are not primarily related to the difference between 'disjointed incrementalism' and an over-ambitious concept of 'synoptic problem solving' (Braybrooke and Lindblom 1963). What is important, instead, is whether analyses (and disagreements) relating to the best way of achieving *common* goals can, or cannot, be effectively separated from disagreement over the *individual* distribution of costs and benefits. If members distrust the fairness of distribution rules, they will be tempted, or even forced, to link substantive and distributive issues. Using their veto on substantive choices in order to improve their distributive position, they must contribute to the interminable haggling over package deals and side payments that are characteristic of all EC decisions. But, of course, distributive issues are legitimate even in a *Gemeinschaft*, and if they cannot be neutralized by agreed-upon rules of fairness, they must somehow be settled in negotiations.

There are, however, many decision situations in which adequate compensation is impossible – either because the losses involved would be of a non-quantifiable, qualitative nature, or because of uncertainty over their future incidence and magnitude, or finally because of the negative-sum character of the decision situation itself. The first case is of considerable importance not only under conditions of ideological disagreement, but even more so when considerations of national 'sovereignty', or *Länder* 'autonomy', or interference with established bureaucratic routines and networks of interaction, come to play a significant role. It is under such conditions that the imperatives of 'conflict avoidance' and 'non intervention' have their strongest impact upon the substance of joint decisions in Germany, and the same mechanisms seem to restrict the directive effectiveness of Community policies and of their implementation (Laffan 1983). The second case seems to be particularly damaging under conditions, labelled the 'interdependence trap' by Paul Taylor (1980, p. 374), when the costs of an advantageous policy proposal are well defined and certain, while the benefits are more diffuse and uncertain. In the third case, finally, the negative-sum character of the overall situation may not be generally appreciated while participants are bargaining over the avoidance of individual losses. It is plausible that these difficulties became more acute when the world economic environment changed from benign to hostile in the 1970s (Zieburta 1982).

In all three cases, however, the outcome is similar: Individual losses expected from a policy option which would be collectively optimal, cannot be adequately compensated through side payments. Under such conditions, therefore, 'bargaining' is likely to lead to solutions which are unable to achieve realizable common gains or to prevent avoidable common losses.

To summarize a perhaps overly involved line of argument, unanimity is a decision rule which can claim welfare-theoretic optimality, most plausibly, for single-shot decisions. In ongoing joint-decision systems, from which exit is precluded or very costly, non-agreement would imply the self-defeating continuation of past policies in the face of a changing policy environment. Thus, pressures to reach agreement will be great. The substance of agreement will be affected, however, by the prevailing style of decision-making. In its ability to achieve effective responses to a changing policy environment, the 'bargaining' style is clearly inferior to the 'problem-solving' style. But the preconditions of 'problem-solving' – the orientation towards common goals, values and norms – are difficult to create, and they are easily eroded in cases of ideological conflict, mutual distrust or disagreement over the fairness of distribution rules. Thus, reversion to a 'bargaining' style of decision making was characteristic of German federalism during the 1970s, and it seems to have been characteristic of the European Community ever since the great confrontations of the mid-1960s. The price to be paid is not simply a prevalence of distributive conflicts complicating all substantive decisions, but a systematic tendency towards sub-optimal substantive solutions. In short, it is the combination of the unanimity rule and a bargaining style which explains the pathologies of public policy associated with joint decisions in Germany and in Europe.

JOINT DECISIONS AND THE DYNAMICS OF EUROPEAN INTEGRATION

At this point, we can return to the concerns raised in the introduction. Why is it that real developments since the mid-1960s – the frustration without disintegration and resilience without progress – have disappointed hopes for a dynamic deepening and widening of European integration and invalidated predictions of an inevitable return to the intergovernmental relations of sovereign nation states? An explanation has been derived from the decision logic inherent in the particular institutional arrangements of the European community. Relating these findings to both the optimistic and pessimistic prognoses of the future course of European integration, the following conclusions appear to be warranted.

First, the early optimism of neo-functional integration theorists was based upon the expectation that a 'new political community, superimposed over the pre-existing ones' would emerge through the gradual shifting of the loyalties, expectations and activities of political elites toward the new European arena (Haas 1958, p. 16). The basic mechanism driving the process of political integration was identified by Ernst Haas in the concept of 'spill over' which, essentially, meant that narrowly defined European decision functions would have lateral effects on other interests which, in turn, would redirect their demands, expectations and, eventually, loyalties to the European political process. As a consequence, the support for European integration among interest groups and political parties would grow, and governments would realize that further sabotage or evasions were politically unprofitable. Hence, the powers of European institutions would be enlarged, with the consequence of further spill overs eventually bringing about a genuine political community and the acceptance of a full-fledged federal authority (Haas 1958, pp. XXXIII/IV, 3–31, 283–317).

While later interpretations by neo-functionalists, including Ernst Haas himself, have been more cautious, differentiating and, ultimately, even agnostic in their predictions (Haas 1964; 1971; Haas and Schmitter 1964; Lindberg 1963; Lindberg and Scheingold 1970; Schmitter 1969; 1970; Scheingold 1970), they have continued to place their primary emphasis upon the interaction between European decisions and the interests, expectations, activities and loyalties of interest groups, political parties, politicians and bureaucrats, in short: upon the perspectives and actions of a plurality of political elites, rather than upon the institutional self-interests of national governments operating within the constraints of particular institutional arrangements at the European level (Bulmer 1983, p. 353). As William Wallace (1982, p. 64–5) has put it: 'The success of the neo-functional approach depended upon national governments not noticing – in effect – the gradual draining away of their lifeblood to Brussels.'

The tendency to treat institutional arrangements not as a powerful independent variable, but merely as the resultant of economic, social and political interactions, was even more characteristic of the older, 'functionalist' school of international organization, as illustrated by David Mitrany's dictum (1975, p. 27) that 'in the last resort, the form of government and its laws and institutions are shaped and reshaped by the restless flux of the community's social pressures.' And the same non-institutional perspective is, of course also characteristic of the 'communications' approach to political integration developed by Karl Deutsch (1953) and his collaborators (Deutsch *et al.* 1957; 1964; Merrit and Russett 1981).

The re-emergence of 'inter-governmentalism' in the European Community after 1966 (Wallace, Wallace and Webb 1977, pp. 24–5; Taylor 1983, pp. 60–92) came as a disappointment to all such theories of political integration, giving rise to several varieties of *ad hoc* explanations emphasizing either changes in 'background' variables external to the theory, or the historical uniqueness of De Gaulle and his personal intervention. By contrast, and with the benefit of hindsight, my explanations assume explicitly that 'institutions do matter'.

Given this premise, the two most powerful institutional conditions affecting the processes of European integration are, first, the fact that national governments are making European decisions and, second, the fact that these decisions have to be unanimous. The 'joint-decision trap' set up by these two conditions is responsible for the pathologies of substantive public policy described and analysed above.

But joint-decision systems are a 'trap' in yet another, and more important sense. They are able to block their own further institutional evolution. This possibility has been overlooked by functionalist and neo-functionalist writers, and even William Riker, the most agnostic student of federalism (1966), had assumed that in any federal arrangement one of two tendencies, 'centralizing' or 'peripheralizing', must eventually win out (1964, p. 6), with the 'structure of the party system' as the controlling variable (1964, pp. 129–36). While peripheralized federalisms will gradually fall apart, centralized federalisms will 'become more like unitary or imperial governments in time' (1964, p. 7). But neither outcome is happening in either the EC or Germany. The institutional arrangements of German federalism are quite stable, and the European Community seems to be securely 'stuck between sovereignty and integration' (Wallace 1982, p. 67). Our studies of joint decisions in German federalism have discovered a mechanism that preserves the institutional status quo: it is the political priority of substantive solutions over institutional reforms.

All through the 1970s, the German federal government was confronted with urgent problems of unemployment and inflation that seemed to require vigorous action at the national level which, however, depended upon the collaboration of the *Länder*. Even though the majority of the *Bundesrat* consisted of *Länder* governments controlled by parties in opposition to the Social-Liberal federal government, collaboration was never flatly refused. If that had been the case, the legitimacy of the *veto* position of the *Bundesrat* could have become a major political issue which might have strengthened centralist forces. As it was, the *Länder* were always willing to compromise on substantive policy, and the federal government was too hard pressed politically to refuse the compromises which were offered. In the process, however, the institutional position of the *Länder* was continuously improved. Fiscal resources were shifted from the federal level to the *Länder*, precisely during the decade when the federal government was more activist and interventionist than ever before. During the same period, the *Länder* have time and again consented to enlarge the substantive responsibilities of the federal government, but they have also increased their own control over the exercise of these responsibilities. In order to avoid this gradual erosion of its institutional position, the federal government would have had to provoke the direct confrontation of the *Länder* over institutional issues. But under the pressure of urgent substantive problems, it was never willing to risk the complete blockage of joint-decision processes in the (uncertain) hope of improving its position in the longer run. Acting as a 'locally maximizing machine' (Elster 1979, p. 4), the federal government contributed to the tightening of the ropes that reduced its own ability to act.

The situation is even more one-sided in the European Community. In the absence of a European government with a popular political base of its own, all possibilities of institutional transformation are entirely determined by the self-interests of national governments. And even those among them which most vigorously support activist and expansionary European policies are likely to hedge their bets when it comes to relinquishing their veto powers. Conversely, the 'reluctant Europeans' among member governments have been much more willing to accept disagreeable compromises on substantive policy than to weaken their own institutional control over the substance of future decisions. As a consequence, the jurisdiction of the Community has expanded, and Community law has achieved the effectiveness of the legal order of a federal state – but the price has been 'an ever closer national control exercised in the decision processes' (Weiler 1982, pp. 46–7).

Thus, the establishment of the European Council should be interpreted as a symbol of the increasing importance of European policy choices and as an attempt to assert the control of national policy generalists over the vertical alliances of policy specialists dominating the Council of Ministers as well as the European Commission. But that only means that it is national heads of government, rather than national ministers, who are likely to tighten their grip in European policy making (Bulmer, 1983). Nor are these conclusions controverted by the packages of compromises and reforms culminating in the 'Single European Act' of 28 February 1986 which seems to have ended the long period of confrontations and deadlock of the 1970s and early 1980s. Spain and Portugal were finally admitted and interim settlements for the budget issues were found. Even more spectacularly, governments committed themselves to complete the 'internal market' – 'an area without internal frontiers in which the free movement of goods, persons, services and capital is assured' – by the end of 1992 (article 13), and they also renewed their aspirations toward an 'Economic and Monetary Union' requiring the convergence of national economic and monetary policies (article 20).

Compared to these substantive commitments, whose implementation continues to depend upon the agreement of national governments, the institutional changes which were adopted seem to fall far short of the visionary goals of achieving 'genuine political unity' through the creation of 'effective democratic institutions' that had been asserted only a year before (Report of the Dooge Committee 1984). To be sure, on a long list of routine decisions, qualified-majority voting in the Council (which always would have been possible) is now explicitly provided for in the Treaty – and it is apparently practised quite frequently, with governments preferring to be outvoted, rather than having to agree formally to an inevitable but unpopular Council decision. It remains to be seen whether the weakening of the pressures toward consensus will be outweighed by the lower threshold of agreement. At any rate, a long list of more important decisions, and all further evolutions of the Treaty structure, are explicitly reserved for unanimous voting, and the general principle under which all members may exercise a veto in matters affecting their vital national interests remains unchallenged. Ironically, the very limited efforts to strengthen the powers of the European Parliament not only have taken the form of adding another institutional hurdle to European decision making, but have reinforced the practical significance of unanimity within the Council (where it is necessary to override objections or amendments of the Parliament).

On the basis of German experience, one would expect that even the formal relaxation of the unanimity rule may not make much of a difference in practice. As long as it is still national governments that are making European decisions, their common interest in preserving their institutional veto is likely to prevail as well (Everling 1980). In that regard, all neo-functionalist hopes that learning processes would lead to an institutional transformation seem to have been misplaced. The 'transformation group' (Piaget 1973, p. 14; Deutsch 1977, p. 23) of a joint-decision system does not seem to include the self-transformation into a simpler system based upon binding majority decisions. Or, as Helmut Schmidt once remarked with a view to German federalism: 'Any attempt to reform a complex constitution can only increase its complexity.'

If that is so, two of the crucial spill-over mechanisms, which neo-functionalist theory expected to create external political pressures for more integration, seem to be blocked or seriously weakened. First, the reorientation of economic, social and political interests toward the European level remains incomplete. As long as European decisions continue to be made by national governments, the interests affected by them will be mediated by national governments as well. Of course, interest groups will also operate at the European level, but ultimately it is still national governments which they will have to persuade.

As a consequence, nationally specific definitions of group interests, and of party-political ideologies, will be maintained and reinforced, rather than amalgamated into European interest associations (Averyt 1976) and European political parties. In that regard, the tendencies toward the segregation of interests and ideologies inherent in federal, as compared to unitary, states are even more pronounced among the member states of the Community (Kirsch 1984, p. 122). By the same token, there is less reason to expect a transfer of the demands, expectations and loyalties of political elites from the national to the European level.

Second, there is much less reason to expect that 'goal frustration' should lead to 'politicization' and, ultimately, to a redefinition of goals and the 'transcendence' to a higher level of political integration (Schmitter 1969, p. 164). If the iron grip of national governments cannot be broken, the decision logic of European institutions will continue to reproduce the substantive pathologies discussed above. Beyond a certain point, surely, political frustration and exasperation over the inefficiency and inflexibility of European policy making, and over its structural inability to respond to crises creatively, may not lead to renewed demands for 'a more perfect union' but, rather, to cynicism and indifference or to a renewed search for national remedies, however imperfect and limited, for the problems which the Community seems to handle so poorly. As was the case with joint policies in West Germany, the dynamic movement toward greater European integration may have been retarded and, perhaps, reversed, not by the ideological strength of nationalism or by the obstructions of a Charles de Gaulle or a Margaret Thatcher, but by the pathological decision logic inherent in its basic institutional arrangements.

But why is it, then, that the Community didn't disintegrate long ago? As in the case of German federalism, an adequate explanation of its continuing resilience needs to consider two levels of interest, functional and institutional. At the functional level, it is clear that at least some of the benefits predicted by the economic theories of integration have in fact been realized. This tends to be more true for the benefits of 'market integration' than of 'policy integration' (Pelkmans 1980) or of 'negative', rather than 'positive', integration (Taylor 1980, pp. 384–5). But as it is uncertain, even in the industrial sector, whether the common market could be maintained in the absence of a substantial commitment to common (and compensatory) policy measures in such areas as the Social Fund, the Regional Fund and Industrial Policy, one probably could not have the one without the other. In other words, to the extent that joint policies are addressing, however inadequately, real problems which could not be handled at the level of member governments, these problems would simply reassert themselves if the joint-policy system were to be dismantled.

The functional argument is not controverted by the fact that not all economic-policy problems can be handled at the Community level (Ziebura 1982), or that some of the smaller European countries outside of the Community (Switzerland, Austria, Finland, Sweden and Norway) have, on the whole, done better during the world-wide recession of the 1970s than similar countries within the Community (Denmark, the Netherlands, Belgium and Ireland). As all of the successful outsiders are dependent upon industrial exports to the Community, they may simply have been free riders profiting from the creation of the common market and from the Community's relatively liberal trade policies in the industrial sector. Exporters of agricultural goods, on the other hand, like Denmark, Ireland, Greece, Spain and Portugal, had every incentive to join the Community in order to evade CAP's prohibitively high protective barriers. Thus, the appeal of economic integration remains alive, and it is even reinforced, at least for the European Left, by the realization that the internationalization of capital markets has destroyed any hopes for Keynesian full employment policies at the national level (Pelkmanns 1980, pp. 344–5; Scharpf 1987, chs. 11–12). Unfortunately, if my understanding of the 'joint-decision trap' is correct, hopes for an effective 'European Keynesianism' are likely to be futile as well.

At the institutional level, the Community is unequivocally supported by the self-interest of the vertical alliances of policy specialists – interest associations, national ministries and parliamentary committees, and the large contingents of specialized lobbyists, bureaucrats and politicians operating at the European level. They all profit from the availability of additional resources, and of additional points of access to political decision processes, providing additional opportunities for playing the game of influence and obstruction which is their *raison d'être*. Of course, they also must cope with the political frustration, among their clienteles or electorates, over the impact of sub-optimal or even counter-productive European policies. But, as in German federalism, the political effect of voter frustration is largely neutralized by the very diffusion of responsibility and accountability which is characteristic of joint-decision systems (Scharpf, Reissert and Schnabel 1976, p. 236).

Similar cost-benefit calculations tend to stabilize the Community from the perspective of national policy generalists – heads of government, finance ministers and parliamentary budget committees – if their countries are among the net beneficiaries of the Community budget. Net contributors, on the other hand, find themselves locked into an ongoing decision system whose direction they could only hope to change significantly by either assuming the burdens and costs of hegemonic leadership or by threatening to leave the Community altogether. As it is, the only pretender to hegemonic status, West Germany, is too weak or too egoistical to assume the burdens of leadership, while confrontation strategies are unlikely to work for countries whose interest in, and attachment to, the Community is known to be very great. Thus, the Community is likely to remain secure as long as care is taken to concentrate net contributions to the Community budget upon those countries which would have most to lose economically and politically by its dissolution and, in particular, by the disintegration of the common market.

By way of summary, it is now possible to define the 'joint-decision trap' more precisely. It is an institutional arrangement whose policy outcomes have an inherent (non-accidental) tendency to be sub-optimal – certainly when compared to the policy potential of unitary governments of similar size and resources. Nevertheless, the arrangement represents a 'local optimum' in the cost-benefit calculations of all participants that might have the power to change it. If that is so, there is no 'gradualist' way in which joint-decision systems might transform themselves into an institutional arrangement of greater policy potential. In order to be effective, institutional change would have to be large-scale, implying the acceptance of short-term losses for many, or all, participants. That is unlikely, but not impossible (Elster 1979). And, of course, the system might be jolted out of its present equilibrium by external intervention or by a dramatic deterioration of its performance which would undermine even its 'local optimality' for crucial participants. Thus, I have not described a deterministic world, even though the logic of the 'joint-decision trap' may provide as close an approximation to structural determinism as one is likely to encounter in the social sciences.

SOME TENTATIVE EXTENSIONS

Our analyses of '*Politikverflechtung*' pose the question of whether or not the findings can be generalized. We tended to emphasize the specificity of the historical case from which the conclusions were derived (Scharpf 1978a) but nevertheless we attempted to formulate the findings in the language of universalistic propositions. The present essay claims that these propositions also help to explain the European experience. In effect, these cases may be instances of a universal decision logic inherent in particular 'patterns', in the sense discussed by von Hayek (1967), of institutional arrangements. This conclusion offers a few speculative suggestions about other areas of potential application.

Clearly, the 'joint-decision trap' is not inherent in all forms of *de facto* unanimous decision making, even if we exclude (as one should) single-shot encounters. By the same logic, one should probably also exclude all forms of ongoing associations from which exit is very easy, either because their benefits are of marginal value to members, or because they could easily be substituted from another source. Furthermore, it seems also appropriate to exclude associations in which the tension between common and individual interests could not arise because member interests are complementary, and costs low in comparison to the benefits of associaton. Cliques, clubs and business consortia might fall into that class. More doubtful candidates for either inclusion or exclusion are organizations with member interests that are partly complementary and partly competitive, but where members are not expecting each other to pursue anything but their own, individual self-interest. Many forms of long-standing vertical relationships between suppliers and customers fall into that category, but also horizontal cartels and 'free collective bargaining' between employers and trade unions. I would also include here the 'co-operation among egoists' in long sequences of the Prisoners' Dilemma and similar real-world situations. In my view, cases in this category would not provide valid tests for the 'joint-decision trap' hypothesis. While an outside observer might perceive potential 'common' interests and, hence, benefits from 'problem solving', participants may have good reasons to define their mutual relations purely in 'bargaining' terms. Being where they want to be, they are not in any meaningful sense in a 'trap'.

But even if we limit the discussion to ongoing joint-decision systems without exit, in which 'common' interests have a normative validity that is separate from, but not necessarily superior to, the individual self-interest of participants, and in which 'problem solving' would be the more efficient style of decision making, we would still cast the net too wide. 'Problem solving' is, after all, a style of decision making that is frequently encountered in decision situations which are formally operating under hierarchical or majority decisions rules, even though there may be *de facto* unanimity for most practical purposes. Indeed, that may be the secret of their success: 'participative management' (as distinguished from '*laissez-faire* management') is likely to profit from the creativity and intelligence of employees precisely because disintegrative tendencies are held in check by a hierarchical authority that has abdicated some, but not all, of its functions. Conversely, formally egalitarian decision situations might profit from the *de facto* hierarchical role of one hegemonic member – as exemplified by the powerfully integrative role of Prussia in Bismarck's Germany. Similarly, one might suspect that 'consociational democracies' and even American-style 'pluralism' would not work quite as well if obstinate minorities did not have to reckon with the possibility that the formal rule of majority decision might still be invoked against them. The precarious stability of 'problem solving', and the tendency to revert to the 'bargaining' style is, thus, likely to manifest itself most clearly in joint-decision systems in which *de facto* unanimity is not backed up by the formal possibility of unilateral or majority decisions or by the clear preponderance of power of a hegemonic member.

Even within these definitional constraints, however, there seems to be a wide range of institutions to which the logic of the 'joint-decision trap' might plausibly apply. Faculty self-government (in the absence of a powerful president or dean) might be one example. Legalized communes of squatters in West Berlin (tied to their houses by the sunk costs of rebuilding them) could be another. Further candidates could be connubia, business partnerships and joint ventures, political coalitions, military alliances, 'neo-corporatist' arrangements and a wide variety of permanent inter-organizational networks. They are all likely to be confronted with tensions between a recognized common interest and the individual self-interest of participants; they all would profit from a 'problem-solving' style of decision making, if only distributive conflicts could, somehow, be neutralized; and they all should be exposed to the entropic push toward 'bargaining'. At the same time, they all should have difficulties in adopting a decision rule (majority or hierarchy) that could avoid reversion to the bargaining style at the expense of membership control over the substance of decisions.

Thus, it should be possible to test the 'joint-decision-trap' hypothesis under an extremely wide variety of institutional conditions. More interesting, from my point of view, would be the opportunity provided by such empirical studies to identify more precisely those factors that are able to influence the changes of decision styles, from 'bargaining' to 'problem solving' and vice versa, in joint-decision systems. Given an increasingly interdependent world, all mechanisms and strategies that might help to avoid the 'joint-decision trap' ought to be of very considerable scholarly and practical interest.

REFERENCES

Abromeit, Heidrun. 1982. 'Die Funktion des Bundesrats und der Streit um seine Politisierung', *Zeitschrift für Parlamentsfragen* 13, 462–72.

Averyt, William F. jr. 1976. *Agricultural interest groups in the European Community: the Comité des Organisations Professionelles Agricoles.* Ph.D. Yale University, May.

Axelrod, Robert. 1981. 'The emergence of cooperation among egoists', *American Political Science Review* 75, 306–18.

Axelrod, Robert. 1984. *The evolution of cooperation.* New York: Basic Books.

Bacharach, S. B. and E. J. Lawler. 1980. *Power and politics in organizations.* London: Jossey-Bass.

Balassa, Bela. 1962. *The theory of economic integration.* London: George Allen and Unwin.

Balz, M., R. Meimberg and M. Schöpe. 1982. 'Agrarstrukturpolitik in der EG – Regionale Entwick-lungsstrategien erforderlich', *Ifo Schnelldienst* 32/82, 10–20.

Baumol, William J. 1982. 'Applied fairness theory and rationing policy', *American Economic Review* September, 639–51.

Bentele, Karlheinz. 1979. *Kartellbildung in der allgemeinen Forschungsförderung.* Königstein: Anton Hain.

Benz, Arthur. 1985. *Föderalismus als dynamisches System.* Opladen: Westdeutscher Verlag.

BMBW. 1982. *Informationen/Bildung/Wissenschaft des Bundesministers für Bildung und Wissenschaft.* Nr. 4/82. Bonn: 22 April.

BMF. 1985. Bundesministerium der Finanzen. *Die finanzwirtschaftliche Entwicklung von Bund, Ländern und Gemeinden seit 1970.* Dokumentation 2/85. Bonn: 31 January 1985.

BMF. 1982. Bundesministerium der Finanzen. *Die Finanzbeziehungen zwischen Bund, Ländern und Gemeinden aus finanzverfas-sungsrechtlicher und finanzwirtschaftlicher Sicht.* Bonn.

Body, Richard. 1982. *Agriculture: the triumph and the shame.* London: Temple Smith.

Bonoma, Thomas V. 1976. 'Conflict, cooperation and trust in three power systems', *Behavioral Science* 21, 499–514.

Borell, R. 1981. *Mischfinanzierungen. Darstellung, Kritik, Reformüberlegungen.* Wiesbaden: Karl-Bräuer-Institut.

Braybrooke, David and Charles E. Lindblom. 1963. *A strategy of decision. Policy evaluation as a social process.* New York: The Free Press.

Breton, Albert and Anthony Scott. 1978. *The economic constitution of federal states.* Toronto: University of Toronto Press.

Bruder, Wolfgang. 1983. *The regional policy of the European Community: problems and perspectives.* MS. Universität Konstanz.

Buchanan, James M. and Gordon Tullock. 1962. *The calculus of consent. Logical foundations of constitutional democracy.* Ann Arbor, Michigan: University of Michigan Press.

Buchanan, James M. 1975. *The limits of liberty. Between anarchy and Leviathan.* Chicago: University of Chicago Press.

Bühl, Walter L. 1984. 'Die Dynamik sozialer Konflikte in katastrophentheoretischer Darstellung', *Kölner Zeitschrift für Soziologie und Sozialpsychologie*, 641–66.

Bulletin der Europäischen Gemeinschaften. Nr. 11, 1984.

Bulmer, Simon. 1983. 'Domestic politics and European Community policy making', *Journal of Common Market Studies* 21, 349–63.

BVerfGE. 1975. Entscheidungen des Bundesverfassungsgerichts. Band 39.

Dahl, Robert H. 1967. *Pluralist democracy in the United States: conflict and consent*. Chicago: Rand McNally.

Dawkins, Richard. 1976. *The selfish gene*. Oxford: Oxford University Press.

Deutsch, Karl. 1953. *Nationalism and social communication: an inquiry into the foundations of nationality*. Cambridge, Mass.: MIT Press.

Deutsch, Karl (with S. A. Burell, R. A. Kann, M. Lee, M. Lichtermann and R. W. van Wagenen). 1957. *Political community and the North Atlantic area*. Princeton: Princeton University Press.

Deutsch, Karl (with P. E. Jacob, H. Teune, J. V. Toscano and W. L. C. Wheaton). 1964. *The integration of political communities*. Philadelphia: Lippincott.

Deutsch, Karl. 1977. 'National integration. Some concepts and research approaches', *Jerusalem Journal of International Relations* 2, 1–29.

DIW. 1984. Deutsches Institut für Wirtschaftsforschung. EG-Haushalt und -Agrarpolitik. DIW Wochenbericht 40/84, 497–501.

DIW. 1984a. Deutsches Institut für Wirtschaftsforschung. *Statt Subventionsabbau neue Hilfen für die Landwirtschaft.* DIW Wochenbericht 25/84, 297–302.

Downs, Anthony. 1957. *An economic theory of democracy*. New York: Harper and Row.

Dunsire, A. 1978. *Implementation in a bureaucracy*. Oxford: Martin Robertson.

Easton, David. 1965. *A systems analysis of political life*. New York: John Wiley.

Elster, Jon. 1979. *Ulysses and the Sirens. Studies of rationality and irrationality*. Cambridge: Cambridge University Press.

Everling, Ulrich. 1980. 'Possibilities and limits of European integration', *Journal of Common Market Studies* 18, 217–28.

Fabritius, Georg. 1978. *Wechselwirkungen zwischen Landtagswahlen und Bundespolitik*. Meisenheim: Anton Hain.

Feld, Werner J. 1980. 'Two-tier policy making in the EC: the Common Agricultural Policy', in Leon Hurwitz (ed.), *Contemporary perspectives on European integration*. London: Aldwich Press.

Franzmeyer, Fritz and Bernhard Seidel. 1976. *überstaatlicher Finanzausgleich und Europäische Integration*. Bonn: Europa Union Verlag.

Frey, Bruno S. 1977. *Moderne Politische Ökonomie*. München: Piper.

Freyer, Hans. 1964. *Soziologie als Wirklichkeitswissenschaft*. Stuttgart: Teubner (First Edition 1930).

Garlichs, Dietrich. 1980. *Grenzen staatlicher Infrastrukturpolitik. Bund/Länder-Kooperation in der Fernstraßenplanung*. Königstein: Anton Hain.

v. d. Groeben, Hans and Ernst-Joachim Mestmäcker. (Hrsg.). 1974. *Verfassung oder Technokratie für Europa*. Frankfurt/M.: Athenäum Fischer.

Haas, Ernst B. 1958. *The uniting of Europe. Political, social and economic forces 1950–1957*. London: Stevens and Sons (1968 edition by Stanford University Press).

———. 1964. *Beyond the nation state. Functionalism and international organization*. Stanford: Stanford University Press.

Haas, Ernst B. and Philippe C. Schmitter. 1964. 'Economics and differential patterns of political integration: projections about unity in Latin America', *International Organization* 18, 705–37.

Haas, Ernst B. 1971. 'The study of regional integration: reflections on the joy and anguish of pretheorizing', in L. N. Lindberg and S. A. Scheingold (eds.), *Regional integration, theory and research*. Cambridge, Mass.: Harvard University Press, 3–42.

Harrison, Reginald J. 1974. *Europe in question: Theories of regional international integration*. London: George Allen and Unwin.

von Hayek, F. A. 1967. 'The theory of complex phenomena', in F. A. von Hayek, *Studies in philosophy, politics and economics*. London: University of Chicago Press.

Heidenheimer, Arnold. 1958. 'Federalism and the party system – the case of West Germany', *American Political Science Review*. September.

Heidenheimer, Arnold J., Hugh Heclo and Carolyn Teich-Adams. 1975. *Comparative public policy*. New York: St. Martin's Press.

———. 1983. *Comparative public policy. The politics of social choice in Europe and America*. Second Edition, London: Macmillan.

Hesse, Konrad. 1962. *Der unitarische Bundesstaat*. Karlsruhe: Müller.

Hesse, Joachim Jens, (Hrsg.), 1978. *Politikverflechtung im föderativen Staat*. Baden-Baden: Nomos.

Höhne, Wilfrid and Günther Horzetzky. 1984. 'Europäische Agrarpolitik: Probleme und Reformansätze', *Gewerkschaftliche Monatshefte* 35, 310–22.

Hoffman, Stanley. 1966. 'Obstinate or obsolete? the fate of the nation-state and the case of Western Europe', *Daedalus* Summer 1966, 862–915.

Hollingsworth, J. Rogers and Leon N. Lindberg. 1985. *The government of the American economy: the role of markets, clans, hierarchies and associative behavior*. MS University of Wisconsin.

Howard, Nigel. 1971. *Paradoxes of rationality: theory of metagames and political behavior*. Cambridge, Mass.: MIT Press.

Hrbek, Rudolf. 1979. 'Politikverflechtung macht an den Grenzen nicht halt. Auswirkungen der EG-Mitgliedschaft auf die föderative Ordnung der Bundesrepublik Deutschland', *Der Bürger im Staat* 29, Jahrgang, Heft 1, 38–43.

Hrbek, Rudolf and Wolfgang Wessels (Hrsg.). 1984. *EG-Mitgliedschaft: ein vitales Interesse der Bundesrepublik Deutschland?* Bonn: Europa Union Verlag.

Johnson, Nevil. 1973. *Government in the Federal Republic of Germany. The executive at work.* Oxford: Pergamon Press.

Jürgensen, Stephan and Schmitz, Peter M. 1984. 'EG Agrarpolitik: Der Streit um den Grenzausgleich', *Wirtschaftsdienst* IV/84, 192–6.

Katzenstein, Peter. 1984. *Corporatism and change. Austria, Switzerland and the politics of industry.* Ithaca: Cornell University Press.

———. 1985. *Small nations as experiments? Experiences from Europe (and other places).* MS Ithaca, February.

Kirsch, Guy (Hrsg.). 1977. *Föderalismus.* Stuttgart: Gustav Fischer.

Kirsch, Guy. 1984. 'Fiscal federalism', *Wirtschaftswissenschaftliches Studium*, März, 118.

Klatt, Hartmut. 1979. 'Die Länderparlamente müssen sich wehren. Möglichkeiten und Ansätze einer Reform des Länderparlamentarismus', *Der Bürger im Staat* 21, Heft 1, 1979, 20–8.

Knott, Jack H. 1981. *Managing the German economy. Budgetary politics in a federal state.* Lexington, Mass.: Lexington Books.

Kohr, Leopold. 1978. *The breakdown of nations.* New York: Dutton.

Kommission für die Finanzreform. 1966. *Gutachten über die Finanzreform in der Bundesrepublik Deutschland.* Stuttgart: Kohlhammer.

Laffan, Brigid. 1983. 'Policy implementation in the European Community: the European Social Fund as a case study', *Journal of Common Market Studies* 21, 389–408.

Lehmbruch, Gerhard. 1967. *Proporzdemokratie: Politisches System und politische Kultur in der Schweiz und österreich.* Tübingen: J. C. B. Mohr.

———. 1976. *Parteienwettbewerb im Bundesstaat.* Stuttgart: Kohlhammer.

Lehner, Franz. 1979. 'Politikverflechtung: Institutionelle Eigendynamik und politische Kontrolle' in Joachim Matthes (Hrsg.), *Sozialer Wandel in Westeuropa. Verhandlungen des 19. Deutschen Soziologentages.* Frankfurt: Campus, 611–25.

———. 1979a. 'Politikverflechtung – Föderalismus ohne Transparenz', *Der Bürger im Staat* 129, Heft 1, 3–8.

Lijphart, Arend. 1975. *The politics of accommodation. Pluralism and democracy in the Netherlands.* Second Edition, Berkeley: University of California Press.

Lindberg, Leon N. 1963. *The political dynamics of European integration.* Stanford: Stanford University Press.

Lindberg, Leon N. and Stuart A. Scheingold. 1970. *Europe's would-be polity. Patterns of change in the European Community.* Englewood Cliffs: Prentice-Hall.

Lindblom, Charles E. 1965. *The intelligence of democracy.* New York: The Free Press.

March, James G. and Herbert A. Simon. 1958. *Organizations.* New York: John Wiley.

Martins, Mario R. and John Mawson. 1982. 'The programming of regional development in the EC: Supra-national or international decision-making?' *Journal of Common Market Studies* 20, 229–44.

Merrit, Richard L. and Bruce C. Russett. (eds.). 1981. *From national development to global community.* London: George Allen and Unwin.

Mitrany, David. 1975. 'A political theory for the new society', in: A. J. R. Groom and Paul Taylor (eds.), *Functionalism. theory and practice in international relations.* London: University of London Press, 25–37.

Mueller, Dennis C. 1979. *Public choice.* Cambridge: Cambridge University Press.

Nash, John F. jr. 1950. 'The bargaining problem', *Econometrica*, 18, 155–162.

Niskanen, William A. 1971. *Bureaucracy and representative government.* Chicago: Aldine-Atherton.

Noé, Claus. 1983. 'Wo sind 19,5 Milliarden DM geblieben? Bemerkungen zu Zielen, Mitteln und Wirkungsweise regionalpolitischer Versuche der Europäischen Gemeinschaft', *Raumforschung und Raumordnung*, 15–20.

Nölling, Wilhelm. 1977. 'Das Programm für Zukunftsinvestitionen', *Wirtschaftsdienst* VIII, 391.

Noll, Peter. 1984. *Diktate über Sterben und Tod.* Zürich: Pendo.

Oates, Wallace E. 1972. *Fiscal federalism.* New York: Harcourt Brace Jovanovich.

Offe, Claus. 1975. *Berufsbildungsreform. Eine Fallstudie über Reformpolitik.* Frankfurt: Suhrkamp.

Olsen, Johan, Paul Roness and Harald Saetren. 1982. 'Norway: still peaceful coexistence and revolution in slow motion?', in Richardson, J. (ed.), *Policy Styles in Western Europe.* London, 47–9.

Olson, Mancur and Richard Zeckhauser. 1966. 'An Economic Theory of Alliances', *Review of Economics and Statistics* 48, 266–79.

Olson, Mancur. 1969. 'The principle of fiscal equivalence: the division of responsibilities among different levels of government', *American Economic Review* May Supplement, 479.

Ostrom, Elinor. 1984. *Multiorganizational arrangements and coordination: an application of institutional analysis.* MS. Workshop in Political Theory and Policy Analysis. Bloomington, Indiana: Indiana University.

Ostrom, Vincent. 1984. *The political theory of a compound republic.* Revised Edition, Bloomington, Indiana: Indiana University.

Ouchi, William G. 1980. 'Markets, bureaucracies and clans', *Administrative Science Quarterly* 25, 129–41.

Parsons, Talcott. 1967. 'Voting and the equilibrium of the American political system', in T. Parsons, *Sociological theory and modern society.* New York: Free Press, 223–63.

Pelkmans, Jacques. 1980. 'Economic theories of integration revisited', *Journal of Common Market Studies* 18, 333–54.

Pentland, Charles. 1973. *International theory and European integration*. London: Faber and Faber.

Pérez-Diaz, Victor M. 1985. *Governability and mesogovernments: regional autonomies and neo-corporatism in Spain*. MS Madrid, February 1985.

Piaget, Jean. 1973. *Der Strukturalismus*. Olten und Freiburg i. Br.: Walter Verlag.

Rawls, John. 1971. *A theory of justice*. Cambridge, Mass.: Harvard University Press.

Reissert, Bernd. 1979. *'Politikverflechtung' in der Europäischen Gemeinschaft*. MS. Wissenschafts-zentrum Berlin.

———. 1984. *Staatliche Zuweisungen und kommunale Investitionspolitik (Politikverflechtung VI)*. MS. Wissenschaftszentrum Berlin.

Richardson, Jeremy (ed.). 1982. *Policy styles in Western Europe*. London: George Allen and Unwin.

Riker, William H. 1962. *The theory of political coalitions*. New Haven: Yale University Press.

———. 1964. *Federalism: origin, operation, maintenance*. Boston: Little Brown.

———. 1969. 'Six books in search of a subject or does federalism exist and does it matter?' *Comparative Politics* October, 135.

Riker, William H. 1975. 'Federalism', in F. I. Greenstein and N. W. Polsby (eds.), *Governmental institutions and processes*. Handbook of Political Science, Vol. 5. Redding, Mass.: Addison-Wesley, 93–172.

Rodemer, Horst. 1980. *Die EG-Agrarpolitik, Ziele, Wirkungen, Alternativen*. Tübingen.

Rothenberg, Jerome. 1970. 'Local decentralization and the theory of optimal government', in Julius Margolis (ed.), *The analysis of public output*. New York: Columbia University Press, 31–64.

Runge, Charles F. 1984. 'Institutions and the free rider: the assurance problem in collective action', *Journal of Politics* 46, 154–81.

Scharpf, Fritz W. 1970. *Demokratietheorie zwischen Utopie und Anpassung*; Kronberg: Scriptor (Nachdruck 1975).

———. 1972. 'Komplexität als Schranke der politischen Planung', *Politische Vierteljahresschrift* 13, Sonderheft 4, 168–92.

Scharpf, Fritz W., Bernd Reissert, and Fritz Schnabel. 1976. *Politikverflechtung. Theorie und Empirie des kooperativen Föderalismus in der Bundesrepublik*. Kronberg: Scriptor 1976.

Scharpf, Fritz W., Bernd Reissert, and Fritz Schnabel (Hrsg.). 1977. *Politikverflechtung II. Kritik und Berichte aus der Praxis*. Kronberg: Athenäum.

Scharpf, Fritz W. 1977. 'Public organization and the waning of the welfare state', *European Journal of Political Research* December, 339.

———. 1978a. 'Die Theorie der Politikverflechtung: Ein kurzgefaßter Leitfaden', in Joachim Jens Hesse (Hrsg.), *Politikverflechtung im föderativen Staat*. Baden-Baden: Nomos.

———. 1978. 'Interorganizational policy studies: issues, concepts and perspectives', in K. Hanf and F. W. Scharpf (eds.), *Interorganizational policy making. Limits to coordination and central control*. London: Sage, 345–70.

———. 1985. 'Beschäftigungspolitische Strategien in der Krise', *Leviathan* 1, 1–22.

Scharpf, Fritz W., Bernd Reissert, and Fritz Schnabel. 1978. 'Policy effectiveness and conflict avoidance in intergovernmental policy formation', in K. Hanf and F. W. Scharpf (eds.), *Interorganizational Policy Making*. London: Sage, 57–112.

Schelling, Thomas C. 1960. *The strategy of conflict*. Cambridge, Mass.: Harvard University Press.

Scheingold, Stuart A. 1970. 'Domestic and international consequences of regional integration', *International Organization*, 978.

Schmidt, Helmut. 1980. 'Ansprache des Bundeskanzlers in der 494. Sitzung des Bundesrates am 12.12.1980', *Stenographische Berichte des Bundesrats, von der 482. bis zur 494. Sitzung*, Bonn, 431–5.

Schmitter, Philippe C. 1969. 'Three neo-functional hypotheses about international integration', *International Organization* 23, Winter, 161–6.

———. 1970. 'A revised theory of regional integration', *International Organization* 24, 836–68.

Schnabel, Fritz, 1980. *Politischer und administrativer Vollzug des Krankenhausfinanzierungsgesetzes*. MS. Wissenschaftszentrum Berlin.

Schultze, Rainer-Olaf. 1982. 'Politikverflechtung und konföderaler Föderalismus: Entwicklungslinien und Strukturprobleme im bundesrepublikanischen und kanadischen Föderalismus', *Zeitschrift der Gesellschaft für Kanada-Studien* 2, 113–44.

Scitovsky, Tibor. 1958. *Economic theory and Western European integration*; London: George Allen and Unwin.

Sen, Amartya K. 1970. *Collective choice and social welfare*. Edinburgh: Oliver and Boyd.

———. 1977. 'Rational fools: a critique of the behavioral foundations of economic theory', *Philosophy and Public Affairs* 6, 317–44.

Sharpe, L. J. 1985. *Territoriality and the European state system*. MS Oxford, March.

Simmert, Diethard B. and Kurt-Dieter Wagner (Hrsg.). 1981. *Staatsverschuldung kontrovers*. Bonn: Bundeszentrale für Politische Bildung.

Slater, Martin. 1982. 'Political elite, popular indifference and community building', *Journal of Common Market Studies* 21, 69–86.

Späth, L., E. Teufel, E. Eppler, and J. Morlock. 1979. 'Föderalismus heute. Regierung und Landtags-fraktionen nehmen Stellung', *Politikverflechtung oder Föderalismus heute. Der Bürger im Staat* 29, Heft 1, 52–8.

Steinle, Wolfgang J. and Karl A. Stroetmann. 1983. 'Gemeinschaftliche Forschungs- und Technologiepolitik als Beitrag zur regionalen Entwicklung Europas', *Raumforschung und Raumordnung* 1983, 57–62.

Streeck, Wolfgang and Philippe C. Schmitter. 1984. *Community, market, state and associations: the prospective contribution of interest governments to social order*. Florence: European University Institute Working Paper 94.

Strohe, Franz-Josef. 1982. 'Zusammenwirken von Bund und Ländern bei der Bildungsplanung', BMF, 1982, 561–80.

Taylor, Paul. 1980. 'Interdependence and autonomy in the European Communities: the case of the European monetary system', *Journal of Common Market Studies* 18, 370–87.

——. 1983. *The limits of European integration*. London: Croom Helm.

Tönnies, Ferdinand. 1963. *Gemeinschaft und Gesellschaft*. Darmstadt: Wissenschaftliche Buchgesellschaft (First Edition 1887).

Trivers, Robert L. 1971. 'The evolution of reciprocal altruism', *Quarterly Review of Biology* 46, 35–57.

Tullock, Gordon. 1965. *The politics of bureaucracy*. Washington, D.C.: Public Affairs Press.

——. 1969. 'Federalism: problems of scale', *Public Choice*, 19–29.

Vobruba, Georg (ed.). 1983. *'Wir sitzen alle in einem Boot'. Gemeinschaftsrhetorik in der Krise*. Frankfurt.

Wallace, Helen, William Wallace, and Carole Webb (eds.). 1977. *Policy making in the European communities*. London: John Wiley.

Wallace, William. 1982. 'Europe as a confederation: the Community and the nation state', *Journal of Common Market Studies* 21, 57–68.

Weiler, Joseph. 1982. 'Community member states and European integration. Is the law relevant?' *Journal of Common Market Studies* 21, 39–56.

Wheare, K. C. 1960. *Federal government*. 4th Edition, Oxford: Oxford University Press.

Ylvisaker, Paul. 1959. 'Some criteria for a ''proper'' areal division of governmental powers', in: Arthur Maass, (ed.), *Area and power. A theory of local government*. Glencoe, Ill.: The Free Press.

Zeh, Wolfgang. 1979. 'Musterfall Gemeinschaftsaufgaben. Erscheinungsformen, Willensbildungsmuster und Ursachen der Politikverflechtung', *Der Bürger im Staat* Heft 1, 15–19.

Ziebura, Gilbert. 1982. 'Internationalization of capital, international division of labour and the role of the European Community', *Journal of Common Market Studies* 21, 127–40.

AFTERWORD: MODES OF EUROPEAN POLICY-MAKING

The Joint-Decision Trap, one of my most cited articles, focuses entirely on the specific "joint-decision mode" of EU legislation (which the Commission has come to describe as the "Community Method"), and on its limited problem-solving capacity. Though the English version was only published in 1988, the text had been written in 1983/84 (i.e., before the adoption of the Single-Market programme). It drew on our studies of policy-making in German federalism, where we had explained the obvious problem-solving deficits of some national programs by their dependence on the (nearly) unanimous agreement of *Länder* governments. Taking the state of the Common Agricultural Policy as an example, the article suggested that under similar institutional conditions intergovernmental conflicts of interest could also explain glaring problem-solving deficits at the European level. With the benefit of hindsight it is now easy to show that the basic explanatory model (which had anticipated George Tsebelis' [2002] "veto players" theory) remains valid wherever its assumed conditions are in force. But the popularity of the article on the citation index surely owes even more to the fact that it was also easy to show that these institutional conditions and interest constellations do not exist everywhere, and that even where they do exist, factors not represented in the model may prevent the expected policy blockades or compromises on the lowest common denominator.

Obviously, not all policy choices at the European level are adopted in the joint-decision mode. In a later article (2001), I distinguished four such modes, all of which are in fact employed in multilevel Europe or in federal Germany. They differ in the degree of institutionalization and hence in the degree to which they constrain the autonomy of lower-level policy choices. The least constraining mode is coordination by "mutual adjustment", followed by the mode of "intergovernmental negotiations", then by "joint decision making" and finally by policies determined in the "supranational-hierarchical" mode.

The mode of *mutual-adjustment* (Lindblom 1965) assumes that member states, acting autonomously in their own interests, will anticipate, and respond to, each others' actions as best as they can. Depending on the underlying interest constellations and strategic options, such "non-cooperative games" will often generate conflictive and unstable interactions – but they may also result in stable patterns of "ecological" coordination, in "path-dependent" development or in dynamic "bandwagons", "races to the bottom" or "races to the top" (Scharpf and Mohr 1997).

Intergovernmental negotiations may achieve coordination through voluntary agreements. Governments are free to join, or abstain, and agreements will only bind those who have accepted them. From a problem-solving perspective, such "coalitions of the willing" will serve the interests of participants and may ignore external effects. By the same token, the realized benefits of membership may induce outsiders to join, just as the foregone benefits of unilateral action may induce members to quit.

The *joint decision system* of the European Union shares some characteristics of the intergovernmental mode – for instance, coordination also depends on agreement among the governments of member states. But it goes beyond it in several respects: First, participation in joint-decision processes is compulsory for those states that have joined the EU. In the typical case, moreover, the formal decision rule in the Council is no longer unanimity but qualified majority and decisions do not only bind those that have agreed. Finally, the rules so adopted have direct effect and may be enforced as "supreme law of the land" by courts in all member states. Moreover, and equally important, member governments are no longer the only "veto players". Even if they were fully agreed, European legislation in the "Community Method" depends on an initiative by the Commission and, in most areas, also on the agreement of a majority in the European Parliament. Under some circumstances, these may indeed facilitate political agreement; under others they may add to the constraints.

The three modes discussed so far are "political" in the sense that policy choices are formally determined by politically accountable actors – national governments in the Council and, in the joint-decision mode, the European Parliament. That is not true of the *supranational-hierarchical* mode where effective European policy choices are adopted unilaterally by the European Central Bank, the European Court of Justice, and the European Commission when it is directly enforcing competition law and when it is launching Treaty infringement prosecutions against member states. In all of these cases, there is of course some basis in the Treaties or in legislation that was formulated in the "political mode" with the participation of member governments. But the interpretation of general formulas is left to independent agents whose choices cannot be corrected by governments: The ECB is institutionally more protected against political intervention than any national central bank ever was, and when the ECJ is basing its decisions on the Treaties, its interpretation could be corrected only by unanimous Treaty amendments that need to be ratified in all twenty-seven member states. In effect, therefore, not only autonomous political action at the national level, but also political legislation at the European level, are carried out "in the shadow" of factual and legal constraints defined by politically independent agents in the supranational-hierarchical mode.

Nevertheless, the joint-decision mode stands out for two reasons: its potential to create effective European solutions and binding rules is significantly greater than that of intergovernmental negotiations, let alone mutual adjustment. And compared to the supranational-hierarchical mode, it provides at least some opportunities to shape and legitimate the exercise of European governing powers through processes of democratic self-determination. Hence the proposition that the capacity of European legislation continues to be constrained by the mechanisms of the "joint decision trap" retains its normative and practical salience even if the perspective is widened to include the plurality of European governing modes.

REFERENCES

Lindblom, C. E. 1965. *The Intelligence of Democracy: Decision Making Through Mutual Adjustment*. New York: Free Press.

Scharpf, F. W. and M. Mohr. 1994. 'Efficient Self-Coordination in Policy Networks – a Simulation Study'. Discussion Paper 94/1. Cologne: Max Planck Institute for the Study of Societies. Reprinted in: Scharpf, F. W. 1997. *Games Real Actors Play. Actor-Centered Institutionalism in Policy Research*. Boulder, CO: Westview, Appendix 2.

Scharpf, F. W. 2001. 'Notes Toward a Theory of Multilevel Governing in Europe', *Scandinavian Political Studies* 24, 1, 1–26.

Tsebelis, G. 2002. *Veto Players. How Political Institutions Work*. Princeton, NJ: Princeton University Press.

Chapter 8

MANAGING NETWORKS IN THE PUBLIC SECTOR: A THEORETICAL STUDY OF MANAGEMENT STRATEGIES IN POLICY NETWORKS

ERIK-HANS KLIJN, JOOP KOPPENJAN AND KATRIEN TERMEER

INTRODUCTION

The importance to government organizations of policy networks for the management of policy processes is clearly illustrated by the failure of the Dutch government to develop and introduce a new passport in the 1980s. In 1981, the Dutch Parliament ratified the EC resolution in which it committed itself to the introduction of a new passport according to EC guidelines by 1 January 1985. Tenders were invited from private companies.

Soon, the Ministries of Home Affairs and Foreign Affairs clashed with the result that no decision was taken regarding which company should be granted the assignment of developing the new passport system. The Ministry of Home Affairs (MHA) represented the interests of local governments and of the state printing office (SDUB), the state-owned printers of the present passport. The MHA therefore wanted a decentralized passport system which would be developed by the state printing office. They felt the municipalities should be involved in the production and distribution of the new passport. The Ministry of Foreign Affairs (MFA), which was responsible for the introduction of the new passport, wanted a centralized system which would guarantee optimal protection against fraud. This system differed to such an extent from the old one that the MFA did not want the existing network of actors to develop it. It was to be developed by the 'KEP-consortium', which consisted of two giants, Kodak and Philips, and one dwarf, Elba, a small printer of high quality stationery.

In 1985, the Prime Minister intervened in order to break the deadlock. He suggested a compromise. The passport would be distributed by the municipalities and the assignment would be a joint venture involving KEP and the SDUB. During the next few months however, KEP and SDUB failed to reach an agreement. In June 1986, the MFA signed a contract with KEP: the MHA had lost the bureau-political battle.

The KEP contract involved the creation of a completely new network. A special plant was to be set up whose exclusive task would be the development of a passport system according to the MFA guidelines. In January 1988, the first new passport was to be distributed, but before that time problems arose. Within a few months, Kodak resigned from the project. Because the role of Philips was rather marginal, Elba became the main contract partner of MFA. In the autumn of 1987, the MHA made every effort to acquire a specimen of the new passport in order to have a reputable examining body assess the extent to which it was proof against fraud. However, since the ministry did not obtain a specimen in time, the introduction of the new passport had to be postponed. In the meantime, Parliament had become suspicious and decided to conduct an inquiry, which resulted in the resignation of two of the politicians responsible. In December 1988, the contract with KEP was cancelled. Banks consequently refused to extend further credit, KEP went bankrupt. The responsibility for the development of a new passport was transferred to the MHA, which started a new passport project in 1990.

Although several factors jointly responsible for the passport débâcle have been suggested, one appears to be particularly important: the way the MFA managed the process. The MFA was wholly committed to its own design for the new passport system. Actors who had different ideas were excluded from the process. Participation was restricted to those of like mind. By creating its own network, the MFA expected to be able to gain absolute power over the passport development process. By doing so, however, it rendered itself completely dependent upon one other partner. When this partner failed to comply with the contract, the project was doomed.

The example of the passport débâcle illustrates that it is impossible, or at least precarious, to ignore the existence of networks. The network context of policy projects renders top-down management inadequate. Policy networks require a different method of governing. However, although in policy science the idea of policy networks as a concept for analysing policy processes has gained popularity, little attention has been paid to the question of how policy makers can manage these processes. The aim of this article is to offer a theoretical exploration of the possibilities and limitations of management in policy networks.

POLICY NETWORKS AND POLICY GAMES

The definition of public policy as being the result of an interaction process between many actors of whom only a few are government bodies has gradually become widely accepted. In policy science there is increasing interest in the idea of policy networks as a concept for describing and analysing the setting in which policy develops and is implemented (Hanf and Scharpf 1978; Rogers and Whetten 1982; Hanf and Toonen 1985; Kaufman et al. 1986; Hufen and Ringeling 1990; Jordan 1990; Rhodes 1990; Marsh and Rhodes 1992; Marin and Mayntz 1991). The logical conclusion of this concept is that when a (governmental) actor tries to govern policy processes, he has to take the characteristics of this network into account.

Networks are described in various ways. One major element common to these descriptions is that they concern more or less long-term relation patterns between dependent actors within which interactions take place (Hanf and Scharpf 1978; Benson 1982; Hufen and Ringeling 1990). We can describe networks, thus, as *more or less stable patterns of social relations between mutually dependent actors which form themselves around policy problems or clusters of resources and which are formed, maintained and changed by a series of games* (cf. Klijn and Teisman 1991). The policy network is the more or less stable context within which separate games about policy decisions take place.

What is meant by a *'game' is a continuing, consecutive series of actions between different actors, conducted according to and guided by formal and informal rules, and which arises around issues or decisions in which actors have an interest* (cf. Allison 1971; Crozier and Friedberg 1980; Rhodes 1981). Policy forms the achieved outcome of these games. The cumulative effect from all the separate games results in specific patterns developing. In this way, policy networks arise around policy issues. Then in its turn the network forms the more permanent framework for subsequent games.

Policy networks: some characteristics

First and foremost, policy networks are characterized by the *actors* who are part of it and their *relations* with each other. An important precondition for these relations between actors to arise and to continue to exist is dependence. Actors are dependent on each other if they are unable to conclude games in a manner satisfactory to themselves without the cooperation of other actors. It is owing to this dependence that actors interact with each other. Through a consecutive series of interactions, a pattern of relations is established. The continuing series of games which take place within the network create and perpetuate a certain balance of *resources* such as powers, status, legitimacy, knowledge, information and money within a network (Benson 1982; Aldrich 1979). The distribution of resources in turn affects future games within the network but at the same time is perpetuated or changed by those games.

A network is characterized not only by its actors, their relations and the existing distribution of resources, but also by the prevailing *rules*. Rules are generalizable procedures which are used in games. These procedures, created by the actors jointly in the course of interaction, regulate the separate games within the network without determining them (Weick 1979; Giddens 1984). Rules regulate the behaviour of actors. They specify matters such as what is and is not acceptable, which positions actors may occupy, which actors may take part in which games, which action interconnects with which position, in what way decisions or policy products should be brought about and what costs and benefits correlate with particular behaviour (see, for example, Ostrom 1986). Rules are often ambiguous and there are many rules in existence at any one time, which means it is not always immediately clear to the players which rules are applicable and how rules which might be relevant should be interpreted. Furthermore these rules, in contrast to chess and soccer rules, for example, are not static. They are interpreted and changed during the interaction between the players (Morgan 1986; Giddens 1984; Burns and Flam 1987).

Actors act on the basis of images and interpretations which they have adopted over a period of time. *Perceptions* are definitions or images of reality on the basis of which actors interpret and evaluate their actions and those of other actors (Weick 1979; Rein and Schon 1986; van Twist and Termeer 1991). On the basis of their perceptions, actors choose to participate in specific games within the network, they choose which objectives they anticipate achieving in those games and they select various strategies in those games. Networks are characterized by specific configurations of perceptions which are related to the history and nature of the network. The extent to which actors share perceptions with each other, however, can vary.

The policy game

Usually, only some of the actors from the network are involved in a game. The actors involved are the *players* in the game. Their aim in the game is to achieve specific objectives. To this end they employ *strategies*, i.e. they gear their actions and the objectives which they pursue to the strategic behaviour and objectives of other actors. A strategy is thus a cohesive series of actions whereby one's own desires and ambitions are linked to the assessment of the desires and ambitions of other actors (see also, for example, Crozier and Friedberg 1980). Generally, an actor will not pursue only one objective in a game, but will try to achieve various objectives simultaneously. The dynamics of the game also offer him the opportunity to discover new and interesting objectives in the course of the game (March and Olson 1976).

The position of the players in the game is not only determined by their chosen strategies and their interactions with other actors but also by the resources from the network which they are able to mobilize in the game. In other words: their power in the game is determined by a combination of the resources which they might potentially mobilize, combined with their strategic abilities to put these resources to use in an actual game. The power of each actor exists and remains in existence on account of the fact that other actors consider him to be powerful. Thus power, like rules, is a construct of the actors in the network.

Policy is a result of interactions between actors in games. *Policy outcomes* are policy measures or policy products brought about in games: for instance, a completed motorway, a reduction in agriculture's waste emissions, concluding a legislation project, contracts or procedures being agreed between actors, but also non-decisions or blockades. A further characteristic of games is that they are highly dynamic. Uncertainty is an intrinsic characteristic of games in networks. This means that during the course of the game actors adjust their strategies to the behaviour of the other actors and that while they are playing they are acquiring knowledge about the feasibility of their objectives (Klijn and Teisman 1991). So, during the game, learning processes also occur in which actors adjust their objectives and perceptions to the options and opportunities perceived by them.

The interactions between games and networks

Networks and games are closely linked. The conceptualization chosen here was inspired by Giddens' structuration theory (1984). The network forms the context within which games develop. It provides the resources and rules which are used by the actors in the games. The network structures the game without determining its outcome. The outcome and/or the policy are after all dependent on the strategies of the players. In their turn, the outcomes of games can, in the long term, change the characteristics of the network. Actors can, for example, influence the rule structure of the network by interpreting the rules in a particular way. The network is not only changed by conscious efforts on the part of actors. Unintended effects of behaviour on the part of actors may also result in changes at network level.

The network is reproduced and changed in games. Thus, the observation that networks are of a stable nature means, in fact, that the actors repeatedly confirm the distribution of the resources, the prevailing rules and the existing perceptions in actual games. Total stability is, theoretically speaking, highly unlikely. Rules, for example, are mostly ambiguous. They require an interpretation from actors in actual games and this contributes to the change in their content.

A MANAGEMENT PERSPECTIVE ON POLICY NETWORKS

As the opening case study illustrates, the management of interaction processes in networks takes shape in situations in which various actors with divergent interests and objectives interact. Network management is aimed at improving game interaction and results (Koppenjan *et al.* 1993). Lynn argues that 'successful public management can be viewed as effective gamesmanship' (Lynn 1981, p. 145). In principle, network management does not serve a central objective, but has a more facilitating role. The manager may be a governmental actor, but he may also be an actor from outside government. It is possible that the role of manager may be performed by someone from outside the policy network, who will operate as a mediator. Although the manager is concerned with the way the policy process develops within the network, it would be a mistake to suppose that he has no interests of his own at stake. It is because the manager has something to gain, that he is willing to invest time and resources in facilitating the process.

Two types of network management

Based on the difference between games and networks described in the previous section, a distinction can be made between game management and network structuring. *Game management* concerns the influencing of interaction processes between, actors, which involves anticipating the limitations and opportunities which occur within the network. In game management, the manager considers the characteristics of the network as a given. *Network structuring* on the other hand, is aimed at effecting changes within the network (cf. O'Toole 1988).

The network manager has four key aspects available to him on each level for influencing games and networks: actors, resources, rules and perceptions. Table 1 shown above gives an outline of the key aspects for management at game level and network level and the corresponding activities. These activities will be further developed in sections IV and V.

GAME MANAGEMENT: PROMOTING AND IMPROVING INTERACTION

Game management is aimed at integrating the actors, resources and perceptions present within the network, bearing in mind the prevailing interaction rules and the distribution of resources. By strategic anticipation of the obstacles and opportunities present within the network, an attempt is made to promote the conditions for joint action or for creating common products. The activities indicated by the term game management are outlined below. They are illustrated by examples drawn from the decision making concerning the expansion of Schiphol, the Dutch National Airport.

Expanding Schiphol Airport

Together with the port of Rotterdam, Schiphol Airport is the 'engine' of the Dutch economy. Until recently, the expansion of the airport occurred more or less autonomously: there was no planned coordination with developments in the local environment. For instance, because municipalities were not involved in the planning process for the airport, they built houses in places that were later to become badly situated in relation to the airport. The expansion of Schiphol's activities conflicted increasingly with the quality of life in the area. Noise has traditionally been an important problem, but over the years, problems such as external safety, soil and air pollution reached the policy agenda.

In 1986, in an effort to keep up with international competition, the airport executive presented the 'Schiphol master plan' for the further expansion of Schiphol in order for it to become one of the few airports in Europe with Main Port status. This involved more than a doubling of the number of passengers and the building of a fifth runway. The

TABLE 1 *Game management and network structuring*

Key aspects:	actors	resources	rules	perceptions
Types of management:				
game management	selective activation	mobilizing resources	anticipating rules	compromising and joint image formation
network structuring	changing relations between actors	changing the distribution of resources	changing the rules	changing norms, values and perceptions

government supported this target on the condition that it was linked to a second goal: the solving of the environmental problems which would accompany such an expansion. The Ministry of Housing, Physical Planning and Environment (VROM) coordinated efforts to develop a plan which would accommodate both targets.

In 1988, a project organization was set up in which relevant parties were invited to participate. It included members from the ministries of VROM, Home Affairs, Transport, Public Works and Water Management, and Economic Affairs, the province of North Holland, the municipalities of Haarlemmermeer and Amsterdam, the Executive of Schiphol Airport and Royal Dutch Airlines (KLM). Environmental groups and representatives of the local residents, however, were not invited. The project began in September 1989, with the signing of a joint declaration of intent, whereby the participants committed themselves to developing a joint plan with regard to the two targets.

Subsequently, participants exchanged information about their preferences, and research was carried out into possible scenarios and their impacts. Two coalitions took shape: the province of North Holland and the municipality of Haarlemmermeer formed the environmental coalition, and the other participants the Main Port coalition. VROM had to adopt a neutral position in order to perform the role of coordinator, and could therefore not openly support the environmental coalition. An attempt to get a joint plan of action accepted failed. Another procedure had to be found. Under the chairmanship of the secretary-general of the VROM (the most highly placed civil servant in that ministry) a selected group of participants negotiated specific issues and their proposals were presented to the other members of the project. If these were not accepted, the process was repeated until they were. In this way a plan of action was formulated on which all the parties agreed. In April 1991, after some final wheeling and dealing, this plan was accepted by all the parties involved.

The plan included a guided expansion of the airport, the re-routing of the forth runway and the construction of the fifth. The capacity of the airport would be used in such a way that noise nuisance would be limited. The demolition of a number of houses and the insulation of others was also agreed on. Furthermore, the agreement included a number of measures in the field of external safety, transport and regional development. It was estimated that the plans would cost about 22 billion guilders.

As a result of this network management, the first step was taken towards the coordinated planning of the future development of Schiphol. It proved to be possible to decide jointly on a plan in a way which might benefit all parties. Although the Main Port coalition had had to accept limits to expansion, it might nevertheless gain because of the reduction in the risk of political mobilization. There were also potential benefits for the environmental coalition, i.e. the reduction in environmental damage. Without interaction, the environmental situation in the area surrounding the airport might have been even worse. Although the results of the project have been promising to date, further success is not assured. For instance, a number of important issues, such as night flights, still need to be resolved. Strategies of game management are discussed in more detail below.

Selective activation of actors
In a policy network there are a variety of actors at work. These actors have diverse interests, perceptions and resources. Starting from these different positions they are involved in processes within the network. This does not mean that they play a role in each process or each game. Game management can involve the inclusion or non-inclusion of actors in policy games. To that end, potential relations between actors need to be activated or

blocked. This strategy is referred to as 'selective activation' (Scharpf 1978; Friend *et al.* 1974). By means of selective activation, the formation of restraining or driving coalitions with regard to specific policy proposals can be strengthened or weakened and blockades can be set up, avoided or broken through.

The success of selective activation depends on a correct assessment of which actors are essential to joint action and the willingness of actors to invest their resources (Scharpf 1978; O'Toole 1988). Actors can be essential because they have an indispensable resource at their disposal, or because their participation confers a desired excess value on the joint action. Actors are undesirable if their presence is not strictly necessary but actually hampers joint action. Furthermore, actors can have at their disposal 'veto power', which affords them the option of blocking interaction processes (cf. Kingdon 1984; Marsh and Rhodes 1992, pp. 249–68).

In the case of Schiphol, the actors relevant to both targets (further development of the airport and the safeguarding of the quality of life in the environment) were activated in order to facilitate the coordinated expansion of the airport, and resulting in a project organization in which 16 parties cooperated. Although this ensured the articulation of a variety of interests and issues, it made joint decision-making difficult. Therefore a second round of selective activation became necessary in which the number of participants was limited. This was effected by creating a working group ('the Inner Circle') within the project organization. And then, of course, there was the problem of the environmental pressure groups and representatives of local residents which were not invited to participate. This means that in a future round of decision making, these groups will have to be involved. However, because they are not committed to the joint plan of action, reaching an agreement will not be easy.

Mobilization of resources

There is a specific distribution of resources within a network. Strategic anticipation of resources demands an exact assessment of the importance of specific resources to the progress and quality of a particular game. The actors who were invited to join the project organization for Schiphol were selected on the basis of their official positions, their expertise, their commitment to the two targets and their capacity to contribute to the creation of political and societal support.

Closely linked to this is the problem of how necessary resources can be mobilized. Mobilizing resources often has its price. Bringing resources and their 'administrators' together in one game, moreover, can cause complications. One possible solution to this is provided by the mobilization of 'supporters', i.e. tapping resources without the administrators of those resources actively participating in the game (Teisman 1992). If the price of mobilizing certain resources or actors is considered too high, replacement of resources can be sought. This assumes that actors do not have a monopoly on particular resources whereby they cannot be passed by. In the case of Schiphol this was effected by deciding to let the environmentalists' viewpoint be represented by governmental organizations instead of pressure groups.

The use of interaction rules

In a game, players use rules. Some of these rules are known and are used consciously. Other rules are followed unconsciously, but are no less compulsory. The manager has to be aware of the prevailing rules, because contravening them disrupts the relations between actors and can lead to blockades in interaction. Knowledge of the rules of the network also makes it possible, based on a number of things that can be regarded as 'obvious', to get games underway quickly and, if necessary, to terminate them.

In the case of Schiphol, the interaction between participants regarding such a strategic issue as the future expansion of the airport was a relatively new experience. Adequate routines for interaction were lacking. This meant that at the start of the process a great deal of energy had to be invested in the development of rules. This was effected by the use of arrangements such as the signing of a joint declaration of intent and a joint plan of action. At certain points in the process, the way interactions were organized became the subject of explicit decision making, for instance when it was decided to establish a working group. In order to play the new game, new rules had to be developed. One may surmise that these rules will eventually become institutionalized and thus part of the network.

Managing perceptions

Actors' perceptions about problems and situations are often divergent. In order to achieve a specific policy objective it may be necessary to harmonize the actors' perceptions (cf. Rein and Schon 1986). This is made possible by an exchange of objectives, executing 'package deals' or – in the case of incompatible objectives – 'agreeing to disagree'. If objectives are not mutually exclusive it is possible to achieve 'consensus building' (O'Toole 1988; Hanf and O'Toole 1992).

One way out of conflicts and deadlocks may involve actors abandoning their original position and pursuing new goals which will benefit both parties. By redefining the issues it is possible in many cases to convert win-lose or lose-lose situations into win-win situations. The game manager will do his best to achieve such a redefining of the aim of the game (Forrester 1989).

Managing perceptions was crucial to the Schiphol project. One implication of attempting to accommodate the two seemingly conflicting targets was that parties had to change their perceptions about their interests and goals and the ways to pursue them. Because the targets were formulated in general terms, there was room for participants to look for common ground for decision making. This process was structured by the formation of the working group (the Inner Circle) in which members' conflicting perceptions were confronted. The results of this confrontation were meticulously communicated to the other members of the project organization. By correlating various problems, goals and measures, a package deal was created. The package deal meant that actors had to accept that they could not optimize their interests. It then became possible to find courses of action from which everybody would benefit.

NETWORK STRUCTURING: CHANGING THE NETWORK

In this section the strategies of network structuring which are available to the network manager will be discussed: strategies aimed at changing the relations between actors, the existing distribution of resources, the prevailing interaction rules and the existing perceptions. They are illustrated by the case of the renovation of post-war housing in the Dutch city of Groningen.

Renovation of post-war housing in Groningen

In the mid-1980s, the renewal of the pre-war housing areas in Groningen, a medium-sized city of 170,000 inhabitants in the north of The Netherlands, had almost been completed.

The renewal of these areas was based on the concept of 'building in the interests of the neighbourhood'. This meant a careful improvement of the existing dwellings for the original residents. The aim was to minimize the demolition of dwellings and to keep the new rents as low as possible. The renovations were carried out as a project: one by one, blocks of dwellings were improved mainly by renovating the existing dwellings.

The renewal of the pre-war housing areas took place within a well organized local housing network. The actors of this network were sections of the Department of Housing, Physical Planning and Environment, housing associations, tenant organizations, politicians, local estate agencies, financial organizations, developers, architects and research organizations.

In one of the neighbourhoods, which consisted of pre-war and post-war dwellings, a project group which also coordinated the improvement of the prewar dwellings started renovating those constructed post-war. They used the same procedures for the post-war dwellings as they had used for the pre-war dwellings. However, dissatisfaction with this method of improvement arose in the project group, which mainly consisted of civil servants. Improvements were mainly carried out on the outside (insulation) although some limited improvements on the inside were also made. The housing association and the civil servants concluded that the dwellings remained much as they had been: relatively small and basic. The improvements which were made did little to enhance their popularity on the local housing market.

In September 1987, spurred on by this discontent, the project group came up with a radical new idea for improving the next block; an idea which had the support of the local council executive. The project group proposed demolishing the block of dwellings together with a number of the adjoining blocks and changing the layout of the neighbourhood. This idea constituted a radical break from the proposals that had been made so far and with the existing, mainly prewar, urban renewal traditions. There were vociferous protests from local residents. The social democratic party, which held a dominant position on the council, agreed with the tenants. Eventually, in 1988, the local council rejected the project group's proposal.

This blockage in the decision-making process was the reason why the local Physical Planning and Housing Department initiated a broad-based process which triggered a discussion on what was to be done about the post-war neighbourhoods. After a period of research and intensive interaction between all parties, in late 1989 a concept policy document was produced in which the 'new policy' was laid down. Its main aims were to increase the differentiation of the housing stock in post-war neighbourhoods (in price, size and dwelling type) by implementing more radical improvements and by building new dwellings. Following discussions and negotiations with housing associations, the document was accepted by the local council in early 1991.

In addition, a new way of decision making was agreed by the various parties. The resultant policy document was to constitute the basis for a policy process at neighbourhood level in which plans were made for each post-war neighbourhood which form the basis of the renovation of these areas. The drawing up of the plans was to be a concerted effort by all the actors concerned. Housing associations would perform a coordinating role in this process. In the period between 1991 and 1993, plans were made for all eight post-war neighbourhoods. On the whole, neighbourhood plans were drawn up in relative harmony. In 1993 and 1994, almost all the neighbourhood plans were passed with little problem by the local council. The deadlock which had existed in 1988 was chiefly resolved by effecting a radical change in the perceptions of the actors on renovating post-war neighbourhoods and by developing new decision procedures. Some of these strategies will be discussed in more detail in the following sections.

Changing the relations between actors
Network structuring can deal with relations between actors within a network. In addition, it can involve introducing new actors and excluding others or changing the relations between actors. The introduction or exclusion of actors can affect the relations between actors within the network. It can result in closed strongholds being broken open, offer scope for new ideas and enable new coalitions to form. Furthermore, this kind of change at the policy network level does not necessarily make itself felt in every game. The exclusion of actors, though, is not always easy to achieve, owing to rights which might be founded on long-standing practices.

Changing the relations between actors can occur in various ways. Usually it is effected by establishing or changing long-term organizational arrangements which affect a number of games within the network. Arrangements in the framework of network structuring might be, for example, the introduction of consultation procedures, the establishment of advisory bodies, entering into long-term or extensive contracts or the setting up of public or private legal persons.

In the case of renovating post-war housing, the local council used this strategy of introducing new actors or explicitly changing relationship between actors. The most important strategy was the attempt to create a smoothly functioning tenants association at neighbourhood level. Until 1988, only small tenants associations existed but no organization was available which could present the interests of tenants in a specific neighbourhood. Local government tried to create such neighbourhood tenants associations by offering all kinds of (subsidy) facilities. In almost every neighbourhood, the forming of a unified tenants association at neighbourhood level occurred very quickly. In all the neighbourhoods these newly created organisations participated in policy processes. This gave the policy processes at neighbourhood level a strong legitimacy and facilitated the acceptance of the plans by the local council.

Changing the distribution of resources
Changing the distribution of resources within the network is aimed at effecting changes in the position of actors in the policy network by bringing about changes in the resources which they have at their disposal: money, formal positions, manpower, information, expertise and legitimacy.

Influencing the resources in the network can be done in several ways. Influencing the resource information can take place by, for example, introducing new data systems or linking existing systems. Thus, legalizing the linking of databases will strengthen the position of various public services in combating the abuse of social services. Expertise and skills can be strengthened by means of training and schooling. Strengthening the legitimacy of actors or the support which they get can take diverse forms. For instance, the government can recognize an organization as a discussion partner, give this organization access to permanent consultative bodies or even grant the organization a legal monopoly.

Strategies to influence the distribution of resources were not a dominant feature in the case of renovating post-war housing in Groningen. Nevertheless, some strategies can be identified which were aimed at effecting minor changes in the resource division. Several subsidy instruments were developed to make the policy process concerning the neighbourhood plans more attractive. Besides the fact that funds were reserved for neighbourhood improvements (on condition that concrete plans were submitted) there was also the possibility for tenants associations to receive subsidies for special activities. These subsidies, which in principle were reserved use over a long period, were intended as an incentive for various actors to participate in the policy process at neighbourhood level.

Changing interaction rules

In spite of the attention focused on the concept of rules (Burns and Flam 1987; Ostrom 1986), the form of management which involves the influencing of interaction rules has received little attention. The idea underlying this concept is that it is possible to steer a process in a particular direction by influencing the interaction rules. Given that actors are often only partly conscious of the rules which determine their behaviour, and that changing the rules is usually a long-winded affair, interaction rules are often difficult to influence.

In the case study, the idea of 'steering by means of procedures' was practised in the sense that new procedures for decision making were agreed upon. But implicit attempts were also made to change the more informal rules of the network. It used to be standard procedure for new initiatives on renovation to be taken by the local Physical Planning and Housing Department. By allowing housing associations to take the initiative in developing neighbourhood plans, the department, supported by the local council executive, tried to call into question the 'given nature' of this informal rule and to stimulate housing associations to take new initiatives.

Changing norms, values and perceptions

Network management can also deal with changing the existing values, norms and perceptions of the actors within the network. By directing 'internalization processes', the manager can attempt to steer the values and perceptions of a target group in the desired direction (in 't Veld 1991).

In addition to persuasion strategies, network management can address itself to the organizing or promoting of an 'open debate' (Majone 1986, p. 457). A more radical, 'tougher' method is that of reframing. Reframing is an intervention which stimulates the actors involved to put their own frame of reference (frame) into perspective and to consider a situation or relation from another frame of reference. Reframing is aimed at effecting an illogical, irrational leap which can be compared to a 'paradigmatic shift'. 'The approach' results in changing perceptions, behaviour and relations', according to Levy and Merry (1986, p. 96). Reframing can be effected by simulations or by organizing a confrontation between actors with new points of view. Striking, shocking events often serve as a 'trigger' for reframing, whether consciously directed or not.

In the case study, reframing strategies were important. In fact, one of the major causes of the initial blockade in the decision making on post-war neighbourhoods were the differences between the various actors' perceptions on renovation. Generally speaking, it can be said that in the beginning most parties had a 'technical orientation' towards renovating post-war neighbourhoods. This orientation emphasized the technical defects of the housing stock and was aimed at making low investments to improve those defects. Conflicts arose when a new orientation became dominant. This 'housing market orientation' stressed the problem that the post-war dwellings did not meet with their inhabitants' preferences and could only satisfy the housing preferences of a very small group of inhabitants who had low incomes. This meant that more radical measures for changing the housing stock of a neighbourhood sometimes needed to be taken. The local Physical Planning and Housing Department succeeded in legitimizing this new orientation by means of an intensive process of research coupled with interaction between all the important actors within the network.

ASSESSMENT OF AND RECOMMENDATIONS FOR NETWORK MANAGEMENT

Notwithstanding the previous arguments, there still remains the question of what should be understood by 'good' network management and which criteria should be employed in determining this. The problem with answering this question is that actors pursue different objectives which, moreover, can change in the course of the policy process. For this reason, the achieving of objectives cannot be a guiding criterion in structuring and assessing network management. In this section a number of norms will be formulated which emphasize the quality of policy processes.

Based on the idea that networks are often characterized by cooperation problems caused by the lack of a dominant decision centre, network management is considered a success if it promotes cooperation between actors and prevents, by-passes or removes the blockades which obstruct that cooperation. This can be effected by taking advantage of the opportunities and avoiding the threats which can occur at game level and through actively influencing opportunities and threats at the level of the network and its environment. This general norm for assessing network management is further developed below based on six properties which are required of 'good' network management.

1   Achieving win-win situations
Instead of concentrating on one actor achieving his objective, network management needs to address itself to bringing about a situation which represents an improvement on the starting position for all those concerned. This does not mean that all those involved will achieve their objectives to the same extent. In many cases it will not be possible to give all the actors a feeling of winning. In such cases, a situation can be fostered which makes non-participation in interactions less attractive than participation (Dery 1984; Teisman 1992, p. 96). Good management contributes to the stimulation of interactions which will lead to such a situation, and to the breaking through of deadlocks which prevent the achieving of win-win situations.

2   Activating actors and resources
Interaction assumes that actors are willing to invest their resources in a joint process. This means that they need to realize the attractiveness of that interaction process. Network management needs to be aimed at promoting that willingness and should therefore stimulate enthusiasm.

3   Limiting interaction costs
The costs of interaction should be kept within reasonable limits. If interaction leads to endless squabbling or trench warfare it can cause participation in the interaction to result in a waste of resources and energy. It is necessary to prevent actors pulling out in disillusionment after an enthusiastic start. Interaction costs should be proportionate to the stake in the game. Network management should be aimed at restructuring, avoiding or ending interactions which lead to win-lose or, lose-lose situations (Koppenjan 1993). In addition, good management of conflicts makes heavy demands on network management.

Suppressing conflicts threatens the quality and transparency of the interaction. Regulation should prevent conflicts becoming dysfunctional and destructive (Termeer 1993).

4   Procuring commitment
In addition to mobilizing actors and resources, network management needs to induce those involved to make a commitment to the joint undertaking. Without this 'voluntary binding', cooperation threatens to founder on the strategic uncertainties which play a role in collective action: the danger that the impact of actions will be shifted onto others or that actors will pull out at crucial moments and leave others with the risks (Olsen 1965). By procuring a form of commitment to the collective action, this danger of withdrawal can be curbed. This commitment from the parties concerned can consist of informal agreements, or of more formal arrangements entering into convenants or contracts or the establishing of autonomous legal persons (Teisman 1992).

5   Political-administrative management
In network management particular attention needs to be focused on political commitment. The functioning of networks, indeed, is sometimes seen as posing a threat to the position of representative bodies such as municipal councils, the Provincial States and Parliament (Hufen and Ringeling 1990, p. 251). The existence of policy networks does not mean, however, that representative bodies are by definition excluded. On the contrary, they are often part of networks. For this reason, good political-administrative management is a part of network management. It is particularly important to link up the various games in which representative bodies are involved with the games which are being played elsewhere in the network. The quality of political-administrative management stands or falls by the manager's 'feeling' for determining which information is relevant and for choosing the correct moment for political-administrative harmonization attempts.

6   The quality and openness of the interaction
Network management needs to do justice to the quality and openness of the interaction within networks (Majone 1986). After all, one of the dangers connected with the functioning of networks is that external effects are produced which are damaging in the longer term, both to those involved within the network and to others not represented within the network. Furthermore, it is necessary to prevent a stranglehold consensus emerging within the network which results in 'groupthink' type situations in which criticism is not accepted and risks and the external impact of decisions are ignored, with all the concomitant repercussions (Janis 1982; 't Hart 1990).

THE MARGINS OF NETWORK MANAGEMENT

Management in policy networks requires a great deal of patience and a feeling for the relations and the options which can be found within the network. The network manager has limited resources at his disposal and is dependent on others. Not all key aspects are equally easy for him to influence. His attempts to influence can be neutralized by the strategies of others. His efforts to improve interaction processes can be in vain. The margins for network management are not always wide. Moreover, the manager is himself part of the network and has his own interests, values and perceptions. This complicates his relation with the other actors.

On the other hand, he can undertake attempts to influence, in the same way as other actors, which means he is not powerless. His interventions can promote interaction, help to restructure the direction of interaction processes and introduce new values, ideas and actors. Network management cannot guarantee better interaction development and better policy outcome but does increase the chances of these things occurring. The opportunities for network management should not be underestimated, either. The fact that many actors are involved in policy processes in networks affords the manager the scope to introduce his own ideas and reactivate stagnating processes. Furthermore, the influence of the – often indirect – management strategies dealt with here, could well be much more radical and far-reaching than those of the classical, more short-term oriented, direct strategies.

REFERENCES

Agranoff R.I. 1986. *Intergovernmental management. Human services problem-solving in six metropolitan areas.* Albany, New York: State University of New York Press.

Aldrich, H.A. 1979. *Organizations and environments.* Englewood Cliffs: Prentice-Hall.

Allison, G.T. 1971. *Essence of decision.* Boston: Little, Brown and Company.

Benson, J.K. 1982. 'A framework for policy analysis' in Rogers and Whetten (eds.) (see below).

Burns, T.R. and H. Flam. 1987. *The shaping of social organization; social rule system theory with application.* London: Sage.

Crozier, M. and E. Friedberg. 1980. *Actors and systems; the politics of collective action.* Chicago and London: University of Chicago Press.

Dery, D. 1984. *Problem definition in policy analysis.* Kansas: University Press of Kansas.

Forester, J. 1989. *Planning in the face of power.* Berkeley: University of California Press.

Friend, J.K., J.M. Power and C.J.L. Yewlett. 1974. *Public planning: the inter-corporate dimension.* London: Tavistock.

Gage, R.W. and M.P. Mandell. 1990. *Strategies for managing intergovernmental policies and networks.* New York and London: Praeger.

Giddens, A. 1984. *The constiution of society; outline of the theory of stucturation.* Berkeley and Los Angeles: University of California Press.

Hanf, K. and F.W. Scharpf. 1978. *Interorganizational policy making; limits to coordination and central control.* London: Sage.

Hanf, K. and Th.A.J. Toonen. 1985. *Policy implementation in federal and unitary systems.* Dordrecht, Boston and Lancaster: Kluwer.

Hanf, K. and L. O'Toole. 1992. 'Revisiting old friends: networks, implementation structures and the management of interorganizational relations' *European Journal of Political Research* 21, 163–80.

Hart, P. 't. 1990. *Groupthink in government. A study of small groups and governmental failure.* Amsterdam and Lisse.

Hjern, B. and D.O. Porter. 1981. 'Implementation structures: a new unit for administrative analysis', *Organizational Studies* 3, 211–37.

Hufen, J.A.M. and A.B. Ringeling. 1990. *Beleidsnetwerken: Overheids-, semi- overheids- en particuliere organisaties in wisselwerking,* *[Policy networks: Interaction of government, quasi-government and private organizations].* 's-Gravenhage: Vuga.

Janis, I.L. 1982. *Groupthink: psychological studies of policy decisions and fiascos.* Boston: Houghton Mifflin.

Jordan, G. 1990. 'Sub-governments, policy communities and networks; refilling old bottles?', *Journal of Theoretical Politics* 2, 319–38.

Kaufmann, F.X., G. Majone and V. Ostrom (eds.). 1986. *Guidance, control and evaluation in the public sector.* Berlin and New York: De Gruyter.

Kingdon, J.W. 1984. *Agendas, alternatives and public policies.* Boston and Toronto: Little, Brown and Company.

Klijn, E.H. 1995. 'Analysing and managing policy networks: a theoretical examination of the concept policy network and its problems', *Administration and Society* (forthcoming).

Klijn, E.H., and G.R. Teisman. 1991. 'Effective policy making in a multi-actor setting: networks and steering' pp. 99–112 in: In't Veld *et al.* (see below).

Koppenjan, J.F.M. 1993. *Management van de beleidsvorming. Een studie naar de totstandkoming van beleid op het terrein van het binnenlands bestuur, [Managing the policy-making process. A study of public policy formation in the field of home administration].* 's-Gravenhage: VUGA.

Koppenjan, J.F.M., J.A. de Bruijn and W.J.M. Kickert (eds.) 1993. *Netwerkmanagement in het Openbaar Bestuur, [Network Management in the public sector],* The Hague: VUGA.

Levy, A. and U. Merry. 1986. *Organizational transformation.* New York: Praeger.

Lynn, L.E. 1981. *Managing the public business.* New York: Basic Books, Inc.

Majone, G. 1986. 'Mutual adjustment by debate and persuasion pp. 445–58, in F.X. Kaufman *et al.* (see above).

Mandell, M.P. 1988 'Intergovernmental management in interorganizational networks' *International Journal of Public Administration* 11, 4, 393–416.

————. 1990. 'Network management: strategic behaviour in the public sector, pp. 35–51, in R.W. Gage and M.P. Mandell (see above).

March, J.G. and J.P. Olsen. 1976. *Ambiguity and choice in organizations*. Bergen: Universitetsforlaget.

Marin, B. and R. Mayntz (eds.). 1991. *Policy networks. Empirical evidence and theoretical considerations*. Frankfurt am Main: Campus Verlag.

Marsh, D. and R.A.W. Rhodes (eds.). 1992. *Policy networks in British Government*. Oxford: Clarendon Press.

Morgan, G. 1986. *Images of organizations*. London: Sage.

Olsen, M. 1965. *The logic of collective action*. Cambridge, MA: Harvard University Press.

Ostrom, E. 1986. 'A method of institutional analysis', pp, 459–79, in Kaufman, Majone and Ostrom (see above).

O'Toole, L.J. 1988. 'Strategies for intergovernmental management: implementing programs in interorganizational networks', *International Journal of Public Administration* 11, 4, 417–41.

Rein, M. and D. Schon. 1986. 'Frame reflective policy discourse', *Beleidsanalyse* 4, 4–19.

Rhodes, R.A.W. 1981. *Control and power in central and local relations*. Farnborough: Gower.

————. 1990. 'Policy networks: a British perspective', *Journal of Theoretical Politics*. 2, 3, 293–317.

Ripley, R.B. and G. Franklin. 1987. (1st ed. 1976) *Congress, the bureaucracy and public policy*. Dorsey: Homewood.

Rogers, D.L. and D.A. Whetten (eds.). 1982. *Interorganizational coordination: theory, research and implementation*, Ames: Iowa State University.

Scharpf, F.W. 1978. 'Interorganizational policy studies: issues, concepts and perspectives', pp. 345–70 in Hanf and Scharpf (see above).

Scharpf, F.W., B. Reissert, and F. Schnabel. 1978. 'Policy effectiveness and confict avoidance in intergovernmental policy formation' pp. 57–114, in Hanf and Scharpf (see above).

Teisman, G.R. 1992. *Complexe Besluitvorming; een pluricentrisch perspectief op besluitvorming over ruimtelijke investeringen, [Complex Decision making; a pluricentric perspective on decision making on spatial investments]*. 's-Gravenhage: VUGA.

Termeer, C.J.A.M. 1993. *Dynamiek en inertie rondom mestbeleid; een studie naar veranderingsprocessen in het varkenshouderijnetwerk, [Dynamics and inertia in the Dutch manure policies; a study of change processes in the pig farming network]*. 's-Gravenhage: VUGA.

Twist, M.J.W. van and C.J.A.M. Termeer. 1991. 'Introduction to configuration approach; a process theory for societal steering', pp. 19–30 in In't Veld *et al.* (see below).

Veld, R. in 't. 1991. 'Autopoiesis, configuration and steering: impossibility theorem or dynamic steering theory' in Veld *et al.* (see below).

Veld, R. in 't, L. Schaap, C.J.A.M. Termeer and M.J.W. van Twist (eds.). 1991. *Autopoiesis and configuration theory: new approaches to societal steering*. Dordrecht and Boston and London: Kluwer Academic Publishers.

Weick, K.E. 1979. *The social psychology of organizing*. (2nd edn.) New York: Addison Wesley.

AFTERWORD: THE MANAGERIAL TURN

THE MANAGERIAL TURN IN POLICY NETWORK THEORY

In 1995, when our article 'Managing Networks in the Public Sector' was published, the concept of policy networks was already quite familiar. With some exceptions (see, for example, Heclo 1978), network were seen as bad news: prohibiting effective, innovative and democratically legitimized policies. The idea that networks could be managed – the core message of our contribution – was relatively new. The article advocated that the potentials of networks could be used in order to arrive at better policies and came up with a set of strategies to do so: game management and network structuring. It was the first English language publication with which we as Dutch network scholars presented our work to the international academic community (to be followed by, for example, Kickert *et al.* 1997 and Koppenjan and Klijn 2004).

The warm welcome the article received in this international public management community stems from the fact that the timing of its publication was just right. At that time the New Public Management (NPM) paradigm was predominant, though widely criticized. Network management, in terms of date of publication preceding the nowadays popular governance narrative, provided a promising alternative to the NPM approach.

Now, 15 years on, it is interesting to look back and to ask what insights presented in our article still hold and what their relevance has been for the continuing debate on networks. We do so below by addressing the following questions:

1) How did the idea of network management evolve conceptually and theoretically?
2) What are the empirical findings of the research on network management?
3) What topics need further exploration?

CONCEPTUAL AND THEORETICAL DEBATES

Since our article a lot of effort has been put into the theoretical elaboration and conceptual clarification of network management. Most attention has been paid to game management or what we currently would call process management (see Mandell 2001; Agranoff and McGuire 2003; O'Toole *et al.* 2007; Meier and O'Toole 2007). This work has resulted in more sophisticated approaches, going beyond somewhat naïve interpretation of the network management repertoire suggestions like '(always) apply process management', 'involving all stakeholders', 'create openness' and 'enhance consensus' (see, for example, De Bruijn and Ten Heuvelhof 2008).

Network structuring or institutional design strategies (Klijn and Koppenjan 2006) aimed at changing the network seem to have received less attention. Since in practice a lot of institutional tinkering is on going on, here lies an important research challenge.

As far as the implications of the concept of network management are concerned, the recent introductions of the concept of meta-governance gives cause for additional reflection. Our 1995 article obviously expressed optimism about the possibilities to manage networks. The same optimism seems to drive the meta-governance discourse (see Sørensen and Torfing 2007). However, the network concept originally referred to the limitations of government's attempts at realizing policies, given their dependencies upon other actors. One may wonder why attempts at network management and meta-governance would not be subordinated to the same limitations. Simply presupposing a meta-position does not make these interdependencies go away. This insight should lead to modesty regarding claims for the possibilities to (meta) govern networks and require further reflection on and clarification of the nature of network management strategies and their effects. So, after 15 years, the need for further conceptual clarification and reflection on the limits of network management persists.

EMPIRICAL RELEVANCE

In the last 15 years a lot of empirical research has been done on network management. Besides the question about what strategies are used and how they are used, the crucial research question was of course if network management strategies matter for achieving good outcomes in complex governance processes.

Many case studies, done in a large variety of countries (such as Australia, USA, UK, Netherlands, Italy, Denmark, France), show that network management is an important, possibly crucial, factor to achieve results in complex governance networks. Case studies showed the importance of network management for involving stakeholders, solving dead-locks, creating new and attractive content for involved actors and facilitating interactions (for an overview, see Klijn et al. 2010). Research also shows that networking is common among managers in governance networks (see O'Toole et al. 2007; Walker et al. 2007). Civil servants are attracted to the concepts of networks (for example, Fleming and Rhodes 2005) since network strategies provide them with alternative ways of dealing with complex policy processes. These findings in case studies have also been confirmed by large N studies on network management and outcomes of governance networks that show clear influence of network management strategies on outcomes (see Huang and Provan 2007; Meier and O'Toole 2007; Klijn et al. 2010).

TOPICS FOR FURTHER EXPLORATION

15 years after the publication of our article we can observe a broad consensus in the scientific community about the importance of network management as a generic way of dealing with complex societal problems. In addition, we know much more about network management strategies and the conditions under which they are effective. Nevertheless, there is still a lot to be discovered. Without pretending to be complete, we think the following issues need further exploration.

Empirical research on what network management strategies are successful, and why, is still limited and needs to be pursued more rigorously and systematically, preferably by supplementing comparative case research with large N-studies

The tension between governance networks and (representational) democracy is a recurrent theme in the literature (see Sørensen and Torfing 2007). More empirical research on whether and how network management or meta governance can contribute to democratic legitimacy is required.

In practice, civil servants encounter institutional barriers when they apply network management strategies. More research is needed to understand how they cope with these difficulties (Termeer 2009). In network studies remarkably little attention is being paid to the role of media. Especially the question of how disruption in political support for governance processes as a result of sudden media attention can be anticipated and dealt with, deserves further attention.

REFERENCES

Agranoff, R. and M. McGuire. 2003. *Collaborative Public Management; new strategies for local governments*, Washington, D.C.: Georgetown University Press.

Bruijn, J.A. and E.F. ten Heuvelhof. 2008. *Management in networks. On multi-actor decision making*, London: Routledge.

Edelenbos, J, and E.H. Klijn. 2006. 'Managing stakeholder involvement in decision-making: a comparative analysis of six interactive processes in The Netherlands', *Journal of Public Administration Research and Theory*, 16, 3, 417–446.

Fleming, J. and R.A.W. Rhodes. 2005. 'Bureaucracy, Contracts and Networks: the Unholy Trinity and the Police', *Australian and New Zealand Journal of Criminology*, 38, 2, 192–205.

Freeman, J.L. and J.P.P. Stevens. 1987. 'A Theoretical and Conceptual Re-examination of Subsystem Politics', in: *Public Policy and Administration*, 2, 1, 9–24.

Heclo, H. 1978. 'Issue Networks and the Executive Establishment'. In: A. King (ed.). *The New American Political System*, American Enterprise Institute for Public Policy Research, Washington D.C.: 87–124.

Huang, K. and K.G. Provan. 2007. Structural embeddedness and organizational social outcomes in a centrally governed mental health service network, *Public Management Review*, 9, 2, 169–189.

Kickert, W.J.M., E.H. Klijn and J.F.M. Koppenjan (eds). 1997. *Managing complex networks: strategies for the public sector*, London: Sage.

Klijn, E.H. and J.F.M. Koppenjan. 2006. 'Institutional design: changing features of networks', *Public Management Review*, 8, 1, 141–161.

Klijn, E.H, B. Steijn and J. Edelenbos. 2010. 'The impact of network management strategies on the outcomes in governance networks', *Public Administration*, 88, 4, 1063–1082.

Koppenjan, J.F.M. and E.H. Klijn. 2004. *Managing uncertainty in networks*, London: Routledge.

Mandell, M.P. (ed.). 2001. *Getting results through collaboration*, Westport, CT: Quorum Books.

Meier, K. and L.J. O'Toole. 2007. 'Modelling Public Management: empirical analysis of the management-performance nexus', *Public Management Review*, 9, 4, 503–527.

O'Toole, L.J., R.M. Walker, K. Meier and G. Boyne. 2007. 'Networking in comparative context: Public managers in the USA and the UK', *Public Management Review*, 9, 3, 401–420.

Rhodes, R.A.W. 1988. *Beyond Westminster and Whitehall: The Sub-central Goverments of Britain*, London: Unwin Hyman.

Rhodes, R.A.W. 1997. *Understanding Governance*, Buckingham: Open University Press.

Sørenson E. and J. Torfing (eds). 2007. *Theories of democratic network governance*, Cheltenham: Edward Elgar.

Termeer, C.J.A.M. 2009. 'Barriers to New Modes Of Horizontal Governance', *Public Management Review*, 11, 3, 299–316.

Walker, R.M., L.J. O'Toole and K. Meier. 2007. 'It's where you are that matters: the networking behaviour of English local government officers', *Public Administration*, 85, 2, 739–756.

Chapter 9

TERRITORIAL ADMINISTRATION AND POLITICAL CONTROL: DECENTRALIZATION IN FRANCE

JEAN-CLAUDE THOENIG

INTRODUCTION

France, up to the late 1970s, was considered to be a quasi-ideal case of the centralized state (De Tocqueville 1856). The rather unexpected – and authoritarian – decentralization policy launched in 1981 by François Mitterrand, then the newly elected President of the Republic, both raised enthusiasm and attracted international attention (Hayward 1983; Page and Goldsmith 1987; Schmidt 1990). During the 20 years that followed, additional modernization decisions were taken by both ruling politicians and central ministries. At the end of July 2004 the conservative majority in Parliament approved a new and relevant transfer of policy domains from the French state to the regions, the *départements* and the communes.

Have the reforms fundamentally changed territorial politics in France? How far has the state role and influence been reduced or transformed? How far have local and regional authorities taken advantage of massive transfers? The purpose of this paper is: (1) to understand the current state of territorial government, its basic characteristics and dynamics; (2) to identify the actual functioning of the vertical relationships between national and sub-national levels; and (3) to understand how public authorities and organizations belonging to the same institutional and territorial level manage horizontal interdependencies. It does not attempt to list the decentralization reforms and describe their formal content nor to explain why France has become so active in modernizing the way it governs sub-national public affairs. Since the 1950s around 420 decrees have been issued by Paris to modernize administrative procedures.

The debate between new localism and new centralism that goes on in a number of European countries may seem quite irrelevant for the understanding of the current French situation. In France, territorial policy-making and politics are basically run and regulated by a polycentric and informal configuration involving national ministries and sub-national authorities so that none of them plays a leading role and none can act in a fully autonomous way. Intricate interdependencies and complex exchanges provide a normative tissue and a political fabric in which the various parties are embedded, and access to which is not easy for outsiders, including citizens.

Social science research had identified informal characteristics, such as cooptation processes, between state agencies and local agents (Grémion 1976). It has also identified the emergence of cities as strong political entities (Thoenig 1987). Cities operated at the margins of the centralized state design well before the 1981 decentralization. They still exist but now in a global setting where the hegemony of ministries in Paris and prefects in the provinces belongs to the past and the centralized model of government in its pure form has vanished.

Research has also suggested that governance dynamics structure approaches apply to both regional and local public affairs (Le Galès and Lequesne 1998). The practice of governance is usually associated with policy networks, issue communities, urban regimes and subsidiarity. Nevertheless, government-from-below practices (Sellers 2002) do not imply a full withdrawal of the state and participative policy-making does not imply that the political class loses control. State apparatus still matters. The innovation here is that it is just one player among many others. Sub-national bodies enjoy much autonomy but they do not act in an autocratic manner.

French decentralization and modernization policies have stopped halfway between centralization and disjointed pluralism models. It is generally agreed that a system operates that is more than just a compromise. The aim of this paper is to characterize the components of this system as well as its inner social and political regulation. A second aim is to explain the roots of its sustainability and legitimacy.

French decentralization and territorial administration coincide with the triumph of elected politicians – over the State's own executive branch (including the government and national bureaucrats such as the prefects). Multiple political office holders control the reform agenda in a rather conservative manner and it could also be said, from a rather selfish perspective. Often described as a half reform because transfer of power from the state to territorial institutions did not include transfer of power from the local political class to citizens and inhabitants, the 1981 decentralization policy enhanced the role of elected politicians (referred to as *grands élus*). Both its sponsors and socialist thinkers of the time such as François Mitterrand, Prime Minister Pierre Mauroy, and Gaston Defferre, the Minister of the Interior, were seasoned agents as well as themselves being multiple office holders. They framed a decentralization scheme that would strengthen the power base both of their colleagues across the country and among the various political parties.

The interpretative model presented below relies mainly on observations and information collected during a series of six empirical field studies carried out between 1991 and 2002. As well as a discussion of the topics covered and the methods used, other sources and recent studies that cover additional facets will be cited.

THE SEVEN BASIC CHARACTERISTICS OF THE DECENTRALIZATION PROCESS

In France, neither hierarchical authority nor bargaining between fully autonomous equals govern the way in which the national state and subnational public authorities manage their actual interdependence and exchange relationships. A relatively old tradition exists that ranks the French case as being both unique and complex (Ashford 1982). To a large degree the idea that it is some kind of exception – in that inter-governmental relationships would be easier to understand in most other democracies – is not convincing. Part of the prejudice may derive from the quite early emphasis made by social scientists on informal processes and actual practices. Having said that, reforms designed and implemented in the last two decades have not exactly made the situation simpler, to say the least.

Territorial policy-making and politics repeatedly suggest the existence and the importance of seven basic characteristics which structure the way territorial affairs are handled as well as the social structure in which public officials are embedded. They blend functional creativity and democratic conservatism, competition mechanisms and cooperation norms, institutional innovativeness and power struggles. The paper sets them out in turn below, covering: (1) the institutional; (2) the central state and the local; (3) competition between public authorities; (4) inter-institutional mechanisms; (5) democratic participation; (6) constraint; and (7) constitutional reforms.

A densely thick institutional web

Sub-national affairs in France are handled by an exceptionally high number of political public authorities all of which have different legal statuses and operate at different geographic levels. France is vertically sub-divided into four main levels: communes, inter-communalities, *départements* and regions. Around 54 000 sub-national public authorities govern at least some jurisdiction dealing with public affairs – one for slightly more than one hundred inhabitants. The institutional density is thus spectacular. The number of communes, for instance, is approximately equivalent to the sum of the communes in all the other country members of the European Union (see appendix 1).

Not many countries encounter such a dense, creative and diverse institutional landscape. Indeed, the contrast with other countries is striking together with the fact that there is in France an often under-estimated importance given to local government compared with national affairs. The conventional metaphor, that France is made of two parts, Paris and the provinces, does not quite hold, although it is true that the periphery has been deprived of institutional means of self-government. Increasing privatization of urban services and public utilities has also occurred (Lorrain and Stoker 1997). Nevertheless, the rise of the market economy has induced neither much outsourcing nor much privatization; in addition, it has not weakened public institutions. About 20 specific institutional statuses exist: municipal councils, general councils for *départements*, regional councils, agglomeration councils, commune councils, inter-municipal syndicates, urban communities, *pays*, and so on. Each has specific policy domains to handle and a specific territory to cover.

At one end of the spectrum are classic democratic jurisdictions, such as the commune, the *département* and the region, where citizens elect the office holders. These bodies have their own administration and raise their revenues directly from taxes. At the other end, France has *ad hoc* configurations whose *raison d'être* is to administer a specific function – collection of garbage, economic development, and so on. These are governed by so-called indirect democratic principles. Participation in them is optional, depending on the discretion of local and regional councils. Their ruling bodies are composed of officials (many of whom can be let go at any time) who are designated by these councils. A variety of hybrids also operate, some being mandatory for the communes (being part of their territory), others not; some being quite institutionalized, others not.

There are both functional redundancies and geographical overlaps. In extreme cases, up to nine sub-national public authorities handle local development policies in the same commune. This results in a piling up of direct and indirect democracy, generalist and functional authorities, and the end result is a sophisticated web of actors and jurisdictions. Despite core values such as equality, uniformity across the territory of the French Republic is not achieved; indeed, the opposite is the case.

State agencies as local operators

Despite decentralization, the central state retains the monopoly of designing and imple-menting change in the status of public sub-national institutions. Organic changes are top-down driven. As an example, consider the fact that the method of selecting, training and paying employees of local authorities – whether city managers or street cleaners – is defined by (national) law. The Ministry of the Interior is in charge of formally designing the standard plans that communes have to enforce for their public agencies.

Central institutions are the major operators on a daily basis for handling local policies; it is as if no clear-cut separation existed between the sphere of local affairs the state is in charge of and the sphere of local affairs that sub-national authorities are in charge of. Most national ministries operate at the grass roots level. To mention just a few of them, they cover domains such as education, agricultural development, crime and law, public health, sports and roads. A huge percentage, 95 per cent, of state employees work outside Paris, and therefore in other locations than those of the national headquarters. Such a ratio is unique within the OECD and EU member states. In addition, many thousands of field agencies are spread across France. The Ministry of Finance, for example, heads five separate administrative networks. Each has specific units at three levels: regional, *départemental* and local. State employees located sub-nationally outnumber sub-national authority employees by 40 per cent. In some domains, they even deliver additional services without being linked to national policies. For instance they may collect taxes on behalf of local authorities, a service for which local authorities pay a fee. In some domains, non-mandatory services are supplied using a market-type of approach. In engineering, national state ministries such as Agriculture and *Équipement* compete with local authority controlled technical agencies and with private sector companies.

Inside the state apparatus partitioning is general practice, whether hierarchically or horizontally arranged. Tasks are subdivided between specialized 'silos' of expertise. Each state field agency has a monopoly over the way it handles a particular geographical area. It also tends to protect its turf from any interference by other state colleagues. This pattern results in a dilution of horizontal cooperation between state agencies. The unitary French state in fact resembles a loosely coupled network. Even the prefect, supposed to be the ultimate incarnation of state authority and the carrier of general interest in each region and *département*, can barely coordinate events.

Competition between public authorities

Perfect centralization defines a world in which order and action are governed from the top. Who does what, when, how and with whom, is non-ambiguous. The French scene suggests that this is not exactly what happens. Neither the regional council nor the general council have some sort of constitutional right over the policies and statuses of lower-level bodies and jurisdictions such as communes. Regions, *départements* and communes are separate independent entities not linked by subordination principles. No one person is entitled to supervise and to act as a trustee for anybody else.

Regions, communes and *départements* may be characterized as generalist in nature. Legally, core competences are assigned to each of them. But the actual division of domains is far more informal as well as being more subtle. Tasks that are mandatory for communes may be delegated to other levels such as syndicates of communes (examples are waste disposal and bus services) or can be sub-contracted to private companies (examples are water management, cemeteries, public transportation). More importantly, a public authority may take the initiative in entering a policy area that is not part of its own core portfolio but belongs to the core domain of another territorial level. Sometimes as many as three, four – or even five – different authorities, all belonging to different levels, fund and provide goods or services for the same territory. Even state field agencies join in the game, adding their own complexity. In such cases they set up a joint policy with a city. They then provide services that either overlap or are surplus to services produced by the same city.

Local authorities take advantage of such legal permissiveness. They define their own agenda of issues and portfolio of domains. To intervene or not in such and such sector becomes a strategic tool used for political purposes. Even in a situation when relatively small amounts of monies are allocated to a domain, the council may invoke the system to show the population that it cares about it. Taking the initiative to appear to cover, at least symbolically, a wide array of projects may satisfy the following tactical purposes: (1) hindering the intervention of potential competitors; (2) putting pressure on third parties to spend their own money in a domain the latter would not have covered spontaneously; (3) increasing both the brand awareness of the council and the image of its political leaders.

Public affairs provide structure in an open market where players might compete either to expand their visibility or control a dominant market share. The formal division of core domains between players does not regulate most of their acts and non-acts, even in domains such as law and crime where precise limits give exclusive ownership to the state police. Local authorities also sign exchange and cooperation agreements with foreign countries. Politically fashionable issues such as sustainable development attract attention from several public authorities while others such as drug addiction remain neglected and thus kept to the lowest required standards. Some institutions and some levels still matter more than others. But the 'cards' keep being redistributed among the 'players'. The division of work and the modes of exchange are diversified across the national territory. Sub-national government is driven by micro-contexts and multiple players who co-produce informal and flexible designs.

A complex set of inter-institutional patterns
In terms of autonomy and coordination, quite extensive use is made of cooperation patterns, although within certain limits. Coordination, as an administrative mechanism by which the centre makes the parts compatible, does not work well. Policies requiring the intervention of various field agencies inside the same jurisdiction are acknowledged to be a nightmare to coordinate and manage. Each ministry tends to keep its own professional culture and to protect its own networks with local public authorities and elite groupings.

Between sub-national public authorities, the picture looks more or less identical. While massive differences exist between authorities of the same territorial level – for instance, between rural and urban communes – in terms of population size, financial resources or functional needs, local councils fight fiercely to remain the sole legitimate and democratically appointed masters of their jurisdictions. Communes or regions are inclined to prefer what could be termed mutual avoidance. Mergers giving rise to enlarged jurisdictions are considered to be the ultimate threat – indeed, considered to be a way of commiting political suicide. There is wide practice of functional coordination, achieved through various institutional arrangements such as communes, because such coordination provides alternative routes to survival.

Hierarchy and politically organized units tend to be weak mechanisms; nevertheless many joint ventures and alliances occur. Both functional interests and *ad hoc* circumstances (more than partisan politics) push autonomous bodies to become limited partners. Since the late 1980s, extensive use has been made of quasi-contractual partnerships and opportunistic joint ventures. Co-funding provides an illustration of the state of territorial government. Research into budgetary processes in two regional councils (Nord-Pas-de-Calais and Limousin) indicates that about two-thirds of the budgets controlled by regional councils are spent for co-developed programmes and allocated to co-funded projects (Gilbert and Thoenig 1997, 1999b). In the 1990s, a single region co-funded an annual average of more or less 1300 single investment projects.

In terms of inter-institutional influence, both the French government and outside authorities such as the European Commission set up strong incentives as well as pro-cedural requirements. Two major formal set-ups for public investment funding are the European Structural Funds and so-called Plan Contracts between the state and the regions (Gilbert and Thoenig 1999a). To be eligible for such multi-annual subsidies, sub-national authorities have to match the funds allocated. Projects are jointly prepared, decided and assessed and there is wide use of co-funding. Taking one regional council as an example, about half the budget was allocated to a co-funded project. Mutualization practices go far beyond formal set-ups. About one-quarter of local projects are funded on an *ad hoc* and one-off basis. In one example, five partners (a village, the *département*, the national Ministry of Agriculture, the local Chamber of Agriculture and the region) each paid one-fifth of the bill to purchase a 1000 euro forest acquisition. Likewise, in another example, two parties (a regional council and an urban community council) spent 16 million euros each to build a state research centre.

Partnerships may be lasting or one-off, formalized or verbal. Cases of tension arising or conflicting situations emerging about the financial contribution of each participant are exceptional. Basically, the parties involved trust each other at every step of the process, from the initial study to the final payment and evaluation. This fact is apparent from direct observation of sessions conducted by two regional councils and corroborated by in-depth interviews of the 42 state or local decision-makers involved (Gilbert and Thoenig 1997, 1999b).

The success of such co-funding practices is really the cause for amazement. Local authorities pro-actively look for issues that could be administered by quasi-contractual partnerships and projects that could become co-funded. State ministries adopt identical strategies. All such agents are pursuing the following: (1) ways of finding opportunities to keep their role; (2) ways of serving as partners; and (3) ways to increase their legitimacy as good citizens of local democracy.

A moderate level of democratic participation

France shows two opposite facets in terms of democratic participation. Only 1 per cent of French inhabitants hold an elected mandate, mainly in rural municipal councils of fewer than 2000 inhabitants. In large urban communes the average percentage does not reach 0.5 per cent per 1000.

As national surveys consistently show, the mayor of a commune is ranked as the political figure French citizens and inhabitants feel closest to (or feel most liking for), far ahead of the President of the Republic, the Prime Minister, the member of the national parliament or the regional council representative they elect. Compared with the state administration, local authorities are perceived to be both more efficient and more responsive. While the commune remains the archetype of localism and 'old roots', the region has become a key element of territorial identity – despite the fact that it has been established as a fully democratic institution for only 20 years (Observatoire Interrégional du Politique 2003).

On the other hand, France does not rank among countries that are experiencing enlivened local democratic participation (Hoffmann-Martinot 2004). Every six years, the electorate shows an increasing lack of interest for municipal as well as regional elections. The electorate also makes more volatile choices in terms of parties and leaders. Voting less and in a more opportunistic way does not imply that people participate more in other political arenas. France has dragged its feet in any participatory revolution. Decentralization from the state to sub-national authorities was not followed by further decentralization from the political class to citizens. On 27 February 2002, the national Parliament voted for an institutional arrangement aimed at increasing direct democracy. The 50 communes that have over 80 000 inhabitants are required to create district councils that are open to the public, the process being managed under close control by local ruling politicians. Overall, more relevant set-ups, such as referenda or councils of citizens, which enjoy real autonomy, might exist here and there. Their very existence will reflect the discretionary initiative of the ruling mayor and will have no legal basis that could ensure continuity.

Performance-constrained actors

Local authorities in general look like typical formal bureaucracies. But this does not by any means imply that they function in a bureaucratic way, perhaps paralysed by rigidities and poor efficiency. The *departments*, quite unanimously, were perceived as being too small and unable to manage modern economic development policies. The creation, from scratch, of regions was clearly considered as the way to provide adequate solutions to this. Surprisingly, since the 1970s, the *departments*, far from remaining authorities that are in terminal decline, have recovered strongly. More generally, territorial jurisdictions have increased their performance ability in a quite spectacular manner. France had been lagging here in terms of local infrastructure investments. While the state had helped a great deal, a major turnaround was nevertheless achieved by the efforts of modernization carried out by the communes, regions and *départements*. Cities on the other hand seem to have submitted to being governed by 19th-century-style administrative clerks, well-trained technicians and modern managers (Lorrain 1989).

A survey made in 1996 of 266 city managers of communes of 15 000 inhabitants or more (this sample being 15 per cent of the total) clearly suggests that by many standards French local public authorities achieve quite acceptable levels of efficiency and effectiveness (Thoenig and Burlen 1998a). Taken on average, they have been quite good at managing what has turned out to be macro-financial crisis periods (Guengant 1995). They have kept their average annual expenses at a lower level than their revenues with neither salary cuts nor lay-offs of staff. Techniques such as management control are widely used professionally. Research carried out on the use of management tools on 487 communes of 12.000 inhabitants each suggests that about 85 per cent of their city managers combine modern human resource policies and analytical accounting techniques (Thoenig 1997). They provide rather better than average public goods and services and at an acceptable cost and within balanced budgets. Sub-national authorities, once considered to be hopeless cases, are today perceived as relevant alternatives to central state control. Miracles, or even solutions, once provided by Paris, are expected today from regions and inter-communalities. Most regions and some cities now have large chunks of money available both for investment and for current expenditure that it seems apparent the national budget no longer has.

Many communes or even *départements* may be too small geographically or too weak fiscally to recruit needed personnel. However, the quasi-market structure described above provides flexibility: if a council lacks resources, it may, at least most of the time, find the help it needs from partners. Such a situation also applies incentive pressure and in addition citizens can compare and benchmark goods and services provided.

Constitutive reforms and incremental changes

Modernization reforms in general occur and are implemented sensitively – that is, in soft ways. Those problems that might imply surgery in order to heal them are not addressed. French politicians see patience and pragmatism as a virtue. The government considers incrementalism to be a wise operating style. The only exception to this was the comprehensive – and brutal – manner in which the 1981 decentralization reform was handled.

Old or redundant institutions are not abolished by the will of the state, top-down. France remains one of the very few European democracies that since the 1940s has not seen its parliament or central government reshape the general map of the communes. No law has been passed to reduce their numbers, despite the fact that about 80 per cent of them host less than 20 per cent of the total population, each of them having fewer than 2000 inhabitants. To decentralize the handling of major sub-national institutional issues to local political elites could well imply that the state is weaker than expected, at least in matters of territorial politics.

Innovation for the most part is generated locally. Paris simply ratifies and legitimizes new solutions that had been built up elsewhere. Even before the law forbidding local authorities to allocate grants to private firms had been abolished, many municipalities had started to intervene in economic development matters. Since 2003, experimentation has been recognized by the French Parliament as a constitutional right of local authorities. Since for many years, experimentation had been practiced sub-nationally, to some extent the state has recognized what was happening and provided an impulse to widen these initiatives.

The more incremental changes are made the more the actual level of autonomy of sub-national bodies increases. Faced with a specific problem the state designs a specific solution. As the result of the increase by Paris of new institutional statuses and bodies devoted to inter-communal cooperation, communes, and indeed *départements*, gain additional zones of discretion. In other words, in terms of choosing which *ad hoc* body to join or not, their opportunities increase.

Unintended consequences do happen. The major winner of decentralization policies may well be the *département* and its general council – considered in the 1970s to be a conservative body terminally in decline – that today plays a key role in social affairs as well as in road infrastructure. Transfers of policy domains from the state to local authorities may not always get unanimous support. Public reaction to the 2002–04 decentralization plan launched by the centre-right government of President Chirac has been in the main either negative or indifferent. Disenchantment is also gaining ground among reform activists and erstwhile supporters.

THE THREE KEY SYSTEMIC PROPERTIES OF DECENTRALIZATION

Characteristics such as thickness, overlap, redundancy and competition, just to name a few of those discussed above, may appear to be obstacles to modernization and rationalization. This may imply that decentralization policies, combined with the rise of urban regimes and the fiscal crisis of the state, rather than solving the paralysis of centralization and arrogance of bureaucracies notable in the pre-1981 situation, has instead, within 30 years, increased chaos and disruption even more.

The fact is, however, that chaos does not prevail. Analysis suggests that some level of integration has been achieved and that some collective action is possible between the various levels and players. Three main social constructs may be identified that provide a latent form of social regulation and political integration: (1) hyper-centralization of power inside local and regional entities; (2) mutual dependence between the state and the sub-national authorities; and (3) the accumulation of electoral mandates. These constructs diffuse implicit but widely shared norms: policy-makers learn by trial and error. These constructs also involve pragmatism and are action-focused. They make the handling of public affairs less volatile and uncertain as well as less complicated. They civilize conflicts, have a civilizing effect overall, and avoid anarchy.

Centralization of power at the sub-national level

Sub-national authorities are formally administered according to a parliamentary model. Inside each commune, *département* or region, citizens elect the members of a council. Acting as a collective body in an identical way to parliament, the council members define policies and supervise implementation. Since the equality principle is institutionalized, each person has one vote throughout this procedure. All decisions and nominations are consensual, resulting from the aggregation of a majority of individual preferences.

In terms of daily practice, local democracy does not function exactly the way legal frameworks define its authority and legitimacy. Both power dynamics come into play and asymmetric relationships emerge. Public affairs in fact are governed in a highly centralized manner. A single role is the most dominant by far, if not hegemonic: that of the president of the council.

This paradox of local power is even more visible in the cities. We carried out a series of case studies with 10 rural and 10 urban municipalities, including in-depth interviews with their elected officials and administrative officers (n = 40), and observation of policy-making processes in 14 communes of more than 15 000 inhabitants in domains such as budget, taxation, infrastructure building and urban renewal policies (Thoenig 1995). To outline the role of the mayor, in France, he or she is chosen from among the municipal council, being elected by that body and chairing its sessions. He also heads the municipal bureau, a political body that is responsible for the execution of the will of the council, and supervises the city bureaucracy. At the same time, the political majority or group delegates to one of its members specific tasks while at the same time, at least to some extent, keeping formal control of that person's acts and non-acts. In most municipalities evidence persistently shows that the mayor, far from being a peer, becomes the leader, in effect the boss of his colleagues. His supporters depend on him far more than he depends on them. Power inside the municipal polity therefore polarizes around the mayor.

To use a metaphor, in terms of a network, a mayor acts as a structural 'hole' within it. He provides integration solutions when these need to be supplied. Municipal centralization combines two skills. The president of the council becomes the main linkage, if not the monopolistic linkage, between multiple arenas and heterogeneous action plans. At the same time he protects the rents he himself benefits from, opposes the emergence of any direct linkage between them that would weaken his control: indeed, if anything, barriers to this happening are strengthened. A policy of divide and rule, partition and integrate fuels the process (see appendix 2).

Four main arenas and action plans come under the control of the mayor or president: (1) administrative agencies; (2) politics and policy-making; (3) relationships with the population at large; and (4) foreign affairs.

Control of administrative agencies

The mayor fully controls municipal public agencies. He hires and fires the city manager (the *secrétaire general*), an administrative officer. Both work closely together, sharing a common interest, and the city manager relies on his exclusive access to the mayor's office. He therefore keeps under strong command a relatively large number of tasks as well as staff. Since the municipality is often the main employer of the commune, this means that a wide electoral base may be available. Mayoral legitimacy and budgetary control are the city manager's key resources in order to establish his hierarchical authority inside the administrative machinery (Thoenig and Burlen 1998a, b). The mayor can rely on the city manager, not only because he appoints him, but also because the latter provides the mayor with a critical resource: the bureaucrats who endorse/ratify his policy preferences. While other city council members sit on the municipal bureau and have the rank of adjunct mayors, most of the time they have no real influence and may even be denied direct access to the municipal agencies. Many mayors are cautious about offering city council members opportunities or rights (permanent office, rights of signature, and so on) that may jeopardize their hegemony. The mayor in fact acts simultaneously as the prime minister as well as the minister for finance, welfare, public works, and so on of the commune. From a broader perspective, then, nobody else in the commune possesses any capacity to run and coordinate the administrative machine.

Control of politics and policy-making

The mayor also controls the agenda of the municipal council and his preferences become those of his political majority. Far from being a representative of a party machine, he acts as the head of a broad coalition. In principle citizens choose candidates for council membership from lists of the competitors. The council itself has the task of electing the mayor from among its members. In fact the candidates for the mayorship are known in advance and made public since their names affect which way a citizen votes.

Given the fact that there are no limits to the number of times council members can be re-elected, a mayor can stay in office as long as he or she wants. He selects the people who join his list for the next election. In France, the setting up of a coalition that reflects the main characteristics of the electorate in terms of gender, age, residence or geographic/ethnic origins, matters a lot. National partisan politics is more a burden than a resource. The first task a new mayor has to achieve is to make his political career immune from interferences of his own party – at the national and even the local level. In terms of local government, the strongest party in fact is not the national party but the party of the mayor. In France a municipal council is therefore structured around two different social roles: the mayor and the members of the council.

Control of relationships with the citizen

A third key domain covers the relationships with the inhabitants of a commune. Mayors and presidents of councils allocate much attention to them. In some cases money is spent to improve their image and to attribute success to some personal characteristic. In the same way, the solution to 'problems' people express is often perceived as a personal favour – linked to the influence and discretionary will of a single actor: the mayor himself – even when the mayor acts strictly according to the law, follows the rules or when in fact third parties have the final decision.

Caring about such relationships and customizing service to individuals means that the mayor has the expectation of getting an electoral return in the future and thus keep his job and keep control. The more a request is individualized, the easier it is for the mayor to either satisfy it – by giving an instruction to the specific agency that handles the matter under discussion (something a council member cannot do) or, alternatively, to provide proof (in cases where delivery is not feasible) that he has tried his best.

A further outcome of this personalized treatment of demands is structural. Dealing with demands singly means that collective action is less likely to emerge and general causes less likely to find advocates. In addition, the mayor controls the situation so that factions inside the municipal council are less likely to be able to pick up requests from the general public and use these as partisan political issues.

Control of foreign relations

Foreign affairs are the fourth and perhaps most decisive factor that allows centralization to occur and to maintain its legitimacy. Many outside public authorities manage policy domains that have consequences for the commune; in addition, they may allocate attention or resources that matter for the mayor as entrepreneur. The mayor in fact builds a monopoly around relationships with key outside institutions. He alone, of all the council members, spends time keeping in touch and negotiating with the general council, the regional council, state agents such as the prefect, public financial institutions in Paris, European Commission representatives, and so on. The mayoral portfolio also includes public utility companies and firms that are potential job providers or urban developers. The wider his network of access to extra-municipal decision makers, the more he can act as a powerful broker – especially perhaps when there is difficulty with more local matters inside his commune. Mayors know in advance what initiatives third parties may take, which opportunities are available, whom to contact in order to speed up a request or to get some extra funding.

Benefits of centralization

Centralization induces long tenures. French mayors could be described as world champions in terms of longevity in power, despite the fact that recent years have seen some higher turnover (Hoffmann-Martinot 2005). On average they remain in power for 13 years. Not to centralize in fact is seen as a way to commit early political suicide.

Centralization also brings about a major relaxation of the principles of checks and balances (Thoenig 1996). A mayor, as president of the general council or of the regional council, acts simultaneously and for many years in succession as the chief executive as well as the head of the legislative branch. The issues at stake are also of a low public visibility so there is always the danger that some form of patronage may develop.

The polarization of power on a single person has dramatically expanded from communes to départements. The case is even more spectacular at the regional level: only 10 years after their creation, 17 out of 21 regional councils were already governed by one dominant integrator: their president. Functional institutions which are run according to indirect democracy procedures – their leaders being nominated by the councils running the member authorities, not by the citizens of their district – should be added to the list. Decentralization from the state has helped diffuse and legitimize centralization in all such sub-national authorities.

State territorial embeddedness: from local co-optation to the institutionalization of collective action

Cross-regulation and co-optation of local actors were key processes used by state bureaucracies to manage territorial public affairs in pre-decentralized France (Thoenig 1975; Crozier and Thoenig 1976). Observation shows that in the current post-centralized system they are still in use, but have lost much of their importance.

In the early 2000s, as in the early 1970s, state administrative hierarchies function in a relatively flexible manner. They show much sensitivity to both local specificities and specific requests, avoiding the imposition of impersonal criteria. Grass roots agents take much license both with rules and with diktats from headquarters. Inside their ministerial hierarchy, agents even behave as advocates of causes and vested interests rooted in the local territory in which they are supposed to act as representatives of state policy, enforcing the will of the state. Flexibility in action and the endorsement of localism are two basic processes that here reinforce one another.

State agents invest much time and care in building up local relational networks and getting support from local elected officials such as mayors of communes or presidents of councils. They may even prefer to help the latter get their problems solved than to exercise control over whether in fact their acts and non-acts conform to the legal and financial procedures defined by the state. For a prefect, a major failure, infinitely worth avoiding, is to lose access to and confidence from the political elites located within his geographical jurisdiction. This also implies that the more state agencies are embedded in the local territorial jurisdictions, the less their state headquarters can control them. Inside the state apparatus itself it is quite difficult to generate hierarchical coordination between bureaucratic silos. In fact, the dominant local elected politician becomes, even without any explicit intervention, the common reference for each of them.

A major function of cross-regulation is to build local political capital. State representatives working in field agencies internalize values and stakeholdings that are shared by local groups. These values and stakeholdings may in many cases be somewhat different from those emanating from the national headquarters. For grass roots agencies, local embeddedness is a resource, not a constraint. Their agents are perceived by those they administer to be human, sensitive, and doing the best they can. In return, state agencies rally local support. As an example of this, the French national police get vital information from the public – as well as invaluable support from the municipalities.

Decentralization pushes national bureaucracies to be even more sensitive to acquiring local political capital. However, compared with the old days of centralization, Paris now has far fewer resources to allocate at a time when local agents were replaced by heads of autonomous institutions. It would seem to be the case that co-optation and cross-regulation are insufficient mechanisms for the state apparatus to remain a relevant player in territorial affairs.

Within the last 20 or so years, most legal and financial controls of sub-national authority acts were transferred from ministries and prefects to autonomous judiciary bodies such as Regional Courts of Accounts. Facing increased competition from private firms, state agencies have also lost their quasi-monopoly on technical and administrative expertise. Several policy domains linked to transportation, social affairs, professional training and economic development have been transferred by the state to local authorities. By comparison, local authorities have increased their resources and their autonomy in a way that is directly relevant to their populations. State public agencies do less by themselves than in the past, distribute less money and rely less on particular technical standards to impose their will. Faced with increasing budgetary shortages, Paris now decentralizes the leftovers of the Welfare State to sub-national authorities.

Secondary analysis of case studies dealing with the inter-organizational management of policies such as forests, industrial and domestic waste collection and treatment, crime and law, regional parks and urban zoning, indicate that a major change has occurred. Another model of governance has been endorsed and developed by the state: the institutionalization of collective action (Duran and Thoenig 1996).

Being less able to pay the piper and call the tune, central government has developed policy tools such as constitutive policies. Specific arenas are supplied to territorial actors to address new issues in a context where traditional jurisdictions are too small and rigid to handle problems flexibly. Thus multiple public and private actors are involved in setting up solutions and implementing them, and as yet untried and perhaps still uncertain technologies are used to handle problems that are difficult to define. Procedures and approaches are set up such as quasi-neighborhood councils and public hearings that enable single issue groups and private interests to express and share some common definition of specific problems. In parallel to democratically elected councils, *ad hoc* policy arenas assume a consultative role. Powerful traditional institutions such as chambers of commerce or agriculture – as well as single-issue groups, economic lobbies and firms – join public agencies and politicians to help identify specific problems and their causes, coordinate efforts to address them and elaborate, in a quasi-consensual manner, an action-oriented blueprint. Non-profit associations, moral entrepreneurs and citizen groups invest both attentive interest and energy. Such participation schemes, one per policy domain, have given birth to a kind of functional or administrative democracy. The result is both more than pure consultation and less than power sharing. In addition, it remains widely understood that the legitimate political bodies retain the final decision and that elected politicians remain in charge.

Such arrangements mean that touchy local issues such as crime and law become co-governed and as it were co-produced – a finding from field research in three different regions, combining in-depth interviews of 64 state representatives (judges and prefects) and 8 mayors, and with direct observation of coordination meetings and the conduct of police interventions in real time (Gatto and Thoenig 1993). Other domains such as transportation (Purenne 2003), economic development (Douillet 2001) and public housing illustrate how common such a phenomenon has become. Even policy domains that were once pure monopolies of the state – such as R&D or higher education – have become extremely sensitive to the emergence of specific wishes and initiatives emanating from the regions.

One key consequence is that the mayor or the president of a territorial council becomes a much stronger actor than before within his own territorial jurisdiction stronger even than the prefect and the state representatives. This undisputed leader now clearly stands as the common denominator between multiple, weakened state units that are no longer to coordinate their functions by themselves. His platform for action and his power stakeholdings shape a cognitive framework each of them deems appropriate and all share.

The surprise perhaps is that nevertheless the state territorial role is still both valued and desired by local politicians. While state field agencies have lost their former hegemony, they still matter for local politicians. One reason is that the stronger local authorities use the weaker bureaucrats for strategic purposes of their own since state field agencies offer access to decision-makers. When third parties are influential in decision-making, both local and regional politicians use their managers as intermediaries, brokers and advocates in order to handle some problems and satisfy some requests. State agencies supply non-partisan mediation so their representatives facilitate local policy-making. Local administrators take advantage of the fact that state bureaucrats, while remaining sensitive to territorial specificities, do not belong to the sphere of politics. In addition, some prestige is linked to their status and their careers are quite immune from outside influences. Mayors who are members of the same syndicate in charge of local development will favour the intervention of an engineer from the Ministry of Public Works to run their joint venture. Technical criteria and advice that are certified by state administrators are considered to be a protection against patronage and discretionary power. A collateral effect of state mediation is that some convergence is ensured between policy areas in neighbouring jurisdictions: similar issues turn up on the agendas. Identical choice criteria are enacted since state agents share a common educational and cognitive background. In many cases communes or regions adopt action frameworks that are designed by state administrations and benchmarked through cross-regulation.

To involve the prefect in municipal affairs or to receive some input from a state engineer allows the mayor not to become too exclusively dependent on the president of the general council and the bureaucracy he heads. The mayor is then able to avoid such things as the *département* or the region becoming too powerful and dictating its own terms. State local presence and intervention guarantees that public affairs, seen in market terms, remain an oligopoly. In addition, as has been mentioned, state representatives are able to offer an alternative channel and rationale both to political agents and partisan intermediaries. The mayor has not to pay a price to more powerful local politicians. Placing trust in the goodwill of a bureaucrat in fact keeps politics out of the picture since the mayor faces no challenge from powerful local politicians. State public agencies also act to calm the wilder forms of open competition between local authorities, their presence preventing the weakest from becoming the captives of the strongest.

The accumulation of political mandates

At the micro level it can be said that presidential and mayoral centralization simplifies government within each sub-national authority. Nevertheless, tens of thousands of autonomous bodies and territories, combined with the absence of a hierarchical structure that makes clear subordination links between them, does not help to facilitate some form of coordination and integration.

At the meso level, a major constitutive process is in operation. Six to seven hundred elected officials – sometimes known as *grands notables* or *grands élus* – provide integration capacity between separate geo-institutional levels and across partitioned territories. In France, these elected officials represent an extremely influential and exclusive club and in order to join it a local administrator or politician needs to accumulate two or more electoral mandates.

French law allows the same person to exert more than one electoral mandate at a time. So, for example, a municipal council member may also be a regional council member as well as a national senator in Paris or a member of the European parliament in Strasbourg. The law applies some modest restrictions to accumulating national/European and local mandates. So, for example, the law forbids anyone being president of a regional council as well as president of a general council. Extensive use is made of accumulation of elected local mandates. Around two-thirds of the members of general councils also act as local mayors, not counting those who are also municipal council members.

Top positions, then, are concentrated in relatively few hands. National as well as European electoral mandates are linked with sub-national electoral mandates. This polarization of authority also occurs between regional mandates and sub-regional mandates such as municipal offices. Accumulation rate is even more impressive when mandates in sub-national authorities not directly elected by the population – such as urban communities and federations of communes – are taken into account and added to the portfolio.

A Matthew effect is at work (Merton 1968). Top mandates go to powerful politicians. To be a mayor of a large city or a president of a regional council increases the probability of simultaneously being a member of the national parliament. A member of the general council is more likely to be the mayor of the most populated commune of his district than a mere member of a municipal council of a small village in the same district. Citizens give a premium to such accumulation. A candidate already holding another elected office has two to three times more chance of being elected than a competitor who is not. About half the presidents of general councils and three quarters of the presidents of regional councils also sit on the benches of the national parliament.

Multiple mandate positions amount to safe jobs. Influence derived from accumulation amounts to more than the sum of the single mandates. The key reason is that their holder can, in one pair of hands as it were, control different resources and at the same time be present at several levels of government. This can range from Paris itself down to the commune. In addition, know-how, information and networks that are linked to one role have connections to those linked to the other roles.

Despite low turnover and the operation of some patronage, accumulation is more an opportunity than a liability. There are several good reasons why voters do not jeopardize the system of accumulation. It provides them with opportunities. Citizens have a direct channel of access to Paris and central agencies via their mayor if he or she also happens to be a senator. Even mayors of surrounding communes may find it helpful to support their colleague who, as well as being mayor and senator, is also a member of the regional council. At grass-roots level, the *grand élu* is expected to be by-passer, broker and advocate of local causes at the highest level.

Grands élus, much like state agents, provide alternative channels of mediation. But they are both more effective and powerful since no accumulation of mandates exists within state hierarchies. To put this another way, a prefect cannot at the same time be his own subordinate and his own superior. In addition, a senator who also is mayor is not imprisoned in a hierarchy as a prefect is. Through such a senator/mayor's mandate, local inhabitants benefit from the extremely short access path to Paris, while, inside state administrative circuits, there may be two or even three anonymous intermediaries or levels to negotiate. The fact that *grands élus* preside at one if not two sub-national councils gives them a second advantage. As has been said, they control more resources and coordinate wider policy domains; neither are they prisoners of silos. A third difference, in France, is linked to democratic legitimacy: state agents are not elected.

Although multiple mandate holders exert more power and influence than state agencies, they do not try to keep state agencies out of the game. They govern in a centralized and personalized manner that is identical to the leadership style adopted by the single mandate elected official. But they do it with more strength, tending to divide and rule. They are the policy integrators, framing long-term horizons and fostering active coordination between multiple actors, private and public. For the same head to wear multiple hats that in a world as politically scattered and institutionally differentiated as the French one, results in a collective solution. To some extent, then, a *grand élu* acts as an institutional facilitator.

The accumulation process also gives birth to a specific style of policy-making. While *grands élus* show their strength in imposing their own preferences – and reward their supporters – they are also keen not to punish their non-supporters too much. Territorial justice is a criterion that often overcomes partisan loyalties, in that there is a feeling that everybody should be entitled to a fair albeit relatively minimal share of the public pie. Communes that are run by opposition parties may even get better treatment from the *grand élu* in his or her role chairing the general council than communes run by friends of his own electoral majority (Gilbert and Thoenig 1997). As much as 89 per cent of regional funds are allocated with neither opposition nor even any debate among political majorities and minorities inside the council (Gilbert and Thoenig 1999b). In France, political majorities are constructed and deconstructed according to criteria that fit neither ideological splits nor partisan coalitions.

POWER BASES AND CONSERVATIVE AGENDAS

Ideological debates about comprehensive redesigns in the field of territorial government have been quite rare since the early 1990s. In terms of their electoral platforms, politicians do not rank this reform as a top priority. Unlike Great Britain and Italy, for instance, French political leaders, left and right, seem to be either relatively cautious if not downright agnostic. So-called 'New' approaches that deal with public management, centralism or localism, are considered, for managerial purposes, with scepticism and, for political reasons, inappropriate.

Modernization of territorial politics and policy-making nevertheless continues to be fuelled by a stream of initiatives and reforms taken at all levels. About 70 relevant new laws or decrees have been issued by the state in the last 10 or so years. Most if not all of them favour incremental change. The sub-national system in France behaves as if there were a kind of blueprint that sets limits on how far changes should go to be acceptable to the polity and it evolves and is driven by adjustments to this blueprint. A kind of implicit action agenda exists, then, and to understand its existence and its content, we have to remind ourselves of the fact that in France there is no explicit legal definition of the domains of territorial affairs the state administration is in charge of.

Agenda setting and political power in France are mainly in the hands of elected politicians whose feet are locally embedded and whose hands are nationally active. Ratios of mandate accumulation during the last 16 or so years, when France has had different legislatures and 5 changes of parliamentary majority, have remained relatively constant. Around 90 per cent of members of Parliament simultaneously hold one if not two elected mandates in sub-national authorities. About half the senators are also busy as mayors. An average of a third of the deputies hold two other local mandates. Even ministers in the Prime Minister's cabinet may hold local mandates, and many do.

To some extent, then, the most powerful political party in France is neither the party of the President of the Republic nor the opposition party. This social configuration regroups informally, so that most of the *grands élus* for a 'party' in which right- and left-wing politicians are equals and colleagues. It benefits from have a key influence in one specific policy domain: territorial government. The accumulation of mandates makes the blending, if not confusion, between local and national agendas and state offices and sub-national offices constraining. State elites care about national and local affairs at the same time. The national political class, then, is made of influential local administrators and vice versa.

Powerful associations are headed by *grands élus* who happen also to be key parliamentary legislators. The most established one is the national association of mayors. Described as the most powerful but invisible political lobby in national local politics (Le Lidec 2001), it gathers together around 85 per cent of the 36 000 mayors. Other associations mobilize the activism of elected politicians according to their mandates: presidents of the regional councils, presidents of general councils, mayors of middle-sized cities or presidents of agglomeration councils. Because party cleavages may differ or their mutual interests may sometime clash as a consequence of increased sub-national institutional differentiation, *grands élus* experience some difficulty to gain consensus among their local constituency for reforms. This is specially the case for senators who are elected not by the population but by local 'colleagues' such as mayors and general council members. The best they can do is to stand against any reform initiative that may jeopardize the current system: for instance a reform that may merge communes or suppress a *département*. Inside their own political party they do fight reform platforms. They also deter governmental initiatives and kill legislative proposals that would destabilize the system currently in place. These so-called 'guardians of local autonomy' share an implicit non-partisan common agenda. Any reform that would modify the five basic properties of the system should be resisted. Their aim is to safeguard the following:

1. Establishing a formal subordination between sub-national authorities, one level having constitutive rights on another level;
2. Forbidding the accumulation of mandates between all levels;
3. Putting an end to centralization of power in the hands of the president of the council, which means more checks and balances, and more decentralization from elected bodies to the population;
4. Abolishing one of the three main sub-national levels (region, *département*, commune);
5. Lowering the influence of the state machinery and putting an end to its operational role in sub-national government.

In 1999–2000, the socialist Prime Minister Lionel Jospin seriously considered bringing the accumulation of electoral mandates of any kind to an end. Polls suggested strong support from public opinion. But he faced an open threat of blackmail inside his own party in terms of sponsorship of his candidacy for the upcoming presidential election. The law he had prepared in order to enforce more democratic participation by the public was never submitted to parliament.

Between 1981 and 2004 relatively massive policy domains and authority have been transferred from the state to sub-national institutions; no relevant transfer of power, however, has ever been considered from the local politicians to the population. The majority of right- as well as left-wing politicians do not support the idea of expanding checks and balances in local government: to have the executive body or the mayor directly elected by the citizens, for example, apart from participation in the election of the council members. Free referenda, initiatives by the population, and any other sort of modern form of citizen participation are considered to be threatening perspectives to representative democracy – and indeed are sometimes labelled 'non-republican' principles.

Twice in recent years state decentralization policies have reinforced institutional differentiation and autonomy between sub-national levels. Prime Minister Jean-Pierre Raffarin had to abandon any attempt to create subordination in the relationship of the *département* *vis-à-vis* the region or the commune *vis-à-vis* the *département*. The first decentralization operation in the early 1980s faced no resistance for two reasons. First, it did not jeopardize the basic properties of the system. During its first hundred days, the then socialist government managed decentralization in an authoritarian manner, depriving Parliament and citizens of either voice or option. In 2002 and 2003 the process turned into a nightmare for the centre-right government. The Prime Minister had consulted extensively with local elites prior to the final draft of the law and its discussion in Parliament. Lacking support from President Chirac, the Prime Minister had to bargain and to make major compromises to get most of the *grands élus* belonging to his own parliamentary majority to approve his law. Any attempt to subordinate either the d*épartement* to the region or the commune to the *département* had to be dropped.

All the options had both consequences and costs: the choices were: (1) to keep both the region and the *département*; (2) to add local functional institutions without massively decreasing the number of communes; (3) to ask the state to fund cities and villages that were fiscally poor; (4) not to decentralize policy domains where budget cuts would be needed. Facing increasingly differentiated institutional interests – regions, *départements*, communes of agglomeration, cities, and so on – the political class seems unable to find a consensus on which level should be favoured and which suppressed. It externalizes the political responsibility to the government in Paris and the financial costs to the state via the Ministry of Finance, that is, the national taxpayer (Gilbert and Guengant 2002). Local authorities such as communes and general councils prefer by far that the state rather than the region or themselves take responsibility for balancing fiscal revenues. So the state, trapped by and in local interests, with grants to local and regional authorities representing the major expenditure after the public deficit, finds itself with a total amount that is currently increasing by 5 per cent per annum.

Territorial government in fact may be close to fiscal collapse, but public debates are still difficult to marshall. Who outside the inner circle of *grands élus* has the legitimacy to express a political voice and is able to suggest alternatives to a system that is so complicated? The setting of the policy agenda is out of the reach of public opinion. The lack of central discretionary authority on state-local financial relationships is just one facet of a much broader picture. National steering by state political or bureaucratic officials of sub-national public affairs, whether by prefects or heads of national ministries, is ineffective. The surprise initiative taken by President Mitterrand and his Minister of the Interior in 1981 was the exception to the rule. The Presidency of the Republic himself is, if not weaker, at least more prudent than one would expect from a political regime such as the French State seems to be on paper (Hayward and Wright 2002). The state administrative elites are rather like Gulliver: their feet are trapped in a local system that is difficult to clarify, simplify and make less costly, either by more localism or by a new centralism.

ACKNOWLEDGEMENT

The author would like to thank Jack Hayward, Ed Page, Guy Peters and Denis Saint-Martin for their comments on an earlier draft of the paper.

REFERENCES

Ashford, D. 1982. *British Dogmatism and French Pragmatism. Central-local Policymaking in the Welfare State*. London: George Allen and Unwin.
Crozier, M. and J.-C. Thoenig. 1976. 'The Regulation of Complex Organized Systems', *Administrative Science Quarterly*, 4, 547–70.

De Tocqueville, A. 1856. *The Old Regime and the Revolution*. Boston: Michael Levy.

Douillet, A.C. 2001. *Action publique et territoire. Le changement de l'action publique au regard des politiques de développement territorial*. Cachan: Ecole Normale Supérieure and GAPP.

Duran, P. and J.-C. Thoenig. 1996. 'L'Etat et la gestion publique territoriale', *Revue Française de Science Politique*, 4, 580–623.

Gatto, D. and J.C. Thoenig. 1993. *La sécurité publique à l'épreuve du terrain*. Paris: L'Harmattan.

Gilbert, G. and J.-C. Thoenig. 1997. *Les co-financements entre collectivités publiques. Une étude prototype*. Paris: Grale-Gapp.

Gilbert, G. and J.-C. Thoenig. 1999a. 'Les cofinancements publics: des pratiques aux rationalités', *Revue d'Économie Financière*, 1, 45–78.

Gilbert, G. and J.-C. Thoenig. 1999b. *Les co-financements entre collectivités publiques dans la région Nord-Pas-de-Calais*. Cachan: Gapp.

Gilbert, G. and A. Guengant. 2002. 'Le risque institutionnel dans la prospective des finances locales', *Economie Publique – Etudes et recherches*, 8, 27–40.

Grémion, P. 1976. *Le Pouvoir Périphérique: Bureaucratie et Notables dans le Système Politique Français*. Paris: Le Seuil.

Guengant, A. (ed.). 1995. *Analyse financière des collectivités locales*. Paris: Presses Universitaires de France et Grale.

Hayward, J.E.S. 1983. *Governing France. The One and Indivisible Republic*. London: Weidenfeld and Nicolson.

Hayward, J.E.S., and V. Wright. 2002. *Governing From the Centre. Core Executive Coordination in France*. Oxford: Oxford University Press.

Hoffmann-Martinot, V. 2005. 'Reform and Modernization of Urban Government in France', in V. Hoffmann-Martinot and H. Wollmann (eds), *Modernization of State and Administration in Europe: A France-Germany comparison*. Opladen: Leske and Budrich.

Le Galès, P. and C. Lequesne. 1998. *Regions in Europe*. London: Routledge.

Le Lidec, P. 2001. *Les maires dans la République. L'association des maires de France, element constitutif des régimes politiques français depuis 1907*. Paris: Université de Paris 1, Department of Political Science.

Lorrain, D. 1989. *Les mairies urbaines et leurs personnels*. Paris: Fondation des villes.

Lorrain, D. and G. Stoker (eds). 1997. *The Privatization of Urban Services in Europe*. London: Pinter.

Merton, R.K. 1968. 'The Matthew Effect in Science', *Science*, 159, 3810, 56–63.

Observatoire Interrégional du Politique (OIP). 2003. *Le baromètre du fait régional*. Paris: OIP.

Page, E. and M. Goldsmith (eds). 1987. *Central and Local Government Relations: a Comparative Analysis of West European Unitary States*. Thousand Oaks, CA: Sage.

Purenne, A. 2003. *L'action publique par le bas. Les transports urbains de la Communauté urbaine de Lyon*. Vaulx-en-Velin: Rives.

Schmidt, V. 1990. *Democratizing France. The Political and Administrative History of Decentralization*. Cambridge: Cambridge University Press.

Sellers, J. 2002. *Governing from Below*. Cambridge: Cambridge University Press.

Suleiman, E. 1978. *Elites in French Society*. Princeton, NJ: Princeton University Press.

Thoenig, J.C. 1975. 'La relation entre le centre et la périphérie en France: une analyse systémique', *Bulletin de l'Institut International d'Administration Publique*, 36, 77–123.

Thoenig, J.C. 1987. *L'Ère des Technocrates*. Paris: L'Harmattan.

Thoenig J.C. 1995. 'De l'incertitude en gestion territoriale', *Politiques et Management Public*, 3, 1–27.

Thoenig, J.C. 1996. 'Pouvoirs et contrepouvoirs locaux: rendre la démocratie aux citoyens', Institut de la Décentralisation (ed.), *La Décentralisation en France*. Paris: La Découverte, 131–42.

Thoenig, J.C. 1997. 'La gestion des services communaux', *Annuaire GRALE-Annuaire des collectivités locales 1997*. Paris: Litec, 17–35.

Thoenig, J.C. and K. Burlen. 1998a. 'Les secrétaires généraux des villes', *Politiques et Management Public*, 1, 141–72.

Thoenig, J.C. and K. Burlen. 1998b. 'The Asymmetric Interdependence between Two Powerful Actors: The CEO and the Mayor in French Cities', in K.K. Klausen and A. Magnier (eds), *The Anonymous Leader – Appointed CEOs in Western Local Government*. Odense: Odense University Press, pp. 188–203.

Worms, J.P. 1966. 'Le préfet et ses notables', *Sociologie du Travail*, 3, 249–75.

APPENDIX 1 *MAIN SUB-NATIONAL PUBLIC INSTITUTIONS*

Main levels:

communes	36.676
'départements'	100
regions	22

A selection of inter-communal authorities:

urban communities	14 (as of 1.1.2002)
communities of communes	2.033 (id.)
agglomeration communities	120 (id.)
'syndicats mixtes'	1.700 (est.)
'syndicats à vocation multiple'	1.900 (est.)
'syndicats à vocation unique'	12.500 (est.)

APPENDIX 2 *THE PRESIDENT/MAYOR AS INTEGRATOR OF THE LOCAL POLITY*

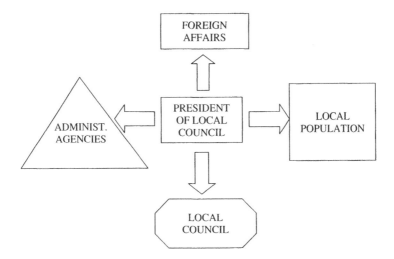

AFTERWORD: TRAPPED IN LOCALISM

While the decentralization policy launched by François Mitterrand in the first part of the 1980s did not generate strong resistance, territorial administration reform has become a very controversial political issue in the last few years.

The 2007 collapse of the banking system and the collateral economic crisis have put heavy pressures on the financial resources available to the French government. The debt of the French State has reached levels – a deficit slightly above 8 per cent and a debt of 80 per cent of the GDP – that are not consistent with the stability criteria defined by the Maastricht treaty.

Despite a rather important package of policy domains transferred to them by the State since the mid-1908s, local authorities do not experience similar budgetary constraints and financial deficits. Between 1996 and 2007, their expenses increased annually by 5.35 per cent, as compared with an average increase of 3.35 per cent of the State budget. More than communes and *départements*, regions were and still are financially at ease in terms of revenues and resources. In 2007 the regions spent 117 per cent more money than in 1996, while the communes had less room for manoeuvre – with increase of only 33.4 per cent. They kept increasing their taxes.

Elected as President of the Republic in 2007, Nicolas Sarkozy promised not to increase national taxes while not to decrease fiscal pressure. Regions and departments should in his view join the national effort of cost cutting and stop acting as free riders. Economies of scale should become a key principle guiding public administration reform nationally and locally. Policy domains – culture, economic development, etc – should be funded by one local authority only, and no longer by two or in some cases three different levels. Regional and departmental councils should cut the monies allocated to their running costs, stop building fancy buildings for their staff, and pay their elected officials as well as their administrative staff less.

In March 2009 a report commissioned by Nicolas Sarkozy to the former Prime Minister Edouard Balladur suggested what was called a simplification of the territorial administration system that could also be politically acceptable. Communes would not be merged. *Départements* and regions would remain distinctive bodies. Nevertheless all the members of the political council running a *département* would also sit on the benches of the regional council. In other changes the latter body would be composed of the elected officials belonging to the councils of the *départements* of a region. These politicians would therefore hold two mandates and be elected by the same voters the same day. This would cut by half the total numbers of councillors in regions and *départements*. This would also imply the creation of new specific electoral districts, namely the *cantons*.

This sophisticated blueprint has not been easy to understand on the part of a rather indifferent public, but it generated a lot of turbulence inside the rank and file of the local and national political class. Open hostility has been expressed both by the left parties and by the centre-right majority of the Senate. Sarkozy's ambition was not only challenged by most of the leaders but also by thousands of local politicians who had been his strongest supporters.

On top of this, several presidents of *départements,* socialists as well as moderates, openly started to challenge the State and to ask courts to oblige Paris to pay its share of the policy domains it should by law contribute to. The State not paying its debts, not holding its promises or transferring more and more expenses to the local budgets, are nowadays suspicions that are openly expressed. *Cumulards* is a pejorative expression for political officials who accumulate two or more mandates, national, regional, communal or at the level of the *département*. Their rebellion is a first in contemporary France.

Another recurrent issue, the abolition of the opportunity for one person to accumulate more two elected mandates or more, is still handled with care if not reluctance by political parties. Centre- and centre-right-wing politicians do not want to take additional risks after their defeat at the regional elections in March 2010. While abolition is supported by public opinion according to the polls, the ecologists are the only party to explicitly insert it in their electoral platform. Members of the socialist party have also endorsed abolition in an internal referendum. Many leaders of the party, at least those who at the same time control the most powerful local federations, are mayors of important cities and also members of the Parliament in Paris, keep expressing their hostility to this idea. They argue that abolition would jeopardize the possibility of the socialists winning a majority at the 2011 elections for the Senate, given the fact that rural districts, traditionally rather centre-right oriented, may fear a reduction of their influence in Paris if electing non-cumulating politicians. While public opinion expresses a lack of overall confidence in the political class, the *cumulard* being a symbol of such a disdain, voters still continue to favour a candidate who already has another mandate to a candidate who has none. Local pragmatism is at work.

In other words, the model presented in the 2005 paper remains robust and able to predict the complex ways politics and policy dynamics interfere and interact in the field of territorial administration in France, which issues make it to the political agenda, which trade-offs reforms have to consider, and how policies will be implemented.

The French case is not just another exotic story. For social sciences dealing with public administration, it offers a heuristic opportunity to study public affairs as a systemic phenomenon, and to address change and stability issues. To define France in terms of a highly path dependent case should not deter analysts from exploring more in depth the logics and stakeholders at work, and the solutions they improvise to satisfy their vested interests while at the same time not jeopardizing public interest too much.

PART III: PUBLIC MANAGEMENT

Chapter 10

A PUBLIC MANAGEMENT FOR ALL SEASONS?

CHRISTOPHER HOOD

THE RISE OF NEW PUBLIC MANAGEMENT (NPM)

The rise of 'new public management' (hereafter NPM) over [at the time of writing] the past 15 years is one of the most striking international trends in public administration. Though the research reported in the other papers in this issue [*Public Administration* 1991, vol. 69, no. 1] refers mainly to UK experience, NPM is emphatically not a uniquely British development. NPM's rise seems to be linked with four other administrative 'megatrends', namely:

 (i) attempts to *slow down or reverse government growth* in terms of overt public spending and staffing (Dunsire and Hood 1989);
 (ii) the shift toward *privatization and quasi-privatization* and away from core government institutions, with renewed emphasis on 'subsidiarity' in service provision (cf. Hood and Schuppert 1988; Dunleavy 1989).
 (iii) the development of *automation*, particularly in information technology, in the production and distribution of public services; and
 (iv) the development of a more *international* agenda, increasingly focused on general issues of public management, policy design, decision styles and intergovernmental cooperation, on top of the older tradition of individual country specialisms in public administration.

(These trends are discussed further in Hood 1990b).

NPM, like most administrative labels, is a loose term. Its usefulness lies in its convenience as a shorthand name for the set of broadly similar administrative doctrines which dominated the bureaucratic reform agenda in many of the OECD group of countries from the late 1970s (see Aucoin 1990; Hood 1990b; Pollitt 1990).

Although ill-defined, NPM aroused strong and varied emotions among bureaucrats. At one extreme were those who held that NPM was the only way to correct for the irretrievable failures and even moral bankruptcy in the 'old' public management (cf. Keating 1989). At the other were those who dismissed much of the thrust of NPM as a gratuitous and philistine destruction of more than a century's work in developing a distinctive public service ethic and culture (cf. Martin 1988; Nethercote 1989b).

NPM's rise also sparked off debate as to how the movement was to be labelled, interpreted and explained. What exactly was the public management Emperor now wearing? Where did the design come from, and did its novelty lie mainly in presentation or in content? Why did it find favour? Was it an all-purpose and all-weather garment? This article attempts to discuss these questions, with particular attention to the last one.

WHAT THE EMPEROR WAS WEARING: THE DOCTRINES OF NPM

Different commentators and advocates of NPM have stressed different aspects of doctrine. But the seven overlapping precepts summarized in table 1 appear in most discussions of NPM. Over the last decade, a 'typical' public sector policy delivery unit in the UK,

TABLE 1 *Doctrinal components of new public management*

No.	Doctrine	Meaning	Typical justification
1	*'Hands-on professional management'* in the public sector	Active, visible, discretionary control of organizations from named persons at the top, 'free to manage'	Accountability requires clear assignment of responsibility for action, not diffusion of power
2	*Explicit standards and measures of performance*	Definition of goals, targets, indicators of success, preferably expressed in quantitative terms, especially for professional services (cf. Day and Klein 1987; Carter 1989)	Accountability requires clear statement of goals; efficiency requires 'hard look' at objectives
3	Greater emphasis on *output controls*	Resource allocation and rewards linked to measured performance; breakup of centralized bureaucracy-wide personnel management	Need to stress *results* rather than *procedures*
4	Shift to *disaggregation* of units in the public sector	Break up of formerly 'monolithic' units, unbundling of U-form management systems into corporatized units around products, operating on decentralized 'one-line' budgets and dealing with one another on an 'arms-length' basis	Need to create 'manageable' units, separate *provision* and *production* interests, gain efficiency advantages of use of contract or franchise arrangements *inside* as well as outside the public sector
5	Shift to greater *competition* in public sector	Move to term contracts and public tendering procedures	*Rivalry* as the key to lower costs and better standards
6	*Stress on private-sector styles of management practice*	Move away from military-style 'public service ethic', greater flexibility in hiring and rewards; greater use of PR techniques	Need to use 'proven' private sector management tools in the public sector
7	Stress on greater *discipline* and *parsimony* in resource use	Cutting direct costs, raising labour discipline, resisting union demands, limiting 'compliance costs' to business	Need to check resource demands of public sector and 'do more with less'

Australia, New Zealand and many other OECD countries would be likely to have had some exposure to most of these doctrines. But not all of the seven elements were equally present in all cases; nor are they necessarily fully consistent, partly because they do not have a single intellectual provenance.

WHERE THE DESIGN CAME FROM: NPM AS A MARRIAGE OF OPPOSITES

One way of interpreting NPM's origins is as a marriage of two different streams of ideas. One partner was the 'new institutional economics'. It was built on the now very familiar story of the post-World War II development of public choice, transactions cost theory and principal-agent theory – from the early work of Black (1958) and Arrow (1963) to Niskanen's (1971) landmark theory of bureaucracy and the spate of later work which built on it.

The new institutional economics movement helped to generate a set of administrative reform doctrines built on ideas of *contestability, user choice, transparency* and close concentration on *incentive structures.* Such doctrines were very different from traditional military-bureaucratic ideas of 'good administration', with their emphasis on orderly hierarchies and elimination of duplication or overlap (cf. Ostrom 1974).

The other partner in the 'marriage' was the latest of a set of successive waves of business-type 'managerialism' in the public sector, in the tradition of the international scientific management movement (Merkle 1980; Hume 1981; Pollitt 1990). This movement helped to generate a set of administrative reform doctrines based on the ideas of *'professional management'* expertise as *portable* (Martin 1983), *paramount* over technical expertise, requiring high *discretionary power* to achieve results ('free to manage') and *central* and *indispensable* to better organizational performance, through the development of appropriate cultures (Peters and Waterman 1982) and the active measurement and adjustment of organizational outputs.

Whether the partners in this union were fully compatible remains to be seen. 'Free to manage' is a rather different slogan from 'free to choose'. The two can conflict, particularly where the NPM revolution is led from above (as it was in the UK) rather than from below. The relative dominance of the two partners varied in different countries even within the 'Westminster model' tradition (cf. Hood 1990c). For example, in the unique circumstances of New Zealand, the synthesis of public choice, transactions cost theory and principal-agent theory was predominant, producing an analytically driven NPM movement of unusual coherence. But in the UK and Australia business-type managerialism was much more salient, producing a more pragmatic and less intellectually elegant strain of NPM or 'neo-Taylorism' (Pollitt 1990, p. 56). Potential frictions between these partners were not resolved by any single coherent or definitive exposition of the joint philosophy. Indeed, the New Zealand Treasury's *Government Management* (1987) comes closest to a coherent NPM 'manifesto', given that much of the academic literature on the subject either lacks full-scale elaboration or enthusiastic commitment to NPM.

WHY NPM FOUND FAVOUR: THE ACCEPTANCE FACTOR

There is no single accepted explanation or interpretation of why NPM coalesced and why it 'caught on' (cf. Hood 1990b; Hood and Jackson 1991 forthcoming, ch. 8). Many academic commentators associate it with the political rise of the 'New Right'. But that on its own does not explain why these particular doctrines found favour, nor why NPM was so strongly endorsed by Labour governments ostensibly opposed to the 'New Right', notably in Australia and New Zealand. Among the possible explanations are the following four.

First, for those who take a sceptical view of administrative reform as a series of evanescent fads and fashions, NPM's rise might be interpreted as a sudden and unpredictable product of 'loquocentric' success (Minogue 1986). (Spann (1981) offers a classic statement of the 'fashion' interpretation of administrative reform.) 'Cheap, superficial and popular', like the industrial 'rationalization' doctrines of the 1930s (Hannah 1976, p. 38, fn. p. 34), NPM had many of the necessary qualities for a period of pop management stardom. A 'whim of fashion' interpretation has some attractions, and can cope with the cycles and reversals that took place within NPM – for instance, the radical shift in the UK, from the 'Heseltine creed' of *Ministers* as the hands-on public managers to the 'Next Steps' corporatization creed of professional managers at the top, with ministers in a strictly 'hands-off' role (cf. also Sturgess 1989). But equally, the weakness of a simple 'whim of fashion' explanation is that it does not account for the relative *endurance* of many of the seven precepts identified in table 1 over more than a decade.

An equally sceptical explanation, but one which better accommodates the recurring or enduring features of many aspects of NPM, is the view of NPM as a 'cargo cult' phenomenon – the endless rebirth, in spite of repeated failures, of the idea that substantive success ('cargo') can be gained by the practice of particular kinds of (managerial) ritual. Downs and Larkey (1986) describe a recurring cycle of euphoria and disillusion in the promulgation of simplistic and stereotyped recipes for better public management in the USA, which shows striking similarities with the well-documented cargo cults of Melanesia (Lawrence 1964; Worsley 1968). However, this explanation cannot tell us why the NPM variant of the recurring public management 'cargo cult' appeared at the time that it did, rather than at any other.

A third, less sceptical, approach might be to view the rise of NPM through Hegelian spectacles and interpret it as an epoch-making attraction of opposites. The opposites in this case are two historically distinct approaches to public administration which are in a sense fused in NPM. One is the German tradition of state-led economic development (*Volkswirtschaft*) by professional public managers, with its roots in cameralism (Small 1909). The other is the Anglo-Saxon tradition of liberal economics, allied with a concern for matching self-interest with duty in administration, that has its roots in utilitarianism (Hume 1981). But, like the 'cargo cult' interpretation, the 'synthesis of opposites' interpretation on its own does not help us to understand why those two distinct public administration traditions should have united *at this particular time* rather than at any other.

A fourth and perhaps more promising interpretation of the emergence of NPM is as a response to a set of special social conditions developing in the long peace in the developed countries since World War II, and the unique period of economic growth which accompanied it (see Hood 1990b and 1991 [then] forthcoming). Conditions which may have helped to precipitate NPM include:

— changes in income level and distribution serving to weaken the 'Tocqueville coalition' for government growth in the electorate, and laying the conditions for a new tax-conscious winning electoral coalition (Tocqueville 1946, p. 152; Peacock 1979; Meltzer and Richard 1981);

— changes in the socio-technical system associated with the development of the lead technologies of the late twentieth-century Kondratiev cycle ('post-industrialism', 'post-Fordism'), serving to remove the traditional barriers between 'public sector work' and 'private sector work' (cf. Bell 1973; Piore and Sabel 1984; Jessop 1988).

— A shift towards 'new machine politics', the advent of a new campaign technology geared towards making public policy by intensive opinion polling of key groups in the electorate, such that professional party strategists have greater clout in policy-making relative to the voice of experience from the bureaucracy (cf. Mills 1986; Hood 1990c, p. 206).

— a shift to a more white-collar, socially heterogeneous population less tolerant of 'statist' and uniform approaches in public policy (cf. Hood and Schuppert 1988, p. 250–2).

The fourth explanation is somewhat 'overdetermined', but it seems more promising than the other three in that it has the power to explain what none of the others can do, namely why NPM should have emerged in the particular time and place that it did and under a variety of different auspices.

AN ALL-PURPOSE GARMENT? NPM's CLAIM TO UNIVERSALITY

Like many previous administrative philosophies, NPM was presented as a framework of general applicability, a 'public management for all seasons'. The claim to universality was laid in two main ways.

Portability and diffusion: First, much the same set of received doctrines was advanced as the means to solve 'management ills' in many different contexts – different organizations, policy fields, levels of government, countries. From Denmark to New Zealand, from education to health care, from central to local government and quangos, from rich North to poor South, similar remedies were prescribed along the lines of the seven themes sketched out in table 1. Universalism was not complete in practice; for instance, NPM seems to have had much less impact on international bureaucracies than on national ones, and less on controlling departments than on front-line delivery units. Moreover, much was made of the need for local variation in management styles – so long as such variations did not challenge the basic framework of NPM (Pollitt 1990, pp. 55–6). For critics, however, much of the 'freedom to manage' under NPM was that brand of freedom in which whatever is not forbidden tends to be compulsory (Larsen 1980, p. 54); and the tendencies to uniformity and 'cloning' under FMI points to possible reasons for the decline of FMI and its supersession by the corporatization creed of 'Next Steps.'

Political neutrality: Second, NPM was claimed to be an 'apolitical' framework within which many different values could be pursued effectively. The claim was that different political priorities and circumstances could be accommodated by altering the 'settings' of the management system, without the need to rewrite the basic programme of NPM. That framework was not, according to NPM's advocates, a machine exclusively tunable to respond to the demands of the New Right or to any one political party or programme (see, for example, Scott Bushnell and Sallee 1990, p. 162; Treasury and Civil Service Committee 1990, pp. ix, 22, 61). In this respect, NPM followed the claims to universality of traditional Public Administration, which also purported to offer a neutral and all-purpose instrument for realizing whatever goals elected representatives might set (Ostrom 1974; Thomas 1978; Hood 1987).

COUNTER-CLAIMS: CRITICS OF NPM

If NPM has lacked a single definitive 'manifesto', the ideas of its critics are equally scattered among a variety of often ephemeral sources. Most of the criticisms of NPM have come in terms of four main counter-claims, none of which have been definitively tested, in spite of the ESRC's 'Management in Government' initiative.

The first is the assertion that NPM is like the Emperor's New Clothes in the well-known Hans Andersen story – all hype and no substance, and in that sense a true product of the style-conscious 1980s. From this viewpoint, the advent of new managerialism has changed little, apart from the language in which senior public 'managers' speak in public. Underneath, all the old problems and weaknesses remain. Implicitly, from this viewpoint, the remedy lies in giving NPM some real substance in order to move from 'smoke and mirrors' to reality – for example, in making output contracts between ministers and chief executives legally binding or in breaking up the public service employment structure, as has happened in New Zealand (cf. Hood and Jones in Treasury and Civil Service Committee 1989–90).

The second is the assertion that NPM has damaged the public service while being ineffective in its ability to deliver on its central claim to lower costs per (constant) unit of service. Critics of this type suggest that the main result of NPM in many cases has been an 'aggrandizement of management' (Martin 1983) and a rapid middle-level bureaucratization of new reporting systems (as in the remarkable growth of the 'performance indicator industry'). Budgetary and control framework changes such as 'top-slicing' and 'creative accounting' serve to destabilize the bureaucracy and to weaken or destroy elementary but essential competences at the front line (see, for instance, Nethercote 1989b, p. 17; Nethercote 1989c). From this viewpoint, the remedy lies in applying to the NPM *system* the disciplines that it urges upon service-delivery bureaucracies but so signally fails to impose on itself – particularly in strict resource control and the imposition of a battery of published and measurable performance indicators to determine the overall costs and benefits of the system.

The third common criticism is the assertion that NPM, in spite of its professed claims to promote the 'public good' (of cheaper and better public services for all), is actually a vehicle for *particularistic* advantage. The claim is that NPM is a self-serving movement designed to promote the career interests of an élite group of 'new managerialists' (top managers and officials in central controlling departments, management consultants and business schools) rather than the mass of public service customers or low-level staff (Dunleavy 1985; Yeatman 1987; Kelleher 1988; Pollitt 1990, pp. 134–7). Implicitly, the remedy suggested by these criticisms is to have disproportionate cutbacks on 'managerial' rather than on 'operational' staff (cf. Martin 1983), and measures to 'empower' consumers, for instance by new systems of direct democracy (cf. Pollitt 1990, pp. 183–4).

The fourth line of criticism, to which most attention will be paid in the remainder of this paper, is directed towards NPM's claim of *universality*. Contrary to NPM's claim to be a public management for all seasons, these critics argue that different administrative values have different implications for fundamental aspects of administrative design – implications which go beyond altering the 'settings' of the systems.

In order for their counter-claim to have any significance, it must be able to survive obvious objections. First, it must be able to show that the objection is more than a semantic quibble about where the line comes between a different programme and a change of 'settings'. For that, it must be able to show that the incompatibility problem lies in NPM's 'hard core' research programme rather than in its 'elaborative belts' (Lakatos 1970). Second, it must be able to show that it is more than a trivial and obvious proposition. In order to survive this objection, it needs to show that there are different management-system implications of different *mainstream*, relatively orthodox values, without reference to values at the extremes of the orthodox belief spectrum (since it needs no elaborate treatise to show that different 'fundamentalist' values have different implications for public management). Third, the 'incompatibility' argument needs to rest on a plausible case that an 'all-purpose culture' either does not exist or cannot be engineered into existence. Unless it can do so, it risks being dismissed for mechanically assuming that there is a particular set of administrative design-characteristics which goes with the ability to achieve a particular set of values. Finally, it needs to show that the debate relates to *administrative values* – values that relate to conventional and relatively narrow ideas about 'good administration' rather than to broader ideas about the proper role of the state in society. Unless the critique of the 'all seasons' quality of NPM relates to administrative values in this sense, it risks being dismissed simply as an undercover way of advocating different *political values* from those currently held by elected governments. A case built on such a basis would not essentially be an administrative design argument, and would neither demonstrate that NPM is incapable of being adapted to promote alternative political values nor that NPM is a false recipe for achieving the narrow 'efficiency' values of the current orthodox agenda.

Most of the orthodox criticisms of NPM in this vein are vulnerable to counter-attack from this last objection. Most academic attacks on NPM have questioned NPM's universality by focusing on the equity costs of a preoccupation with cost-cutting and a focus on 'bottom line ethics' (Jackson 1989, p. 173). For instance, a focus on outputs allied with heavy 'hands-on' demands on managers is often claimed to downgrade equity considerations, particularly in its implications for the ability of female managers to reach top positions in the public service (cf. Bryson 1987; Pollitt 1990, pp. 141–2). A focus on disaggregation and a private-sector PR style is likewise often claimed to reduce the accessibility of public services by increasing the complexity and opacity of government (Nethercote 1990c), and increasing the scope for buck-passing and denial of responsibility, especially for disadvantaged consumers. However, any simple dichotomy between 'efficiency' and 'equity' can be countered by NPM's advocates on the grounds that 'efficiency' can be conceived in ways which do not fundamentally conflict with equity (cf. Wilenski 1986), and that equity values could perfectly well be programmed in to the target-setting and performance indication process, if there was strong enough political pressure to do so.

THREE CLUSTERS OF ADMINISTRATIVE VALUES

In administrative argument in the narrow sense, the rival values in play typically do not fall into a neat dichotomy. At least three different 'families' of values commonly appear in debates about administrative design, and these are summarized in table 2 below (cf. Hood and Jackson 1991 forthcoming). Broadly, the 'sigma' family of values relates to *economy* and *parsimony*, the 'theta' family relates to *honesty* and *fairness*, and the 'lambda' family relates to *security* and *resilience*.

The trio corresponds roughly to the management values used by Susan Strange (1988, pp. 1–6) in her account of the evolution of different regimes in the international sphere; and at least two of the three correspond to the groups of values given by Harmon and Mayer (1986, pp. 34–53) in their well-known account of the normative context of public sector organization. It cannot be claimed that these values are esoteric or extreme, or that they are not 'administrative' values.

TABLE 2 *Three sets of core values in public management*

	Sigma-type values KEEP IT LEAN AND PURPOSEFUL	*Theta-type values* KEEP IT HONEST AND FAIR	*Lambda-type values* KEEP IT ROBUST AND RESILIENT
STANDARD OF SUCCESS	*Frugality* (matching of resources to tasks for given goals)	*Rectitude* (achievement of fairness, mutuality, the proper discharge of duties)	*Resilience* (achievement of reliability, adaptivity, robustness)
STANDARD OF FAILURE	*Waste* (muddle, confusion, inefficiency)	*Malversation* (unfairness, bias, abuse of office)	*Catastrophe* (risk, breakdown, collapse)
CURRENCY OF SUCCESS AND FAILURE	*Money and time* (resource costs of producers and consumers)	*Trust and entitlements* (consent, legitimacy, due process, political entitlements)	*Security and survival* (confidence, life and limb)
CONTROL EMPHASIS	*Output*	*Process*	*Input/Process*
SLACK	*Low*	*Medium*	*High*
GOALS	*Fixed/Single*	*Incompatible* 'Double bind'	*Emergent/Multiple*
INFORMATION	Costed, segmented (commercial assets)	Structured	Rich exchange, collective asset
COUPLING	*Tight*	*Medium*	*Loose*

Sigma-type values: match resources to defined tasks: In the 'sigma' family come administrative values connected with the matching of resources to narrowly defined tasks and circumstances in a competent and sparing fashion. Such values are central, mainstream and traditional in public management. From this viewpoint, frugality of resource use in relation to given goals is the criterion of success, while failure is counted in terms of instances of avoidable waste and incompetence. If sigma-type values are emphasized, the central concern is to 'trim fat' and avoid 'slack'.

Classic expressions of sigma-type values include:

(i) 'just-in-time' inventory control systems (which avoid tying up resources in storing what is not currently needed, pushing the onus of accessible storage and rapid delivery on to suppliers);
(ii) payment-by-results reward systems (which avoid paying for what is not being delivered); and
(iii) administrative 'cost engineering' (using resources sparingly to provide public services of no greater cost, durability or quality than is absolutely necessary for a defined task, without excessive concern for 'externalities').

The principal 'coin' in which success or failure to realize sigma-type values is measured is time and money, in resource costs of consumers and producers.

It can be argued that an orthodox design for realizing sigma-type values would closely parallel the 'mechanistic' structures which have frequently been identified in contingency theory as applicable to defined and stable environmental conditions (cf. Burns and Stalker 1961; Lawrence and Lorsch 1967). Since the 'sigma' group of values stresses the matching of resources to defined objectives, the setting of fixed and 'checkable' goals must be central to any design for realizing such values. The fewer incompatible objectives are included, the more readily can unnecessary fat be identified and removed. Equally, the more that the control emphasis is on output rather than on process or input, the more unambiguous the waste-finding process can be. To make output control a reality, two features are necessary. One is a heavy emphasis on output databases. Such an emphasis in turn requires a technological infrastructure of reporting which will tend to make each managerial unit 'tightly coupled' in informational terms. The other is the sharp definition of responsibilities, involving separation of 'thinking' and 'executing' activities and the breakup of organizations into separate, non-overlapping parts, to come as close as possible to the ideal of single-objective, trackable and manageable units. It follows that information in such a control system will be highly segmented and valuable, so that it will be guarded with extreme care and traded rather than given away. These design characteristics map closely on to the recipes offered by the corporate management strain of NPM.

Theta-type values: honesty, fairness, mutuality: 'Theta-type' connotes values broadly relating to the pursuit of honesty, fairness and mutuality through the prevention of distortion, inequity, bias, and abuse of office. Such values are also central and traditional in public management, and they are institutionalized in appeal mechanisms, public reporting requirements, adversary bureaucracies, independent scrutiny systems, attempts to socialize public servants in something more than 'bottom line ethics' or a high 'grovel count' (Self 1989). From this viewpoint, success is counted in terms of 'rectitude', the proper discharge of duties in procedural and substantive terms, while failure is measured in terms of 'malversation' in a formal or substantive sense. If theta-type values are placed at centre stage, the central concern is to ensure honesty, prevent 'capture' of public bodies by unrepresentative groups, and avoid all arbitrary proceedings.

Classic expressions of theta-type values include:

(i) recall systems for removing public officials from office by popular vote;
(ii) 'notice and comment' and 'hard look' requirements in administrative law (Birkinshaw, Harden and Lewis 1990, p. 260);
(iii) independent anti-corruption investigatory bodies such as the 1987–9 Fitzgerald Inquiry which effectively brought down the Queensland government in 1989 (cf. Prasser, Wear and Nethercote 1990).

The 'coin' in which success or failure is measured according to theta-type values may be partly related to 'balance sheet' items (insofar as dishonesty and abuse of office is often linked with palpable waste of resources), but also involves less tangible stakes, notably public trust and confidence and the ability to exercise citizenship effectively.

Putting theta-type values at the centre of the stage has implications for organizational design which are different from an emphasis on 'sigma-type' values. Where honesty and fairness is a primary goal, the design-focus is likely to be on process-controls rather than output controls. Goals, too, are less likely to be single in nature. 'Getting the job done' in terms of aggregate quantities is likely to be supplemented by concerns about *how* the job is done (cf. March and Olsen 1989, pp. 47–52).

Hence 'double bind' elements (Hennestad 1990) may be central to goal setting, with line management under complex cross-pressures and with control operating through a shifting-balances style (Dunsire 1978). The cross pressures and 'double bind' process may operate through the activities of independent adversary bureaucracies, rather than with corporate objectives settled in a single place – for example, in the Hong Kong style of independent anti-corruption bodies. Similarly, concern with process may cause the emphasis to go on the achievement of maximum *transparency* in public operations – for example, extensive public reporting requirements, 'angels' advocates' (the practice of incorporating representatives of 'public interest' groups on corporate boards), freedom of information laws, 'notice and comment' procedures, rather than simple 'bottom line ethics'.

Indeed, the logical conclusion of putting theta-type values first in designing public management would be to minimize the ability of those in high office to sell or distort public decisions as a result of 'capture' by particular groups – for example, by the entrenchment of adversarial processes within the bureaucracy or by greater use of direct democracy in public decision-making (Walker 1986; Pollitt 1990, pp. 183–4).

Lambda-type values: reliability, robustness, adaptivity: 'Lambda-type' values relate to resilience, endurance, robustness, survival and adaptivity – the capacity to withstand and learn from the blows of fate, to avoid 'competency traps' in adaptation processes (Levitt and March 1988; Liebowitz and Margolis 1990), to keep operating even in adverse 'worst case' conditions and to adapt rapidly in a crisis.

Expectations of security and reliability are central to traditional public administration values, and have often been associated with the choice of public rather than private organization for the provision of a hazard-related task. Perhaps the classic historical case is of the Venetian arsenal and *Tana* as instruments for ensuring the security of Venice's maritime power by direct state production of ropes and vessels (cf. Lane 1966).

From the viewpoint of lambda-type values, success is counted in terms of resilience and reliability, while failure is measured in terms of catastrophe, breakdown and learning failure. If lambda-type values are placed at centre stage, the central concern is to avoid system failure, 'down time', paralysis in the face of threat or challenge.

Classic expressions of lambda-type values include:

(i) *redundancy*, the maintenance of back-up systems to duplicate normal capacity;
(ii) *diversity*, the maintenance of quite separate, self-standing units (to avoid 'common mode failure', whether in technical terms or in terms of 'groupthink'); and
(iii) *robustness*, use of greater amounts of materials than would ordinarily be necessary for the job (cf. Health and Safety Executive 1988, p. 11).

The 'coin' in which success or failure is measured in lambda-type values includes security, survival and the robustness of basic assumptions about social defence mechanisms.

Orthodox discussions of learning problems and catastrophes tend to focus on specific failings of individuals rather than systemic or structural factors in organizational design (Turner *et al.* 1989, p. 3). But some tentative pointers to the administrative design implications of putting lambda-type values at centre stage can be gleaned from three closely related literatures: 'contingency theory' ideas about structural factors related to highly uncertain environments (cf. Lawrence and Lorsch 1967); the literature on the organization of socially created disasters (Dixon 1976; Turner 1976 and 1978; Perrow

1984); and the developing and related literature on 'safety culture' (Westrum 1987; Turner *et al.* 1989).

Some of the ideas to be found in this literature about the engineering of adaptivity and error-avoidance are contradictory. A case in point is the debate about 'anticipation' versus 'resilience' (Wildavsky 1988). Moreover, Perrow (1984) claims that for some technologies, administrative design for error-avoidance is impossible, even if safety is highly valued. However, much of this literature tends to relate error-generation, capacity for resilience and learning failures to three elements of institutional structure

  (i) degree of *integration* – the extent to which interdependent parts of the system are linked in decision and information terms rather than isolated into separate compartments, each trying to insulate itself independently against system failure;
 (ii) degree of *openness* in the culture or management system, avoiding authoritarian barriers to lateral or systemic thinking and feedback or learning processes; and
(iii) the extent to which there are systemic pressures for *misinformation*, rather than sharing of information, built in to the organizational process.

From the perspective of this literature, an organizational design which maximized lambda-type values would need to involve: multiple-objective rather than single-objective organization (van Gunsteren 1976, p. 61); a relatively high degree of 'slack' to provide spare capacity for learning or deployment in crisis; a control framework which focused on input or process rather than measured output in order to avoid building up pressures for misinformation; a personnel management structure which promoted cohesion without punishing unorthodox ideas; a task division structure organized for systemic thinking rather than narrow compartmentalization; and a responsibility structure which made mistakes and errors admissible. Relatively loose coupling and an emphasis on information as a collective asset within the organization would be features of such a design structure.

Compatibility: From this discussion, as summarized in table 2, one fundamental implication is that these three sets of mainstream administrative values overlap over some of their range, like intersecting circles in a Venn diagram. For example, dishonesty frequently creates waste and sometimes leads to catastrophe. Frugality, rectitude and resilience may all be satisfied by a particular set of institutional arrangements in some contexts.

However, the discussion also suggests the hypothesis that any two out of the three broad value sets may often be satisfied by the same organizing principle for a set of basic administrative design dimensions; but that it is hard to satisfy *all three* value sets equally for any of those dimensions, and probably impossible to do so for all of them. Put simply, a central concern with *honesty* and the avoidance of policy distortion in public administration may have different design implications from a central concern with *frugality*; and a central concern with *resilience* may also have different design implications. If NPM is a design for putting frugality at centre stage, it may at the limit be less capable of ensuring honesty and resilience in public administration.

IMPLICATIONS FOR NEW PUBLIC MANAGEMENT

The work of the ESRC's Management in Government Initiative has helped us to identify the specific forms that NPM took in the UK and to trace its history. But, like many research initiatives, it has perhaps been more successful in prompting the critical questions rather than in answering them definitively. Two key questions in particular seem to deserve more examination, in order to 'put NPM in its place' intellectually.

First, NPM can be understood as primarily an expression of sigma-type values. Its claims have lain mainly in the direction of cutting costs and doing more for less as a result of better-quality management and different structural design. Accordingly, one of the key tests of NPM's 'success' is whether and how it has delivered on that claim, in addition to succeeding in terms of rhetorical acceptance. We still have remarkably little independent evidence on this point, and work by Dunsire et al. (1988) has some path-breaking qualities in that it is a serious attempt to develop indicators of organizational structure and control systems in a way that helps us to understand how privatization and corporatization works. It offers tentative evidence for the proposition that a shift in management structures towards decreased command-orientation and increased 'results-orientation' is associated with improvements in productivity. But the results obtained so far are only indicative: the study does not test fully for 'Hawthorne effects' or secular trends, and it has no control groups. We need much more work in this vein.

However, the critics' questioning of NPM's universality also offers a way of putting NPM in its place and involves crucial claims that need proper testing. Even if further research established that NPM was clearly associated with the pursuit of frugality, it remains to be fully investigated whether such successes are bought at the expense of guarantees of honesty and fair dealing and of security and resilience.

Broadly, NPM assumes a culture of public service honesty as given. Its recipes to some degree removed devices instituted to ensure honesty and neutrality in the public service in the past (fixed salaries, rules of procedure, permanence of tenure, restraints on the power of line management, clear lines of division between public and private sectors). The extent to which NPM is likely to induce corrosion in terms of such traditional values remains to be tested. The effects of NPM 'clones' diffused by public management 'consultocrats' and others into contexts where there is little 'capital base' of ingrained public service culture (as in many Third World countries and perhaps in Eastern Europe too) will be particularly interesting to observe. The consequences for 'theta-type' values are likely to be most visible, since the effects are likely to be quicker and more dramatic there than in countries like Australia and the UK which are still living off 'public service ethic' capital.[1]

Equally, the extent to which NPM's precepts are compatible with 'safety engineering' in terms of 'safety cultures' deserves more analysis. NPM broadly assumes that public services can be divided into self-contained 'products', and that good public management requires de-emphasis of overarching externalities and emphasis on running services within given parameters. Whether the emphasis on cost-cutting, contracting-out, compartmentalizing and top-slicing is compatible with safety culture at the front line needs to be tested. The new breed of organizationally created disasters over the past fifteen years or so, of which some dramatic examples have occurred in the UK, suggest that the issue at least needs investigation.

Only when we can test the limits of NPM in terms of relatively narrow *administrative* values can we start to establish its proper scope and put it in its historical place.

NOTE

[1] I owe this idea to a suggestion by Dr. John Baker of John Baker and Associates.

REFERENCES

Arrow, K. J. 1963. *Social choice and individual values*. New Haven: Yale University Press.

Aucoin, P. 1990. 'Administrative reform in public management: paradigms, principles, paradoxes and pendulums', *Governance* 3, 115–37.

Bell, D. 1973. *The coming of post-industrial society*. New York: Basic.

Birkinshaw, P., I. Harden and N. Lewis. 1990. *Government by moonlight: the hidden parts of the state*. London: Unwin Hyman.

Bogdanor, V. (ed.). 1987. *The Blackwell encyclopaedia of political institutions*. Oxford: Blackwell.

Bryson, L. 1987. 'Women and management in the public sector', *Australian Journal of Public Administration* 46, 259–72.

Burns, T. and G. M. Stalker. 1961. *The management of innovation*. London: Tavistock.

Carey, B. and P. Ryan. (eds.) 1989. *In transition: NSW and the corporatisation agenda*. Sydney: Macquarie Public Sector Studies Program/Association for Management Education and Research.

Carter, N. 1988. 'Performance indicators: "Backseat Driving" or "Hands Off" Control?' *Policy and Politics* 17.

Castles, F. G. (ed.) 1989. *The comparative history of public policy*. Cambridge: Polity.

Day, P. and R. Klein. 1987. *'Accountabilities'*. London: Tavistock.

Dixon, N. F. 1979. *On the psychology of military incompetence*. London: Futura.

Downs, G. W. and P. D. Larkey. 1986. *The search for government efficiency: from hubris to helplessness*. Philadelphia: Temple University Press.

Dunleavy, P. J. 1985. 'Bureaucrats, budgets and the growth of the state', *British Journal of Political Science* 15, 299–328.

———. 1989. 'The United Kingdom: paradoxes of an ungrounded statism', pp. 242–91 in F. G. Castles (ed.) *The comparative history of public policy*. Cambridge: Polity.

Dunsire, A. 1978. *Control in a bureaucracy*, vol. 2 of *The execution process*. London: Martin Robertson.

Dunsire A., K. Hartley, D. Parker and B. Dimitriou. 1988. 'Organizational status and performance; a conceptual framework for testing public choice theories', *Public Administration* 66, 4 (Winter), 363–88.

Dunsire, A. and C. C. Hood. 1989. *Cutback management in public bureaucracies*. Cambridge: Cambridge University Press.

Gustafsson, B. (ed.) 1979. *Post-industrial society*. London: Croom Helm.

Hannah, L. 1976. *The rise of the corporate economy*. London: Methuen.

Harmon, M. and R. Mayer. 1986. *Organization theory for public administration*. Boston: Little, Brown.

Health and Safety Executive. 1988. *The tolerability of risk from nuclear power stations*. London: HMSO.

Hennestad, B. W. 1990. The symbolic impact of double bind leadership: double bind and the dynamics of organizational culture', *Journal of Management Studies* 27, 265–80.

Hood, C. C. 1976. *The limits of administration*. London: Wiley.

———. 1987. 'Public administration' in V. Bogdanor (ed.) *The Blackwell encyclopaedia of political institutions*. Oxford: Blackwell.

———. 1990a. 'Public administration: lost an empire, not yet found a role' in A. Leftwich (ed.) *New directions in political science*. Aldershot: Elgar.

———. 1990b. 'Beyond the public bureaucracy state? Public administration in the 1990s', inaugural lecture, London School of Economics, 16 January 1990.

———. 1990c. 'De-Sir-Humphrey-fying the Westminster model of governance' *Governance* 3, 205–14.

———. 1991 (forthcoming). 'Stabilization and cutbacks: a catastrophe for government growth theory?' *Journal of Theoretical Politics*.

Hood, C. C. and G. W. Jones 1990. 'Progress in the government's Next Steps initiative'. Appendix 6 in HC 481, 1989–90, 78–83.

Hood, C. C. and M. W. Jackson. 1991 (forthcoming). *Administrative argument*. Aldershot: Dartmouth.

Jackson, M. W. 1989. 'Immorality may lead to greatness: ethics in government' pp. 160–77 in S. Prasser, R. Wear and J. Nethercote (eds.) *Corruption and reform: the Fitzgerald vision*. St. Lucia: Queensland University Press.

Jessop, B. 1988. 'Conservative regimes and the transition to post-Fordism', *Essex Papers in Politics and Government* No. 47, Department of Government, University of Essex.

Kast, F. E. and Rosenzweig, J. E. 1973. *Contingency Views of Organization and Management*. New York: Science Research Associates.

Keating, M. 1989. 'Quo vadis: challenges of public administration', address to Royal Australian Institute of Public Administration, Perth, 12 April 1989.

Kelleher, S. R. 1988. The apotheosis of the Department of the Prime Minister and Cabinet', *Canberra Bulletin of Public Administration* 54, 9–12.

Lakatos, I. 1970. 'Falsification and the methodology of scientific research programmes' pp. 91–196 in I. Lakatos and A. Musgrave *Criticism and the growth of knowledge*. Cambridge: Cambridge University Press.

Lakatos, I. and A. Musgrave. 1970. *Criticism and the growth of knowledge*. Cambridge: Cambridge University Press.

Lane, F. C. 1966. *Venice and history*. Baltimore: Johns Hopkins University Press.

Larson, E. 1980. *Wit as a weapon: the political joke in history*. London: Muller.

Lawrence, P. 1964. *Road belong cargo*. Manchester: Manchester University Press.

Lawrence, P. R. and J. W. Lorsch. 1967. *Organization and environment*. Boston: Harvard University Press.

Leftwich, A. (ed.) 1990. *New directions in political science*. Aldershot: Elgar.

Levitt, B. and J. G. March. 1988. 'Organizational learning'. *Annual Review of Sociology* 14, 319–40.

Liebowitz, S. J. and S. E. Margolis. 1990. 'The fable of the keys'. *The Journal of Law and Economics* 33, 1–26.

March, J. G. and J. P. Olsen. 1989. *Rediscovering institutions: the organizational basis of politics*. New York: Free Press.

Martin, J. 1988. *A profession of statecraft? Three essays on some current issues in the New Zealand public service*. Wellington: Victoria University Press.

Martin, S. 1983. *Managing without managers*. Beverly Hills: Sage.

Meltzer, A. H. and S. F. Richard. 1981. 'A rational theory of the size of government'. *Journal of Political Economy* 89, 914–27.

Merkle, J. 1980. *Management and ideology: the legacy of the international scientific management movement*. Berkeley: California University Press.

Mills, S. 1986. *The new machine men*. Ringwood: Penguin.

Minogue, K. 1986. 'Loquocentric society and its critics', *Government and Opposition* 21, 338–61.

Nethercote, J. R. 1989a. 'The rhetorical tactics of managerialism: reflections on Michael Keating's apologia, "Quo Vadis" ', *Australian Journal of Public Administration* 48, 363–7.

———. 1989b. 'Public service reform: Commonwealth experience', paper presented to the Academy of Social Sciences of Australia, 25 February 1989, University House, Australian National University.

———. 1989c. 'Revitalising public service personnel management', *The Canberra Times* 11 June.

Niskanen, W. A. 1971. *Bureaucracy and representative government*. Chicago: Aldine Atherton.

Ostrom, V. 1974. *The intellectual crisis in American Public Administration*. Alabama: University of Alabama Press.

Peacock, A. 1979. 'Public expenditure growth in post-industrial society', pp. 80–95 in B. Gustafsson (ed.) *Post-industrial society*. London: Croom Helm.

Perrow, C. 1984. *Normal accident: living with high-risk technologies*. New York: Basic.

Peters, T. and R. Waterman. 1982. *In search of excellence*. New York: Harper and Row.

Piore, M. J. and C. F. Sabel. 1984. *The second industrial divide*. New York: Basic.

Pollitt, C. 1990. *Managerialism and the public services: the Anglo-American experience*. Oxford: Blackwell.

Prasser, S., R. Wear and J. Nethercote (eds.). 1990. *Corruption and reform: the Fitzgerald vision*. St. Lucia: Queensland University Press.

Scott, G., P. Bushnell and N. Sallee. 1990. 'Reform of the core public sector: New Zealand experience', *Governance* 3, 138–67.

Self, P. 1989. 'Is the grovel count rising in the bureaucracy?' *The Canberra Times* 14 April, p. 11.

Spann, R. N. 1981. 'Fashions and fantasies in public administration', *Australian Journal of Public Administration* 40, 12–25.

Strange, S. 1988. *States and markets: an introduction to international political economy*. London: Pinter.

Sturgess, G. 1989. 'First keynote address' pp. 4–10 in B. Carey and P. Ryan (eds.), *In transition: NSW and the corporatisation agenda*. Sydney: Macquarie Public Sector Studies Program.

Thomas, R. 1978. *The British philosophy of administration*. London: Longman.

Tocqueville, A. de 1946. *Democracy in America*. London: Oxford University Press.

Turner, B. A. 1976. 'How to organize disaster', *Management Today* March 56–7 and 105.

———. 1978. *Man-made disasters*. London: Wykeham.

———. 1989. 'How can we design a safe organization?' paper presented at the Second International Conference on Industrial and Organizational Crisis Management, Leonard N. Stern School of Business, New York University, November 3–4.

Turner, B. A., N. Pidgeon, D. Blockley and B. Toft. 1989. 'Safety culture: its importance in future risk management', position paper for the Second World Bank Workshop on Safety Control and Risk Management, Karlstad, Sweden, 6–9 November.

Treasury and Civil Service Committee. 1990. Eighth report of Session 1989–90 *Progress in the Next Steps initiative*, HC 481, London: HMSO.

van Gunsteren, H. R. 1976. *The quest for control: a critique of the rational-central-rule approach in public affairs*. London: Wiley.

Walker, G. de Q. 1986. *Initiative and referendum: the people's law*. Sydney: Centre for Independent Studies.

Westrum, R. 1987. 'Management Strategies and Information Failure' pp. 109–27 in J. A. Wise and A. Debons (eds.) *Information systems failure analysis*. NATO ASI Series F Computer and Systems Science, Vol. 3. Berlin: Springer.

Wildavsky, A. 1985. Trial without error: anticipation vs. resilience as strategies for risk reduction' CIS Occasional Papers 13. Sydney: Centre for Independent Studies.

Wilenski, P. 1986. *Public power and public administration*. Sydney: RAIPA/Hale and Iremonger.

Wise, J. A. and Debons, A. (eds.) 1987. *Information systems failure analysis*. NATO ASI Series F. Computer and Systems Science, vol. 3. Berlin: Springer.

Worsley, P. 1968. *The trumpet shall sound*. 2nd. ed. London: MacGibbon and Kee.

Yeatman, A. 1987. The concept of public management and the Australian state in the 1980s', *Australian Journal of Public Administration* 46, 339–53.

AFTERWORD: FROM FASHION TO MAINSTREAM

Deservedly or otherwise, 'A Public Management for All Seasons?' is my single most cited work and has often been given as a reference to early usage of the term 'New Public Management' (although it was not in fact the first time I used that phrase in print; for that, see Hood 1989). Indeed, there are reasons to believe that the paper has become one of those documents that are more commonly cited than read, because it is often cited to imply (wrongly) that I was a pioneering advocate of New Public Management rather than a sceptical commentator arguing that no single approach to organization and management could satisfy all administrative values in all circumstances.

The paper grew out of my 1990 inaugural lecture ('Beyond the Public Bureaucracy State') as Professor of Public Administration and Public Policy at LSE. That lecture attracted academic attention at the time, was reported in the press and even caused the then UK Cabinet Secretary to ask to see me, but it was far from the first discussion of 'managerialism' in government and public services. After all, James Burnham (1942) had produced his *The Managerial Revolution* over forty years earlier; there had been numerous commentaries on public-service managerialism in the subsequent decades, particularly in the 1960s and 1970s (such as Peter Self's (1971) critique of the 'cult of management' in the Maud and Fulton reports of the 1960s in Britain); and Christopher Pollitt's (1990) *Managerialism and the Public Services* delineated many of the same features of public service managerialism that are discussed in 'A Public Management for All Seasons?'

The reason for coining the neologism 'New Public Management' at that time was that a term was needed to characterize a new (or at least recycled) set of doctrines of how to manage the state which combined Burnham-style managerialism with economic rationalism. Terms like 'Thatcherism', much used back then, could not adequately capture that phenomenon, because the developments concerned were not specific to the UK (and indeed the approach was arguably taken further under centre-left Labour governments in Australia and New Zealand than in the UK at that time) and because such changes were promoted by both right and left political parties in government.

The early 1990s were also a time when management and managerialism, long important in city and local government, was coming to be more heavily stressed in central or national government in Britain. To be sure, it had been crucial to the conduct of the state machine in the two World Wars, but after World War II with the release of the managers brought in from business to orchestrate the wartime economy, the civil service reverted to a more policy-focused vision of its role and competencies. The reaction against that style had perhaps reached its height in Britain when 'A Public Management for All Seasons?' was written. As a sign of those times it is worth recalling that the late Sir Peter Kemp (the senior civil servant then responsible for the UK government's executive agency programme) refused to use the word 'administration' at all to describe the work of executive government, insisting on the term 'management' instead.

But that was then, this is now. Is the paper of any more than antiquarian interest today? Certainly, it represents an early 'traits' approach to NPM that soon came to be refined by more systematic empirical and comparative work, for example, by Michael Barzelay (2000) and Christopher Pollitt and Geert Bouckaert (2004). And indeed ever since the term was coined (and flogged to death on the conference circuit), scholars have eagerly lined up to pronounce the death of NPM and its replacement by other big ideas – such as 'Digital Era Governance' (Dunleavy *et al.* 2006), 'the New Public Governance' (Osborne 2010) or simply a reversion of the neo-Weberian state after the supposed excesses of managerialism.

Of course time does not stand still in the world of administrative ideas. Fashions alter, new words and phrases displace the older ones. But despite continuing attacks on NPM as an 'ideology', many of the ideas and practices referred to in 'A Public Management for All Seasons?' have become mainstream in the working of executive government, and indeed there has been much refinement of them since then. Nor are the administrative doctrines that the term NPM was coined to summarize likely to disappear off the face of the earth, especially during another period of strong pressures for cost-saving and therefore for managers who can control the bottom line in service delivery. Reflecting on British experience some forty years ago, Richard Chapman and Andrew Dunsire (1971: 17) noted that there had always been a tension between a 'Benthamite and Taylorite (F.W., not Sir Henry) tradition' and a 'Macaulayite and Bridges tradition'. The same tension can be found in public administration and management in many other countries. The 'New Public Management' was a development firmly in the former tradition, and while there was inevitably a counter-reaction to it, that Benthamite and Taylorite approach to public administration is likely to be as recurrent a strain of future thinking about public services and government as it has been in the past.

REFERENCES

Barzelay, M. 2000. *The New Public Management*, Berkeley, CA, University of California Press.

Burnham, J. 1942. *The Managerial Revolution*, London, Putnam.

Chapman, R.A. and A. Dunsire. (eds). 1971. *Style in Administration: Readings in British Public Administration*, London, Allen and Unwin.

Dunleavy, P.J., H.Z. Margetts, S. Bastow and J. Tinkler. 2006. *Digital Era Governance: IT Corporations, the State and E-Government*, Oxford, Oxford University Press.

Hood, C. 1989. 'Public Administration and Public Policy: Intellectual Challenges for the 1990s' *Australian Journal of Public Administration* 48, 4, 346–58.

Osborne, S.P. (ed.). 2010. *The New Public Governance: Emerging Perspectives on the Theory and Practice of Public Governance*, London, Routledge.

Pollitt, C. 1990. *Managerialism and the Public Services: The Anglo-American Experience*, Oxford, Blackwell.

Pollitt, C. and G. Bouckaert. 2004. *Public Management Reform*, 2nd edn, Oxford, Oxford University Press.

Self, P. 1971. 'Elected Representatives and Management in Local Government: An Alternative Analysis' *Public Administration* 49, 3, 269–77.

Chapter 11

THE COMPETENT BOUNDARY SPANNER

PAUL WILLIAMS

INTRODUCTION

This paper explores the major factors that influence the effective collaborative behaviour and competence of key agents managing within inter-organizational theatres – the boundary spanners. The discussion is framed within the UK public policy context where the persistence of a number of complex problems is being tackled through partnership and collaborative interventions. A critical review of the disparate and cross-disciplinary literature, both institutional and relational, is examined and used to explore a range of perspectives, themes, concepts and models that help to illuminate the behaviour patterns and competency profiles of practising boundary spanners.

This is followed by a detailed account of the research findings of a study that is aimed at identifying and understanding the competency framework for boundary spanners including the bundle of skills, abilities and personal characteristics that contribute to effective inter-organizational behaviour. Prominent in the emerging framework are the building and sustaining of relationships, managing within non-hierarchical environments, managing complexity and understanding motives, roles and responsibilities. The paper concludes with a discussion about areas for future research.

THE MORPHOLOGY OF PUBLIC POLICY PROBLEMS

The public policy landscape is characterized by a host of complex and seemingly intractable problems and issues – community safety, poverty, social inclusion, health inequalities, teenage pregnancies, urban regeneration, substance misuse, climate change and homelessness – an ever growing and assorted list of community concerns. Such issues have been referred to as 'wicked' because they 'defy efforts to delineate their boundaries and to identify their causes, and thus to expose their problematic nature' (Rittel and Webber 1973, p. 167); Trist (1983) simply sees them as 'messes'. 'Wicked issues' appear to possess a number of inherent properties:

- They bridge and permeate jurisdictional, organizational, functional, professional and generational boundaries. They are often capable of metamorphosis and of becoming entangled in a web of other problems creating a kind of dense and complicated policy swamp.
- They are socially constructed because the conceptualization, causes and analysis of problem structures are a function of the unique perspective or gaze of individual stakeholders, of which there are many in dense policy spaces such as with health, poverty or social disadvantage. Schon (1987) and Stone (1997) refer to the act of 'framing' because 'depending on our disciplinary backgrounds, organizational roles, past histories, interests, and political/economic perspectives, we frame problematic

situations in different ways' (Schon 1987, p. 4). In addition, the ripple effect of interdependent problems often makes it difficult to disentangle root causes, and even trace many policy outcomes back to specific interventions despite the current penchant for evidence-based practice.

• Wicked issues are not amenable to optimal solutions. Many are not entirely solved or remain intractable and real progress is dependent on systemic change not short-term fixes.

• Finally, this kind of problem does not 'yield readily to single efforts and is beyond the capacity of any one agency or jurisdiction' (Luke 1998, p. 19).

It is instructive to frame an understanding of 'wicked issues' in the language and thinking of non-linear theories such as complexity and chaos theories developed in the physical sciences. Complex social problems such as crime or health inequality are not amenable to linear thinking which assume a simple relationship between inputs and outcomes. On the contrary, relationships are non-linear. Outcomes are difficult or impossible to predict; responses can be disjointed from causes and a change in the causal agent does not necessarily elicit a proportional change in some variable it affects. It may elicit no response, a dramatic response or a response at certain levels of cause. The metaphors of complexity theory – strange attractors, birfucation, edge of chaos and possibility space – may offer useful ways of exploring and understanding complex societal problems in the future.

ORGANIZATIONAL FORMS

Assuming that a large number of problems presenting themselves in the public policy arena in Britain today bear a close resemblance to the characteristics of a 'wicked issue', it is appropriate to consider the best form of managerial and organizational response necessary for their treatment. I argue that a postmodern rather than a classical form of organization is more likely to be in tune with this particular policy challenge for reasons that are summarized in table 1. Firstly, given that the problems are cross-boundary in nature, the focus of organizational action needs to move from a preoccupation with intra-organizational imperatives more to a commitment to the building of inter-organizational capacity. Secondly, thinking about 'wicked issues' requires a language that reflects relationships, interconnections and interdependencies – holistic thinking. This is not the prevailing discourse of classical organizations that are underpinned by notions of rationality, linear thinking, task differentiation and functionalism. Bureaucratic forms of organization which champion the virtues of rationality, professionalism and compartmentalism are anathema to the

TABLE 1 *Modern and postmodern forms of organization*

	Modern	Postmodern
Domain	Intra-organizational	Inter-organizational
Metaphor	Mechanistic	Systems
Form of government	Administration	Governance
Form of organization	Bureaucratic	Networking, collaboration, partnership
Conceptualization	Differentiation; tasks and functions	Interdependencies
Decision-making framework	Hierarchy and rules	Negotiation and consensus
Competency	Skills-based professional	Relational
Solutions	Optimal	Experimentation, innovation, reflection

challenge of interdependencies. Forms of organization and governance that are designed around collaboration, partnership and networking appear to be more suitable for the task.

Inter-organizational capacity is unlikely to flourish in organizational structures that are based on hierarchical control and power. New capacities are needed to manage conflict, inter-personal behaviour and fragmented and contested power relations. Within the realms of inter-agency activity, where 'organizational sovereignty loses credibility and conviction' (Clegg 1990, p. 19), decision-making models must reflect consensus formation and trust building. Difficult problems invite new ways of working and thinking, and whereas 'most people will come to this trapped or constrained by conventional organizations, labels and assumptions, what is needed is a willingness to entertain the unconventional and pursue the radical' (Clarke and Stewart 1997, p. 5). A presumption towards innovation, experimentation, risk taking and entrepreneurship is welcome in the battle against complex problems, in contrast to the preoccupation with finding a single 'right' solution.

Finally, the skills and competency profile of individuals who are focused on the management of interdependencies will not be professional or knowledge-based, but rely more on relational and inter-personal attributes designed to build social capital. They will build cultures of trust, improve levels of cognitive ability to understand complexity and be able to operate within non-hierarchical environments with dispersed configurations of power relationships.

THE HEGEMONY OF 'JOINED-UP' GOVERNANCE

The New Labour government in Britain has embraced the analysis of 'wicked issues' with some alacrity and grounded many of its public policy interventions on holistic planning, joined-up government and cross-cutting approaches. An emerging inter-organizational hegemony is promulgated and manifested in terms of multi-agency, multi-disciplinary and cross-boundary programmes across the policy spectrum. A flood of new initiatives bears witness to this approach – Health, Education and Employment Action Zones, New Deal for Communities, City Challenge, Local Strategic Partnerships and many more. One commentator refers to a condition of 'initiativitis' (Fitzpatrick 1999, p. xiii) to describe this type of policy making.

However, it seems that the prevailing policy discourse at both a theoretical and empirical level is quite often confined to a narrow discussion of the effectiveness and sustainability of new inter-organizational structures and mechanisms. I argue that this fixation at the organizational and inter-organizational domain levels understates and neglects the pivotal contribution of individual actors in the collaborative process. The research and analysis that follows argues that the effectiveness and success of inter-organizational ventures rests equally with the people involved in the process and their ability to apply collaborative skills and mind-sets to the resolution or amelioration of complex problems. I am supported in this view by other researchers. Poxton, reflecting on the experiences of primary health and social care partnerships, concludes 'a new policy environment and new organizational arrangements should make co-operation and collaboration easier than it has been in the past. But real success will depend as much on the determination and creativity of practitioners and managers as it will on Government edict and structural change' (Poxton 1999, p. 3). Bardach, also, maintains that it is 'clear that whatever else might help explain success in the collaborative process, the efforts and creativity of what I call purposive practitioners is an essential explanatory ingredient' (Bardach 1998, p. 6).

A mixture of flamboyant and insightful descriptions are sometimes ascribed to people who manage across boundaries including networker, broker, collaborator, cupid, civic entrepreneur, boundroid, sparkplug, collabronaut and boundary spanner (Thompson 1967). Some occupy designated boundary spanning or cross-cutting posts such as health promotion managers, anti-poverty officers, community safety co-ordinators and the like. The majority of people are employed in mainstream jobs in which the participation in collaborative exchanges with people in other agencies and organizations is increasingly important to the realization of their own personal or organizational objectives.

However, the literature is not particularly forthcoming on the nature, characteristics and behaviour of these boundary spanners. The emphasis is rather more on managing within organizations as well as on the development of professional expertise.

THEORIES OF INTER-ORGANIZATIONAL RELATIONS

Although this paper has a micro-level focus, a consideration of inter-organizational theorizing at an institutional level is warranted and instructive as it offers perspectives and hints to behaviour patterns relevant to the role of individual actors in the collaborative process. There is no consolidated body of inter-organizational theory and a 'striking characteristic of research on inter-organizational relations is the astonishing variety of disciplines, research paradigms, theoretical perspectives and sectoral focuses within which it is researched' (Huxham and Vangen 1998, p. 1). The literature too is characterized by 'a cacophony of heterogeneous concepts, theories, and research results' (Oliver and Ebers 1998, p. 549). However, Grandori (1997) detects the prevalence of economic and sociological macro-analytical approaches to the subject.

Oliver and Ebers (1998) attempt to identify 'structural beacons in the messy landscape of inter-organizational research' through a review of the pertinent literature. They conclude that resource dependency and network models dominate the theoretical approaches, while considerations of power and control prevail with regard to outcomes. They emphasize the predominance of motivation and interaction in the processes linking antecedents with outcomes. In the case of inter-organizational network research, they find that the theoretical stances are polarized between a social network perspective, which looks at the structural properties of networks, and a governance perspective that focuses on 'attributes of both the networked actors and the form and content of their relationships within a particular institutional context' (Oliver and Ebers 1998, p. 569).

Grandori (1998) suggests that interfirm co-ordination modes can be explained by the core variables of task complexity, environmental uncertainty, task-related competence, behavioural trustworthiness, task interdependence and resource interdependencies. Oliver (1990), on the other hand, lists the critical contingencies of relationship forming as asymmetry, reciprocity, efficiency, stability and legitimacy. Ebers (1997) contrasts Inter-organizational networks with other form of organizing such as markets and firms. They 'institutionize recurring, partner-specific exchange relationships of finite duration (often based on goal accomplishment) or of unspecified duration among a limited number of actors' (Ebers 1997, p. 21); actors within them individually retain residual control over resources but sometimes jointly decide on their use; processes of negotiation are used to co-ordinate resource allocation decisions, and a wide range of information is shared between organizations.

The network metaphor is a highly integrative mechanism between different levels of analysis and Ebers (1997) identifies three types of micro-level ties that represent key core concepts:

1. resource flow and activity links;
2. information flows, especially to address issues of complexity and uncertainty. The role of catalysts or informational intermediaries is considered to be highly influential in shaping and facilitating network form because they act as brokers to allow information symmetry and 'as mutually trusted lynchpins between social groups, human catalysts can bridge and help overcome informational asymmetries, establish a common set of expectations, and facilitate goal adjustment' (Ebers 1997, p. 31); foster co-operation and exchange; act as neutral arbitrators in conflict resolution; and reduce communication costs and uncertainty. The role played by catalysts is also associated with innovation and entrepreneurship because of a greater access to external partnering, critical resources and information (Dodgson 1994; Ahuja 2000);
3. mutual expectations between actors, particularly trust.

Managing within networks occupies the focus of a number of researchers (Kickert and Koppenjan 1997; O'Toole *et al.* 1997) and is described as 'promoting the mutual adjustment of the behaviour of actors with diverse objectives and ambitions with regard to tackling problems within a given framework of interorganizational relationships' (Kickert and Koppenjan 1997, p. 44). The major activities include intervening/restructuring network relations, joint problem solving and negotiating integrative strategies. Game management strategies such as brokering and facilitation are much in evidence. O'Toole *et al.* (1997) highlight the demands of network management at different phases of the policy-making process. Although there may be similarities with other stages, they suggest that the implementation phase is characterized by managing across and through different functional networks; working in a multi-party and multi-level environment and understanding the complexity of assembling all the pieces of the implementation jigsaw. This entails a very focused and problem-solving mode of engagement.

Some models of inter-organizational relationships present a typology of different structural forms (Alter and Hage 1993) and others visualize this type of activity unidimensionally along a continuum of varying degrees of sophistication from co-operation to collaboration, reflecting the changes in the intensity of the interaction and the magnitude of the reconfiguration of power relationships (Taylor 2000; Mattesich and Monsey 1994; Hudson 1998; Pratt *et al.* 1999).

Much of the research focus on inter-organizational relations is on motives, contingencies and structures and less on processes. An exception to this is theories that map joint working in terms of a sequence of defined stages or phases. Gray (1989) proposes a 3-stage model – problem setting, direction setting and implementation – using this approach, and Lowndes and Skelcher (1998) refer to a four-stage life cycle of partnerships. Ring and Van de Ven (1994) propose a cyclical model of network development that emphasizes socio-psychological factors as much as managerial proficiencies. It may be that a different set of boundary spanning skills and styles are appropriate for different stages as is suggested by Snow and Thomas (1993) with phase-specific broker roles. A final approach centres on the identification of particular factors, barriers or conditions that are influential in determining the success or failure of collaborative encounters – critical performance factors such as shared vision, communication, teamwork and so on. Huxham and Vangen

(1999) prefer to concentrate on the key themes in collaborative practice such as trust, leadership, accountability and power, some of which are process-orientated and others that are structural in nature such as ambiguity, complexity and dynamics.

PROFILING BOUNDARY SPANNERS

The literature on boundary spanners is by no means extensive or consolidated. However, it is possible to identify a number of themes and perspectives that permeate the research that is available from a number of different disciplines and traditions.

The boundary spanner as reticulist

Friend *et al.* (1974) identify a cluster of reticulist or networking skills and judgements and emphasize the importance of cultivating inter-personal relationships, communication, political skills and an appreciation of the interdependencies around the structure of problems and their potential solutions. Webb refers to individuals 'who are especially sensitive to and skilled in bridging interests, professions and organizations' (Webb 1991, p. 231), and Degeling (1995) sees reticulists as 'entrepreneurs of power' who understand coupling, interdependencies and fissures in strategically located players. Trist visualizes them as facilitating communication over 'social ground rather than between institutionalised figures' (Trist 1983, p. 280), although a knowledge of how to operate within the formal organizational system is equally essential. One report refers to 'special' people in networks who play a role in 'bringing unlikely partners together, in breaking through red tape, and seeing things in a different way' (LGMB 1997, p. 10).

Hosking and Morley (1991) summarize the functions of networking as gaining information, achieving influence to help implement the actor's agenda and to exchange with others, co-operation and resources. Effective networking enables a boundary spanner to understand the social constructions of other actors, and how they 'define the issue in relation to their own values and interests, knows what "outcomes" and processes each would value, knows who needs to be involved, knows who could mobilize influence, and so on' (Hoskins and Morley 1991, p. 228). It is the basis for successful negotiation.

Networking takes place through inter-personal relationships and this can result in a blurring of professional and personal relationships. Some research (LGMB 1997; Ring and Van de Ven 1994) views this process of social bonding as a positive feature in terms of sharing values, gaining trust and so on. An opposite view (LGMB 1997) warns of the potential downside of informality and an over-reliance on personal relationships, the tensions of multiple accountabilities, the inherent fragility of personal relationships and the negative effects of the formation of cliques.

The boundary spanner as entrepreneur and innovator

Complex public policy problems tend not to be amenable to tired traditional or conventional approaches. Their resolution demands new ideas, creativity, lateral thinking and an 'unlearning' of professional and organizational conventions and norms. The entrepreneurial and innovative capacities of boundary spanners are emphasized by Challis (1988) who highlights the defining characteristic of flexibility, and Leadbeater and Goss who refer to 'civic entrepreneurs' as 'creative, lateral thinking rule-breakers who frequently combine a capacity for visionary thinking with an appetite for opportunism' (Leadbeater and Goss 1998, p. 15). Similarly, deLeon evokes the image of public entrepreneurs as mavericks or 'catalysts who bring together problems and solutions that otherwise would bubble chaotically in the conventional currents of modern policy streams' (deLeon 1996, p. 508). Kingdon (1984), also, underlines the importance of 'policy entrepreneurs' who are skilled at coupling problems, policies and politics, particularly opportunistically in response to opening 'policy windows'.

The boundary spanner and otherness

Boundary spanners are characterized by their ability to engage with others and deploy effective relational and interpersonal competencies. This is motivated by a need to acquire an understanding of people and organizations outside their own circles – to acknowledge and value difference in terms of culture, mind-set, profession, role and 'gaze'. Trevillion views boundary spanners as 'cultural brokers' who need to understand anothers' organization and to 'make a real effort to empathize with, and respect anothers' values and perspectives' (Trevillion 1991, p. 50); Engel concludes that, because much interorganizational activity takes place in teams, the people involved need to practice empathy and that 'communication underpins and permeates the entire construct of capability for collaboration' (Engel 1994, p. 71); and Hornby alights on the notion of 'reciprocity' which she considers is manifested 'in respect and concern for the individual, gives value to mutual understanding and the building of mutual trust' (Hornby 1993, p. 160). The dynamics and dilemmas of support relationships in boundary management is considered to be a difficult because boundary spanners 'must be adept at breaking down boundaries between themselves and recipients to listen empathetically and build trust; they also need to enforce boundaries to protect themselves from enmeshment with the recipient's problems' (Bacharach et al., 2000, p. 706). This is a balancing act between inclusion and separation, dependence and autonomy.

The boundary spanner and trust

Trust is often isolated as one of the most important factors to influence the course of interorganizational relations. Webb is forthright in his assertion that 'trust is pivotal to collaboration. Attitudes of mistrust and suspicion are a primary barrier to co-operation between organizations and professional boundaries: collaborative behaviour is hardly conceivable where trusting attitudes are absent' (Webb 1991, p. 237), and 'trust is thought to be a more appropriate mechanism for controlling organizational life than hierarchical power' (Sydow 1998, p. 31). It is a highly contested notion that is the subject of a substantial body of theory from a variety of disciplines (Giddens 1991; Lane 1998; Boon 1994; Lewicki and Bunker 1996; Cummings and Bromily 1996; Das and Teng 2001).

Various models of trust implicate the concept with faith, predictability, goodwill and risk taking. Others suggest that it can be derived from calculation, value and norms or common cognition. Bachmann (2001) refers to trust as a mechanism for coping with uncertainty and complexity, and there are theories that position trust at both a personal and system level. Bachmann (2001) is also anxious to stress the relationship between trust and control, both being mechanisms for co-ordinating social interactions. Similarly, Hardy et al. distinguish between real and simulated trust, and attempt to disentangle the two heavily loaded notions of trust and power. They suggest that most functional interpretations of trust 'ignore the fact that power can be hidden behind a façade of "trust" and a rhetoric of "collaboration" and can be used to promote vested interests through the manipulation and capitulation of weaker parties' (Hardy et al. 1998, p. 65). Newell and Swan (2000) submit that different types of trust interrelate in particular ways depending on the motives holding actors together in a network. Lastly, from a practical point of view, there is an important question to be resolved in relation to the building and sustaining of trust. Vangen and Huxham single out expectation forming and risk taking as the main determinants of a model that envisages a cyclic process because 'each time partners act together they take a risk and form expectations about the intended outcome and the way others will contribute to achieving it. Each time an outcome meets expectations, trusting attitudes are reinforced. The outcome becomes part of the history of the relationship, so increasing the chance that partners will have positive expectations about joint actions in the future' (Vangen and Huxham 1998, p. 8).

The boundary spanner and personality

The literature is peppered with innumerable references to the personalities, character, traits and disposition of boundary spanners. There are suggestions that they are personable, respectful, reliable, tolerant, diplomatic, caring and committed – to name but a few. Fairtlough (1994) writes that 'diplomacy, tact, dispassionate analysis, passionate sincerity, scrupulous honesty; the boundary spanner needs an impossible string of virtues', and Beresford and Trevillion (1995) consider that collaborative values to be characterized by honesty, commitment and reliability. The proposition is, perhaps, that good collaborative behaviour is a function of particular personal attributes – an assumption that is grounded in the personality school of thought which argues that people are different because of defining characteristics, personalities or temperaments (Eysenck 1994).

Unfortunately, trait theories are found to be poor predictors of behaviour, and a second school of thought associated with cognitive psychology interprets individual differences in terms of different cognitive styles and processes (Brunas-Wagstaff 1998). The significance of personality remains a highly contested intellectual domain and the question, 'is an effective boundary spanner born and not bred', will continue to attract keen debate.

The boundary spanner as leader

The boundary spanning challenge impinges significantly on leadership styles. Luke (1998) offers a critical comparison of leadership styles between traditional and collaboratively inclined organizations and this is illustrated in table 2. The sovereign and charismatic leader, who enthuses firm and directive leadership, is sharply contrasted with a more facilitative and catalytic approach displayed by leaders in partnership arenas. He identifies certain foundational skills that are essential for 'catalytic leaders' – these are thinking and acting strategically, interpersonal skills for facilitating a productive working group or network, and underlying character. Kanter (1995), also, profiles cosmopolitan leaders of the future as integrators, diplomats, cross-fertilizers and deep-thinkers.

TABLE 2 *Contrasts between modern and postmodern styles of leadership (after Luke 1998)*

Modern leadership	Postmodern leadership
Hierarchical	Non hierarchical and inter-organizational
Evokes followership	Evokes collaboration and concerted action
Takes charge; seizes the reins of an organization	Provides the necessary catalyst or spark for action
Takes responsibility for moving followers in certain directions	Takes responsibility for convening stakeholders and facilitates agreements for collective action
Heroic; provides the right answers	Facilitative; asks the right questions
Has a stake in a particular solution or strategy	Has a stake in getting to agreed-upon outcomes, but encourages divergent ways to reach them.

The preoccupation of the New Labour government in Britain, with joined-up approaches to policy making, has spawned a number of reports and studies that refer to individual skills and competencies. One government report concludes that civil servants need to be better at working across organizational boundaries and 'alter their mindsets from a culture of tribal competitiveness to one of partnership' (Cabinet Office 2000, p. 42). This report also advocates the promotion of 'culture-breakers' to act as catalysts for cross-cutting behaviour. Another report judges that in local government 'new skills and capacities are essential, particularly strategic capacities, and skills in listening, negotiation, leadership through influence, partnership working, performance management and evaluation' (DETR, 2000, p. 7). Capacity building is considered to be especially important, as are brokering, networking, resource packaging and building trust. Finally, Jupp (2000) addresses the neglected issue of training and development in partnership working. He notes that, traditionally, management training is concentrated around managing in hierarchical situations and more recently, in managing contracts. In contrast, the emphasis should now move to developing key partnership skills such as brokerage, facilitation, negotiation and coordination and project management.

RESEARCH METHODOLOGY

New empirical research has been undertaken by the author to explore the management of interdependencies inherent in collaborative and networked forms of governance. This research set out to identify, describe, categorize and understand boundary spanning competencies and effective collaborative behaviour. The fieldwork and data collection consists of two interconnected phases (table 3). Phase 1 is directed to an initial identification and categorization of boundary spanning competencies together with a short attitudinal investigation. The concept of 'competency', which is often used promiscuously (Sandberg 2000), in this context, is taken to mean, 'an underlying characteristic of a person in that it may be a motive, trait, skill, aspect of one's self-image or social role, or a body of knowledge which he or she uses' (Boyatzis 1982, p. 21).

To start with, surveys of three types of boundary spanner operating in different policy areas – health promotion specialists, crime and community safety co-ordinators

TABLE 3 *Details of fieldwork*

	Phase 1			Phase 2
Geographical area	UK	Wales	Wales	Welsh local authority area
Sample	Environmental & local Agenda 21 co-ordinators	Crime & community safety co-ordinators	Health promotion specialists	Partnership managers
Type of organization	Local authority	Local authority	Health authority and NHS Trust	Local authority; Health authority; NHS Trust; Police; Voluntary sector; Probation service; Youth offending partnership
Research method	Postal survey	Postal survey	Postal survey	In-depth interviews
Sampling method	Opportunistic	Opportunistic	Opportunistic	Snowball
Sample size	469	22	10	15
Response rate (%)	50	54	100	100

and environmental and local agenda 21 co-ordinators – were undertaken using postal questionnaires. They were selected opportunistically through personal contact between the author and three national networks. This enabled effective access to individual contacts and a potentially enhanced response rate. The policy framework and institutional contexts for all three samples was comparable, involving managing across traditional boundaries and tackling complex problems within a variety of multi-agency initiatives.

Phase 2 sharpened the focus of the research with a more intensive exploration and understanding of the potential determinants of effective boundary spanning framed within a particular geographical area. The area selected was a unitary local authority in South Wales within which a variety of different agencies were collaborating across a range of policy areas. The policy and governmental context was broadly similar to that in other local authority areas throughout the UK where partnership working is high on the political agenda. A sample of boundary spanners operating at a strategic level was chosen for interview using personal contacts in the study area to identify the main actors managing in multi-agency partnerships addressing key problem areas – health, social care, crime and young people. The findings from Phase 1 were used to inform the topic guide for a series of in-depth and semi-structured interviews. Topics covered included motivations for partnership working; the management of boundary spanning roles; personal skills and competencies for collaborative working; evidencing effectiveness through critical incidents; barriers and problems in cross-boundary activity; and training and development.

THE ART OF BOUNDARY SPANNING

The research findings indicate that, as far as boundary spanners are concerned, there are a number of key factors and influences implicated in effective collaborative working, and they involve the use of particular skills, abilities, experience and personal characteristics. It is particularly evident, also, that there is considerable overlap and interdependency between the various factors and individual variables, and typically, they are deployed in different permutations depending on particular circumstances.

Building sustainable relationships

A necessary part of interorganizational working involves building and sustaining effective personal relationships. Collaborative encounters involve the management of difference. People from a variety of organizational, professional and social backgrounds assemble to pursue mutually beneficial agendas, and this demands an investment in time to forge an effective working relationship and a readiness to visualize reality from the perspective of others. The development of interpersonal relationships is part of a process of exploration, discovery and understanding of people and the organizations they represent – a search for knowledge about roles, responsibilities, problems, accountabilities, cultures, professional norms and standards, aspirations and underlying values. The quality of this information is invaluable in allowing boundary spanners to identify potential areas of communality and interdependency. The medium for this process of enquiry and knowledge exchange is the quality and durability of personal relationships. The respondents to the research draw particular attention to a number of factors in this process.

Communicating and listening

The value of basic and effective oral, written and presentational communication skills cannot be overestimated. The ability to express oneself, and one's position with clarity, is considered to be essential, as is the choice and use of language. The problem associated with the use and interpretation of 'professional' languages and jargon is recognized as an area in need of sensitive management in order not to undermine, patronize, mislead or give offence to others. The search for shared meanings is particularly acute in partnership arenas. Communication is also a two-way process and receiving information – listening – is considered as important as information giving. References are made to 'active listening' which is expressed as a willingness or openness to be influenced by the views of other people.

Understanding, empathizing and resolving conflict

Relationship building is described as a process that occurs over time – an interaction that seeks to illuminate the perspectives, roles, problems, priorities, motivations, styles and values of prospective partners. One view is that this must involve a balance between how much to invest in the personal as opposed to the strictly work relationship. Time is clearly a significant factor here, as is regular exposure to, and engagement with, partners. It is also felt that a state of understanding can proceed to a higher, and potentially more rewarding level, the condition known as empathy. However, it is accepted that, notwithstanding the potential benefits of this end state, a working relationship can still be maintained at a lower level of 'understanding'. The acid test of a robust relationship is considered to be the ability to manage conflict and criticism – the potential to disagree and fallout, but a willingness to move on without harming the relationship.

Personality

The conversations with boundary spanners around building and sustaining relationships inevitably invite references to defining personality traits, characteristics and personal values. Respect, honesty, openness, tolerance, approachability, reliability, sensitivity and many others are viewed as desirable qualities, and the 'best' boundary spanners are considered to be those with an easy and inviting personality, particularly those who are able to divest themselves of their organizational and professional baggage.

Trust

Not surprisingly, trust is raised as a key variable within exchange relationships, acting as a kind of currency or lubricant. The study confirms the conclusion of the literature review that the notion has no universally agreed meaning and, moreover, is often taken for granted and internalized. However, there is consensus that trust must underpin effective relationships at both an individual and organizational level. A number of meanings are attributed to the notion, including that it entails a reciprocal risk-taking involving the giving and receiving of information not widely accessible in the public domain. The risk is, that if the person entrusted with this information misuses it, then some harm could befall the informant. It is conceptualized as a process of 'opening-up' or exposing oneself, and of dependency testing. If it passes the tests of reliability, delivering on promises, not being underhand and being honest, the relationship moves on to a possibly more enduring state of 'deep trust'. This description of trust is very indicative of the calculative model referred to in the literature. Other comments suggest that individuals approach trust in one of two ways. Either by assuming that people are trustworthy from the outset and proceeding accordingly or, believing that people are naturally guarded and even devious, and testing whether this proves to be a self-fulfilling prophesy.

Trust is considered essentially to be a condition that is constituted in the relationship between individuals, although by implication and on the basis of the aggregated behaviour of individuals representing it, organizations can acquire a reputation for being more or less trustworthy. This evidences the difficulty of disentangling personal from institutionalized forms of trust.

Managing through influencing and negotiation

Collaborative environments are characterized by power relationships that are more contested and dispersed than is often the case in traditional bureaucracies where power, authority and control over resources are often exercised by individuals drawing on their position and status in the hierarchy. There is an acute awareness amongst the boundary spanners interviewed that they lack direct lines of authority over other partners, and the atmosphere of interorganizational working needs to be set within decision-making models that are premised on consensus, equality and win-win solutions. The skills needed to be effective in these arenas are felt to be influencing, bargaining, negotiation, mediation and brokering.

Influencing is about being persuasive and diplomatic; always being constructive and non-judgemental; leading on some occasions but facilitating in others; and of being acutely aware of the political and personal sensibilities surrounding exchanges. The potential for effective influencing stems from the nature and robustness of personal relationships, and the dynamics often change depending upon whether the encounters are dyadic or in groups, private or in public. Collaboration involves a great deal of negotiation – over aims, funding proposals, operational programmes, priorities, resource allocation and so on. It is seen by a number of survey respondents as a process that is both convoluted and very time consuming, particularly in collectives involving a number of partners. Effective boundary spanners can expect to enter such arenas having to compromise and make careful judgements about the balance between benefits and disbenefits for themselves and other organizations. It is a far from altruistic exercise and needs to be 'hard-nosed', particularly around detailed operational, contractual, financial and delivery considerations as they impact on individual organizations.

A skill that frequently appears in the conversations with the interviewees is the ability to successfully broker solutions or deals between a number of different parties. This requires considerable expertise in influencing and negotiation, but also the perceived legitimacy to act objectively and openly for others – the honest broker role. Brokering effective deals epitomizes, perhaps, the essence of a successful boundary spanner as it depends on the employment of a range of competencies and skills – an acute understanding of interdependencies between problems, solutions and organizations; an interpersonal style that is facilitating, respectful and trusting; and a drive to devise solutions that make a difference to solving problems on the ground.

Networking

Partnership environments are characterized by networked forms of governance and, certainly, networking is the predominant *modus operandi* of choice of the boundary spanner. Within the particular interorganizational domain studied, there is a well-developed network of key 'movers and shakers' – primary nodes in the network – which make partnerships work. It consists of a reservoir of people active at a strategic level, representing different agencies and organizations who are referred to as 'the usual suspects' because of their appearance on many different partnerships. This has considerable advantages in terms of the accumulated investment of inter-personal relationships and social capital. There are clear benefits of being a member of an interorganizational network, including being at the leading edge of information, having access to new ideas, gossip and happenings in other sectors, professions and organizations, and being able to seek support from and influence people in other organizations. A network offers members the benefit of 'being in the loop' for information of all sorts, about emerging resource opportunities, changing government priorities, impending changes, potential scandals, new needs – the raw material for constructing a joined-up agenda.

Networking occurs at and around meetings, but is most effectively undertaken outside formal decision-making structures, especially in conversations. There is a general view that the 'real' business of partnership work is effected within the framework of these personal exchanges. It is where difficulties are shared, aims agreed, problems sorted out, deals struck and promises made – all out of the public gaze. Crucially, this is where interorganizational imperatives are translated into the organizational realities of individual participants, and where the progress of formal events are mapped out in advance and choreographed.

The extent to which networking involves the blurring of professional and personal boundaries is contested. One view is that a strictly professional relationship is perfectly tenable, but another argues that a more personal relationship will increase the potential, quality and richness of the interchange. The dangers of tight and exclusive networks are recognized, particularly in terms of their potential to become institutionalized through processes of group normalization and shared values leading to 'blindness' in certain areas. Questions are also raised about the inherent fragility of networks that are reliant on personal relationships, and the problems encountered when key boundary spanners are removed from a network as a result of a job shift or breakdown in relationships.

Managing complexity and interdependencies

The interviews with boundary spanners confirm that interorganizational management is a highly complex business. In addition to dealing with often-disparate bodies of technical knowledge and professional expertise, actors are faced with making sense of the structure and process of collaboration. This demands an appreciation of connections and interrelationships which are manifested in different ways at different stages in the partnership process. At the planning and formulation stage, the relevant links involve partner search, problem diagnosis, defining roles and responsibilities, negotiating goals and developing cross-cutting agendas; at the implementation and delivery stage, they are about contracts, agreements, protocols and budgeting; and at the evaluation stage, they involve joint accountabilities and the measuring of outcomes. Although the boundary spanners interviewed operate primarily at a strategic level, they are acutely aware of the need to cross the boundary between strategy and implementation, to ensure that policy intentions are translated into problem solving on the ground. In fact, most profess a commitment to achieving real change in the face of difficult problems and issues.

The study isolates three main contributory factors to an ability to manage interdependencies – interorganizational experience, transdisciplinary knowledge and cognitive capability. The value of accumulated 'on-the-job' interorganizational experience is considered to be possibly the main source of understanding. It is the constant exposure to others that enables an understanding of their viewpoints, constraints, cultures, working practices and so on to be stored. Also highly regarded is a track record of employment in different types of organization and sector. The belief is that experience of different cultures, ways of working, roles and responsibilities and past networks – insider knowledge – is invaluable for both making connections and understanding the motivations, mind-sets and behaviours of colleagues in partner agencies.

On the question of technical knowledge, there is a view that boundary spanners need to be knowledgeable in one area of expertise to act as a kind of passport of legitimacy for engaging with people from other organizations – harnessing the power that is associated with knowledge. Another view is that boundary spanners need to be 'a jack of all trades and master of none'. It is suggested that the best boundary spanners do not have a conventional professional or career profile, are less constrained by the attendant baggage, and are not perceived as direct threats to the status of the more professionally grounded practitioners of this art. Numerous references are made to the desirability of having 'analytical ability', 'being able to think laterally', 'taking a holistic view', 'understanding the big picture' and of 'strategic thinking'. Whether these abilities are rooted in experience or a function of a particular cognitive style is a matter of debate.

The ability to be creative, innovative and entrepreneurial is important in joint working environments, particularly where the design of effective solutions to complex problems, the skillful negotiation of sustainable partnership agreements involving a number of different agencies, and the mobilization of resource packages is needed. Interviewees highlight the value of opportunism as well as the ability to collaboratively fashion new solutions to previously intractable problems. In addition, the successful mobilization or levering-in of resources is considered to evidence well-developed entrepreneurial skills. A powerful image of Kingdon's (1974) 'policy entrepreneurs' is invoked by a number of respondents who are adept at coupling solutions to problems, and of often being ahead of the agenda with 'Blue Peter' solutions already prepared in anticipation of future political/ resource opportunities or opening 'policy windows'.

Managing roles, accountabilities and motivations

Boundary spanners are acutely conscious of the configuration of roles and responsibilities between agencies within an existing or emerging inter-organizational domain, and appreciate the political and professional sensibilities that encompass them. This accumulated knowledge of 'who does what' is vital in the management of partnerships and provides the basis on which potential connections and interrelationships can be identified and explored, both at the strategy formulation stage and for detailed operational programming.

The management of multiple accountabilities is viewed as an area of tension that requires delicate judgement. Boundary spanners are particularly confronted with the accountability interface between their role as organizational representative and that of partner in a multi-agency environment. These accountabilities may be conflicting at times and the situation may be confounded by perceived accountabilities to service users or deep-rooted value systems such as the public service ethos. Boundary spanners interviewed in the survey are adamant about the first call on their responsibility – that is, to their employing organization. However, it is felt that the way in which this is discharged needs to recognize the other sources of accountability. A poor partner is perceived as one who slavishly or dogmatically ploughs a representative furrow in partnership arenas and, irritatingly, has to 'report back' everything to the home organization. Conversely, the more effective partners are those who are empowered, within certain negotiated parameters, to engage constructively with other partners. They have a feel for what may or may not be acceptable to their home organizations and are ready to play the partnership game. Understanding the parameters and constraints of each partner is considered to be highly important.

The interorganizational relations' literature offers a number of explanations to the triggers for partnership working, and some of these resonate well with the individual motivations that are expressed by people in the survey. I conceptualize these as hegemony, resource opportunity and mandate. Collaboration as hegemony embraces the view that interorganizational working is the only way for dealing with complex and interrelated problems that cross artificially created administrative and jurisdictional boundaries. It is the most effective and efficient way of using an organization's resources, avoids duplication and overlaps, and can produce synergistic outcomes that can only be achieved through 'whole-systems' approaches. This model of collaboration also includes the deep-rooted motivation expressed by some boundary spanners of a commitment to service users or citizens as the basis for service delivery – as opposed to approaches based on the convenience of existing bureaucratic structures and administrative arrangements.

Collaboration as resource opportunity reflects the resource exchange model in which organizations seek to work in partnership in order to realize their own internal goals through accessing resources from other organizations. This practice is certainly increasing outside the sphere of 'natural partnerships' with the advent of more cross-cutting issues. The third source of collaborative motivation is mandated. Central government is committed to the concept of interorganizational working and is anxious to encourage, persuade, empower or coerce all organizations, particularly in other tiers of governance, to be similarly committed. New legislation, advice, guidance, funding regimes and initiatives are geared to partnership working. The problem occurs where coercion and prescription conceals the true motivations of individuals and organizations. The rhetoric of collaboration may be fuelled but insincere; convenient or fragile relationships may result.

CONCLUSION

It is hoped that the value of this paper lies in the fact that it provides a much needed focus on the individual actor within the field of interorganizational relationships, while the strength of the empirical research lies in its attempt to build a framework of competency-based variables and factors that influence effective collaborative engagement, behaviour and management. The research reinforces many of the images that dominate the relational literature – the boundary spanner as network manager; the importance of building effective personal relationships with a wide range of other actors; the ability to manage in non-hierarchical decision environments through negotiation and brokering; and performing the role of 'policy entrepreneur' to connect problems to solutions, and mobilize resources and effort in the search for successful outcomes.

The empirical research also resonates with institutional level perspectives and theorizing on interorganizational relationships. The network metaphor is certainly a powerful integrating mechanism across all levels of analysis, and the micro-level ties identified by Ebers (1997) can be clearly seen – the management of expectations between actors through the medium of trust, and the ability of catalysts to cope with highly complex and ambiguous information. Individual motivations of boundary spanners, whether mandated or voluntary, have clear parallels with domain level perspectives, and there is an appreciation at the micro-level of the different phases in the collaborative process.

It is recognized that the research presented in this paper is by no means definitive and important questions remain unresolved. There needs to be more specific evidence to link the use of a particular set of competencies or collaborative behaviour to outcomes. The interorganizational literature is particularly poor in this area. It is comparatively strong on antecedents, motives and structures, but weak on processes and effectiveness. Methodologies that link competency to impact, performance and effectiveness need to be explored and developed, particularly in relation to comparisons with other forms of organizing. Although the boundary spanners involved in the research cover different policy areas, organizations and types of partnership, the research does not explore possible differences and contrasts. The role and behaviour of boundary spanners within different contextual and institutional situations needs further examination. Again, many partnerships typically proceed through various stages of development, and are manifested at both a strategic and operational level. The skill demands of each of these phases, and the relationship between strategic and operational boundary spanners, represents an interesting avenue for further exploration. A deeper understanding of the dynamics of boundary spanners' interventions would also be an invaluable contribution. These and many other questions offer potentially rewarding pathways for future research.

Finally, there are practical benefits from this type of research. In the current British policy climate, which extols the virtues of partnership working, a clear recognition and understanding of effective boundary spanning capacities is essential to inform the training, development and education of current and potential practitioners. There is a current dearth of opportunities on collaborative working and this needs to be addressed as a matter of some urgency.

There is little doubt that 'the fashioning of collaborative relationships of substance is a job for talented practitioners' (Hudson 1993, p. 375) and much greater attention needs to be focused on their contribution within inter-organizational relationships than has been the case in the past. It is hoped that this paper will stimulate further research in this important aspect of public policy in the future.

ACKNOWLEDGEMENT

The author is very grateful to the anonymous reviewers for their very helpful and constructive comments and suggestions to an earlier draft of this paper.

REFERENCES

Ahuja, G. 2000. 'Collaboration networks, structural holes, and innovation: a longitudinal study', *Administrative Science Quarterly*, Vol. 45, 425–55.

Alter, C. and J. Hage. 1993. *Organizations working together*. Englewood Cliffs, NJ: Prentice Hall.

Bacharach, S.B., P. Bamberger and V. McKinney. 2000. 'Boundary management tactics and logics in action: the case of peer-support providers', *Administrative Science Quarterly*, Vol. 45, No. 4, 704–736.

Bachmann, R. 2001. 'Trust, power and control in trans-organizational relations', *Organization Studies*, Vol. 22 No. 2, 337–365.

Bardach, E. 1998. *Getting agencies to work together*. Washington, DC: Brookings Institution Press.

Beresford, P. and S. Trevillion. 1995. *Developing skills for community care*. Aldershot: Arena.

Boon, S. 1994. 'Dispelling Doubt and Uncertainty: Trust in Romantic Relationships', in S. Duck (ed), *Dynamics of relationships*. London: Sage.

Boyatzis, R. 1982. *The competent manager*. London: Wiley.

Brunas-Wagstaff, J. 1998. *Personality: a cognitive approach*. London: Routledge.

Cabinet Office. 2000. *Wiring it up*. London: Cabinet Office.

Challis, L., S. Fuller, M. Henwood et al. 1988. *Joint approaches to social policy*. Cambridge: Cambridge University Press.

Clarke, M. and J. Stewart. 1997. *Handling the wicked issues – a challenge for government*. Birmingham: University of Birmingham.

Clegg, S.R. 1990. *Modern organizations*. London: Sage.

Cummings, L.L. and P. Bromily. 1996. 'The organizational trust inventory (OTI)' in R.M. Kramer and T.R. Tyler (eds), *Trust in organizations*. London: Sage.

Das, T.K. and B-S. Teng. 2001. 'Trust, control, and risk in strategic alliances: an integrated framework', *Organization Studies*, Vol. 22 No. 2, 251–83.

Degeling, P. 1995. 'The significance of 'sectors' in calls for urban public health intersectoralism: an Australian perspective', *Policy and Politics*, Vol. 23 No. 4, 289–301.

deLeon, L. 1996. 'Ethics and entrepreneurship', *Policy Studies Journal*, Vol. 24 No. 3, 495–510.

DETR. 1999. *Cross-cutting issues affecting local government*. London: DETR.

Dodgson, M. 1994. 'Technological collaboration and innovation', in M. Dodgson and R. Rothwell (eds), *The handbook of industrial innovation*. Cheltenham: Edward Elgar.

Ebers, M. 1997. 'Explaining inter-organizational network formation', in M. Ebers (ed.), *The formation of inter-organizational networks*. Oxford: Oxford University Press.

Engel, C. 1994. 'A functional anatomy of teamwork', in A. Leathard (ed.), *Going interprofessional*. London: Routledge.

Eysenck, H.J. 1994. 'Trait theories of personality', in S.E. Hampson and A.M. Colman (eds), *Individual differences and personality*. London: Longman.

Fairtlough, G. 1994. *Creative compartments*. London: Adamantine Press.

Fitzpatrick, D. 1999. 'Drowning in a sea of initiatives', *New society*, 26 April, pp. xiii–xiv.

Friend, J.K., J.M. Power and C.J.L. Yewlett. 1974. *Public Planning: the inter-corporate dimension*. London: Tavis-tock.

Giddens, A. 1991. *Modernity and self-identity*. Oxford: Polity Press.

Grandori, A. 1997. 'An organizational assessment of interfirm coordination models'. *Organization Studies*, Vol. 18, No. 6, 897–925.

———. 1998. 'Editorial', *Organization Studies*, Vol. 19 No. 4, v–xiii.

Gray, B. 1989. *Collaborating*. San Francisco: Jossey-Bass.

Hardy, C., N. Phillips and T. Lawrence. 1998. 'Distinguishing trust and power in interorganizational relations: forms and facades of trust', in C. Lane and R. Bachmann (eds), *Trust in and between organizations*. Oxford: Oxford University Press.

Hornby, S. 1993. *Collaborative care*. Oxford: Blackwell.

Hosking, D-M. and I.E. Morley. 1991. *A social psychology of organizing*. London: Harvester Wheatsheaf.

Hudson, B. 1993. 'Collaboration in social welfare: a framework for analysis', in M. Hill (ed), *The policy process: a reader*. London: Harvester.

———. 1998. *Primary health care and social care: working across organizational and professional boundaries*. Leeds: Nuffield Institute for Health.

Huxham, C. and S. Vangen. 1998. 'What makes practitioners tick?: understanding collaboration practice and practising collaboration understanding', Workshop on Interorganizational Collaboration and Conflict McGill University Montreal.

Huxham, C. and S. Vangen. 1999. 'Building trust in inter-organizational collaboration', *Organization Studies*.

Jupp, B. 2000. *Working together*. London: Demos.

Kanter, R.M. 1997. 'World-class leaders', in F. Hesselbein, M. Goldsmith and R. Beckhard (eds), *The Leader of the future*. San Francisco: Jossey-Bass.

Kickert, W.J.M. and J.F.M. Koppenjan. 1997. 'Public management and network management: an overview', in *Managing complex networks*. London: Sage.

Kingdon, J.W. 1984. *Agendas, alternatives, and public policies*. Boston: Little, Brown and Company.

Lane, C. 1998. 'Introduction: theories and issues in the study of trust', in C. Lane and R. Bachmann (eds), *Trust in and between organizations*. Oxford: Oxford University Press.

Leadbeater, C. and S. Goss. 1998. *Civic entrepreneurship*. London: Demos.

Lewicki, R.J. and B.B. Bunker. 1996. 'Developing and maintaining trust in work relationships' in R.M. Kramer and T.R. Tyler (eds), *Trust in organizations*. London: Sage.

LGMB. 1997. *Networks and networking*. London: LGMB.

Lowndes, V. and C. Skelcher. 1998. 'The dynamics of multi-organizational partnerships: an analysis of changing modes of governance', *Public Administration*, Vol. 76, 313–33.

Luke, J.S. 1998. *Catalytic leadership*. San Francisco: Jossey-Bass.

Mackintosh, M. 1993. 'Partnership: issues of policy and negotiation', *Local Economy*, Vol. 7 No. 3, 210–44.

Mattessich, P.W. and B.R. Monsey. 1994. *Collaboration: what makes it work*. St. Paul, Minnesota: Amherst H. Wilder Foundation.

Newell, S. and J. Swan. 2000. 'Trust and inter-organizational networking', *Human Relations*, Vol. 53 No. 10, 1287–328.

Oliver, C. 1990. 'Determinants of interorganizational relationships: integration and future directions', *Academy of Management Review*, Vol. 15 No. 2, 241–65.

Oliver, A.L. and M. Ebers. 1998. 'Networking network studies: an analysis of conceptual configurations in the study of inter-organizational relationships', *Organization Studies*, Vol. 19 No. 4, 549–83.

O'Toole Jnr., L.J., K.I. Hanf and P.L. Hupe. 1997. 'Managing implementation processes in networks', in *Managing complex networks*. London: Sage.

Poxton, R. 1999. *Working across the boundaries*. London: King's Fund.

Pratt, J., P. Gordon and D. Plampling. 1999. *Working whole systems*. London: King's Fund.

Ring, P.S. and A.H. Van de Ven. 1994. 'Developmental processess of cooperative interorganizational relationships', *Academy of Management Review*, Vol. 19, 90–118.

Rittel, H. and M. Webber. 1973. 'Dilemmas in a general theory of planning', *Policy Sciences*, 4, 155–69.

Sandberg, J. 2000. 'Understanding human competence at work: An interpretative approach', *Academy of Management Journal*, Vol. 43 No. 1, 9–25.

Schon, D.A. 1991. *The reflective practitioner*. Aldershot: Ashgate.

Snow, C.C. and J.B. Thomas. 1993. 'Building networks: broker roles and behaviours', in P. Lorange, B. Chakravarthy, J. Roos and A.H. Van de Ven (eds), *Implementing strategic processes: change, learning and co-operation*. Oxford: Blackwell.

Stone, D. 1997. *Policy paradox: the art of political decision making*. New York: Norton and Co.

Sydow, J. 1998. 'Understanding the constitution of interorganizational trust', in C. Lane and R. Bachmann (eds), *Trust in and between organizations*. Oxford: Oxford University Press.

Taylor, M. 2000. *Top down meets bottom up: neighbourhood management*. York: Joseph Rowntree Foundation.

Thompson, J.D. 1967. *Organizations in action*. New York: McGraw-Hill.

Trevillion, S. 1991. *Caring in the community*. London: Longman.

Trist, E. 1983. 'Referent organizations and the development of inter-organizational domains', *Human Relations*, Vol. 36 No. 3, 269–84.

Vangen, S. and C. Huxham. 1998. The role of trust in the achievement of collaborative advantage, presented at the 14th EGOS Colloquium, Maastricht.

Webb, A. 1991. 'Co-ordination: a problem in public sector management', *Policy and Politics*, Vol. 19 No. 4, 229–41.

AFTERWORD: BRINGING BACK AGENTS

I was motivated to write my original paper by a strongly held view that the empirical and research literature on collaboration was heavily biased towards macro-level and structural perspectives, and comparatively silent on the role and contribution of individual actors. This view was informed by an extensive review of the literature, and influenced by conversations with many policy-makers and practitioners interviewed in the course of my research studies. Inevitably, this view has to be framed within the highly contested structure/agency debate and the degree to which individual actors have the ability to shape the outcomes of social action, compared with the extent to which contextual factors define the range of available actions. My general view of UK public policy is that government tends to place undue faith in structural reform and reconfiguration, statutory direction, regulation and financial incentives to shape the direction of collaborative activity. However, although structures and institutional arrangements can help and hinder collaborative efforts, key actors – the boundary spanners – are especially instrumental in achieving particular outcomes in practice. There is merit, then, in putting the spotlight on these individuals, to recognise and evaluate their contribution through an examination of their training and development, rewards, incentives and appraisal mechanisms. Certainly, there is a pressing need for research that explores the complicated interweaving and alchemy between structural and agential factors, and the manner in which different factors, including boundary spanners, constrain and enables action (Williams and Sullivan 2009).

The working environment for boundary spanners – inter and intra sectoral collaboration – continues to spread and deepen across UK public policy, particularly as a response to the intractability of 'wicked issues', and the exhortation and legislation by national government to plan and deliver public services that are efficient, effective and grounded in the needs of citizens and service users. However, the results from this form of working are not altogether convincing, and it often appears to be driven by a degree of faith and optimism underpinned by an unquestioning acceptance of the virtues of collaboration itself. This situation arises partly because of the lack of attention that is given to evaluation in the policy process, despite the rhetoric of 'evidence-based' policy-making, and is compounded by the inherent conceptual, methodological and practical problems of undertaking this kind of research.

In time honoured fashion, my original paper concluded with a plea for more research into this comparatively neglected area of inter-organizational studies. However, the intervening years have not seen any sustained interest by academics and policy-makers. Although there has been a steady accumulation in the knowledge base of collaborative working, the balance has not shifted to an individual level, and new contributions are largely empirical rather than theoretical. The most recent handbook on inter-organizational studies (Cropper *et al.* 2008) does not include an integrated perspective on the role of individuals within the collaborative process, although it does pick up on specific themes such as power, trust, leadership and identity which are relevant at an individual level. However, the field is not barren, and valuable contributions have been made by Sullivan and Skelcher (2002) who make specific reference to 'boundary spanners and reticulists' in a discussion of building capacity for collaboration, and the specific roles and importance of this cadre of actors is highlighted in a variety of good practice guides and handbooks that have been prepared to help policy-makers and managers work in this mode of governance. Also, Noble and Jones (2006) take up the challenge of a lack of focus on people in the collaborative process with a useful contribution that examines managerial challenges within different stages of a public-private partnership using 'sensemaking' to understand different processes, and finally, Kingdon's (1995) model is used as the basis of a paper (Oborn *et al*. 2010) to develop the role of the policy entrepreneur and agency in London's health service.

An interesting stream of literature emanating from the USA centred on the notion of 'collaborative public management' (Agranoff and McGuire 2003) does acknowledge the changing role of public managers in a collaborative context (O'Leary and Bingham 2009) although this contribution does raise the perennial problem of defining 'boundary spanners'. Are they a special class of actor, with a dedicated role, or is anyone who engages in boundary spanning activity a boundary spanner? The picture is complicated by a view that individuals within organizations with cross cutting functions and skills beyond those of mainstream managers (Wright 2009) can also be referred to as boundary spanners; and, operating within hierarchical frameworks can be achieved more effectively by styles and skills that are associated more with collaborative settings such as building trust, developing inter-personal relationships, networking, and sharing power. So, are boundary spanners operating within organizations similar to those managing within collaborative contexts? The question of whether boundary spanners evidence a set of distinctive skills, competencies and abilities remains contested, particularly as they are invariably required to work in multiple forms of governance and need to switch behaviours accordingly. More research is needed to explore boundary spanning roles and behaviours in different policy areas, different stages of the policy process, and within different collaborative forms and contexts. This research might profitably explore the use of different methodologies, such as 'Q' methodology (Watts and Stenner 2005) to understand how actors understand the skills and behaviours of boundary spanners.

On reflection, although there has been some progress since the original publication of this paper, the main challenges still remain. The area of enquiry is as relevant as ever, agential factors such as the nature and contribution of boundary spanners are still under-represented in the literature and research, and there is a continuing need to explore and understand the role and contribution of this cadre of individual actors – the boundary spanners.

REFERENCES

Agranoff, R. and M. McGuire. 2003. Collaborative Public Management: New Strategies for Local Governments. Washington, D.C.: Georgetown University Press.
Cropper, S., M. Ebers., C. Huxham and P. Smith Ring. 2008. *The Oxford Handbook of Inter-Organizational Relations*. Oxford: Oxford University Press.
Kingdon, J.W. 2003. *Agendas, Alternatives, and Public Policies*. London: Longman.
Noble, G. and R. Jones. 2006. 'The Role of Boundary-Spanning Managers in the Establishment of Public-Private Partnerships', *Public Administration*, 84, 4, 891–917.
Oborn et al. (2010 forthcoming) 'Policy entrepreneurship in the development of public sector strategy: The Case of the London Health Service Review', *Public Administration*.
O'Leary, R. and L.B. Bingham. 2009. *The Collaborative Public Manager*. Washington, D.C.: Georgetown University Press.
Sullivan, H. and C. Skelcher. 2002. *Working Across Boundaries: Collaboration in Public Services*. Basingstoke: Palgrave.
Watts S. and P. Stenner. 2005. 'Doing Q-methodology: theory, method and interpretation', *Qualitative Research in Psychology*, 2, 1, 67–91.
Williams, P. and H. Sullivan. 2009. 'Faces of Integration', *International Journal of Integrated Care*, 9, 1–13.
Wright, C. 2009. 'Inside Out? Organizational Membership, Ambiguity and the Ambivalent Identity of the Internal Consultant', *British Journal of Management*, 20, 3, 309–322.

Chapter 12

THE PUBLIC SERVICE ORIENTATION: ISSUES AND DILEMMAS

JOHN STEWART AND MICHAEL CLARKE

WHAT IS THE 'PUBLIC SERVICE ORIENTATION'?

Local authorities search for a sense of purpose that can drive forward management and motivate their staff. The answer may lie in words so familiar that their meaning has been lost: public service.

The activities of a local authority are not carried out for their own sake, but to provide service for the public. Under the pressures of resource constraint, the essential rationale of public service can easily be overlooked. Yet whatever the level of resources available to local government, or whatever the activities undertaken by local authorities, their justification lies in service for the public. This article sets out the implications for management in local government of the public service orientation which sees service for the public as the key value.[1]

The public service orientation recognizes that:

— a local authority's activities exist to provide service for the public
— a local authority will be judged by the quality of service provided within the resources available
— the service provided is only of real value if it is of value to those for whom it is provided
— those for whom services are provided are customers demanding high quality service
— quality of service demands closeness to the customer.

These values have to be expressed in day to day management action. If service for the public really is taken as the key value for management in local government, managers must:

— know the services wanted by the public
— be close to the customer
— seek out customer views, complaints and suggestions.

The public service orientation challenges those senior managers who:

— judge the quality of service by organizational or professional standards rather than by customer standards
— devote little time to learning about the customer away from the central office in which they work
— provide no training for staff on quality of customer service
— do not involve customers in decisions on the services provided or projects undertaken

— have not considered whether reception arrangements help the customer.

If public service means service for the public, does management in local government really provide quality of service? How does management know whether it does or not?

An orientation for our times

The public service orientation not only meets present management needs, but responds to new pressures:

— The Audit Commission has rightly advised local authorities to ensure that their management is guided by vision or shared values. Service for the public provides such a vision and such a value. If accepted, the difficult and demanding task is to work out the implication for management structure, management systems and management styles.
— Many local authorities face problems of staff morale. Under continuing attack, faced with the problems of cutback and constraint, and deprived of growth there is uncertainty of purpose. The public service orientation provides a sense of purpose. Whatever the level of resources, the commitment is to the highest possible quality of service.
— There is a search for value for money. That search cannot be successful if the emphasis is on cost alone. *Value* must also be striven for. The public service orientation provides that drive. Value is found in service provided. The task is to appraise the performance of the local authority not by cost alone but also by the quality of service provided.
— The legitimacy of local authorities has been eroded and this decline in acceptance is shared with other public services. It is as if the public service is seen as serving the organization rather than the public. The public service orientation can build public confidence. The task is for the local authority to be close to the customer.

THE MANAGEMENT CONSEQUENCES

If accepted, the public service orientation must become part of the day-to-day working of local authorities. That requires commitment by senior management. The public service orientation must govern management processes and management structures and management style. Management must:

— have the capacity to analyse service for, the public
— be close to the customer
— open up the authority to the public
— make service for the public the guiding management criterion.

How any local authority meets these requirements must be worked out in that authority. Service for the public is not service for an abstraction, but service for a particular public with its own views, ideas and demands. It is to its own customers that an authority has to be close.

Analysis of service

The local authority must see its activities as justified only by the service provided. Analysing services in this way is a first step.

The immediate questions for analysis are:

— what are the services provided by the authority for its public?
— who are the customers for each of those services – actual and potential?

The activities of the authority are analysed not by organizational arrangements or by professional requirements, but by the service provided.

The questions are not easily answered. Management has tended to work to organizational rather than in service terms. The authority is inclined to look inward and this analysis forces it to look outward.

Key characteristics of the service can be identified among which are:

— speed of service
— extent of consumer choice
— coverage
— discrimination of need
— quality of service
— sensitivity to complaints.

The local authority will emphasize, in practice, one characteristic rather than another. Quality may be sacrificed for speed of service or for comprehensive coverage. There is an organizational choice, often made implicitly or by the traditions of past practice. Analysis of service makes explicit the choices made in the weight given to characteristics.

For the service-centred authority, the issues must be overt; it is important to know, for example, whether the weight given by the local authority to quality as opposed to speed, is the weight given by the customer. There may be reasons for a difference. But the authority should know:

— what the customer wants from a service, and
— whether the authority provides it.

Close to the customer
The customer, whether called client, tenant, user or public, can help the authority decide whether the authority has got it right. The question to be asked is:

— Are we providing what the customer wants?

The local authority may then still want to ask the question:

— Are we providing what the customers need?

But the second question must be grounded in the understanding provided by the answer to the first question and cannot be answered by the authority alone. The authority that tries to answer the second question without regard to the first, does not provide service *for* the customer, but *to* the customer.

A local authority close to its customers might be expected to:

— hold citizen surveys to establish public satisfaction with existing services
— ask for suggestions from the public for improving services

— seek out complaints about inadequate services
— test public attitudes to levels of expenditure and taxation and to the allocation of expenditure to different services
— introduce quality monitoring of services by customer panels meeting for regular discussion with staff
— involve customer panels in preparing briefs for all building projects, as when tenants help in the design of new housing
— introduce project review in which user views are sought on completed building projects
— carry out market research on customer reaction to proposed changes in service, as when bus travellers are asked views on alternative bus designs
— maximize customer choice, so that wherever possible, the customers can choose the service they want
— provide customers, consumers and users of services with standard of service statements and encourage them to evaluate the service by that standard
— above all encourage its management to look and to listen to the customer, watching the authority and watching its work.

Once the authority accepts that it has to get close to its customers, and to listen to what they say, then there will be no shortage of initiatives. The listening authority learns quickly. There are a variety of ways of collecting views and suggestions from the customer. The problem is not *how* to get close to the customer but to want to do so.

Closeness to the customer by itself is not enough. Closeness is for learning and learning certainly comes from suggestion, complaints, opinions, customer choice and action in use. But learning must feed into the working of the authority and must be enforced in the management processes of the authority. For example:

— the budgetary process of the authority may require that any submission of departmental estimates contain a summary of work done to learn customer views on existing services and on proposed changes in those services.
— any proposal for a capital project could contain a statement both of how customer views will be obtained for the design process and of how and when the project will be evaluated after completion
— performance review procedures can be structured around customer views.

Opening up the authority
A local authority that provides service for the public, must be open to the public. Too often and in too many ways the local authority closes itself off from the public.

— buildings, by their impersonality grandeur or scale, can deter
— directions on access may be meaningful for those who already know their way, but not for those who are lost in the corridors of power
— forms confuse the uncertain and unsure
— offices can be geographically as well as organizationally remote from those who most need them
— notices can be written more for the organization than for those who read them
— reception arrangements can be exclusion arrangements for those who step with hesitation through the doors.

In these and many other ways, the local authority describes itself to its public. Often messages tell the public of closure not openness. A local authority needs to understand the message it gives.

By surveys, by client evaluation, by direct experience, by pilot testing and above all by listening, senior management in a local authority can learn how it closes. Then they can start to learn how to open.

A local authority committed to the public service orientation will emphasize the need to:

- turn official language into understandable language and test that understanding
- emphasize form design for easy completion and test that ease of completion
- review buildings and offices to ease public access and watch for discouragement
- decentralize for ease of access and learn the response
- make reception arrangements, helping arrangements and encourage helping
- train staff for the open authority and learn from the customers of the organization.

The management principle

Service for the public becomes the management principle for the authority. It requires that:

- methods of work are designed to meet customer needs rather than organization needs
- all existing activities should be appraised by the criteria of service for the public
- all new policy proposals should be judged by the service provided for the public
- staff should be appraised, whether through formal or informal processes, by the quality of their service for the public (helpfulness; dealing with complaints quickly; seeking public views; proposals for better public service)
- organizational structure and management systems should be reviewed to support service to the customer. Key questions could be:

    - is senior management close to the customer or isolated by organizational hierarchy?
    - does the division of activities between and within departments reflect organizational needs rather than the needs of service for the public?
    - where in the budgetary process is service for the public emphasized?
    - does policy planning start from the customer?

Positive staff policies

The public service orientation requires a positive staff policy, for it is only through staff that service for the public can be achieved. A message has to be given and heard. Service for the public matters. The message cannot be heard unless it is given and reinforced in many ways and at many times.

A positive staff policy requires:

- emphasis on the value which is placed on service for the public. This can be achieved by staff newsletters, briefing groups, meetings, visits by senior management and in the day-to-day flow of business. The local authority that does not show its staff its key values, can hardly be surprised if they do not know what they are.

— involvement of staff from all organizational levels, in quality appraisal groups to review service provided
— the encouragement of staff initiative in service for the public, spreading information through the authority on what has been achieved
— staff training courses to build specific skills in:

  — analysis of service
  — market research
  — form design
  — better English

— seminars to build staff understanding of the implications of service for the public
— staff development programmes that go beyond courses and seminars. Planned experience can give understanding of public attitudes and encourage learning.

ISSUES IN THE PUBLIC SERVICE ORIENTATION

The foregoing proposals for the public service orientation raise a number of important questions. Such questions include:

— Doesn't the emphasis on service for the public concentrate too much on particular views and ignore the wider public interest?
— How does the public service orientation differ from the idea of public participation?
— The public may know what they want but not what they need. Must that not involve both political and professional judgement?
— Is not a councillor elected to make judgements on behalf of the public? Should not a local authority give a lead to its public?
— Doesn't an emphasis on the 'customer' ignore the distinctive nature of the public sector?
— What happens when a customer does not want a service? Doesn't an authority have to enforce regulation and control?

These questions have to be raised even by sympathisers with the public service orientation. Indeed a strength of the public service orientation is that it brings such issues into the open – for they are implicit in every action by a local authority – even if there are no final answers.

Broadly, however, our view is that the public service orientation will work not against local democracy, based as it is on the representative system and public accountability but will give real meaning to such processes which, without an emphasis on service for the public, can become theoretical constructs. Nevertheless there are dilemmas which are raised by the questions and must be faced. The dilemmas may be resolved in different ways in different authorities, but they cannot be ignored.

The distinctive contribution of the public service orientation
There are several issues which distinguish the public service orientation from other approaches.

Service **for** *not to the public*

All local authorities provide public services, but they may provide services *to* the public, rather than *for* the public. Service *for* the public places emphasis on those for whom the service is provided. Service to the public places emphasis on the service. The danger is that services *to* the public are provided without regard for the views of those for whom the services are provided. It is not that the services are not meant to help the public, but that those who provide them believe they know either *what the public wants* or *what the public needs.*

No local authority would ever argue that they provide services without regard to public views. More often it is argued that the authority knows the public's views.

'An experienced officer has a good understanding of what the public wants.'
'Good councillors know their patch.'
'We don't go far wrong.'

But, just when the authority, its councillors or its staff think they know what the public wants, danger starts. If one knows, one does not need to find out: a sign of the enclosed organization.

The enclosed authority builds its own image of what the public wants. 'The authority has to build houses for the average tenant but the average tenant does not exist. A good architect forms a view of what the average tenant wants.' A local authority operates with a generalized image of the public built up over time. That generalized image can quickly become an obstacle to learning what members of the public want from the services they receive.

If the authority already knows, there is no need to learn. Yet even if the authority recognized it had only an imperfect knowledge of what the public wants, it may still regard it as unnecessary to find out more. Although it may not know what the public *wants*, it believes it knows what they *need*. If that belief is held sufficiently strongly then the views of those who receive the service are irrelevant.

'The authority has to act in the public interest.'
'The authority must pursue the policies on which it was elected.'
'It is good professional practice.'

The public interest can become an abstraction that is pursued regardless of public views. Professional practice can too easily become an end pursued without change in a world in which both circumstances and public attitudes are changing and where a new professional response is demanded.

The public service orientation still requires the consideration of the public interest, political purposes and professional requirements. Needs have to be assessed as well as expressed. Service *for* the public means, however, that needs should not be regarded as separable from the views, wishes and 'felt' needs of those for whom they are provided.

There is and always will be a continuing dilemma. There is a necessary choice between the views of those for whom a service is provided and views held within the organization. The local authority has the power to impose its own views. It acts with the legitimacy given by the political process, with the authority of professional knowledge and in the name of a wider public interest. The authority has to regulate and enforce. It will take action to place a child in care. It will impose smoke control and environmental standards. When the local authority so acts, it acts on behalf of one set of customers against other customers. Nothing in the public service orientation lessens that need. What the public service orientation requires is clarity in the authority as to the customers in whose name regulation and enforcement is applied as well as those against whom they are applied.

Service *for* the public means that the views of the public for whom the service is provided are seen as critical, although not necessarily decisive in every instance. Departures from those views however require justification.

A focus on the customer and the citizen

The public service orientation focuses on those for whom the services are provided. Individuals, families, and organizations are customers who are entitled to good service. They are also citizens who are entitled to be treated as such. The emphasis is both on the *customer* for whom the service is provided and on the *citizen* to whom the local authority is accountable. Customer and citizen are entitled to respect, and a public service orientation has a special obligation to show that respect, whether or not their interests are identical in any given case.

The local authority must show respect by concern

— to make access to the authority easy
— to make reception arrangements helpful
— to ensure delivery of service is geared to the needs of the customer
— to increase the capacity of the organization to respond
— to explain its services and the reasons that underline their provision
— to give priority to complaints.

It is not always clear who are the customers for a particular service. The customer may not be those on whom the service has an immediate impact. The real customers of trading standards are those who buy the goods inspected, not those who provide them. There may be more than one customer of a service. The customers of schools can be the children themselves, the parents, the future employers and the public at large. Focus on the issue of *'who is the customer?'* is an essential step in clarification in the public service orientation.

Only if general respect is translated into behaviour towards the individual can it be regarded as meaningful. Customers and citizens are entitled to explanation: for instance, about the nature and level of services provided and about why an individual case does or does not fit the general policy.

Local authorities are institutions constituted for collective decision-making. This can mean that the individual or small group can easily be ignored. Yet a collective view has to be tested against views held by individuals, before it can be assumed to be widely held. The stress on the customer and citizen should not be regarded as an attack on collective decision-making, but rather as asserting the need to test that view. Yet there will remain a dilemma between the collective view, even when grounded in actual views, and the views of particular individuals. That dilemma is inherent in collective decisions. It is right that the authority be aware of it.

The public service orientation distinguished from consumerism

The public service orientation is a challenge to the public sector to think positively about those who use its service. They should not be thought of as clients dependent on the public sector, but as customers demanding a high standard of services and attention.

It is a mistake, however, to treat a public-sector organization as if it were identical to some other form of organization. The public sector in general and local authorities in particular have their own purposes and their own rationales. To put forward this argument is not to take a position on the size of the public sector. One can argue that the public sector should be larger or smaller than at present. What it does is to recognize that services have been placed in the public sector to be run on a different basis from those in the private sector and that the implications of this decision need to be thought through.

In the public sector service is provided subject to considerations determined by the political process rather than by considerations simply of the market place. Even where it has been decided that a service within the public sector should be subject to certain market forces, that in itself is a decision made in the political process.

The customer of a public service is not the same as the customer of a service in the market. The customer does not necessarily buy the service; the customer may have a right to receive the service; the customer may be compelled to receive the service; customers may be refused a service because their needs may not meet the criteria laid down. The conditions of service are not determined by the resources available to the customer but subject to special conditions laid down by a political process.

In the public sector the nature of the services provided is not determined by the market. Services may be provided free of charge or at a subsidized rate. Issues about rationing can arise and criteria of need may have to be laid down. Choices have to be made between conflicting demands: they are made not by decisions subject to the market but subject to the political process. The customer influences that process as a citizen.

Concern for the citizen as well as the customer distinguishes the public service orientation from the concern for the customer that should mark any service organization. For this reason issues such as participation and public accountability are raised in any discussion of the public service orientation. Thus the public service orientation is *not merely consumerism.*

The public service orientation applies wherever responsibility for a service lies in the public sector, however it is delivered. If a service is, for example, contracted out or provided in partnership with another agency, it does not remove the responsibility of the local authority to its citizens for that service. A private firm providing the service on behalf of the local authority has a contractual responsibility to the authority not to the citizen. The local authority remains responsible for the service to its citizens. However, the firm can be required to provide good service to the customers, whether that customer is the local authority itself or members of the public. The public service orientation requires from the local authorities a concern for the customer in setting and monitoring the contract, but they will expect the contractor to discharge that concern.

Public services and the political process
Service for the public is provided subject to the political process of the authority. A local authority has limited resources and has to determine how to allocate them. The choice between the amount to be spent on libraries as opposed to roads maintenance is a choice between differing values. In local authorities it is not an individual choice about the use of resources, but a collective choice made through the political process. The aim should be to provide the best possible service with those resources.

The political process determines not merely the resources available, but the nature of the services to be provided. Policies are laid down setting directions for the authority, its services, the criteria determining access to those services, and the method or methods by which they are to be provided. The public service orientation requires that both in policy formulation and in implementation, those for whom services are provided are not forgotten nor are the citizens to whom accounts are given. Collective processes are not contradicted by individual needs, rather they are informed by them.

But what are the implications of the public service orientation for the political process? Four implications are paramount. They affect:

— policy formulation
— the framework and the nature of service provision
— public accountability and public participation and, as a result,
— the relationships between councillors, staff and public.

Informing the process of policy formulation

The political process itself provides a channel of views and opinions, but they are limited channels. Councillors are, because of their election, entitled to speak as representatives of the public; however, they are not entitled to claim that they automatically know what the public think about each of the services provided. From their many contacts with the public they will learn much but not all. Surveys have shown that over three-quarters of the public have never raised an issue with a councillor. Councillors committed to the public service orientation will use their own knowledge, and other knowledge of the public's concerns, but they will also seek out new ways of learning. The authority committed to the public service orientation will above all seek to open the authority to new contracts with its public.

Some authorities have commissioned general surveys of public attitudes towards the local authority and its service; that is a useful but limited step. Its very generality is its limitation. It is more important to go beyond the general to the particular. Learning is required from the actual or potential customers of particular services. Dialogue should be opened up between the authority and its public as the Swedish example suggests (see Clarke and Stewart 1985b).

Setting the framework

Informed by the public service orientation, the political process determines the nature of the services to be provided and the resources available. The necessity of political decision-making does not remove the need for the public service orientation in the operation of the service; rather it strengthens it. Whatever the policy, however great or small the level of resources, the aim can still be the best quality of service achievable.

The idea of the public service orientation has been interpreted by some as little more than asking the public what they want. The answer to such questions is usually 'more' and, consequently, the idea is inextricably linked with expanding services. This assessment misses the point. At whatever level services are set and within whatever broad parameters they are being provided (and these are political decisions) there should be a concern for quality of provision and for the effectiveness of their delivery. Quality and effectiveness are central to providing service for the public.

The public service orientation requires:

— focus on access (design and location of buildings, information, letters, forms)
— attention to customer views and a determination to seek them out
— search for and welcome to suggestions

— priority to complaints
— attention to detail
— explanation of refusal so that customer and citizen know where they stand.

These requirements are likely to be realized only if those who deal directly with the public understand the policy they are applying, have a capacity to respond to the public's problems as they are presented, and have organizational support. Policy should not unnecessarily be turned into over-detailed specification, though there will be times when the political requirement for a service has to be specified in detailed rules governing the allocation of a service. A housing allocation, for example, has to follow a rigorous points scheme in order to secure fair and equal treatment.

The public service orientation does not rule out the need for detailed specification of the nature and condition of a service. It requires that such conditions be the subject of clear political decisions, made in full awareness that narrow limits are being set on the capacity of staff to respond helpfully to the public's problems. The public service orientation does not resolve the issues of specification against discretion. It requires that the issue and the balance between them are faced.

To set wider limits for the staff who have to deal with the public does not remove the concern of councillors. Many councillors are involved with the individual problems of members of the public. They test the performance of the local authority in the complaints they receive. To give wider discretion to staff does not lessen that interest of councillors. The discretion is provided not for its own sake but to give service for the public in carrying out the policies of the authority. Both have still to be judged by the councillor, and for that judgement the councillor is accountable.

The implication that staff require greater discretion to provide a responsive service is another issue to be confronted. Not only does discretion, once given, have to be supported managerially and politically but it has to be both properly defined and prepared for. Discretion without definition is not likely to serve much purpose; similarly, staff who are not trained to cope with discretion are unlikely to perform well.

Distinguishing the contribution of public participation

Public participation is the involvement of the public in the process of decision-making. Often enough involvement is at the level of consultation, rather than as a partner in decision-making. The public is consulted about proposals for a new town development, for an urban renewal scheme or over a new system of public transport. The decision remains with the local authority which may take more or less account of the process of consultation.

Public participation can go further than consultation. It can go as far as the use of a referendum or, on a smaller scale, the handing over of part of a local authority service to be run by the users of the service, as with tenants control of estate management or user-control of a sports facility.

Public participation in some of its forms can, however, focus too much on the collective community view with the result that the individual is lost sight of. Views expressed by a few members of the public at a meeting do not always represent the views of customers and citizens. Representatives of tenants, or users engaged in running activities themselves, require a public service orientation for they too can forget the public they serve. It may be argued that they are less likely to do so being close to tenants and users. But such representatives can too readily assume they 'know' because they are tenants and users, yet that may mean only they know what they themselves want. The public service orientation does not mean the introduction of a particular form of public participation. It does not mean that decisions are removed entirely from either professionals or politicians. It does challenge, however, the right of either to define unilaterally what the customers want and need without regard to their views.

The impact on relationships
The public service orientation highlights the triangle of relations between

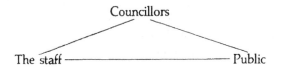

It raises the issues of

- — whether the councillors (even with the assistance of the staff) have enough knowl-edge of, and take sufficient account of, the views of the public both as customer and as citizens
- — whether the councillors have allowed sufficient scope and discretion within the limits of their policy requirements for staff to provide good service for the public as customers
- — whether the councillors provide both directly and through staff sufficient explana-tion to provide a basis for public accountability.

The public service orientation raises a further issue. Are there times when the public should decide for themselves? In other words, are our current forms of representative democracy adequate? We return to this issue below.

Organizing for the public service orientation
The staff provide service *to* the public. They do not necessarily provide service *for* the public. At the counter or in the community, the staff can easily be seen as concerned more to impose than to respond. Such perceptions are far from universal. There are many instances of good service for the public. Yet even where such perceptions are felt, the problem may not lie in the staff but in the organizational conditions. Good service is provided at the counter or in the street, but good service depends upon organizational support. There are many organizational issues raised by a focus on service *for* the public. We note four in particular:

- — rules and procedures
- — hierarchy
- — professionalism

and the relationships which underpin them.

Procedures may restrict the capacity of staff, professional and non-professional, to provide service for the public. They may limit the capacity to respond to problems and issues as they are presented. They may be necessary to ensure that the policies laid down by the council are carried out, and may be a way of ensuring that limited resources are allocated to those most in need.

Although the procedures may be defended and defensible on these grounds, the justification may be more formal than real and it does not follow that all procedures will be so justified. One test is whether the procedures are seen as fair by most of the public affected by them. Thus, a points allocation system for housing will normally be accepted as fair by applicants for housing even though there may be arguments about the points. The existence of rules for the allocation of scarce resources will normally be seen as fair. The existence of rules as such does not prevent good service, provided service carries explanation and the explanations bring general although not universal acceptance of their necessity. Rules are justifiable, but they must *be* justified. Their fairness can be reviewed in public dialogue.

Bureaucracy does not operate by rules alone, but by hierarchy. Cases may have to be referred upwards; virement may be limited. The hierarchy operates not because of rules, but in their absence. Issues are referred up the hierarchy because rules are not laid down. In the eyes of the public it is remote decision-making by 'them'. Lack of discretion at the point of contact or close to the public can limit the capacity for good service.

Many local authority staff are professionals who deal with the public in accordance with their acquired knowledge and skills. The views of the public can be discounted and stress laid on the professional approach as though that were enough. Professionalism can provide a good service for the public, if the public is listened to. If the professional solution is unthinkingly imposed, professionalism merely provides service *to* the public.

Professionalism has come under increasing challenge. On the one hand it is challenged politically, as councillors begin to question the validity of professional judgement. There is a public challenge as the authority for professional decisions is increasingly questioned. Professional skills and knowledge provide the basis for the professional to make an important contribution, but a contribution which many feel should not be made in isolation. There may be a requirement for new forms of relationships between the professions and public and a new form of professionalism that sees the public less as dependents but as partners.

There is a rationale for the inward or upward looking organization. Local authority staff, both professional and non-professional, are responsible through the organizational hierarchy to committee and council. They are subject to political control. The necessity of political control can be used to justify rules laid down, limited discretion and the hierarchical control of professionals and others, and yet that political control can easily become a formality rather than a reality.

The public service orientation does not deny the necessity for rules, hierarchy or professionalism. It questions their dominance and past forms.

Representative democracy: the need for new relations between politicians, staff and public

Representative democracy can be used to justify organization that provides service to the public rather than for the public. Phrases such as 'The committee insist' or 'Public accountability requires' can justify the emphasis on the organization that looks upward through the hierarchy not outward to the public. Although representative democracy provides the means by which the organization looks outward to the public, it can lead to an emphasis on the public as an abstraction rather than on members of the public.

We suspect that too great a burden is being placed on the principle of representative democracy, if it is assumed that through this means alone public service can be secured.

Indeed it leads to a burden of hierarchical control. The number of tiers in hierarchy, the detailed rules, the agendas of decision can all make service for the public difficult; they can also substitute form for the reality of political control.

The assumption can be too readily made that the primacy of political control based on representative democracy is the only legitimate means of expressing public views. This assumption rules out any role for participative democracy, just as it also leads to an organizational framework that restricts the capacity to build service for the public. Consideration must at least be given to the possibility of the public deciding for themselves: of the collective will being expressed directly instead of indirectly.

Perhaps more immediately the public service orientation demands a new view of the triangle of relationships. Thus, the relationship between staff and public is affected by the relationship between staff and politicians. The issues raised are

— whether the forms in which policy are expressed prevent or encourage service for the public by the staff?
— whether control systems discourage service for the public without necessarily ensuring control by the political process?
— whether the hierarchies through which political control is expressed cause the organization to look inwards rather than outward?
— what the balance is between the professional's relationship with the politicians and the relationship with the profession?
— whether professionalism gets in the way of taking sufficient account of the public as customer and citizen?

It is important to consider not only the pairs of relationships but the set of relation-ships and to look at them in terms of service for the public. A holistic approach is required.

The dilemmas of the public service orientation
The public service orientation raises issues about the role of the local authority and the services it provides. Because the public service orientation focuses not on the organization but on the public as customer and citizen, it raises issues that can easily lie hidden in the day-to-day workings of a local authority that believes it acts in the public interest but rarely checks that belief against the reality of members of the public. Moreover, although this article has focused on local government, both the orientation and the issues raised are relevant to the public service generally.

There is no easy resolution of the issues raised. There are dilemmas as to the choice to be made between:

— the assumed public interest and the expressed public interest
— the public interest in general and the interest of the individual member of the public
— between the public as collective and the public as individual
— between representative democracy and participatory democracy
— between the public as customer and the public as citizen
— between uniformity in policy implementation and responsiveness in practice
— between the use of professional skills and knowledge and the views of the client.

The choices made can and will vary from authority to authority and from circumstance to circumstance, but the public service orientation requires that greater weight is given to the views of the public in any choice made. The authority that is committed to developing the public service orientation must be prepared to see these issues raised. The public service orientation does not, for example, demand the rejection of any wider concept of the public interest or of professional judgement, but a recognition that both have to be tested against public views.

— In what circumstances, if any, should the authority's view on what the public *needs* override what the public wants?
— Is service to the public ever more appropriate than service for the public?
— Can concern for community views mean neglect of individual views?
— Does the principle of representative democracy exclude any development of participatory democracy?
— How does the customer of a local authority service differ from the customer of a private firm?
— Does the public service orientation challenge or support the political process?
— Can the requirements of political control be reconciled with responsiveness to the public?
— Are the rights of the public as citizens different from the rights of the public as customers?
— Does the duty of councillors to represent the public mean that they speak for the public?
— When does the public service orientation deny professionalism and when does professionalism deny the public service orientation?
— Should the wider public interest always override the views of individuals?
— How is that wider public interest judged?
— How far can customer choice be extended for a public service?
— Does the fair and impartial implementation of policy prevent responsiveness to individual needs?

Finally the implications of the public service orientation can be considered against concrete issues facing the authority. For example:

'One area of the county has always appeared to the chief officers to be neglected, "almost backwater", lacking many of the facilities of other areas. The county is considering how transport facilities can be improved and development undertaken. Yet there is every indication that in that area the people living there do not seek that development.'

In what circumstances and for what reasons is that development justified?

'Prospective tenants placed high on a council's waiting list have turned down three offers, which means they no longer have priority.'

Is that rule justified?

The contribution of the public service orientation is to open up an enclosed organization and there is no better way to open it up than to question.

NOTE

1. This article is the product of a series of papers produced for, and published by, the Local Government Training Board which have set out the case for a public service orientation. The paper draws upon the reaction to the original papers and on interviews with chief officers about their initiatives. See: Clarke and Stewart 1985a, 1985b, 1986a and 1986b.

REFERENCES

Clarke, M. and J. Stewart. 1985a. *Local government and the public service orientation: or does a public service provide for the public?* Luton: Local Government Training Board, August, mimeo.

———. 1985b. *The service programme: report on a visit to Sweden.* Luton: Local Government Training Board, October, mimeo.

———. 1986a. *The public service orientation: developing the approach.* Luton: Local Government Training Board, April, mimeo.

———. 1986b. *The public service orientation: issues and dilemmas to be faced.* Luton: Local Government Training Board, mimeo, August.

AFTERWORD: NO MORE CUSTOMERS

When we wrote, first, about the Public Service Orientation twenty five years ago, we did so to encourage public services to look outwards and to be more responsive. Looking back on our work in the light of developments since we can see two major problems. On the one hand we were probably over-simplistic in the use of language – to the detriment of our basic theme. On the other, while we argued strongly for attitudinal, behavioural and cultural change in public service organizations, we undoubtedly underestimated the magnitude of the changes involved and the need for constant renewal. We now have a suspicion that confusion of language may have further aggravated or inhibited the organizational change agenda.

Our concept of the public service orientation stressed the need for public service organizations to look outwards to the public served rather than inward to the organization. The phrase itself was not widely adopted and has faded into disuse, but the basic argument has been widely accepted. Its relevance in 2011 is as great as it was in the mid nineteen-eighties. It has been – and continues to be – echoed in the policies of each of the major parties. And yet...

Looking back on the original article, we can now see that overuse of the word 'customer' can mislead. At the time we could see the potential for this and entered a number of cautionary remarks. We are clear that the use of the word by us and by others has had an impact in opening up what we described as 'enclosed' organizations. The word undoubtedly commanded an attention that was necessary at the time. The danger was and is that it does not adequately describe the nuanced relationships of public service organizations and their service users. While the ideas of the 'customer' and 'customer service' stimulated developments in public management and in service delivery, they have themselves became a barrier to further development. We now believe that their very simplicity gets in the way of an analysis of the multiplicity of different relationships between the services and those who use them, benefit from them or are affected by them. Without such analysis it is impossible to understand the different approaches required in the management of those relationships.

The word 'customer' carries with it assumptions based on the private sector and the market: of an individual customer choosing whether or not to purchase goods and services and being treated accordingly. Such assumptions do not adequately fit the complex requirements of the public domain and the different relationships which are entailed in serving a range of publics. We suggest it can be very far from clear who the 'customer' of a particular service is. Is the customer of the school the child, the parent, the future employer; whom? Or is it all of them? It is self-evidently more than one of these; consequently, their varying needs or wishes have to be balanced in the search for the public interest.

In some services there are collective customers rather than individuals. A free service has to be rationed and some so-called 'customers' do not receive the services they want. On the other hand there are some services that the public are compelled to receive. In some cases the interests of different members of the public can be in conflict with one another – as in many planning decisions (and here it is difficult to see how they can all be described as 'customer'!).

Some services exist to maintain order and use the power of coercion to order the relationship with members of the public who, incidentally, are unlikely to see themselves as 'customers'. 'Customers' do not choose to pay taxes, but can be compelled to do so. A series of different words better describe the many relationships involved: patient, passenger, client, applicant, defendant, tax-payer, even prisoner. Our contention is that the approach of management and staff is not one-dimensional but should be based on the nature of the relationship sought.

In the original paper, and in the work which followed from it, we argued for a systematic approach to these relationships and for an understanding of the way in which the 'enclosed' organization impeded effective delivery. We suggested that the need to make the organization outward facing and responsive implied particular objectives embedded in organizational leadership and in service management; in HR policies and training and development; and which must permeate the culture of the organization. While we made clear that all of this implied a massive challenge to any organization, we underestimated its scale and the need for it to be a continuing process.

We can now see how partial effort has not adequately re-shaped culture and approaches, how relatively simplistic models of 'customer care' borrowed from a private sector (often retail) context have failed to go beyond the superficial and how more strategic interventions and objectives have had an initial impact but then been allowed to slip back, the job having apparently been 'done'. There are few examples of a real appreciation of the multiplicity of service relationships and the gearing up of the organization to meet them in their richness rather than in over-simplification. We think it likely that a better understanding of those relationships and their differences would have made it more likely that organization development initiatives would have been better designed and implemented.

But there is more even than this recognition of diversity and difference. We have suggested that the peculiar nature of the public domain requires not just recognition of the distinctive kinds of service relationship, but also the special relationship expressed in the idea of citizenship. This marks out the involvement of the public in the processes of government (and public service delivery) in a way that has no parallel in the private sector. A customer of a service is also a citizen, but a citizen is not necessarily a customer of a particular service. As citizens, people have a right to be informed, to speak about and to be listened to in relation to decisions about the shaping of services, irrespective of whether they are direct users, and so regarded as 'customers'. One need not be a 'customer' of a school or the planning system to have views which have a right to be heard. A focus on customers, however nuanced, that neglects citizens and citizenship weakens rather than strengthens the public domain.

Although we directed attention to these issues in the original article, the domination of the word 'customer' and of the practice of the private sector has meant that they have been neglected in both the discourse and practice of public management. The failure to confront has meant that the dilemmas identified in the article have not been faced and, therefore, resolved. While public participation has been emphasized by the Government – significantly more, it has to be said, in relation to local government and other public agencies rather than its own activities – it has not resolved the central dilemma embedded in the relationship between participatory and representative democracy.

It is as if participatory democracy can be considered in isolation from representative democracy. There was one exception with the 2008 Department of Justice Paper setting out *A National Framework for Greater Citizen Engagement* which confronted the issue – but had no obvious impact on Government policy. Failure to consider that issue properly creates a barrier to the development of participatory democracy by ensuring that its place in the system of governance remains unclear. In turn this leads to a neglect of the question of how representative democracy can be strengthened notwithstanding the fact that it will surely continue as the basis of government in a complex society.

There remain equally unresolved dilemmas about choice, not least between the public interest in general and the interests of the individual members of the public or the public as collective. We need to find ways of seeing how differences can be reconciled, failing which we have to find a balance between different requirements, needs, interests and objectives – a task which lies at the heart of the public domain. The problem has been that too often such issues are considered in isolation, without an endeavour to see them strategically and 'in the round'.

Far from resolving these dilemmas they still lie at the heart of public management. They are exacerbated by other issues we touched on. The growth of partnership, for instance, which can pose another set of barriers, reinforcing opacity rather than transparency. Similarly, the fragmentation of the public sector through the growth of new agencies for the delivery of public services creates dilemmas for 'joined-up' government and the requirement to meet the needs of those who don't fit the 'boxes' into which public services are divided. These may further reinforce the tendencies to be enclosed and inward-looking rather than outward-looking and responsive.

We are in no doubt that there is still an important agenda to be tackled. On the one hand, there needs to be a more sophisticated approach to the defining and designing of service relationships (and an eschewing of the simplistic notion of 'customer'); on the other, there is the need then to take a systematic and strategic approach to ensuring that public service organizations are capable of delivering accordingly and being genuinely outward looking and responsive. Tackling the latter is a formidable task in itself. At the same time there needs to be proper awareness of the importance of citizens and citizenship in the public domain and of the need to address the other dilemmas we pointed to in our original article.

Chapter 13

'PORTRAIT OF A PROFESSION REVISITED'

BARON WILSON OF DINTON

On the walls of my private office hang the photographs of my seven distinguished predecessors as Secretary of the Cabinet. I sometimes find myself staring at them for inspiration, not always successfully I admit.

A week or two ago I found myself looking at the great Lord Bridges, Secretary of the Cabinet and War Cabinet from 1938 to 1946. I wondered what he would have made of it if in the space of a week one of his predecessors had published an article in *The Spectator* advertised as 'The Descent of the Civil Servant' and another had appeared on the Frost programme to reassure the world that the Service was still in good shape.

Both predecessors, Lords Butler and Armstrong, I hasten to say, were acting in the most supportive spirit and spoke from what for all of us is a deeply shared view of the role of the Civil Service. But, staring at Bridges, I could see a bubble emerging from his mouth enquiring: what precisely is happening on your watch, Sir Richard?

This a good question which deserves an answer.

What follows is my own analysis, although the Government is of course publicly committed to a Civil Service Bill which I shall come to later. Not everyone will agree with what I say. But the issues need to be aired.

SERVING THE GOVERNMENT OF THE DAY

To begin at the beginning, civil servants are employed by the Crown out of money voted by Parliament to maintain the functions of the State in accordance with the wishes of Parliament within the framework of the law.

Because the government of the day commands a majority in Parliament, the Civil Service works under the direction of that government, executes the programme of that government and owes its loyalty to that government. But the Service is not simply the creature of any government: the Crown in Parliament is supreme.

Because governments change, policies change, functions change and laws change; and the Civil Service changes too. It has never remained the same for long. But it has established over time an important character which I would argue makes it an institution of value and a force for good in public life, provided always that it continues to perform well.

CHARACTER OF THE SERVICE

How would I define its character?

First, integrity. I believe that it is a real benefit to the nation to know that the permanent body of men and women at the core of the State are committed to public service and to the conduct of public affairs with integrity. I do not intend to imply that others lack integrity. I simply make the point because there is ample evidence abroad of the harm that can follow if public servants lack this tradition.

Second, political impartiality. I believe that there is real benefit in having a non-partisan Civil Service. This is not because politics is a dirty business. I have worked for a great many politicians for 35 years and I know them to be decent, honourable people as a breed.

It is however fundamental to the working of our constitution that governments should use the resources entrusted to them, including the Civil Service, for the benefit of the country as a whole and not for the benefit of their political party; and that opposition parties should feel confident that this position is being respected. The non-political character of our Civil Service underpins that convention. Very few countries have such a Civil Service. It is an asset which I believe politicians of all parties value.

Third, merit, by which I mean ability to do the job plus the right personal qualities. We turned our face long ago against patronage. There is real benefit in recruiting and promoting permanent civil servants on the basis of merit rather than their political loyalty or personal connections. Again this is not because political loyalty in itself is bad: it is not. But the vital thing is to get the best people into key jobs. The merit principle does this and underpins political impartiality.

Fourth, the ability to work for successive governments. The permanence of a non-political Service carries with it a commitment to certain standards of conduct and discretion which ensure that it can provide loyal service to whatever government is in power, responding flexibly to new political priorities. It also ensures that there is in every government department a body of knowledge and experience – a corporate memory – which is at the disposal of every government, however inexperienced. I believe this to be to the public good too, all the more so given that much of our constitution is unwritten.

And finally, public service. What attracts many people to the Civil Service is the wish to make a contribution to the community. We have some of the best, most challenging jobs in the economy, at every level. This gives us a deeply committed workforce.

THE CIVIL SERVICE IS IN TRANSITION

Now let me turn to the question: what is happening on my watch?

The short answer is: fundamental change which is not widely understood. The Civil Service is in transition. Quite apart from the demands of governments, the external world is changing at a pace which affects all governments which come to power. Globalisation, science and technology, changes in social attitudes and behaviour, the power of the media: all are powerful forces.

The work of the Civil Service lies at these frontiers, and in particular at the frontiers of constitutional change, management change and political change. It is in a sense a shock-absorber at the heart of the State.

MODERNISATION

The need to modernise is at the top of our agenda. This is not new, but more than ever it is challenging.

The world of Sir Humphrey has long since gone. We are not a static force, resisting change from the trenches. We cannot afford to be. We have to earn our keep afresh with every new government. The size and shape of the Service left by one government may not meet the needs of the next.

It is a sobering thought that for over 30 years every government has pressed the Civil Service to improve its performance. We have done a lot to meet this demand: the Service which I leave is very different from the Service which I joined in 1966. And yet the pressure for further improvement is great.

UNITS OVER THE YEARS

The Fulton Report in 1968 set the ball rolling with an agenda which was hugely influential. It culminated in the major decentralisation of management functions to departments and agencies in the 1990s, the Continuity and Change White Paper in 1995 and the steady move to more open government. The Office of Public Service Reform set up last year is in the direct line of descent of this tradition.

There has been constant pressure to improve policy-making. Mr Heath set up the Central Policy Review Staff with a remit to take a 'synoptic view' across government. Its successors – the Policy Unit in Number 10 in the 1980s and 1990s, and now the Forward Strategy Unit, the Performance and Innovation Unit, the Social Exclusion Unit – have all reflected a need felt by successive Prime Ministers to challenge the thinking and strategy of departments, and to handle more effectively issues that cut across departments.

There has been constant pressure to cut red tape and reduce the burden on business. The Deregulation Unit was established under Mrs Thatcher. The fight still goes on in the Regulatory Impact Unit and its Task Force.

There has been a continuous search for efficiency. The Efficiency Unit under Mrs Thatcher devised 'Next Step' agencies in which over half the Civil Service now work. Later there was the drive for market testing and privatisation. Over twenty-five years the size of the Civil Service dropped by about 40 per cent from 746 000 to 480 000.

Finally, there has been the growing recognition of the needs of the consumer. The Charter Mark Unit set up under Mr Major still continues. The present government has committed itself to major improvements in the quality of key services, supported by the Delivery Unit in the Cabinet Office.

Units at the centre of government are not new. I am not suggesting that they have now reached some final, perfect form. The centre of government has always evolved and searched for new ways to be effective. The search will continue. I am just making the point that establishing new Units at the centre of government to tackle long-standing problems is an old practice.

The message from governments for over 30 years is clear: the Civil Service must modernise and change if it is to remain fit for purpose. We have accepted this and taken it to heart.

CURRENT REFORMS

What is different now is the scale of what is required to meet the present government's programme of delivery?

Any organisation in any sector would be challenged to do what we have set out to do on education, health, crime and transport. Just consider what is involved in the National Health Service, with a workforce of around one million people, the largest in Europe, one of the largest in the world save only for the Indian Railways.

I and my permanent secretary colleagues recognised this challenge in December 1999 when we published a major five-year programme of reform. We are only halfway through it but we have met or exceeded all our targets so far.

We are opening up the Service to talent. We have increased the number of Senior Civil Service vacancies put out to open competition by 88 per cent in two years: two-thirds were filled from outside. Nine out of thirteen posts at permanent secretary level have been put out to open competition since the reform programme was launched: five have been filled from other sectors. We have brought in over 100 secondees to do prominent key tasks. We have organised 4000 interchange opportunities in the past year. We are on track to meet our diversity targets.

We are radically improving our management. We have introduced a new system for managing pay and performance in the Senior Civil Service, offering high rewards for the best performers. Everyone at this level, including permanent secretaries and me, receive feedback on their performance from staff, colleagues and managers. And we are strengthening our leadership: the first 100 people have now embarked on our new Public Service Leaders Scheme.

We are competing for talent in a tough market. But people want to work for us. In a survey published last week, three Government departments featured in the top twenty-five organisations graduates wanted to join. We still attract the brightest and best: we had 11200 applications for 250 places in our general fast stream competition in 2000.

We are winning prizes. The Knowledge Network, a project led by the Office of the e-Envoy, won a prestigious award for Best Management Practice in IT last year. The Inland Revenue at Cumbernauld won a UK Business Excellence Award in 2000. Central government has been rated first above 14 other employment sectors for its work in championing and investing in women's progress.

We know there is much more to do, but we have a very good story to tell so far. I commend our leaflet *The Service is changing*.

A LOT MORE TO DO

There are of course still many questions we need to address.

Do we need an even greater flow in and out of the Service? Probably yes. How do we get the people we need to do the job now without necessarily keeping them for life? The search for a greater variety of employment patterns is rising up the agenda.

What skills do we need in the 21st century? Traditionally we have encouraged those required for high-quality advice to Ministers. Increasingly we need top-class managers who can deliver large-scale services and projects. Do we need to do more to equip our people to give them new skills and experience? Certainly.

Are we paying enough attention to leadership skills and teams at the top of departments? Until recently, no; but that is changing. Are we tough enough in confronting poor performance? Answer, not yet.

Has the delegation of management functions to departments made cross-departmental working harder, for instance on IT systems? How do we get more movement between departments, particularly at the senior levels? How do we maintain our drive for diversity? Are our recruitment systems – and salaries – fit for purpose? Is the personnel function in departments sufficiently professional?

These are all questions that I and my permanent secretary colleagues know we have to tackle, and are tackling. As always with rapid change, people inside and outside get worried that we are losing old values, throwing out the baby with the bath water. My permanent secretary colleagues and I are as committed as anyone to these values. But we know that the best way of protecting them is to move with the times and to show that we can rise successfully to the challenges we face in a modern world.

CONSTITUTIONAL CHANGE

Modernisation is not the only kind of challenge.

I believe that when the history books come to be written they will say that we are living through a period of great constitutional change. Our entry into Europe in 1973 was a big constitutional event. Over 30 years the implications of membership have broken across Whitehall like a wave in slow motion, as department after department has gradually recognised that the European dimension is integral to its daily business.

Devolution to Scotland, Wales and Northern Ireland was a big constitutional event. It happened extraordinarily quickly and with apparent ease. But it has required the Civil Service not only to set up the new administrations but also to define new relationships and new ways of working between administrations, and to evolve new loyalties and new accountabilities.

I believe that the Human Rights Act, the Data Protection Act and the Freedom of Information Act will in a different way prove to be important constitutionally because of their potential to affect the relationship between the individual and the State and to alter the ways in which governments and civil servants do their business, internally as well as externally.

The relationship between central and local government is changing. By a complex process over twenty years or so central government is now held responsible by the public for the quality of services delivered locally – education, for instance, or policing – even though statutorily and constitutionally they are not primary responsibilities of central government.

Indeed, central government now sets national standards for many major public services which are delivered, not by the Civil Service, but through local government, other public bodies, the voluntary sector and even in some cases the private sector. Ministerial accountability has become an extended concept.

One can argue that the decision of the electorate to leave one political party in power for eighteen years was a significant constitutional event. We can be proud of the way the Civil Service managed the handover from one government to another in 1997, under Robin Butler's leadership. It went well. But long periods of opposition mean a longer period of learning for all concerned when a new generation of Ministers finally comes to power.

It is perhaps part of the great British tradition that we make big constitutional changes as if we were under anaesthetic and only notice them gradually after many years. It is perhaps part of the tradition of the Civil Service to present to the world a calm picture of business as usual while paddling away furiously under the surface to make things work.

Neither tradition should obscure the fact that change is taking place, that the Civil Service is at the heart of it and that it is, I believe, managing it well. I shall come to the idea of a Civil Service Act. But seen in the perspective I have just described, such an Act would be one piece in a much larger constitutional jigsaw which over a longer timescale is greatly altering the world of the Service.

THE POLITICAL ENVIRONMENT

The political environment in which the Civil Service operates is also changing.

This brings me to the charge that the Civil Service has become politicised. 'Politicisation' is a difficult term because it is so often used without definition. I would like to address some of the main concerns.

PERMANENT APPOINTMENTS

First, the charge has been made over the years that Ministers want civil servants who are 'one of us' or alternatively 'cronies', depending on which decade you are in.

In practice there is no evidence that Ministers want the permanent civil servants who work for them to share their political views. I have never known a politician who has shown the blindest bit of interest in which political party I voted for, and I have never heard of a colleague experiencing such an interest either.

What Ministers are interested in, quite rightly, is having competent people working for them, the best people to do the job. The eternal challenge for the Civil Service is to win the trust of the government of the day in its ability to serve them well. It requires a constant supply of able rising stars in every field. But that is not politicisation.

NOT BEING DRAGGED INTO THE POLITICAL ARENA

Second, I do not believe that the Civil Service is being politicised by allowing itself to be dragged into the political arena.

Senior civil servants often work closely with politicians in an intensely partisan political environment. We have always done so. We are impartial but we cannot ignore politics or pretend that they do not exist.

This comes as a surprise to some people. There was a complaint a while ago that the Civil Service was being politicised because it was being used to implement the political manifesto of the Government. That is what we are there for.

To pull off this trick, of working closely with politicians in a fierce partisan environment without being drawn into politics, the relationship between civil servants and Ministers has to be one of mutual trust and understanding. This is central to the Civil Service Code, and to the effectiveness of any government. Anyone who has run a large organisation knows that the success of the top team depends crucially on loyalty and trust.

We ought perhaps to ask whether the dangers of drawing civil servants into the political arena are growing. The political environment now includes much more news coverage around the clock, more competitive, more aggressive, more questioning, less respectful of authority.

The public profile of civil servants is becoming more prominent. Our degree of scrutiny by Parliament is becoming more real, not least as Select Committees grow in importance. Our actions are becoming subject to greater public comment, as if we were figures in our own right rather than servants of the government. We have a strong gene against this.

The trap is obvious. If permanent civil servants were to become public figures in a way which led Parliament and the media to look to them for their personal views and advice to Ministers, as opposed to the policies and views of the Government they serve, it is easy to imagine how loyalty and trust could be eroded.

This is a question both of principle – we are there to serve the government of the day – and professionalism. The pressures for politicisation would become much stronger if political appointees were the only people the Minister could trust.

I think the Civil Service has been remarkably successful in avoiding being drawn into the political arena over the years. But the importance of the Civil Service Code and the boundaries which it draws around behaviour is very great if we are to continue to maintain a correct relationship with successive governments.

Leaking

Perhaps the biggest threat to mutual confidence over the last decade or two has come from unauthorised leaking.

Given how much happens in government it is striking that there are relatively few serious leaks. The great majority of civil servants understand the importance of trust. But just a handful can do great harm by leaking against the government of the day. It is deeply corrosive when it happens, under whatever government, and I strongly condemn it.

I believe however that there needs to be a better avenue of redress for people who are discontented for whatever reason, to reduce the temptation to leak to the press or the Opposition. At present the avenue of redress leads through an individual's line manager to the permanent secretary and beyond that to the Head of the Civil Service or the First Civil Service Commissioner. People see this route as too daunting, 'too nuclear' as one individual said to me.

That is why I would like the Civil Service Commissioners to have a more formal responsibility for ensuring that there are effective, accessible arrangements in place for individuals with grievances in departments, and for taking a more active role if things seem to be going wrong, although equally we must not put them into the position of having to investigate or refuse to investigate every unsubstantiated allegation that gets thrown up. Their role should be internal, free from partisan external pressure.

Using the resources of government for Party advantage

Let me return to the issue of politicisation.

It is a longstanding convention that governments must not use the resources of the State improperly to gain Party political advantage. Here again, I do not believe the Civil Service is being politicised. But for many years the conditions in which we operate have been slowly changing, not least because of the pressure on all political parties to maintain a permanent level of campaigning between elections.

Thomas Szasz, the American writer, once said:

> In the animal kingdom, the rule is, eat or be eaten; in the human kingdom, define or be defined.

This is certainly true in modern politics. No government can afford to ignore how it is being defined in Parliament and the media.

It is this perhaps that gives an edge to allegations about 'spin'. It has always been the case that the actions and words of government have a political significance. No one has ever seen this as a problem for the Civil Service provided that presentation was handled in a proper way for the purposes of government, not Party.

Here again, I believe that the Civil Service has done well in advising successive governments about what is acceptable, and governments have accepted that advice. But the issues and judgements perhaps become more difficult over time.

Certainly the demand for high levels of professionalism in the Government Information and Communications Service have become ever greater, simply because in this media age any major organisation must take seriously the press and media, and deal with them professionally.

Special advisers

Finally, I would like to come the question of special advisers about whom all sorts of concerns have been expressed.

I am conscious that anything I say – or do not say – on this subject is liable to be misinterpreted, either as an attack on the Government, or a rearguard action to protect Civil Service interests, or a mouthing of words given to me by somebody else. None of these is true.

Let me be clear. Special advisers have long been part of our political system, and as an institution they are here to stay. In my view we should take a positive approach to their role, bring them in from the shadows, put them on a proper footing, as clearly as we can, and recognise that they have a legitimate contribution to make to the working of government as it is evolving.

I believe it is right that Ministers should be able to have special advisers to act as their political eyes and ears, help the department understand the mind of the Minister, work alongside officials on the Minister's behalf and handle party-political aspects of government business. They can help protect the Civil Service against politicisation.

I think a debate about their role is useful. I welcome the consultation document issued by the Wicks Committee. The debate needs to address the facts. For instance, only Ministers who attend Cabinet are allowed to appoint special advisers. The usual limit is two each.

There are 81 special advisers compared with 3429 members of the Senior Civil Service. Most special advisers are not 'spin doctors'. There are 11 out of the 81 who are employed primarily in the field of communications and perhaps another 30 who, as well as policy development, deal with presentation and speeches without necessarily talking to the press themselves. But most contribute behind the scenes in ways that could by no stretch of the imagination be called spin. These are the facts. The question is: what should be the framework within which they operate?

Framework for special advisers

I would like to test out six propositions as a contribution to the debate.

First, as I say, we should accept that special advisers are now established as a proper and legitimate feature of the constitutional framework within which Cabinet Ministers work.

Second, as the Government has already agreed, there should be a limit on the number of special advisers in each government, set by Parliament at the beginning of each new Parliament.

Third, rather than engage in abstruse discussions about what special advisers can do, we should say clearly and firmly what they cannot do and, beyond that, leave each Cabinet Minister to determine how they want to deploy them.

I think it should be possible reasonably briefly to define the things which special advisers must not do. For instance, without trying to be exhaustive, I have in mind the following.

Special advisers should not behave illegally or improperly. They should observe the same standards of conduct expected from permanent civil servants other than of course those relating to impartiality and the ability to serve future governments. The Special Advisers' Code already sets out standards.

Special advisers should not ask civil servants to do anything improper or illegal, or anything which might undermine the role and duties of permanent civil servants as described in the Civil Service Code. This means for instance that they should not do anything to undermine the political impartiality of civil servants or the duty of civil servants to give their own best advice to Ministers.

Special advisers should not have any role in the recruitment and promotion of permanent civil servants, or in their line management including the assessment of their performance and pay. Acting as eyes and ears, they are an extension of the Minister, not part of the permanent department.

If this general approach were adopted, the debate could then be about the precise boundaries of what was and was not acceptable, in relation to special advisers both in departments and Number 10 where special conditions apply.

This may sound a negative approach. But by defining the area of what was not acceptable it would free up Ministers to deploy their special advisers as they wished within the framework which had been created. We might consider whether the Minister should agree with the permanent secretary, who as Accounting Officer has responsibility for the governance of the department, what role each special adviser would play, and with what authority, from the outset of each appointment, though this would need to be thought through.

I believe we can do more to help special advisers play their role effectively, for instance through proper induction training. We are now organising this.

Fourth, there should be an effective grievance procedure for any civil servant who felt that a special adviser was abusing his or her position. I have already touched on the role the Civil Service Commissioners might play.

Fifth, special advisers should work under the direction of the Minister who appoints them. They should account to that Minister and to the Prime Minister who authorises their appointment. The Minister should be able to ask the permanent secretary to handle some aspect of a special adviser's management if necessary. But the basic responsibility for special advisers, for their selection and their actions, should rest with the Minister who is accountable to Parliament for them.

Finally, where a Minister wants an expert adviser who is non-political and needed solely because of a particular expertise, this should fall outside the special adviser system and be handled through the Civil Service Commission, perhaps on a short-service contract.

These are the main propositions which I would suggest for discussion. If they, or something like them, were to be generally acceptable, they could be embodied in a Civil Service Act.

ARGUMENTS AGAINST AN ACT

Let me turn finally to the question whether we now need a Civil Service Act.

A certain amount depends of course on what it would do, but general opinion over the years has been against an Act, regardless of what it said. Let me briefly run through the arguments against an Act.

First, it is said, the Civil Service is an institution of great pragmatism that evolves over time and works best without being hamstrung by legislation. Second, it is unwise to stir things up if you are unsure what demons you may accidentally unleash in the process. Third, 'if it ain't broke, don't fix it'. For all the media comment, so the argument runs, things are still working well. What is it that suddenly requires a Bill? Fourth, an Act would achieve nothing. Many of the things which would be in a Bill already have the force of law through Orders in Council. If there are issues, they are issues about behaviour. Legislation would add nothing except perhaps greater legalism in the relationship between Ministers and civil servants which would be a pity.

Finally, a Civil Service Act would make no sense unless it was part of a larger piece of legislation which covered the constitutional position of Ministers themselves and of government: in short, a written constitution, something which I hasten to add is not in contemplation.

CASE FOR AN ACT

These arguments have weight but over the last decade the balance has gradually been tipping the other way.

I myself do not think for a moment that an Act would solve everything. In particular, it would be no guarantee of good behaviour. It would be modest and useful rather than earthshaking. But I would welcome it. Let me summarise why.

As I have explained, the Civil Service for some years now has been going through great change, partly constitutional, partly managerial, partly in the political environment. It faces even greater change now because of the challenge of improving the quality of public services.

An Act could provide a forward-looking framework for the continued development of the Civil Service. Ministers and the public are entitled to expect that the Service has the people and the culture to perform at a high level of effectiveness. Recruitment, and the role of the Civil Service Commissioners who oversee the principles of recruitment, is at the heart of this. The Act would put the Commissioners onto a statutory basis, as the Government has promised.

The process of change occasionally throws up issues about the conventions which underpin the Civil Service, not just under this government but previously. These issues are many and varied: they concern for instance the role of special advisers, the role of Ministers in management matters, the principles governing Government communications and publications, opening up the Civil Service to outsiders, modernising recruitment, structures, ways of working, and so on.

Very often these issues are about boundaries, the boundaries between what is and is not acceptable, the boundaries between Government and party, grey areas where judgements are difficult and different people acting in good faith may properly come to different conclusions.

There is a danger that if we continue to leave these issues unattended they will fester. They could increasingly become rubbing points, matters of political controversy used to embarrass governments, damaging the Civil Service and perversely making it more difficult to bring about the changes which are needed.

A Civil Service Act could play a positive role in providing a framework for clarifying the boundaries, easing the rubbing points and providing a confident basis for accepting the kind of modernisation I have described without the fear that something important was being lost.

Finally, an Act would bring the Civil Service more directly under the oversight of Parliament.

WHAT WOULD THE ACT COVER?

What specifically would the Act cover? This is for debate; but I would make it short and brief, and cover five main things.

First, it should take power by regulation to define the Civil Service. At present there is no definition of a civil servant. Second, it should recognise on its face the fundamental principles of selection and promotion on merit and the political impartiality of the Service. Third, it should provide for the Civil Service Code and the Special Advisers' Code to be given legal force by regulation subject to the approval of Parliament. Fourth, it should put the role of the Civil Service Commissioners onto a statutory footing, both as guardians of the principles governing recruitment and in relation to grievances under the Codes, as I mentioned earlier, making their annual report to Parliament.

Finally, it would implement the Government's commitment to the regulation by Parliament of the number and the role of special advisers. There are aspects of this which need more thought. The Government plans to issue a discussion paper. But in essence the Act would bring together and codify a great deal of work which has already been done in these areas, not least by the Cabinet Office on the two Codes and by the Civil Service Commissioners on recruitment.

It would be an Act rooted in the need to serve present and future governments and the public, and not a vehicle for vested interests or nostalgia. It would be based on a broad consensus of cross-party support and informed opinion, and not become a political football. It would be framed in a way which supported the modernisation of the Civil Service without making its management rigid or inflexible. If we can meet these requirements – and I think we can – it would be another building block in our ambitions to modernise the Civil Service.

CONCLUSION

I started with Bridges and I will end with him.

His celebrated Rede lecture, *Portrait of a Profession*, in 1950 painted a picture of a Civil Service which had changed with the times but developed a strong and enduring character and culture which he believed provided the country with outstanding governance.

If he were to return today he would, I suspect, be astonished by the world in which the modern Civil Service works. But he would recognise the enduring character of the Service.

He might ask whether people were still proud of the Civil Service. I would have to remind him that he said, rightly, that the British are not fond of authority and that civil servants must be content to be ranked as figures of fun with mothers-in-law and Wigan pier.

But the question needs to be asked. People going through great change deserve encouragement when they do well. I would like to pay a warm tribute to the quality and character of the Civil Service and to the way in which civil servants at all levels have responded to the call for change in the time that I have had the privilege to be their Head. They are marvellous people.

I think we can be confident that the Service will in Bridges' phrase continue to be one of the most worthwhile, if also perhaps one of the least understood, of professions. We can be confident that it will continue to serve different governments well, that it will go on changing to meet the needs of the times and that it will retain its enduring character.

A Civil Service Act would not alter that. It would free us up to get on with the job within a clearer framework. In the words of the Northcote–Trevelyan report, 'A few clauses would accomplish all that is proposed in this paper, and it is our firm belief that a candid statement of the grounds of the measure would insure its success and popularity in the country'.

It has been my aim [today] to provide this candid statement; and it is also my answer to Bridges' portrait hanging on my wall.

Thank you [for listening so patiently].

AFTERWORD: CONTINUITY AND CHANGE

This article, originally delivered as a lecture before an invited audience, came at the end of my career as a civil servant. It aimed to reconcile the traditional values of the civil service with constant pressures for modernisation, and to argue for a Civil Service Bill, something which has now been enacted.

The date was 26 March 2002. There was mild turbulence around the relationship between Ministers and civil servants, mainly the result of the Sixsmith affair (see Blunkett 2006). David Blunkett (2006: 354) had told the Cabinet in February 2002 'Well, I think if we're going to have legislation that protects the civil service from the government, could we build into it protection for the government from the civil service?' I was still Secretary of the Cabinet but the then Prime Minister, Mr Tony Blair, was actively considering my successor. I knew my influence would wane and I wanted to drive a stake into the ground to show how far we had reached on legislation before I stood down. Not everyone agreed on the need for a Bill. I thought that a public statement like this, subsequently published in *Public Administration*, might make it that bit more difficult to ignore.

In earlier days I had rather liked the way in which the constitutional position of the civil service depended on conventional understandings between civil servants and Ministers. It seemed very British. But, as I explained in the lecture, I had become convinced that the balance of argument had tipped the other way. New Ministers and their advisers might not always know the conventions. Having to argue things from scratch is not always easy: issues of principle may arise in minor situations where their assertion may seem 'nitpicking' but giving way may create awkward precedent. I realised how vulnerable the civil service would be if it were ever faced with a serious challenge to its fundamental values.

I did not want to overstate the case for a Bill. It would be no guarantee of good behaviour. But it would be a modest and useful measure.

Number 10 had cleared the lecture although they would have preferred me not to give it. In the event it did not cause difficulty. But the *Times* report was accompanied by a cartoon showing Mr Blair cheerily waving me goodbye and Alastair Campbell saying to Jonathan Powell behind the door of Number 10: 'Has he gone yet?' There were other small indications. In the lecture I described the civil service as 'a shock-absorber at the heart of the State'. I meant the sort of role which the civil service has performed so well this year when the coalition government was formed, smoothing the transition of a new government to power. Mr Blair in a speech in February 2004 interpreted the metaphor differently. He said:

'We need a Civil Service which aims to amplify the implementation of successful change rather than, as sometimes in the past, act as a shock absorber in order to maintain the status quo.'

But I was arguing for *both* traditional values *and* a willingness to change. I saw a Bill as a means of securing the former, while freeing up the Service to modernise to meet the needs of governments.

Arguing for legislation should not have been controversial. In 1997, before the General Election, the Labour Party and the Liberal Democrats had made a joint commitment to a Civil Service Act. The Government had confirmed in July 2000 that it would introduce legislation, in a response (collectively agreed) to the Committee on Standards in Public Life (Cm 4817 2000), I was given permission to inform the Public Administration Select

Committee (PASC) that there would soon be a consultation document. Indeed we drew up proposals about what it should say, reflected in my lecture.

There were pressures for a Bill from outside. The Committee on Standards in Public Life (2003) gave it dogged support. The PASC under its chairman, Tony Wright, was a strong champion, hosting a debate on the subject (see http://www.civilservant.org.uk/pasc1003.pdf) and publishing its own draft Bill in January 2004. There were questions in the House of Lords, and Lord Lester introduced Bills.

And yet progress was slow. It took until November 2004 for the Government to publish a consultation document in the form of its own draft Civil Service Bill. It did nothing much more until Mr Gordon Brown, as new Prime Minister, promised in July 2007 to bring forward civil service legislation (see Secretary of State for Justice and Lord Chancellor 2007). There was then a further two-year pause before provisions were included in the Constitutional Reform and Governance Bill. This wended its way slowly through Parliament, gathering more and more constitutional measures, until it received its Second Reading in the House of Lords on 24 March 2010, just in time for the dissolution of Parliament and the General Election of 2010. The provisions on the civil service were never debated in Committee in the Lords but mercifully reached the Statute Book in the 'wash-up' in the last days of that Parliament.

Most of what this lecture argued for is in The Constitutional Reform and Governance Act 2010 (c.25). It puts the Civil Service Commission on a statutory footing, requires civil servants to be recruited on the basis of merit and fair and open competition, specifies functions which special advisers may not undertake (including the management of civil servants), requires the publication of Codes for the civil service and special advisers, and so on. It does not limit the number of special advisers, but it is interesting to note that the Coalition Agreement published by the new Government promises that it 'will put a limit on the number of Special Advisers'.

All this is now history. Why did it take so long to get these provisions on the Statute Book, given that there was so much agreement? One reason is that this legislation has never been a pressing political priority. It is hard for any Bill to make progress without a political champion inside the government. There may have been a worry that introducing a Bill might imply confirmation that there was indeed a problem about the role of special advisers and lead to embarrassment.

It is also just possible that not everyone in their heart-of-hearts really likes the Trevelyan – Northcote reforms. Recruitment processes aimed at selection on merit can seem Dickensian to a Minister who would prefer to import someone more partisan who is known to them and immediately available. The American system can look very attractive, particularly if you only select the bits you like. In recommending legislation 156 years ago, Messrs Northcote and Trevelyan understood that the battle against patronage is never completely won. After all, Mr Disraeli, who disliked their reforms but was unable to block them, created the post of First Civil Service Commissioner for a friend who needed money. It is good that we have got them on the Statute Book at last.

REFERENCES

Blunkett, D. 2006. *The Blunkett Tapes: My Life in the Bear Pit*. London: Bloomsbury Press.

Blair, T. 2004. Speech on civil service reform given by the then Prime Minister on Tuesday 24 February 2004 (http://www.guardian.co.uk/politics/2004/feb/24/Whitehall.uk1).

Committee on Standards in Public Life. 2003. *Defining the Boundaries within the Executive*. Ninth Report. CM 5775 London: The Stationery Office.

Secretary of State for Justice and Lord Chancellor. 2007. *The Governance of Britain*. CM 7170 London: The Stationery Office.

NAME INDEX

SUBJECT INDEX